Adobe®
Photoshop® Lightroom® 5
Streamlining Your Digital Photography Process

Adobe®
Photoshop® Lightroom® 5
Streamlining Your Digital Photography Process

ROB SYLVAN & NAT COALSON

WILEY

Adobe® Photoshop® Lightroom® 5
Streamlining Your Digital Photography Process

Published by
John Wiley & Sons, Inc.
10475 Crosspoint Blvd.
Indianapolis, IN 46256

ISBN: 978-1-118-64521-5

Manufactured in the United States of America

10 9 8 7 6 5 4 3 2

For general information on our other products and services or to obtain technical support, please contact our Customer Care Department within the U.S. at (877) 762-2974, outside the U.S. at (317) 572-3993 or fax (317) 572-4002.

Wiley publishes in a variety of print and electronic formats and by print-on-demand. Some material included with standard print versions of this book may not be included in e-books or in print-on-demand. If this book refers to media such as a CD or DVD that is not included in the version you purchased, you may download this material at http://booksupport.wiley.com. For more information about Wiley products, visit www.wiley.com.

Library of Congress CIP Data: 2013939156

Credits

Acquisitions Editor
Courtney Allen

Project Editor
Jennifer Bowles

Technical Editor
Mark Sirota

Editorial Director
Robyn Siesky

Business Manager
Amy Knies

Senior Marketing Manager
Sandy Smith

**Vice President and
Executive Group Publisher**
Richard Swadley

**Vice President and
Executive Publisher**
Barry Pruett

Project Coordinator
Katie Crocker

Indexing
Broccoli Information
Management

Book Designer
Erik Powers

About the authors

Rob Sylvan is a photographer, trainer, and author based in New Hampshire. In addition to serving as the Lightroom Help Desk Specialist for the National Association of Photoshop Professionals, he provides academic support to KelbyTraining.com subscribers. Rob also writes the Under the Loupe column for the Lightroom section of *Photoshop User* magazine.

Rob is the author of many photography-related books, including *Lightroom 2 for Dummies*, also published by Wiley. He teaches a four-week Lightroom class at PPSOP.com, is a founding member of the stock photography co-op Stocksy.com, and is on staff at thedigitalphotoworkshops.com.

For more information about Rob, and to stay up-to-date with Lightroom, head over to www.lightroomers.com.

Nathaniel Coalson is a fine art photographer and mixed media artist based in Colorado, USA, and Leicester, England. Nat has worked professionally in photography, imaging, and printing since 1987; his work has been exhibited extensively, received numerous awards, and is held in private and corporate collections. Nat is an Adobe Certified Expert on Lightroom and Photoshop and an experienced teacher, speaker, and mentor, teaching photographers and artists working at all levels. He is the author of many photography-related books including *Nature Photography Photo Workshop*, published and distributed worldwide by Wiley.

For Grampy and Cookie

Acknowledgments

My deepest thanks go to Nat Coalson, the original author of this book, who kept it updated through Lightroom 4. Nat is an incredible photographer and gifted teacher. Thank you for providing such a strong foundation upon which to build. I am grateful for the opportunity to update this work for Lightroom 5.

Any book that has reached the final stage of being published is actually the work of many hands (eyes, brains, and hearts, too) behind the scenes. I owe everyone at Wiley a great deal of gratitude, but specifically Courtney Allen, Jennifer Bowles, Mark Sirota, Robyn Siesky, and Erik Powers, who were instrumental in getting this book finished, looking so great, and out into the world. Thank you all.

I am grateful for all that I have learned from my friends at the National Association of Photoshop Professionals, the Digital Photo Workshops, the fantastic staff and instructors at Photoshop World, and countless numbers of fellow photographers. You all have taught and inspired me over the years.

I also want to thank my wife, Paloma, for being the love of my life and my number one supporter during this project; my son Quinn, for assisting me on many shoots and being the subject in many more; and my family, friends, and neighbors—Ea, Avery, William, Adrienne, Emma, Julia, Paige, Ella, John, Kris, Gabby, Ed, Jaylin, Alden, Hayden, Charlie, Dan, Raymond, Maggie, Kayla, Justin, Jayda, Nekos—for being a part of the book in large and small ways.

Special thanks to Michelle at Crackskulls Coffee & Books for keeping me caffeinated throughout this project.

CHAPTER 01
Getting Started

01

GETTING STARTED:
Foundations for success

WELCOME TO LIGHTROOM 5

Adobe Photoshop Lightroom is a full-featured software program for digital image management and processing, designed for professional and serious amateur photographers alike. As the official Adobe press release explains, Lightroom enables photographers to "import, manage, enhance, and showcase" all their photos and videos. Lightroom 5 is a major upgrade and is recommended for all previous users as well as those just getting started with Lightroom.

Lightroom's integrated approach to handling the entire digital photography workflow offers photographers significant advantages over other individual programs. However, if you also want to use other software, Lightroom also integrates very well with other programs—you can use Lightroom as the hub of your image processing system and easily jump over to other software (including Photoshop) to perform specialized tasks as needed. That said, once you've mastered Lightroom, you may find you rarely—if ever—need to use other software to process the vast majority of your photos.

Figure 1-1

What's New in Lightroom 5

- **Major changes to minimum system requirements**
- **Smart previews that offer new options for your Lightroom workflow**
- **A new type of local adjustment called Radial Filter**
- **Non-circular healing comes to the Spot Removal tool**
- **Sensor spot visualization function for easier removal**
- **Support for importing files in PNG format**
- **Transparency support on export and edit in Photoshop**
- **A true full screen mode**
- **New smart collection and Library Filter criteria**
- **User configurable overlays for Loupe and Develop**
- **Aspect ratio crop overlays**
- **Improved Book module text tools, page numbers, and custom user pages**
- **Video can be added to slideshows**
- **DNG Validation**
- **Overall performance improvements**
- **Raw format support for new cameras**
- **Improved perspective correction with Upright**
- **Improved Lens Corrections and new lens profiles**
- **More consistency throughout the user interface**

In this chapter I introduce core Lightroom concepts and explain the screen interface. If you're new to Lightroom, I strongly recommend you read this chapter before proceeding through the remainder of the book as you'll find learning Lightroom much easier with the fundamentals described in the following sections. (If you're an experienced Lightroom user, you may be able to skip most of this and go straight to other chapters.)

 Internet access required for some features
Lightroom 5 is dependent on the web for some features. In particular, the Map module depends on Internet access for core functionality (it pulls map data from Google) as does the program's Help files, which are online. Also, to upload books to Blurb from the Book module you need to be online. Lightroom can also automatically check for new updates to the program and notify you when they become available for download.

 Language support
Lightroom 5 is available with support for many languages (the Read Me file contains more information about this). You are prompted to choose a language during installation, but you can also change this setting via the Lightroom preferences.

 Lightroom and Adobe Photoshop Camera Raw
Many photographers use Lightroom in conjunction with the full version of Photoshop and the Adobe Camera Raw plug-in. For full compatibility you need to maintain the latest versions of all software. The Read Me that comes with the Lightroom 5 installer has more information on compatibility between the software versions. See Chapter 5 for more about using Lightroom with Photoshop.

 Lightroom and PSE
If you want to do more with your photos than what Lightroom can directly provide and you don't own Photoshop, it's hard to beat the combination of Lightroom and Photoshop Elements (PSE). PSE offers the most essential functionality of the full version of Photoshop at a very low price, and with both programs installed on your computer you have an enormous range of capabilities.

How to use this book

This book is not meant to be *read* as much as it is meant to be used, presumably while at your computer with Lightroom running. Of course, you can learn about some features by reading about them, but in most cases you'll learn the fastest when you follow along on your computer as you read the steps and descriptions. Also, due to inherent space limitations, some of the screenshots used for the illustrative figures are small—you'll find it easier to learn if you're looking at Lightroom full-size on your own computer display.

 Download all figures
All figures in this book are available for download at:
www.lightroomers.com/lightroom5book

PREREQUISITES
The content of this book assumes you have at least basic- to intermediate-level computer skills, are comfortable managing files on hard drives and removable media, and understand

01

common computer operations such as copy/paste and manipulating dialog boxes. (If you're just learning to use a computer, Lightroom is probably not your best choice of software.) I also assume you have a fundamental working knowledge of your camera.

CHAPTER STRUCTURE

The chapters in this book are segmented by module and key features, and are generally sequenced in the order you might use Lightroom. In particular, the first few chapters—Import, Library, Develop, and Export—are presented in the order you'll approach your photo processing workflow. The content pertaining to the output modules—Book, Slideshow, Print, and Web—will be useful on an as-needed basis; there's no specific order in which you'd use these modules. The Map module, which won't be for everyone, is sandwiched in between the other modules. The last chapter, covering the advanced use of Lightroom catalogs, will come in handy when you've gained a basic working knowledge of Lightroom, and especially when you are ready to take your workflow to the next level by using multiple catalogs. The Appendix contains additional information, mainly for advanced users, and is intended to address specialized questions and topics not everybody will be concerned with. The Appendix also contains a list of my favorite shortcuts and links to helpful websites, as well as a glossary of terms.

Each chapter starts with an overview of what will be covered, and then a basic, suggested workflow is presented using a step-by-step approach. These workflows are mainly included to give you an idea of the typical tasks involved; after reading the rest of the chapter you'll no doubt begin developing and refining your own workflows. Following the introductory workflow, each module, window, panel, and control is explained in detail, based on the general order of how the screen interface is presented. The chapters all finish with suggestions for next steps and things to consider for maximizing your effectiveness using Lightroom. Throughout the chapters I've also sprinkled in my own comments and opinions; take them as you will.

FINDING WHAT YOU'RE LOOKING FOR

Because of the way each chapter is structured, you can easily look up general topics using the Table of Contents, and the opening page of each chapter also lists the main topics included in that part of the book. In certain cases, looking up a topic in the Index will give you a better overview of where that topic is addressed.

There is a fair amount of intentional repetition to solidify key concepts. Also, you will note that because some features are shared by multiple modules (such as the color picker) I've chosen to elaborate on the functionality in one chapter, and then refer back to that on the relevant pages in other chapters. My hope is that you won't have to jump around too much, but even though working with Lightroom can be done in a fairly linear way, explaining the tools can't be done this way because of the amount of overlap between some of the module controls.

If you're new to Lightroom you will benefit from working through this book in a linear fashion. Although the material is mostly presented in sequence based on workflow, it may also be helpful to jump from one topic to another as needs dictate. You can use this book to learn Lightroom from the ground up, or refer back to something later. When you have a basic familiarity with the software and workflow, you can later refresh your knowledge by going straight to the section or page containing the shortcuts, tips, and techniques appropriate for the task at hand. Before long, you'll know Lightroom inside and out—and that's when the real fun begins!

Get the book spiral bound

It would be wonderful if we could release this book in spiral-bound form, but it's not logistically feasible with a publication such as this. Instead, I highly recommend you take this book to your nearest copy shop or office supply store to have them chop the spine off and put on a plastic coil binding. This allows the opened book to lay flat on your computer desk while you're working through the material. If you plan to use the book frequently, you might also add a durable, clear plastic cover.

ICONS

Throughout the book, I've placed small tidbits of additional information for your consideration. Although these are separate from the literal descriptions of Lightroom's essential functionality, they are derived from my own experiences with Lightroom, my work with countless clients and students, and extensive, ongoing research into best practices in Lightroom and digital photography in general. I've done my best to put these icons in context with the steps in the workflow where they are most relevant. They are denoted by small graphic elements and colored text, as described below:

New in Lightroom 5: Throughout the book I've highlighted in bold the main features new to this release of Lightroom.

Tip

These offer common best practices in digital photography and imaging, ways to speed up your workflow, methods of processing, and suggested ways to approach various tasks.

Reminder

Reminders are generally tips found in multiple places in the book.

Preference

I've noted important Lightroom Preferences near the descriptions of the controls they affect. As the name implies, a Preference comes down to your personal choice; in most cases I explain my own way of working in order to create a framework for your own decision making.

Warning

Warnings are strong cautions against doing something a certain way, or explanations of potentially tricky aspects to watch out for.

Shortcuts: Mac and Windows

Lightroom is full of keyboard shortcuts and I've tried to include those that I think you'll find most useful. I strongly recommend you try to memorize and use the most common

01

shortcuts—using the keyboard to work in Lightroom can eliminate many manual steps and makes performing tasks much faster. The Mac shortcut is listed first, followed by the Windows shortcut.

The shortcuts in this book are based on Lightroom 5, though most of them also work in earlier versions, and most will continue to work in future versions. Some of these shortcuts are not included in Lightroom Help or other official documentation. This increases the possibility they may change from one version release to another. In a printed book, I can't guarantee that the accuracy of the published shortcuts will last forever. There's a list of some of the most useful shortcuts at the end of the book.

⟐ Module shortcuts

Each module has a screen available listing the most commonly used shortcuts for that module. To view this screen, use the menu command at Help→[Module Name] Shortcuts…or use the ⌘+/ or Ctrl+/ shortcut!

⟐ Lightroom Queen shortcuts lists

Victoria Bampton, aka The Lightroom Queen, maintains the most comprehensive and up-to-date lists of Lightroom shortcuts available. If you want to learn all the shortcuts for speeding up your workflow, you can't do better than her lists. You can download them at www.lightroomqueen.com/keyboard-shortcuts.

KEYBOARD VARIATIONS

On Mac, the Apple key and ⌘ (Command, or cmd) are the same. On Windows, Control and Ctrl are the same. (In some cases, the Control key is also used on Mac.) Option on Mac is the same as Alt on Windows.

Workflows

Each chapter contains one or more suggested workflows, presented step-by step.

⟐ What is a workflow and why should I care?

The term *workflow* simply describes a sequence of steps to produce a specific result. Understand that there is no single workflow that is right for everyone. The workflows I've included are meant to be fast, simple, and straightforward. By necessity, this means that at times I've left something out because it is too complex to address in the context of the steps. Over time, you will create your own workflows based on the tasks you need to accomplish with your photography.

Example Lightroom workflow

To give some context to the detailed explanations that follow in this chapter, following is an overview of a typical Lightroom workflow:

Step 1. Capture digital photos.

Step 2. Copy photos to a hard drive and import them to a Lightroom catalog.

Step 3. Organize photos in the Library module.

Step 4. Back up your photos and catalog.

Step 5. (Optional) Plot photo locations in the Map module.

Step 6. Enhance and optimize photos in the Develop module.

Step 7. Export finished photos for specific purposes.

Step 8. (Optional) Create Books, Slideshows, Prints, and Web Galleries.

Step 9. Update your backups!

Of course, each of these steps is actually comprised of multiple tasks, the specifics of which vary depending on circumstances. These tasks—and time-saving shortcuts and techniques—are explained in detail in the following chapters. If you perform each phase of the workflow similarly every time, you will soon be able to think several steps ahead. This facilitates better decision making, dramatically speeds up your work, and ultimately allows the highest possible quality for your photographic work.

GETTING MORE HELP

Situations may arise for which you need more help than what's provided in this book. Adobe can be a good place to start, but there is a vast number of other resources run by Lightroom enthusiasts (and most of them free) available online. I've included a comprehensive list of links in the Appendix.

BUILT-IN LIGHTROOM HELP

From within Lightroom, you can access Adobe's online help system, which is quite thorough on many topics. It's in the same place on Mac and Windows, under the Help menu→Lightroom Help (F1). (Requires Internet access.)

Configuring your computer for Lightroom

Before you install Lightroom you should be sure your computer is up to snuff. Lightroom is a powerful application, and as such can sometimes be quite demanding on computer resources. Most importantly, make sure your computer meets the minimum system requirements, which have changed significantly in version 5.

In all but a couple of very minor ways, working with Lightroom is essentially the same on Mac and Windows. I use a Windows desktop and Mac laptop, and my Lightroom experience is the same on both. Some of the menu commands are in different places, and there are some differences in the way that Lightroom works with the file systems on different operating systems. But all in all, you should expect a great experience with Lightroom regardless of your operating system. Just a heads up—with a couple of exceptions, all of the screen images in this book were made on a Mac.

01

LIGHTROOM 5 SYSTEM REQUIREMENTS

The current minimum requirements for Lightroom 5 are in the following list. If your computer doesn't meet or exceed these, you won't be able to install the program.

WINDOWS

- Processor: Intel Pentium 4 or AMD Athlon 64

- OS: Microsoft Windows 7 with Service Pack 1 or Windows 8

- RAM: 2GB

- Hard disk: 2GB of available hard disk space

- Media: DVD-ROM drive

- Display: 1024 x 768 monitor resolution

MACINTOSH

- Processor: Multicore Intel processor with 64-bit support

- OS: MAC OS X 10.7 (Lion) or MAC OS X 10.8 (Mountain Lion)

- RAM: 2GB

- Hard disk: 2GB of available hard disk space

- Media: DVD-ROM drive

- Display: 1024 x 768 monitor resolution

Note: On all systems, an active Internet connection is required for web-based services (Map module, uploading Books, etc.).

 Help→System Info

Once Lightroom is installed and running correctly, you can see a summary of your system info using this command under the Help menu.

RECOMMENDED COMPUTER SETUPS

As you might expect, the minimum system requirements are usually far from the *ideal* setup. And as a digital photographer, you owe it to yourself to work with the most capable tools you can afford—your computer is no exception. You've probably spent lots of money on your camera gear; why skimp on your digital darkroom? What follows here is a summary of my recommendations for setting up your computer as a photo processing workstation. The Appendix also includes a section on optimizing Lightroom's performance.

RAM (AKA MEMORY)

As noted in the minimum specs, Lightroom can technically run with 2GB RAM, but honestly, you won't have a pleasant experience working with this limited amount of memory. 4GB is really the practical minimum, and if you can bump this up to 8GB or more you'll see a huge difference in speed and stability.

COMPUTER DISPLAYS

You will have the most success processing your photos if you use a good quality display. The differences in quality and accuracy between monitor makes and models can be significant. Generally speaking, I think you can expect to spend a minimum of $500 for a monitor suitable for photography work. I highly recommend displays from NEC and Eizo; with the range of products available from these two companies there's really no need to consider other brands. (I currently use—and absolutely love!—the NEC MultiSync 2690WUXi, which is reasonably priced and has a very wide gamut.) Also of critical importance is calibrating and profiling your display; see the section on color management later in this chapter.

 Using Lightroom with dual monitors

Lightroom provides support for a Secondary Display; this is an additional window containing a different set of controls from the main application display window. The most common use for the Secondary Display is showing a large preview while the main window shows smaller previews. Using the Secondary Display is the only practical way to utilize a second window in Lightroom, and is discussed further later in this chapter and in Chapter 3.

HARD DRIVES (AKA STORAGE)

It's important that you plan out your photo storage system carefully, accounting for your current needs and budget along with a plan for growth. Over the coming years your photo library may grow to hundreds of thousands—or even millions—of images! If you're not already using a good organizational system, now is the time to start.

At this point, magnetic and solid state (SSD) hard drives are the most practical options for storing your photo library. Magnetic hard drives are inexpensive and the capacities of the most common drive sizes (500GB, 1TB, 2TB) will be enough for most people, at least for now. The prices for SSD drives are coming down, but with relatively limited capacities and higher costs they are still impractical for most digital photography storage systems. That said, SSD drives do have real speed advantages for the operating system and storage of your Lightroom catalog (and its associated files).

In addition to the recording format, the other main choice in hard drive systems is whether to use single drives or RAID units. RAID storage uses multiple disks that appear to your system as a single volume. RAID systems can also be configured to automatically copy files between the disks in the system to provide transparent backup capability. RAID is just one component of a proper backup system designed to protect against inevitable disk failure.

 Use dedicated disk drives for your image library

Regardless of the drive format you choose, it's best to *not* store your image files on your system disk. (The system disk is the hard drive that contains your operating system, and usually also contains your applications and other programs.) I strongly recommend you store your photo library on disk drives used only for that purpose. If you currently are storing your photos on the system disk (such as in the default Pictures folder), I recommend you set up new drives to use only for your imaging work.

External drives provide the most flexibility—they are highly portable and can be moved to another computer as needed. External USB, FireWire (IEEE 1394), and Thunderbolt interfaces usually provide adequate read/write times when using Lightroom. (I currently use 3TB single drive external units.)

It's easiest to use fewer, larger disks for your entire image library: one or two large-capacity disks are much easier to manage than many small ones. More importantly, a single master hard drive also facilitates easier backups. As your library grows and your disks fill to capacity, I recommend you simply transfer your photo library to progressively larger drives.

When I'm buying new hard drives, I buy enough storage capacity to grow into for at least the next 18 months. I always buy drives in pairs (at minimum and, ideally, in triplicate). One is the master working drive, on which are stored all my original working files. The second drive is the working backup, which is updated after every work session. The third drive is an archive, updated less frequently than the working backup and stored off-site. When considering brands, I prefer to stick with those that are well-known for reliability; I've had great experiences with Seagate and Western Digital.

About asset management

Asset management is all about how you name, organize, store, and back up your image files. Asset management plays a crucial role in your ability to find, work with, and share your photos. For most photographers this is certainly not the most fun or exciting part of the process, but it's not optional—if nothing else, the sheer volume of digital photographs you make requires you to develop and implement a comprehensive system for managing your images.

ORGANIZING AND NAMING YOUR IMAGE FILES

At one point or another one of the most daunting challenges all photographers face is deciding how to arrange their image files into folders and what to name files and folders. The most important thing is to create a standardized system and use it consistently. Take some time to develop a good plan that you can start using now. You can later decide whether you need to go back and rework your old image archives to conform to the new system.

There are lots of differing opinions about how image files should be named and organized; this is an area where your personal preferences play a significant role in your decisions. In the end, the system has to make sense and work for you. It doesn't make sense to adopt someone else's strategy if it only causes you confusion and the risk of misplacing or losing files. That said, there are some widely accepted best practices for how to organize and name your files and folders:

- Every file and folder in your image library must have a unique name.

- Give files and folders *meaningful* names. The filenames assigned by your camera are useless in a structured storage system.

- In your names, include a formatted date, such as YYYYMMDD.

- Include some kind of identifier as to what the folder/file contains. For the nature photographer, using the names of locations and/or subject matter makes sense.

- Use sequence numbers (or serial numbers) to differentiate files from a single shooting session.

- Name and group folders and subfolders according to their date or content.

- When possible, give your folders and the files they contain the same base filename.

- The system must be able to scale (grow exponentially) over time.

You can learn more about using Lightroom for asset management in Chapters 2 and 3.

Installing Lightroom

There are two ways to install Lightroom: from a DVD or a downloaded package. Whether you're using a Mac or Windows machine, the installation process and end results are essentially the same. Following are overviews of the installation processes, along with some things you should know when starting out. Installing Lightroom is not complicated; you will probably be able to finish the installation using only the on-screen instructions provided by the installer. (Complete installation instructions are provided in the Read Me file that comes with the Lightroom installer package.) If you are unable to install Lightroom, consult Adobe's documentation and/or technical support.

Download installers
Any software application that comes on a DVD has a limited shelf life; Lightroom is no exception. If you've purchased Lightroom as a DVD, I suggest that in the future you'll be much better off downloading the updates from the Adobe.com website. Provided there's a fast enough Internet connection available, it's almost always best to download installers from the manufacturer's website, mainly because you're assured of receiving the most current version.

Antivirus software issues
It's been reported that Norton Antivirus and MacAfee may incorrectly identify Lightroom files as potential threats. If you use these software packages, check their settings and be sure to allow access to the Lightroom catalog and other files, or temporarily disable them during the installation process.

Installing on multiple computers
Your license for Lightroom allows you to install the application on up to two computers using the same serial number. (This can include different operating systems; I have one installation running on a Mac laptop and one on a Windows desktop. You'll need to use different installer packages, but the serial numbers are platform-independent so you can use the same number for both installations.)

01

ABOUT REVERSE GEOCODING

The first time you open a new or upgraded catalog, you'll see a message asking if it's OK to enable reverse geocoding (see **Figure 1–2**). This is a privacy setting and is used for the Map module—it's entirely optional. If you choose to enable it right away, the feature will be active the first time you switch the Map module. You can enable or disable Reverse Geocoding at any time using the Catalog Settings dialog box.

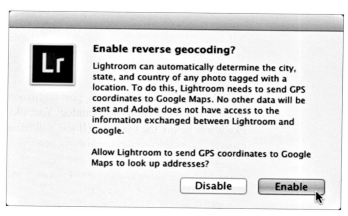

Figure 1-2

Reverse Geocoding and Catalog Settings are discussed in detail in Chapters 6 and 11.

INSTALLING LIGHTROOM FOR THE FIRST TIME

When you install Lightroom for the first time using the default settings, the Lightroom program is placed in your Applications folder (Program Files folder on Windows) on your system drive and the Lightroom configuration files (presets, templates, etc.) are placed in another directory, depending on your operating system.

Lightroom uses a database file, called a catalog, to manage your files and store the work you do on them. The first time you run Lightroom, if no previous catalogs are found, you are prompted to enter a name and location for your default catalog (see **Figure 1–3**). The default is your Pictures folder on the system drive; this is usually OK. Later, you might consider keeping your catalog on the same drive where all your photos are stored. (For an introduction to catalogs, see the section later in this chapter and for lots more, read Chapter 11.)

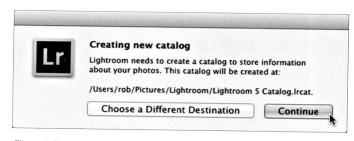

Figure 1-3

UPGRADING LIGHTROOM FROM A PREVIOUS VERSION

Upgrading from previous versions of Lightroom can be more complicated than doing a fresh installation for the first time. When you upgrade Lightroom, the new application itself is installed as if it was for the first time; the previous version of Lightroom remains intact, so you'll have both versions on your computer. Your custom preferences, presets and templates also remain untouched, but new Lightroom default presets may be added to the folders.

Before you jump right in to upgrading, there are a few important things to understand. First and most critical, every time you upgrade Lightroom to a major release (3, 4, 5, etc.) you must also upgrade the catalog. You can upgrade a copy of a Lightroom catalog from any older version to a newer version at any time (though you typically only do this once).

WHAT HAPPENS DURING A CATALOG UPGRADE

During the upgrade, a copy of your catalog from the old version is created, and the copied catalog is modified to support Lightroom's new features. No changes are ever made to the previous version catalog! Your old catalog is still on your hard drive exactly like it was before the upgrade. (If you still have the earlier version of the Lightroom program on your computer, you can open the old catalog just like before.) If you're not careful about this, you could end up working in several different catalogs without knowing it. It's also possible you might upgrade your old catalog multiple times, with each upgrade producing another copy of your old catalog. For these reasons, I strongly recommend that after you've successfully installed Lightroom 5, upgraded your catalog, and confirmed everything looks like it's running OK, you should uninstall the previous version of Lightroom and remove your old catalogs from your hard drives. (If this makes you nervous, just be sure to make backups first.)

Note: If you try to upgrade the same catalog more than once, Lightroom will let you know, and will give you the option of using the previously upgraded catalog to avoid creating multiple redundant copies.

HOW TO UPGRADE A CATALOG

To upgrade your catalog, all you need to do is install the new version of Lightroom and launch the program. Lightroom will find your old catalog and prompt you to upgrade (see **Figure 1–4**). In

Figure 1-4

the upgrade window, be sure the correct catalog is selected for upgrading. By default, Lightroom will create the new catalog in the same folder as the original. If you're using the default catalog name, Lightroom will automatically change the name of the new file to reflect the current version. (For example, Lightroom 4 Catalog would become Lightroom 5 Catalog.) You can choose a different location or filename by clicking the Change button. When you're ready, click the Upgrade button to allow Lightroom to update the selected catalog.

Note: If Lightroom doesn't automatically find your old catalog and simply opens a new catalog, you can find it manually from the File→Open Catalog menu in Lightroom 5 and this will trigger the same upgrade process.

Upgrade from Beta catalog

If you used the Beta version of Lightroom 5, you can upgrade that catalog to the full 5 release version, or you can just import it into your Lightroom 5 catalog via the File→Import from another catalog menu (this is covered in greater detail in Chapter 11).

⚠ **About old Lightroom plug-ins**

Adobe doesn't typically change anything in Lightroom's program code that would inherently cause older plug-ins to fail; however, depending on the way those plug-ins were themselves coded, they may or may not work correctly in the new version.

MOVING LIGHTROOM TO A NEW COMPUTER

If you're going to install Lightroom on a new computer, first copy your old catalog to that computer. Then install Lightroom from scratch. When you open it for the first time it will find your old catalog and prompt you to upgrade. See Chapter 11 for lots more about working with catalogs.

REMOVING AND REINSTALLING LIGHTROOM

If something goes wrong during the installation, or if any time in the future you need to remove Lightroom, the process is fairly straightforward, but is different on Mac and Windows machines. On Mac, you can usually just drag the Lightroom application to the Trash and then reinstall. On Windows, in general, you should always use the Programs and Features Control Panel to uninstall Lightroom.

Note that it's very rare for something to actually be wrong with the Lightroom program. If Lightroom isn't running correctly it's usually a problem with the preference file or the catalog, not the program itself. In these situations, uninstalling and reinstalling won't make any difference. Chapter 11 offers suggestions for troubleshooting catalogs. I have a tutorial on my blog on how to replace the Lightroom preference file: www.lightroomers.com/replacing-the-lightroom-preference-file/745

Lightroom Fundamentals

When the Lightroom application is running, it constantly pulls in data from a number of sources (see **Figure 1–5**). Lightroom's main strengths are derived from the fact that it uses a database (the catalog) for most of its operations. Under the database model, all your edits to photos are totally non-destructive—the original pixel data in the files on disk is never modified. Using catalogs also allows powerful search and filtering capabilities. Lightroom excels at batch processing; you can quickly and easily apply stored settings to many photos at once using presets, templates, and sync operations. Also, within the catalog you can make unlimited virtual copies and collections of photos without needing to duplicate the original files on the hard drive.

Along with the organizational power of the catalog, Lightroom's processing engine provides very high image quality. When the controls are used correctly, Adobe's rendering of raw image data—as well as essential processing routines such as sharpening, noise reduction, and making enlargements—are second to none.

Lightroom Application

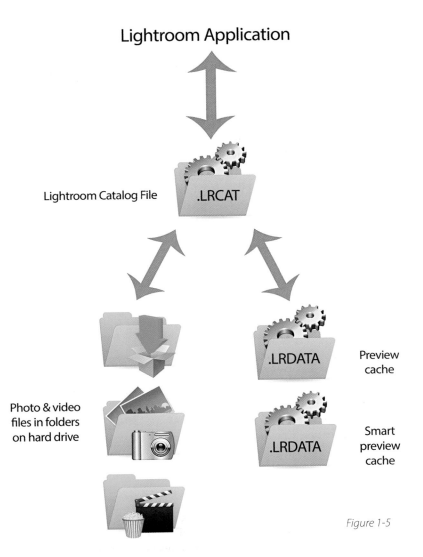

Lightroom Catalog File — .LRCAT

.LRDATA — Preview cache

Photo & video files in folders on hard drive

.LRDATA — Smart preview cache

Figure 1-5

INTRODUCTION TO LIGHTROOM CATALOGS

Any time you're working in Lightroom, you're working within a catalog. A Lightroom catalog is a SQLite file with the extension .lrcat. When you launch Lightroom, it looks for a catalog to load. If you've never moved the default catalog, or haven't created a new one, you will be working within the default catalog. However, you can make additional catalogs and store them on any hard drive, even one that's different from where your image files reside. The name and location of catalog files have no direct effect on Lightroom's operation, so you can name your catalog whatever you like, and put it on any local hard drive you choose. (Keeping your master catalog on the same external hard drive with the image files makes backups easier.) You can't open a Lightroom catalog over a network, and it can be opened by only one person at a time.

01

Image files must be imported into a Lightroom catalog before you can work with them, during which Lightroom creates records of the photos within the catalog. (Importing photos is covered in Chapter 2.) It might help to think of a Lightroom catalog like a department store catalog: it contains all the information *about* the items but *not the items themselves*. It's critical that you maintain the links between the Lightroom catalog and the actual files stored in folders on your hard disk, and this is done by performing all your file management tasks (moving, renaming, and deleting) inside of Lightroom.

Since a Lightroom catalog contains records of the photos and videos you've imported, but not the files themselves, all the work you do in the catalog is done by reference. As you work, Lightroom continually reads from each image file and/or video clip on the hard drive. Lightroom continually renders previews, which are also saved on the hard drive, in a special folder next to the catalog file. The previews you see in Lightroom are generated using the current adjustment instructions. All this information is stored in the catalog, along with the Develop history, collection membership, virtual copies, etc., and you can also choose to save each photo's adjustment instructions and custom metadata out to the XMP metadata space inside each photo on the hard disk. Lightroom never modifies the actual pixels in the source files.

Working with catalogs is covered extensively in Chapter 11.

 Essential file maintenance

If your catalog is lost, deleted, or corrupted, the work you've done in the catalog may become inaccessible. This is why it's imperative to: a) save your metadata to disk as you work, b) keep your catalog clean and optimized, and c) make regular backups of your catalog and image files.

 Catalog corruption

If you don't have a lot of experience using databases—especially for image editing and management—it may come as a shock if a problem with the Lightroom catalog makes the work you've done to your photos inaccessible. It is entirely possible that a Lightroom catalog could become corrupted and not be able to be opened or worked with in any way. In the vast majority of cases, a problem with the Lightroom catalog does not mean there's a problem with the image files.

SUPPORTED FILE FORMATS

Unlike Photoshop, which can open and save a dizzying array of image, graphic, and video file formats, Lightroom is designed to work only with the most common formats generated by a digital photography workflow. Lightroom can import, process, and export the following types of files:

- **Raw:** Raw captures from nearly all modern digital cameras

- **DNG:** Adobe Digital Negative

- **JPEG (JPG):** (Joint Photographic Experts Group) compressed image files

- **TIFF (TIF):** (Tagged Image File Format); 8 bit, 16 bit, and 32 bit may contain layers and vector elements

- **PSD:** 8-bit and 16-bit Photoshop documents (only those saved with the Maximize Compatibility option enabled)

- **PNG: New in Lightroom 5:** The ability to import PNG (Portable Network Graphic) files

- **Video formats:** Digital movies from most popular cameras and smartphones including MOV, MPG, AVI, and AVCHD (MTS and MT2S only)

 PNG support

PNG files can now be imported, managed, and edited in Lightroom. Transparent areas in a PNG file will appear white inside of Lightroom. If you want to export copies of an edited PNG file from Lightroom you'll want to choose TIF or PSD format to preserve transparency (more on this in Chapter 5).

MAXIMUM DIMENSIONS

Lightroom can import image files up to **65,000 pixels per side or 512 megapixels.** Files with dimensions that exceed this specification and other unsupported files will not be imported; you'll receive a warning dialog containing a list of files that couldn't be imported.

 Files in CMYK mode

Lightroom can import files in CMYK color mode, but any Develop adjustments you apply to them will be done using Lightroom's internal RGB color space. Lightroom cannot convert files to the CMYK color space on export.

RAW FORMAT SUPPORT

Raw files come from your camera with a format specified by the camera manufacturer; common examples are Canon's .CR2 and Nikon's .NEF formats. Native raw files are encoded and cannot be directly modified. And though they may have the same file extension, raw files from different cameras are often programmatically different from one another: a .CR2 file from a 5D Mark II is different than one from a 50D.

Raw files in your camera model's native format must be recognized by Lightroom for you to work with those files. Adobe's imaging software supports nearly all digital cameras available on the market, and support for new models is continually updated. However, when a new camera model is released, there may be a period of time during which your raw files cannot be read by Lightroom. If Lightroom can't import your raw files, this may be the reason. Raw file format compatibility is addressed in incremental software updates to Lightroom. You'll need to shoot raw+JPEG (Lightroom can import the JPEGs), or use the software from your camera manufacturer until an update to Lightroom/Camera Raw is released.

Lightroom respects XMP during import

If you're importing raw files with .xmp sidecars or TIF/PSD/JPG/DNG with embedded XMP metadata, Lightroom will read any compatible metadata settings from them and the images will be added to the catalog with those settings applied. This is discussed further in Chapter 3.

ABOUT COMPOSITE IMAGES

Any photo that is made of more than one original capture is called a composite. Without using additional plug-ins, Lightroom can't produce composites. To combine multiple images you need to get them out of Lightroom and into other software, such as Photoshop. Processing individual images that will become part of a composite requires special consideration. If during processing you start thinking of combining multiple exposures—in any fashion and for any reason—you need to start considering exports and external editors, covered in Chapter 5.

For now, as you're looking at processing individual images in Lightroom, learn to make the most of the tools available. You may find that in some cases—especially those that at first glance appear to require blending exposures—can be fully accomplished in Lightroom. You will find images that in the past may have required compositing now can be successfully processed with a single capture in Lightroom.

LIGHTROOM PREVIEWS

During an Import, and at other times while working in Lightroom, Lightroom reads the pixel data from image files and creates image previews, which are referenced by the catalog. The previews are temporary JPEG files created in several sizes. Lightroom renders new previews whenever necessary while you're working on photos. Note that for raw files, the image data must be demosaiced and rendered to produce the preview. (There's more about these processes in Chapters 3 and 4.)

For now, you just need to know that Lightroom's image **preview files are stored outside the catalog in a separate package with a name that ends in "Previews.LRDATA".** When you're working on a photo in Lightroom, its previews are continually updated but the actual pixel data in the source file is never altered.

A quick overview of Lightroom's previews:

- **Minimal:** Used for displaying thumbnails (the smallest previews).

- **Standard:** Used for larger, single-image previews in the main preview area.

- **1:1:** The largest previews in Lightroom, 1:1 refers to one screen pixel per one image pixel. You'll often be looking at 1:1 previews as you zoom in to look more closely at a photo.

Previews can be purged, deleted, and re-rendered at any time, as long as Lightroom can find the original files on disk. Lightroom can't build new previews from missing files, or files stored on offline volumes. Previews are explained in context at various places throughout this book.

SMART PREVIEWS

New in Lightroom 5: A new type of (optional) preview, called a smart preview, has been added. A smart preview is a copy of the source photo that is converted to a type of DNG file (DNG format is covered in more depth in the Appendix) that uses a lossy form of compression (similar to the compression used in JPEG files) to make the file size smaller. In addition, the pixel dimensions of a smart preview are reduced to 2540 pixels on the longest side (if the source photo is larger than that) to further reduce file size. This combination of lossy compression and reduced pixel dimensions is intended to be a good compromise between file size and quality. **Smart previews are stored in their own separate package alongside the catalog and regular preview cache with a name that ends in "Smart Previews.LRDATA".** The other reason they are converted to DNG is so that they remain fully editable raw photos, and this is the most important part. We now have the ability to store a lightweight version of our raw photos right alongside the catalog file and always have them with us.

Why is that so important you ask? Well, if you have a situation where the original source photos are offline (such as on disconnected external drive), but you had previously rendered smart previews of the offline photos, then Lightroom allows you to continue working with those photos as if they were still online. That's right, you can head to the Develop module and make adjustments to the smart preview and Lightroom will continue to store those adjustments in the Lightroom catalog (while updating the appearance of the preview), and whenever the source files become available to the catalog again (such as when you connect that external drive) Lightroom will automatically associate those adjustments to the original files as if they were there all the time. As an added bonus, the existence of smart previews helps speed up the loading process of photos into the Develop module even when the source photos are online.

The benefits are not limited to the Develop module, though; you can work with smart previews in all of the modules and even export copies (keeping in mind the limitations of the smaller pixel dimensions). Due to the smaller pixel dimensions of the smart previews, when you zoom to 1:1 you are looking at the 100% view of this smaller file, so you might want to save pixel peeping activities such as noise reduction and sharpening for when you have the original files online.

In Chapter 2 we look at how to create smart previews during import. In Chapter 3 we explore how to create smart previews after import, as well as how to delete them and identify which photos already have smart previews. In Chapter 11 we see how smart previews can be created during catalog export to create a relatively lightweight and mobile travel catalog that allows you to leave your source photos at home.

 Be mindful of available disk space
While smart previews can open new doors to exciting workflows, it is important to keep in mind that they will take up additional disk space on the drive where your catalog is stored. You can monitor the size of the smart preview cache from the File Handling tab of the Catalog Settings (more on this in Chapter 11).

01

HOW LIGHTROOM USES PROFILES

Lightroom makes use of three main types of profiles that help create the best possible rendering of your photos. Camera profiles describe the color and tone characteristics of specific image sensors and processors. Lens profiles help correct for flaws in the optical properties of individual camera lenses. ICC profiles describe the color reproduction of different printers and monitors. Using the correct profiles you can be assured of the highest possible quality from your work in Lightroom. These are discussed at length in the chapters where they're most relevant: Develop, Export, Book, and Print.

LIGHTROOM PRESETS AND TEMPLATES

Throughout the program, Lightroom provides presets and templates to store settings and layouts. Generally speaking, presets store settings; templates store formatted layouts. This distinction is not critical; throughout Lightroom you'll see frequent references to presets and/or templates, and the use of one term versus the other is somewhat inconsistent. What's important to understand is that presets and templates can save you lots of time by applying previously saved settings to your photos.

The default Lightroom installation comes with many built-in presets and templates. As you work with Lightroom, you should also save your own as this will dramatically speed up your workflow. You can also use presets and templates made by other people; see the Appendix for links.

PRESETS FOLDER

The Lightroom presets folder is an important folder on your hard drive that you may access frequently the more you use Lightroom. To get there quickly, open the Lightroom Preferences (under the Lightroom menu on Mac and the Edit menu on Windows) and on the Presets tab, click the button for Show Lightroom Presets Folder. We look at using presets and templates throughout the book.

USING PRESETS AND TEMPLATES FOR BATCH PROCESSING

A batch is a group of files that are all processed using the same criteria. Lightroom gives you lots of ways to apply file-specific, variable data to your batch-processed photos, such as a unique filename for each one. This is mainly done using templates. When processing many images at one time, the choices you make become increasingly important. Effective batch processing requires planning ahead and thinking carefully about the correct settings.

ABOUT LIGHTROOM PREFERENCES

In many scenarios the default Preference settings used when Lightroom is installed are ideal. However, when you've worked with Lightroom for some time, there may be settings you want to change to suit your computer configuration or work habits. On a Mac, Lightroom's Preferences are accessed under the Lightroom menu. On Windows, they're under the Edit menu. Spend some time getting to know the options available in the Preferences dialog boxes; they are fairly straightforward, and with an understanding of Lightroom's interface and functionality the settings you want to change will become more evident. In the chapters that follow, key preferences are explained in context of a particular aspect of the workflow, and there's also more about Preferences in the Appendix.

Saving and backing up your work

As you work on your photos, Lightroom automatically saves your adjustments in the catalog and continually generates screen previews based on the adjustments that have been applied. Your original file (regardless of its format) remains unaltered, giving you unlimited flexibility for changing your mind later. However, storing all your editing instructions only in the Lightroom catalog carries some risk. For example, if you do all your processing in Lightroom and the catalog becomes corrupted (and you haven't made backups) you could lose that editing data, requiring the work to be redone. This is why you should consider the option of saving your work to the photo's own metadata when working in Lightroom.

SAVE METADATA TO FILE

When you save metadata to files, in addition to being stored in the Lightroom catalog, the metadata processing instructions for the adjustments you make are stored with the photo. This can be done using sidecar files (for camera raw formats) or by saving metadata in the actual files themselves (for all other formats). Saving out the metadata helps ensure 1) your work won't be lost and 2) your edits travel with the original file wherever it goes. Even when you save metadata adjustments into a file, the pixel data is not changed: the metadata is stored in a separate part of the file and can be read back in when Lightroom (or other software compatible with XMP format metadata) loads the image. To Save Metadata to File, use the command on the Metadata menu or the shortcut ⌘+S or Ctrl+S.

BACKUP AND ARCHIVAL

Every computer user knows that backing up your files is critical. Still, I'd be negligent if I didn't remind you *to actually do it*. And by doing it, I mean not only creating backup copies, but actually going through the process of restoring from your backup to ensure that you know how to do it and (more importantly) that your backups are working. People accidentally lose important computer data every day. Usually it's because of user error (deleting something unintentionally) but equipment failure is also common. In the digital photography workflow there's absolutely no excuse to risk losing all your work. I can't overemphasize the need for creating a practical system for backing up your work and updating your backups frequently. When a hard drive fails mechanically or its data become corrupted, if you're prepared, you will be back on track quickly. **Update your backups after every work session!**

BACKING UP LIGHTROOM CATALOGS

Lightroom offers the ability to make a backup of a catalog file and test its integrity. Lightroom catalog backups are done when you exit the program; you should, at least occasionally, allow these backups to be performed. **During a Lightroom backup, only the current Lightroom catalog is backed up—the image files are not copied.**

Lightroom backup settings are found in the Catalog Settings dialog box. When Lightroom asks if you want to do a backup, you can specify the location for the backup file (see **Figure 1–6**). The default location for the backup is right alongside your working catalog, but **I highly recommend that you choose an alternative location on a separate**

drive from your working catalog.
The backups are automatically
placed in subfolders named with
the date and time.

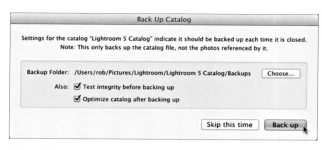

Figure 1-6

 **Keep only the most recent one
or two catalog backups**
Go to your backups folder to
periodically delete old ones after
verifying that your current backup
copies are in working order.

BACKING UP IMAGE FILES
As is discussed repeatedly
throughout the book, you should
always maintain at least two
current copies of each of your
photo and video files on separate
media (see **Figure 1–7**). The
easiest way it to set up two hard
drives, one as the master working
library and the other as its mirror
image. If possible, store a third
backup at an alternate location. Update these backups frequently.

Master
Working
Drive

Working
Backup
(Local)

Archive
(Off-site)

Figure 1-7

Syncing drives
I recommend you use backup software that can synchronize data between hard drives.
During a sync, the files on each drive are compared, and only the files that have changed
are copied. See the Appendix for links to recommended software.

Cloud backups
Depending on the size of your photo library and the frequency with which you back up
large numbers of files, using cloud storage services might be a viable option. Many of
these services allow you to create your initial backup by sending a hard drive for them to
copy files to the server, which is much faster than waiting the potential weeks it might
take to copy a large image collection over the Internet.

Essential troubleshooting
As with any software application, things can and sometimes will go wrong when you're
working in Lightroom. If you're diligent about backing up your work you need not fear
any situation Lightroom may present. Following are some general guidelines for handling
trouble with Lightroom.

WHAT TO DO AFTER A CRASH
If Lightroom unexpectedly quits on you, or you have to force quit or restart your
machine, you need to proceed with care the next time you launch Lightroom. While
Lightroom has a catalog open, a lock file is placed in the catalog folder to ensure other
programs on your computer can't tamper with the Lightroom data. After a crash, the

previous lock file may remain, and you may also see a Journal file. **Do not delete the Journal file!** Lightroom will use it to help restore the previous work session when the program is restarted.

However, if after a crash, you attempt to open your catalog and you get the message that the catalog is already open by another program you should try moving the file with the .LOCK extension out of the folder where your catalog is stored, and then double-click the .LRCAT file to open the catalog again. Sometimes a crash causes that LOCK file to linger when it shouldn't, which prevents you from reopening the catalog.

Also, in these situations, there is the possibility of catalog corruption. If Lightroom tells you the catalog is corrupt and needs to be repaired, let it proceed. After a successful repair, optimize and back up the catalog. If the repair is unsuccessful, or the catalog is acting quirky, you may need to restore a previous catalog backup to use as your new master working catalog. See Chapter 11 for more information about recovering corrupted catalogs.

 Avoid force-quitting Lightroom whenever possible

If you experience what appears to be a crash in Lightroom, especially if you can still move the cursor, give it a few minutes to see if the application and/or operating system recover from the condition. Force-quitting Lightroom at any time and for any reason dramatically increases the likelihood of data corruption. Of course, sometimes force-quitting can't be helped... keep good backups!

The Lightroom Workspace

When you launch Lightroom, the main window opens with the same settings and image selections that were in use when you last quit the program (see **Figure 1–8**). Following is an overview of the Lightroom screen layout, tools, and controls. The specific operations of these are detailed in the chapters that follow.

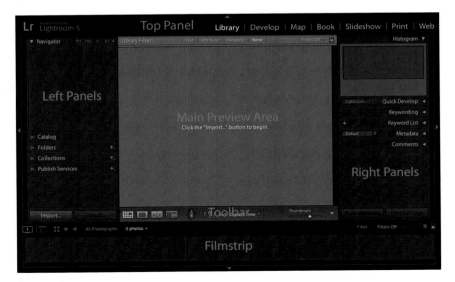

Figure 1-8

01

MAIN APPLICATION WINDOW

Lightroom's main window opens when you launch the program. This is where you'll do most of your work. The appearance of the main application window is highly customizable.

SCREEN MODES

The main Lightroom application window has four screen modes:

- **Normal:** A floating, resizable window. May or may not fill your entire screen. Resize the window by clicking and dragging its sides or corners. Move the window by clicking and dragging the title bar at the top.

- **Full screen with menubar:** Fills your screen with the Lightroom application window. This window is not resizable.

- **Full screen:** Like the above, but the main menu bar at the top of the screen is hidden. (On Windows, the Taskbar is hidden as well; this is my preferred screen mode.) As needed, put your mouse cursor at the top of the screen to access the menu bar. When you're finished, move away from the menu bar and it becomes hidden again. Press Shift+F to cycle through these first three screen modes in turn. Note, the old shortcut of pressing the F key now takes you to Full Screen Preview instead of cycling through the screen modes.

- **Full Screen Preview: New in Lightroom 5:** There is a true full screen mode that takes your photo to full screen and hides everything else. Press F to jump into and out of Full Screen Preview.

LIGHTS OUT

Lights Out dims or hides all the interface elements to show only the photo previews (see **Figure 1–9**). If no photographs are selected, all the thumbnails will remain visible in Lights Out. If one or more photos are selected, those will remain visible while the unselected photos will be hidden. There are three Lights Out modes:

- **Lights On:** This is the default state, where all interface elements and photographs are shown at full strength.

- **Lights Dim:** The interface is dimmed (by a percentage you can set in Lightroom Preferences).

- **Lights Out:** All interface elements are hidden by a solid color (also specified in Preferences).

Lightroom Interface Preferences

Many of Lightroom's interface options can also be customized in the Lightroom Preferences (under the Lightroom menu on Mac and the Edit menu on Windows).

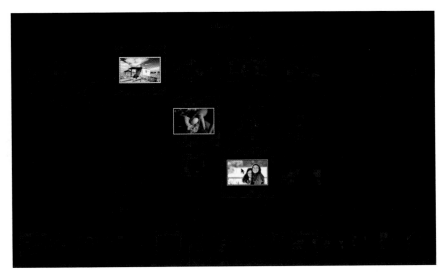

Figure 1-9

SECONDARY DISPLAY

Lightroom offers support for dual monitors using the Secondary Display feature (see **Figure 1–10**). Open the second window by clicking the button on the upper left side of the Filmstrip. The Secondary Display is a pared-down version of the main window and has its own layout and controls. (You can also play slideshows in the second window; see Chapter 8.) You can open the Secondary Display window even with only one monitor.

Figure 1-10

01

MODULES

All work in Lightroom is done in one of seven modules. The modules provide tools and commands specific to each phase of the workflow. The modules can be accessed using the Module Picker to the right of the top panel (see **Figure 1–11**) or by using various keyboard shortcuts.

Figure 1-11

LIBRARY

This is where you organize, sort, and manage your images. Library is also where you edit video in Lightroom. A limited subset of processing controls is provided in the Quick Develop panel. See Chapter 3 for more information about Library.

DEVELOP

Here you can process your photos to perfection. Cropping and straightening, tone and color adjustments, noise reduction, sharpening, creative effects… the list goes on and on. The Develop module is the core of Lightroom's image processing power; see Chapter 4.

MAP

Using the Map module you can view the locations where your photos were taken. You can use the Map module to add and edit location data as well as integrating GPS data using tracklogs. See Chapter 6.

BOOK

The Book module allows you to create sophisticated book designs and upload them directly to Blurb and/or output them as PDF and JPEG files. See Chapter 7.

SLIDESHOW

In the Slideshow module you can design presentations for playback within Lightroom or exporting as video, PDF or JPEG files. See Chapter 8 for information about working in Slideshow.

PRINT

Lightroom's Print module gives you a variety of tools to create custom layouts and make high-quality prints. See Chapter 9.

WEB

In Lightroom's Web module, generating Web galleries in HTML or Flash format is quick and easy. See Chapter 10.

MODULE TIPS

Each module has its own set of Tips (see **Figure 1–12**). You'll see them the first time you enter each module under a new installation of Lightroom, and then they go away. To see Module Tips at any time, use the command under the Help menu.

MAIN PREVIEW AREA

Figure 1-12

In Library and Develop, photos are shown in the center of the Lightroom window (see **Figure 1–13**). In the output modules this area is used to preview the current layout. The size of the preview area is variable, based on the visibility and sizes of the panels.

Figure 1-13

 Preview background options
Right-click or Ctrl+click in the main preview background to change color and texture options (see **Figure 1–14**).

PANELS

Around the main preview area, the Lightroom application window is divided into four panels (see Figure 1–8). Lightroom's panels contain the majority of controls you will use to process your photos. Note that panels can't be undocked, moved, or floated in the main window; they are always in the same position. However, they can be hidden

Figure 1-14

27

01

and resized as described below. **The contents of the left and right panels change within each module.** Generally, left panels are used for organizing, batch processing, and accessing presets and templates, while right panels contain tools used for applying specific settings to photos or output layouts. The top panel (Module Picker) and bottom panel (Filmstrip) remain consistent throughout all the modules.

TOP PANEL

The top panel contains the Identity Plate (left) and the Module Picker (right). During processing, Lightroom's progress indicators are also displayed in the Identity Plate area.

IDENTITY PLATES

At the far left of the top panel is the main Identity Plate (see **Figure 1–15**). You can customize it with your own text or graphic files. The main Identity Plate can be used in slideshows, Web galleries, and print layouts, and in those modules you can also create additional Identity Plates.

Figure 1-15

APPLY A CUSTOM IDENTITY PLATE

Use the menu command under Lightroom menu➔Identity Plate Setup (Mac) or Edit... ➔Identity Plate Setup (Windows) to customize and save identity plate presets using the main Identity Plate Editor (see **Figure 1–16**). Custom Identity Plates are stored within the catalog file, and as such are unique to each catalog. I sometimes use this to display the name of the catalog to serve as a reminder of which catalog I am using. Also see Chapters 8, 9, and 10 for more about using Identity Plates in the output modules.

To turn off the custom identity plate, simply uncheck the box in the Identity Plate Editor.

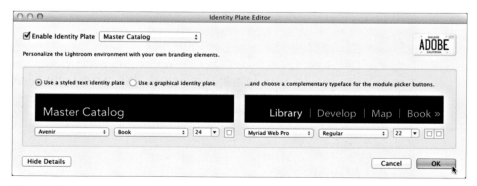

Figure 1-16

THE ACTIVITY VIEWER AND MULTITHREADING

When Lightroom is working on a process, the main Identity Plate is replaced with the Activity Viewer, which shows one or more progress bars (see **Figure 1–17**). Lightroom is multithreaded, which means it can multitask: several operations can be performed at

the same time. If more than one process is going, multiple progress bars are shown; you can click the triangle on the right side of the progress bars to see the individual operations, and can also then access the cancel button to stop the process.

STOPPING A PROCESS

To stop a process, click the small X at the right side of the progress bar.

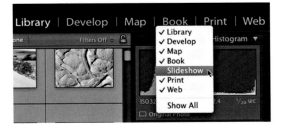

Figure 1-17

 Move on to other tasks

There is usually no need to wait for a process to complete before moving on to another task. For example, if you are in the middle of an import, you can still work on images already in the Library. If you're exporting a Web gallery, a batch of images, etc., the same applies.

THE MODULE PICKER

Right-click or Ctrl+click on a module name in the top panel. From the pop-up menu, you can hide and show individual modules from the list (see **Figure 1–18**).

LEFT AND RIGHT PANELS

The contents of the panels are different for each module. Generally, the left panels provide access to files and

Figure 1-18

templates within each module. The right panels in Library and Develop include tools for modifying the photo(s). In the output modules, the right panels contain controls for changing layout settings.

HIDING AND SHOWING PANEL GROUPS

The combined assemblages of the left and right module panels are typically referred to as panel groups (or panel sets). To hide a panel group, click its outer edge. Click again to show it. Or, when a panel group is hidden, you can temporarily show it by hovering your mouse cursor over the collapsed panel at the outer edge of the window (when it is set to Auto Hide/Show, which can be enabled or disabled). Auto Hide/Show allows you to temporarily access the panel group to make whatever changes are necessary, and when you move the cursor away, the panel group is hidden again. (I personally find that behavior annoying and prefer to use the Manual setting.) Right-click or Ctrl+click a panel edge to set options for Auto Hide/Show and syncing between opposite panels (see **Figure 1–19**). **Panel states for each module persist until you change them.**

Figure 1-19

The top panel and Filmstrip can also be hidden in the same manner. Alternatively, you can press the Tab key to hide/show both the left and right panel groups simultaneously, or press Shift+Tab to hide/show the left, right, top, and Filmstrip all at once.

CHANGE PANEL SIZE

Panels can be resized by dragging their edges. Wider panels show longer file and template names and provide greater sensitivity for adjustment sliders. Narrower panels make more room for photos in the preview area. To change the width of a panel group, position your mouse cursor over the inside edge of any panel; the mouse cursor changes to a double arrow (see **Figure 1–20**). Click and drag to resize the panel. Note that all panels have a minimum and maximum width.

Figure 1-20

Show the panels you use; hide the others

I usually work with different panel groups hidden in each module. For example, in Library, I prefer to keep the right panel hidden and the left panel showing. This is because the left panel provides access to files in Folders and Collections, which I use a lot. I less frequently use the Library right panel to make metadata edits to files (mostly keywords). Conversely, in the Develop module, I usually work with the left panel hidden and the right panel showing, because the tools I use most often are in the right panel.

EXPAND AND COLLAPSE INDIVIDUAL PANELS

In addition to hiding and showing the entire left and right panel groups, individual panels can be expanded and contracted (see **Figure 1–21**). Click anywhere in the top bar of each panel to hide or show its contents (it's not necessary to click directly on the triangle).

Figure 1-21

EXPAND ALL AND COLLAPSE ALL

Right-click or Ctrl+click on the panel header and select Expand All or Collapse All to open or close all the panels in the group.

HIDE AND SHOW INDIVIDUAL PANELS

The individual panels in the left and right panel groups can be hidden and restored from the main panel track as you see fit. Right-click or Ctrl+click on a panel header, and then make selections from the contextual menu to show or hide individual panels or select Hide All/Show All (see **Figure 1–22**).

Note: The Navigator, Preview, and Histogram panels cannot be hidden.

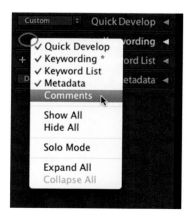

Figure 1-22

SOLO MODE

When you enable Solo Mode, opening one panel closes all the others. This is my preferred way of working. While in Solo Mode you can hold the Shift key while clicking another panel header to open additional panels, which can be handy at times.

Right-click or Ctrl+click on any of the panel headers; select the option from the pop-up menu to enable Solo Mode (see **Figure 1–23**). The Triangle icon on the panel header changes to a dotted pattern to indicate Solo Mode is active.

Option+click or Alt+click on any panel header to open that panel and simultaneously toggle Solo Mode.

Figure 1-23

NAVIGATOR PANEL

The Navigator (see **Figure 1–24**) is in the first position of the left panel group in the Library and Develop modules (this panel is replaced with Preview in the output modules, where it functions a bit differently). The Navigator shows a preview of the selected photo, or the target photo if multiple photos are selected. The Navigator panel can be used to select zoom levels, or ratios of magnification. Selecting a zoom level in the Navigator enlarges the photo preview to that size.

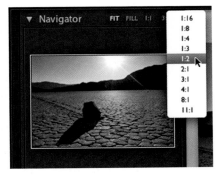

Figure 1-24

Zoom ratios

Unlike other programs that specify magnification level with a percentage, Lightroom's zoom levels are based on the ratio of image pixels to screen pixels. 1:2 is one screen pixel to two image pixels. 4:1 is four screen pixels to one image pixel, and so on.

The preset zoom ratios are:

- **Fit:** Fits the entire photo into the main preview area.

- **Fill:** Expands the photo so that the entire preview area is filled. The sides of images may not be visible.

- **1:1:** One image pixel for one screen pixel.

- **User-selected setting:** The fourth zoom ratio setting uses the last custom zoom level you selected. Clicking this ratio also displays a pop-up menu for you to choose the custom zoom level (see Figure 1–24).

01

Move around an enlarged preview with the Navigator
When zoomed in to a photo, drag the white box in the Navigator preview to change the area shown in the main preview (see Figure 1–24).

Preview presets in Navigator
The Navigator offers more than just a preview. For instance, in Library, moving your mouse over folders or collections will show the first image in that source in the Navigator. And in Develop, Navigator shows previews of presets. Just roll your mouse cursor over the presets in the list, and Navigator will show you what that preset looks like applied to the selected image.

FILMSTRIP (BOTTOM PANEL)
The bottom panel, called the Filmstrip, shows thumbnails for the images in the current image source (see **Figure 1–25**). The Filmstrip remains the same throughout all the modules. You can change the order of photos in the Filmstrip and the display of the thumbnails. There's more about this in Chapter 3.

Figure 1-25

FILMSTRIP NAVIGATION CONTROLS
At the left of the top part of the Filmstrip are navigation controls. The square icon is a shortcut to Library Grid view mode; next to that are arrows to go forward and back.

Change the size of Filmstrip thumbnails
Drag the top edge of the Filmstrip to resize it; this changes the size of the thumbnails.

Double-click to toggle size
When you've resized the Filmstrip, you can double-click the top of it to toggle between the two most recently used sizes.

PANEL CONTROLS
Within the panels, Lightroom provides several types of software controls to edit and process your photos. Most can be manipulated using either your mouse or the keyboard. Some require you to select from a menu; others let you type directly into text boxes.

DISCLOSURE TRIANGLE BUTTONS
Throughout Lightroom's panels there are very small and easily overlooked black triangle-shaped buttons (see **Figure 1–26**). These open and close a subsection of the panel, revealing or hiding more controls.

ARROW BUTTONS

These are found on the Quick Develop panel (see Figure 1–26). While most of Lightroom's settings are absolute (applying a specific value), the arrow button controls are relative—they are applied on top of whatever settings are already present. The single arrow buttons apply changes in smaller increments than the double arrows. See Chapter 3 for more about Quick Develop.

SLIDERS

Particularly in Develop, the sliders (see **Figure 1–27**) are the most common method of making adjustments to photos. Lightroom's sliders can be adjusted in several ways:

- Drag the slider with your cursor.

- Scrub the slider's numeric value left and right using the mouse.

- Position your cursor anywhere over the slider and then use the up and down arrow keys to increase or decrease the value.

- Double-click a slider to Reset it to its default value.

- Double-click the field and type in a numeric value.

TEXT ENTRY FIELDS

There are text fields in many panels throughout the modules. To enter text, click on the field and type. Always be sure to press Enter or Return when you're done typing text into a field anywhere in Lightroom. This reduces the chance of accidentally typing something into a text box when you're trying to use a shortcut. If you change your mind typing into a text or dialog box, or to deactivate a tool, press Esc to cancel.

Figure 1-26

Figure 1-27

01

TOOLTIPS

Place your cursor over part of the interface and let it remain for a few seconds (without moving or clicking) to see a pop-up tooltip telling you what that control does. If there is a keyboard shortcut for the tool or command, it will also be shown in the tooltip (see Figure 1–26).

PANEL SWITCHES

Most panels that provide controls for image adjustments (and Filmstrip filters) provide a small switch that allows you to disable/enable the adjustments for that panel. Like a light switch, up is "on" and down is "off" (see **Figure 1–28**). Look for these switches in numerous places throughout Lightroom's interface. In some cases, they may be oriented left/right. In all cases, they perform the same function: enabling and disabling the effects of that panel or control.

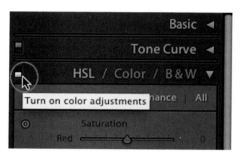

Figure 1-28

PANEL SCROLL BARS

When multiple left and right panels are open, their contents are often too long for all the panels to show on the screen. In this event, scroll bars appear to allow you to move up and down within the panel track (see **Figure 1–29**). Click and drag the bar to scroll, or use your mouse wheel.

PANEL END MARKS

The panel end mark is an ornament that can appear at the bottoms of the left and right panel groups (see **Figure 1–30**), and is designed to let you know there are no more panels below. In Lightroom 5 the default setting is None, and only one panel end mark graphic is provided as an alternative. I prefer to leave them hidden to reduce screen clutter, but you can right-click or Ctrl+click anywhere below the last panel and select the panel end mark (Small Flourish) from the list.

Figure 1-29

 Custom panel end marks

From the panel contextual menu, select Go to Panel End Marks Folder. You can find custom panel end marks on the web, or create your own in Photoshop (PNG is a good format for these). Put the image files in the folder and your custom files will then show in the list. One clever idea for end marks I saw once was from John Beardsworth, who made

Figure 1-30

a graphical reference key for the meaning of rating stars and color labels in his workflow (check out his article here: www.lightroomsolutions.com/articles/panel-end-markers).

MENUS, COMMANDS, AND SHORTCUTS

Lightroom's main menu bar changes from one module to the next. In this way, Lightroom is like seven programs in one! To memorize all the commands available in Lightroom requires using and remembering all the different menus in each module. (However, there are some shared menus and commands that remain constant throughout the modules.)

As you're learning to use Lightroom, frequently look at the menus, commands, and shortcuts available in each module. This will not only give you a better grasp of the full functionality available in Lightroom, it will speed your work as you memorize the locations and shortcuts for specific commands. As with Lightroom's menus, each module has its own shortcuts, and some shortcuts in different modules share the same key. Shortcuts are shown next to the corresponding commands in menus (see **Figure 1–31**).

Figure 1-31

01

➡️ **Many shortcuts are toggles**

In Lightroom, many of the keyboard shortcuts turn tools on and off or make items active/inactive. This is a toggle control.

CONTEXTUAL MENUS

Lightroom is full of contextual menus (see **Figure 1–32**). Using them is essential to speeding up your work. A contextual menu's contents are determined by the context in which you clicked. Depending on where you click, contextual menus appear showing the commands most useful and appropriate for the object clicked. Though this book provides many keyboard shortcuts, I use contextual menus as much or more than the keyboard. I work with a tablet and stylus, and a right-click or Ctrl+click is often faster than switching to the keyboard.

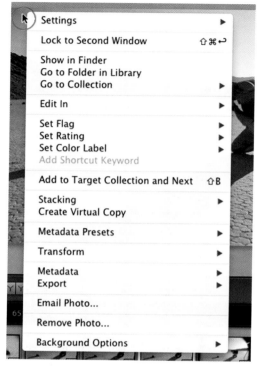

Figure 1-32

TOOLBARS

Each module has its own Toolbar containing various tools for that module (see **Figure 1–33**). The Toolbar is shown at the bottom of the main preview area and can be hidden and shown. Most of the tools and functions on the Toolbar can also be performed using shortcuts; once these are committed to memory, it's possible to work most of the time with the Toolbar not showing. Simply press the T key to hide (and show) the Toolbar.

Figure 1-33

CHANGE WHAT SHOWS IN THE TOOLBAR

At the right side of the Toolbar is a button that activates a menu that you can use to customize the contents of the Toolbar specific to each module (see Figure 1–33). The Toolbars for each module are described in those chapters.

WORKSPACE QUIRKS

Many of Lightroom's interface widgets are very small and—using various shades of gray, black, and white—can be easily missed. Get in the habit of looking closely at the Lightroom interface to discover the full set of controls. Unfortunately this low contrast color scheme cannot be changed.

OPTION OR ALT

In many areas of Lightroom's interface, holding the Option or Alt key reveals additional functions, such as hidden controls, buttons, and options. For example, the Quick Develop panel in Library shows additional controls when Option or Alt is held down. The Sharpening panel in Develop has uses for Option/Alt. And, holding Option/Alt changes the Export button to Export Catalog. Memorize the most important places the Option/Alt key is useful, and then as you're working, periodically press the key and watch how it changes the options on the screen. Many otherwise hidden functions become readily available.

 Hide-and-seek interface widgets

Throughout Lightroom there are controls that will show only if they are relevant to the selected photo or photos. In cases where these controls don't apply, they are hidden from view.

How to ensure accurate color for your photos

Color management refers to an integrated system of computer hardware and software working together to translate color from one device to another in a controlled way. For your photos to look their best, implementing color management is a critical aspect of successfully going from capture to print with the best possible quality.

The color management system (CMS) is built into your computer's operating system— on Mac it's ColorSync and on Windows Vista and 7 it's WCS. The CMS handles color management at the system level and is responsible for translating color values to and from your image files and output devices. Lightroom is color-managed by default and there are no color settings to configure. (Lightroom uses a 16-bit, proprietary color space for internal processing.)

CALIBRATING AND PROFILING YOUR DISPLAY

The most important step in achieving accurate color in your photos is working on a calibrated and profiled display. If you're using a properly calibrated and profiled display, you can trust that the colors you see on-screen in Lightroom are accurate.

01

Calibrating your display corrects its output settings. Profiling makes an ICC profile for use by the CMS. Calibrating and profiling your display must be done with a combination of dedicated hardware and software. Software alone (such as Adobe Gamma) is not sufficient. You must use a dedicated measurement device for accurate calibration. I use and recommend the X-Rite i1 (Eye One) and Color Munki systems for this; see the Appendix for links.

USING COLOR PROFILES

A color profile describes a color space—the range of available colors and their numeric values. Profiles can be embedded in image files. The embedded profile tells the color management system the parameters for translating the photo's colors to different devices—printer, monitor, etc. When Lightroom generates new files, profiles are always embedded by default. The Print and Book modules allow you to choose the color profiles to be used, as does the Export window. To ensure consistent color, whenever you're saving files out of Lightroom, you should always use the correct color profiles for the intended use. See Chapters 4, 5, 7, and 9 for more about working with color profiles.

Lightroom always respects and preserves profiles embedded in imported image files. For files with no embedded profile, sRGB is used. Video files do not have embedded profiles and thus cannot be color managed.

Next steps

Now that you've got a solid foundation in how Lightroom works, let's jump right in and import some photos! Chapter 2 describes how you can import photos from your hard drive and from a camera or memory card.

Process in Lightroom, not in-camera

Though many current camera models offer varying levels of processing within the camera itself (brightness, contrast, color, and sharpness controls; black and white conversion; etc.), it's almost always best to do the image processing in Lightroom, not in the camera.

Consider post-processing while you are shooting

Once you're comfortable quickly changing settings on your camera while shooting, start to consider how you will process the file later. Taking production issues into account while you're shooting will help you get better captures and make post-processing easier.

CHAPTER 02

Import

02

IMPORT: Indexing photos and videos with Lightroom catalogs

To work with photos and videos in Lightroom you must first import them. During the import, Lightroom reads the files on disk and creates a database entry for each file. These records are stored within the currently open catalog. A catalog record contains all the information *about* the image or video file—but *not the file itself* (refer to Figure 1-5 back in Chapter 1).

Regardless of the settings you use for the import, the actual images and video files are never stored inside the catalog. They are always stored outside the catalog, in a folder on your hard disk.

The image data from the imported files is not stored in the catalog, either. A Lightroom catalog only stores textual and numeric data: filenames, paths to their locations on disk, and all associated metadata (such as keywords and adjustment settings) are saved in the catalog as text entries. (There's no functionality provided to directly access this data; you only see the effects of the data—visually—as you work in the Lightroom modules.)

Lightroom never alters the original image data in the files on the hard drive.

As you work, Lightroom continually renders and saves previews for the photos and videos, using the current settings applied within the catalog. Previews are constantly being updated. Always remember that you are never looking at the actual file on disk—you're seeing a preview rendered in Lightroom, in real-time, based on the current settings. Lightroom continually references the files on disk, renders updated previews to your display, and stores your changes as metadata within the catalog. To permanently apply any changes, new files must be exported. (Exporting is discussed in Chapter 5.)

In this chapter, we cover the three most common scenarios you'll encounter for indexing files with a Lightroom catalog: importing from a hard drive, importing from a camera or other device, and shooting tethered (with your camera connected to the computer). Other alternative import scenarios are also discussed toward the end of the chapter.

You'll also get an in-depth look at all the functions and controls provided by the Import window, where you choose files to be imported and specify how Lightroom will handle the files (and metadata) during the import.

> ## What's New in Import
>
> - **Create Smart Previews on import**
> - **Tethered Capture update**

 Brush up on the fundamentals

If you are new to Lightroom and have skipped over Chapter 1, I strongly encourage you to review the Introduction to Lightroom Catalogs section in Chapter 1 to get up to speed on critical concepts required for having a successful Lightroom experience.

Really think about what you're doing
If importing is done incorrectly, it can lead to frustration, wasted time, and even potential loss of files. If at all possible, you should read and understand the contents of this chapter before you import a lot of files into Lightroom. Otherwise, expect to have lots of cleaning up to do later in the Library module.

 ## Overview of Import workflow
Step 1. Choose the source of the photos and videos to be imported (refer to Chapter 1 for an overview of supported file formats).

Step 2. Set the import method for how the files will be handled.

Step 3. If files are being copied or moved, choose the destination hard drive and folder.

Step 4. (Optional) Specify additional processing and addition of metadata to be performed by the import.

 At home versus on the road
Your import processes will likely vary when you use multiple computers; for example, if you use a laptop while traveling and a desktop computer at your studio. In Chapter 11 you can learn a lot more about working with multiple catalogs and computers.

What to do before importing
Prior to importing photos to Lightroom, you should devise a system for organizing and naming your files—you really don't want to have your photos and videos strewn all over your hard drives in multiple locations using different naming schemes. Setting up a well-organized digital storage system for your files will make your work easier—and provide peace of mind. Good "information architecture" can also dramatically accelerate your workflow.

Organize your files and folders as much as you can before importing them to Lightroom. Ideally, you won't import a bunch of junk just to be deleted later. You can use the Mac Finder, Windows Explorer, Adobe Bridge, or any other file browser you already own to organize your files.

At the very least, before you import photos, think carefully about 1) where the image files are now, 2) where you ultimately want them to be, 3) and what kinds of additional batch processing you might want to do during the import.

Once photos and videos have been imported to Lightroom, you should always do any further reorganizing from within Lightroom. Otherwise, Lightroom will not be able to keep track of the changes, and you'll end up with lots of missing files and folders in the Lightroom catalog. This is probably the biggest self-inflicted problem I see new Lightroom users create for themselves. Working with files and folders is covered in detail in Chapter 3.

 Download all figures
All figures in this book are available for download at:
www.lightroomers.com/lightroom5book

FOLDER AND FILE ORGANIZATION

Your photo and video files will always be contained within folders stored on one or more hard disk drives. No matter how many files and folders you have now, this number will increase significantly over time and your filing system must scale effectively with this growth.

Since you can't avoid the requirement for at least some basic level of organization on the hard drive, you need to be in control and aware of folder structures and naming conventions. Otherwise, you're likely to waste a lot of time looking for images, moving files around, wondering which file is which, and potentially deleting important files by accident.

How we arrange and name our files is one of the more subjective aspects of the digital photography workflow. Of course, you should use a system that fits your personal preferences and style of working, but following a few standard guidelines will make your system easier to manage.

1. On any given hard drive, store all photo and video files in subfolders under one main, top-level folder. This makes it much easier to keep your catalog links intact, especially when moving your image library to other drives. My main folder is called "ImportedPhotos" with subfolders underneath, named by year (see **Figure 2–1**).

2. Use as few subfolder levels as are necessary to support your ideal organizational structure. The number of nested folders (those within other folders) can easily get out of hand. You don't want to have to drill down through numerous levels of folders to get to an individual file.

Figure 2-1

3. Use descriptive names for folders and files. The names automatically assigned by your camera are not useful. At some point in your workflow, you should change the names of folders and files to give them meaningful names.

4. Use the same base names for folders and the files they contain. Think of a folder and the files it contains as a group. Give the folder a good name and use that same name as the basis for the files inside.

5. Each folder and file should have a unique name. This is a fundamental principle of information architecture, and one that you probably know from experience. If you have multiple, different files using the same name, things can get very confusing, very fast. If you always name files using the subject or location, the date (and time), a unique sequence number, plus helpful identifying descriptions such as dimensions, color space, or intended purpose, it's easy to assign unique names to every file. See the examples in the next section.

6. Keep only one copy of any given file on each hard drive. Just like with multiple files of the same name, keeping multiple copies of the same file in different places really causes problems. Don't duplicate the same file in different folders—with Lightroom, this is almost always unnecessary. If you need to save multiple versions of a photo for different purposes, be sure all filenames are unique and indicative of each file's unique properties. (However, with Lightroom, you will usually not need multiple, derivative files on disk. You can make unlimited variations of any single file on disk—without actually copying the original image file—using virtual copies (VCs). (VCs are discussed at length in Chapter 4.)

7. Keep all files from a single shooting session together in one folder. For any given shooting session, I make one folder, where I keep my original raw captures, plus layered master files from Photoshop and any final derivatives, such as those made for printing. Separating files by their file type takes lots of extra effort with very questionable benefits. Using metadata, there is usually no reason to make separate folders for raw, PSD, TIFF, JPEG, or MOV files. And doing so violates guideline number 5; for example, you could end up with many different subfolders with only the name "TIFF." You can easily find and sort photos by file type—and all kinds of other criteria—using Lightroom. (All imaging software is going this way; metadata is much more powerful and flexible than folder-based systems for search and retrieval.) If you've been in the habit of using folders for each file type, I recommend you try to break the dependence on elaborate folder structures and instead work toward more fully exploiting Lightroom's capabilities. The exception to this might be cases where you're exporting files for a particular purpose, such as sending to a client, etc., which is covered in Chapter 5.

There might be situations where just dumping everything into Lightroom and sorting it out from there is the most efficient way.

Importing files for the first time: Add

Assuming you already have many photos on your hard drive(s), the first step to building your Lightroom catalog is to import your existing images and video files. To do this, it's best to simply Add the files to the catalog, without creating copies or moving them to a new location during the import. The following workflow describes the basic steps necessary to import photos and videos from a hard drive to a Lightroom catalog. Referenced settings are described in detail later in this chapter.

Step 1. Open Lightroom. If this is the first time you've used Lightroom, no photos will be present, just the text *Click the "Import…" Button to begin* will be visible in the middle of the window (see **Figure 2–2**).

Step 2. In the Library module, click the Import… button at the bottom of the left panel (see Figure 2–2), or use the Import Photos and Video command under the File menu (or the keyboard shortcut). This opens the Import window.

Step 3. On the FROM Source panel on the left side of the screen, select the folder containing the photos to be imported (see **Figure 2–3**). You can use the Include Subfolders option to also import photos in lower-level folders.

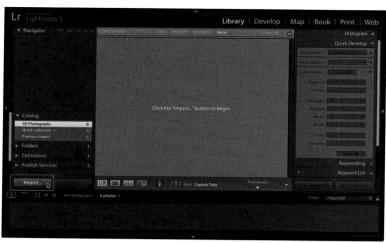

Figure 2-2

Step 4. In the main preview area in the center of the window, confirm the photos to be imported (see **Figure 2–4**). You can use the scroll bar at the right to preview all the photos to be imported. If Lightroom can't read a file its thumbnail will show a gray box or the text, "Preview unavailable for this file" (refer to Chapter 1 for a list of supported file types).

Figure 2-3

Step 5. At the top center of the Import window, make sure the Add button is highlighted (see **Figure 2–5**). This import method simply indexes the files in the current catalog, without moving or copying the files. At the top right of the window, the TO section should read "My Catalog."

Step 6. On the right side of the window, go to the panel labeled Apply During Import and make sure Develop Settings and Metadata are set to None, and the Keywords field is blank (see **Figure 2–6**). Since you don't know at

Figure 2-4

Figure 2-5

this point what metadata might already have been applied, it's best to leave this blank for now, and add metadata as necessary later, which we'll discuss in Chapter 3.

Step 7. Take another look around the Import screen to be sure everything's correct, then click the Import button at the bottom right (see **Figure 2–7**), or press Return or Enter. This starts the import.

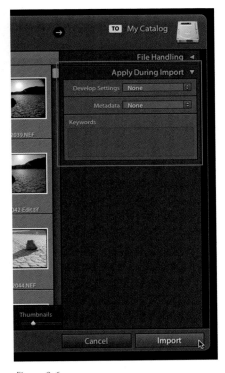

Congratulations! You've just introduced Lightroom to your existing library of photos and videos. From this point forward you will manage those files from inside of Lightroom. In addition, from this point forward you will be most likely importing new photos from your camera's memory card, so let's take a closer look at that workflow.

 ## Copy files from a camera

After you've completed a shoot or filled up a memory card, you should download the files to your computer and back them up as soon as possible. Lightroom facilitates this and much more: you can use Lightroom to handle the transfer of files from your camera to your hard disk and subsequently import them to the Lightroom catalog. You can also import photos from your phone or other mobile device using this method.

Figure 2-6

You can't import files from a removable device using the Add method. Photo and video files stored on any removable media—memory cards, cameras, smartphones, etc.—must be copied onto a hard drive first in order to be imported to Lightroom. Remember that Lightroom always needs to have access to the files in the catalog in order to export full size copies and pass copies along to external editors, and for you to be able to fully evaluate

Figure 2-7

the photos at 1:1 or greater zoom levels. So, the imported files must be stored on a hard drive connected to the computer, either directly or on a local network.

Lightroom 5 allows us to create Smart Previews (covered in Chapter 1), which allows us to work with our photos inside of Lightroom while the original source files are offline. This is a fantastic new addition to Lightroom, but it is still critical that you always know where your source files are located, and that you can easily reconnect them to the catalog

02

when you need to perform tasks that exceed the scope of the Smart Preview as I outlined above. In other words, Smart Previews are very useful, but you still need to manage and protect the original source photos.

The one necessary component of this workflow is allowing Lightroom to copy the files from the device onto a hard disk. Optionally, during this type of import, Lightroom can also rename the copied files, create new folders on the hard drive, convert raw files to DNG, and apply metadata. As you can see, copying files with a Lightroom import gives you many powerful batch-processing capabilities. If you do all the preceding steps, your photos will appear in the Lightroom catalog preloaded with metadata and looking great. With the automated batch processing done during the import, you will be able to move quickly through editing the shoot and finish your work in Develop with minimal effort.

Use the following steps to copy files from your memory card (or other device) to your hard drive and add the copied files to the Lightroom catalog. The individual settings included in the steps are described in much more detail later in this chapter.

Step 1. Open Lightroom. If you have previously imported photos, make sure the correct catalog is open by confirming the contents of the Folders panel or checking the location in the Catalog Settings dialog box (it's important to become familiar with where your catalog is located on your drive, and it's critical that you always know which catalog you have open). If this is the first time you've used Lightroom, no photos will be present, just the text *Click the "Import…" Button to begin* will be visible in the middle of the window (see Figure 2–2).

Step 2. Connect the device. If you're copying files from a digital camera, it's best to use a card reader, if possible—this is faster, more reliable, and safer than transferring directly from the camera (no pesky camera drivers to worry about and no danger of the camera battery running out in the middle of a transfer).

Step 3. Lightroom might detect the connection to the card or device and open the Import window automatically (check the Appendix for a discussion of how to set up the preferences for this). If not, click the Import button (at the bottom of the left panel in Library) to open the Import window.

Step 4. The removable device should automatically be selected in the Source panel at the top left of the Import window (see **Figure 2–8**). If not, select it from the Source panel in the Devices section.

Step 5. In the main preview area in the center of the window, check the photos to be imported

Figure 2-8

02

(see **Figure 2–9**). If the files are already in this catalog, they will be dimmed and unavailable for selection because the Don't import suspected duplicates box in the File Handling panel is checked by default (more on this later). If Lightroom can't read a file its thumbnail will show a gray box or the text "Preview unavailable for this file." You can sort the previews using a variety of methods, including Media Type. Use the scroll bar at the right to confirm all the photos to be imported. If there are files you don't want copied/imported, you can uncheck them in the preview.

Figure 2-9

Figure 2-10

Step 6. At the top center of the Import window, make sure the Copy button is highlighted (see **Figure 2–10**). This import method copies the files from the card or device and then imports the copied files to the catalog.

Step 7. At the top right of the window, the TO section lists a default hard drive and folder location (see Figure 2–10). To choose a different location for the copied files, click the TO button, and then either choose another destination if it's listed in the recent sources, or choose Other Destination… to select a different folder on a hard drive. Skip down to the Destination panel near the bottom right of the Import window (see **Figure 2–11**). You need to confirm the destination for the copied files; use the directory list to see a preview of the folder where the files will be copied and, if necessary, change the folder creation settings on the Destination panel. Detailed instructions for working with destination folders are provided later in this chapter.

Figure 2-11

Step 8. (Optional) On the File Handling panel at the top right, you can enable the option for Make a Second Copy To: if you want to make an additional backup during the copy (see **Figure 2–12**). Use the pop-up menu to choose the backup location. (Make sure backups are saved onto a different hard drive than the master copies.) **New in Lightroom 5:** You can also choose to have smart previews created during import (we'll discuss this further in the section on the File Handling panel in this chapter).

Figure 2-12

Step 9. (Optional) On the File Renaming panel, tick the check box if you want to rename the copied files (see **Figure 2–13**) and choose the file naming template to be applied.

Step 10. (Optional) On the Apply During Import panel you can specify additional metadata to be applied to the files as they are imported: Develop Settings, Metadata, and Keywords (see **Figure 2–14**).

Figure 2-13

Step 11. Look over all the settings on the Import screen to make sure everything is correct, then click the Import button at the bottom right of the window (see **Figure 2–15**), or press Return or Enter. This starts the import.

 Back up right away
Sync your backups immediately after an import completes. Confirm the integrity of the imported/copied files (usually, just quickly scrolling through them is sufficient) and make a backup to a second hard drive or a DVD.

Figure 2-14

 Format the card in the camera
After you've downloaded your files to a hard drive and confirmed your backups, format the memory card in the *camera* before each new shooting session.

 Avoid modifying or deleting the files on the card using your computer
Your computer file system and the file system on the memory card do not necessarily get along. It is safest to never manipulate the files on your memory card from your computer. Deleting, moving, renaming, or modifying folders on the card increases the risk of data corruption. Most importantly, the generally accepted best practice is to **never format the card using your computer.** This can render the card unreadable by the camera.

Figure 2-15

What happens during an import

When you initiate an import, the Import window closes and returns you to the Library Grid view, with the Catalog panel showing the Current Import (which becomes Previous Import once complete) source by default (see **Figure 2–16**). However, there is a new option in the Preferences that gives you the option to have Lightroom return you to the last folder or collection you were in before the import started (these settings are covered in greater depth in the Appendix). If you're copying files, Lightroom makes copies first, and then adds each file to the catalog. Lightroom reads each file being imported, creates a new record in the catalog, applies any optional metadata you've specified, and renders previews for the image or video.

Figure 2-16

With the top panel open, the progress indicator at the left displays the approximate amount of processing remaining for each stage of the import, along with messages describing the current operation in progress (see Figure 2–16).

A photo thumbnail appears in Grid and Filmstrip as each file is added to the catalog. You can begin working on newly imported photos and videos as soon as they are visible in the Library Grid view—you don't need to wait for an import to finish work on files already in the catalog. You can switch from the Current Import source to another image source—or to any other module—while an import is in progress. (However, you can't start another import until the current one finishes.)

 Import failures

If Lightroom fails to import any files, a dialog box appears at the end of the import with a list of which files failed and why, along with buttons to show the failed files in Mac Finder or Windows Explorer.

STOPPING AN IMPORT IN PROGRESS

If you start an import and realize you made a mistake or change your mind about something, you can cancel the import. However, it's often best to let the import finish and clean up after the fact.

If you decide to stop an import in progress, click the X next to the progress indicator in the Library module (see Figure 2–16). **After clicking once, wait for Lightroom to finish what it's doing.** (You can remove the incorrectly imported files later; see Chapter 3 for information about deleting files.)

Most importantly, if you're doing an import and the Lightroom application seems to freeze, or hang, be patient. If at all possible, don't force-quit Lightroom, or click anywhere else on the screen during this time. Most often, Lightroom can recover in a moment or two.

The Import window

When you click the Import button or use the File→Import Photos and Videos… menu command or shortcut, Lightroom opens a window where you configure all the settings for the current import (see **Figure 2–17**). (If the Import window doesn't look like the example shown in the figure, you're probably viewing it in compact mode; click the large triangle button at the bottom left corner to expand the window to the normal view. The compact Import window is discussed later in this chapter.)

Figure 2-17

At any time, you can click the Cancel button (or press the Esc key) to close the Import window and cancel the import without initiating any action. Once an import has begun, this window closes automatically.

The top panel of the Import screen contains the following info displays and controls:

- **FROM:** The Source from which the files are being imported

- **Import Method:** How the files will be handled

- **TO:** The Destination where files in the import will end up

The arrows depict the import processing sequence.

FROM: Select a source

Use the Source selection to specify the location of the files to be imported. If removable media is connected, it will automatically be selected here. Otherwise, the default Pictures folder, or the folder used for the previous import, will be selected. Clicking the FROM menu opens a list of recent sources for quick retrieval (see **Figure 2–18**).

When you've selected a source, the FROM text updates to show the source file path. Any image or video files contained in the source will be shown in the main preview area in the center of the window. If no image or video files of the supported formats are found in the selected source, No Photos Found is displayed in the preview area. Note that this is dependent on the condition of the Include Subfolders option described in a following section.

Figure 2-18

Source

This panel at the top left of the Import window shows a list of sources on the available media (see **Figure 2–19**). If it's not expanded, click the panel header to open it. Sources are grouped by type, with removable Devices at the top and Files (computer media) listed below.

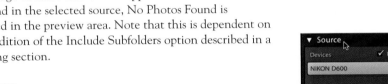

Figure 2-19

DEVICES

When you connect a digital camera, smartphone, or memory card that contains photos, the device will be shown here. The directory structure for Devices is not accessible. Click the name of the device to see the photos in the main preview area. With a device selected, you can check the Eject after import box to permit a safe removal of the media after the import has completed.

 Some AVCHD videos won't show in Devices
If you can't see .mts format videos in the main preview when using the Devices source, navigate to the correct folder in the Files lists and you should be able to find them there.

FILES

This section of the source panel lists all attached media containing a directory structure created by a computer file system. Hard disks, network drives, CD/DVD discs, and removable flash media such as USB thumb drives are all displayed here. (Some memory cards and digital cameras appear in both Files and Devices.)

VOLUME BROWSERS

Each volume is listed separately, with a collapsible header at the top. Click the name of the volume to expand it and drill down through the folders to locate the items you want to import. Click a folder to select it in the list. The items that will be imported are shown in the main preview area in the center of the screen.

Use the disclosure triangles

A faster way to drill down is to click only the disclosure triangles to the left of the folders, which expands the folder without causing Lightroom to display all the files in the folder. Then, select the lower level folder you were looking for.

DOCKING FOLDERS

To make folder lists more manageable, the Files list includes a Dock Folder option. This hides the subfolders above the chosen folder, making it easier to navigate within the panel.

Double-click a folder to dock and undock it, or right-click or Ctrl+click on a folder name, and in the pop-up menu, check or uncheck Dock Folder. This hides or shows the other folders.

If you don't want to dock or undock folders from one another, make sure to just single-click to select them.

Select multiple folders in the Source Files list

⌘+click, Ctrl+click, or Shift+click to select multiple folders for import. This also works to import photos from multiple memory cards at once if you have a card reader with multiple card slots. Just scroll down the Source list until you see each card listed as a volume, and select the folders containing the files you want to import.

ADDING A NETWORK DRIVE

By default, only local volumes (those connected directly to your computer) are shown in the Source panel. To add a network drive, first be sure you're connected with the necessary permissions. On Mac, click the FROM button and choose Other Source (see Figure 2–18). On Windows, click the + button next to Source and select Add Network Volume. Navigate across your network to select the desired volume or subfolder. The network drive will then be shown in the Source panel, where you can choose folders the same way as with local disks. Lightroom can work with photos stored on a network drive. It is just the catalog file that has to be on a local drive.

INCLUDE SUBFOLDERS

When you select a folder from a File source, you can also import files contained in any subfolders underneath the parent folder. This option is enabled by a control called *Include Subfolders*. If the contents of the subfolders are not shown (see **Figure 2–20**), click the Include Subfolders check box at the top of the Files list or the button in the main preview area (see **Figure 2–21**) to show the contents of all subfolders. You

Figure 2-20

can also right-click or
Ctrl+click on individual
folders to change the
option for just that folder.
(Clicking the Source panel
check box is a global option
affecting all folders.)

 Drag and drop to import
You can drag and drop files
and/or folders onto the

Figure 2-21

main Lightroom application window while in the Library module, or onto the program
icon. The import dialog box will open with the images selected as the Source.

Import method

In the center of the top panel, click one of the text
buttons to set how Lightroom handles the files during
the import: Copy as DNG, Copy, Move, or Add (see
Figure 2–22). When you select one of these options,
another line of text underneath will provide a short
description of what that option does. You'll most often
use Copy or Add. Be sure to double-check this setting for every import!

Figure 2-22

COPY AS DNG

This method converts raw files to Adobe's DNG format and then imports those DNG
files. If the raw files have XMP sidecars, those instructions will be integrated into the
metadata for the new DNG file. The settings used to convert to DNG during import are
specified in Preferences. DNG is discussed further in the Appendix.

COPY

When you select the Copy method, Lightroom copies the files from the source to a
new destination folder on the hard drive and imports the copied files. This is the most
common method for importing files from a camera, mobile device, or removable media.
It's very important that you carefully specify the Destination for the copied files! This is
explained in more detail later in this chapter.

MOVE

This is similar to copy, with a twist: Lightroom copies the source files to a new location
and imports the copies… and then deletes the old files at the original location. It's not a
common method; use with care.

ADD

With the Add import method, Lightroom only indexes the source files in the catalog.
You can apply basic metadata and Develop settings, but nothing is done to the original
files on disk—they're left where they are. This is the most common import method
to use for files already on a hard drive. Add is the only import method for which the

Destination settings are unavailable, since you're not doing anything with the files themselves, and you can't rename files using the Add method.

IMPORT METHOD AND PANEL OPTIONS

The panels and options on the right side of the Import window change depending on the import method you've selected. If you're using Add, only File Handling and Apply During Import are available. When using the Copy as DNG, Copy, and Move methods you will have additional panels and options for File Renaming and Destination.

 **Manual copy now, Lightroom import later**

Situations may arise in which manually copying your files from the camera to the hard drive is more desirable than using a Lightroom import to perform the download. For example, if you're pressed for time, a manual download using the Mac Finder or Windows Explorer (or better yet file syncing software that validates the copy, see the Appendix for links) is the fastest way to simply copy the files from the card to the hard drive—you can deal with the Lightroom stuff later. A manual copy allows you to make backups right away, and may provide immediate verification (or indication of any problems) with the files on the card or device. When you've manually copied files this way, during the eventual Lightroom import you can use the Add method.

Main preview area

The preview area in the center of the screen displays the photos and videos selected for the current import. The previews are shown in groups based on their type; at the top of the window are options

Figure 2-23

for choosing what's displayed in the preview: All Photos, New Photos, and Destination Folders (when copying or moving). (See **Figure 2–23**.) You can expand or collapse each group of previews by clicking the header bar. Even with the default All Photos, this bar can be collapsed. If you select a source and can't see any previews in the center of the window, make sure the preview panel is expanded by clicking the header.

All Photos: Includes the previews for all the photos and videos in the selected source.

New Photos: Automatically hides previews for any photos already in the current catalog.

Destination Folders: When using an import method other than Add, this separates the previews based on how the copied files will be grouped into subfolders based on the current import method and the settings in the Destination panel (see **Figure 2–24**). This view is useful when importing new files from a camera.

Figure 2-24

SOURCE CONTENT PREVIEWS

From the selected source, Lightroom only shows thumbnails for files it can import (see **Figure 2–25**). Files with unsupported formats are not visible at all. Photos and videos that have already been imported to the current catalog are dimmed (when Don't import suspected duplicates is checked in the File Handling panel). If Lightroom can't display a preview, its thumbnail shows the text "Preview unavailable for this file." Files for which Lightroom cannot display a preview may show only a gray box in the thumbnail or may display an error message when attempting to display previews. You will likely not be able to import any of these files—if the Import window doesn't show it, Lightroom won't import it.

The size, order, and grouping of the previews are dependent on the settings in the Toolbar.

TOOLBAR

At the bottom of the main preview area there's a Toolbar with additional options for managing previews (see **Figure 2–26**).

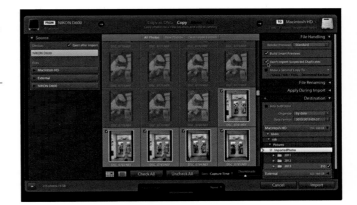

Figure 2-25

VIEW MODES

Click the buttons to switch between Grid and Loupe view. These Grid and Loupe views—and the associated zoom functions—are essentially the same as those in the Library module and are covered thoroughly in Chapter 3.

Figure 2-26

CHECK ALL/UNCHECK ALL AND CHECK VIDEOS/UNCHECK VIDEOS

Click a button to either check or uncheck all the files available in the current source. Hold Option or Alt, and the buttons change to Check Videos and Uncheck Videos.

SORT

Change the Sort Order with the controls to the right of the Toolbar. You can sort the previews by Capture Time, Checked State, File Name, or Media Type (see **Figure 2–27**). When this menu is set to OFF, the default sorting for each device is used. Note that the selection in the Sort menu affects the grouping of previews in Grid view, including those that have and have not been imported.

Figure 2-27

Disappearing previews?

Scroll down to the bottom of the preview area. If you apply a sort order other than OFF, each group of previews will first be based on whether those items are already in the catalog or not, and then sorted based on the selected setting. Often, you must scroll through all the previews to get a clear understanding of what's happening with the previews.

THUMBNAILS

You can change the size of the Grid thumbnails using this slider or the keyboard shortcut.

GRID VIEW

To switch to the thumbnail Grid, press G, or click the Grid view button on the toolbar, or double-click a Loupe preview. Use the scroll bar at the right side of the preview area to view all the thumbnails (see **Figure 2–28**). It's always a good idea to at least take a quick look at the previews to confirm what photos will be imported.

Figure 2-28

LOUPE VIEW

To see a larger preview of a single photo, double-click a thumbnail in Grid view, or press the E key, or click the Loupe view button on the toolbar. You can zoom in and out on a preview by clicking with the magnifier tool, (see **Figure 2–29**) pressing the Spacebar, or using the slider on the Toolbar.

Figure 2-29

CHECK BOXES

To include or exclude photos from this import, you can click to activate or deactivate their check boxes (see **Figure 2–30**). Or, with a large Loupe preview showing for a single image, click the check box in the Toolbar to include or exclude the file from the import.

Figure 2-30

CHECKING AND UNCHECKING MULTIPLE ITEMS

To check or uncheck multiple photos all at the same time, first use the Shift, ⌘, or Ctrl key to select their thumbnails. Holding the Shift key allows you to select a range of contiguous thumbnails; the ⌘ or Ctrl key lets you choose any noncontiguous thumbnails from anywhere in the preview. Selected thumbnails are indicated with a lighter cell color around the thumbnail preview and the currently active photo is highlighted. **Simply selecting or deselecting thumbnails by clicking on the cells does not change their checked statuse**s.

With multiple photos selected, clicking a check box on any one of the selected files will include or exclude all of the selected items (see Figure 2–30). The Check All and Uncheck All buttons make it easier to change multiple photos at once.

 Add everything in hard drive folders

When you're importing photos from a hard drive, it's best to clean up the folders first, as explained at the beginning of this chapter. Once you've done this, when you're importing, I strongly recommend you import everything in each folder—you can change or delete files later if necessary. If you exclude files from an import using the Add method, your Lightroom catalog will be out of sync with what's on the hard drive, which we don't want—this is discussed further in Chapter 3.

IMPORT STATUS AND STATISTICS

A display at the bottom left corner of the Import screen displays information about the current process and indicates how many photos are marked for import and the total aggregate file size of the batch (see **Figure 2–31**).

Figure 2-31

TO: My Catalog or folder Destination

At the top right of the Import window, the TO section shows the location for the imported files, depending on the import method in use. If you're using a Copy or Move method, this will show the name and folder path for a hard disk (see **Figure 2–32**). If you're using Add, it will say My Catalog (see **Figure 2–33**). (It would be more accurate if it said "This Catalog," since you can only import to the currently open catalog.)

Figure 2-32

Figure 2-33

SELECTING A DESTINATION FOR COPIES

If you're copying or moving files, click the TO button to open a pop-up menu with a default list of folder locations on your system disk, plus any other recent hard drives where you've copied files during Lightroom imports. You can also choose a specific hard disk and folder by selecting Other Destination… from the pop-up menu (see **Figure 2–34**)—this is one of the easiest ways to ensure your files end up where you want them.

02

File Handling

On the File Handling panel near the top right side of the window (see **Figure 2–35**), you can choose the type of previews rendered during the import, elect whether or not to have Lightroom ignore suspected duplicate files, and optionally make a backup copy of the original source files.

Figure 2-34

RENDER PREVIEWS

As Lightroom reads the pixel data from imported image files, new previews can be rendered. With the Render Previews menu options you can specify the type of preview that will be rendered as part of the import process (see **Figure 2–36**). The main benefit to rendering previews during import is that it can speed up the workflow later.

Keep in mind that Lightroom will always generate any necessary previews on the fly as it needs them. When you're working with photos, this can cause a slight delay in the response of the program as new previews are built. This is especially true for 1:1 previews, which can take from a few to many seconds to render.

Regardless of the previews you choose to render during import, you can also initiate preview rendering yourself at any time later in the workflow, using the commands described in Chapter 3.

Figure 2-35

Figure 2-36

MINIMAL

By selecting Minimal, Lightroom will use the smallest previews embedded in the photos or render only small thumbnails during the import if no previews are available. Use this option to have your import complete in the shortest time possible. Lightroom will later render Standard Size or 1:1 previews as you work.

EMBEDDED & SIDECAR

Select this option to have Lightroom use the largest available previews contained in the original files. If no previews are available Lightroom will render new ones as needed. This is particularly intended for raw and DNG files. Lightroom will later render Standard Size or 1:1 previews as you work.

STANDARD

Select this option to have Lightroom generate thumbnails and standard-sized previews during import. Standard previews are used to show photos full-screen in all modules except Develop. Lightroom will later render 1:1 previews on a case-by-case basis when you zoom to 1:1 or greater. (You can set the size and quality used for standard previews in Catalog Settings→File Handling.)

1:1

Select this option to have Lightroom render 1:1 previews (the largest size) during import, along with thumbnails and standard previews. This can significantly extend the time required to complete the import, but later, working with the photos in Library and Develop may be noticeably faster.

When it comes to rendering previews you either pay now (longer import time) or pay later (Lightroom works in the background while you work). Lightroom has to always render its own previous eventually. You can learn more about Lightroom previews in Chapter 3.

BUILD SMART PREVIEWS

You were introduced to the new smart preview feature in Chapter 1. You can check the Build Smart Previews box (see Figure 2–35) to have Lightroom build the smart previews as part of the import process. You can always build smart previews any time after import via the Library menu (more on this in Chapter 3).

DON'T IMPORT SUSPECTED DUPLICATES

Also on the File Handling panel, you have the option for Don't Import Suspected Duplicates (see Figure 2–35). Lightroom will compare the new photos being imported with those already in the catalog and will skip those that are suspected to be duplicates. The criteria for this comparison includes filename, capture time, and file size. When checked, if all of these criteria match any photos in the catalog, those files will be grayed out on the Import dialog and excluded from import

If you have two files with the same name, but they're stored in different folders, have different captures times and file sizes, then Lightroom will import them both,

MAKE A SECOND COPY TO:

By enabling this option, you can make a backup copy of the original source files after the new files are copied and imported (see Figure 2–35). Check the box, and then click the text below to choose the location. To the right of the panel is a small triangle button that opens a list of recent backup folders, along with an option to clear the list and another link to Choose Folder. Note that it's the original, unprocessed files that get duplicated to the backup location, not the copies that get imported to the catalog.

This is really intended to be a short-term backup of your memory card to a second drive so that you can have confidence your photos are safely in two locations before formatting the memory card and taking more photos. This is not intended to be a long-term backup solution for your photos. Lightroom never updates the photos created as a second copy, and it is up to you to manage these duplicates. When I do use this feature I always go back and delete the second copies once I know my full system backup program has had time to include my new photos.

File Renaming

Renaming your photo and video files is one of the marks of a good imaging workflow. In most cases, using the default filenames assigned by camera is inadequate. When you use

02

a copy/move import method, Lightroom can rename the files on the fly, prior to importing them to Lightroom. This way, the new copies have meaningful names before they're imported. Check the box to rename files, and then you can modify the options on the File Renaming panel (see **Figure 2–37**).

If you forget this step, make a mistake, or change your mind, you can always rename your files again later.

TEMPLATE

Renaming files during import is accomplished using filename templates. To choose a filename template, select a template from the menu (see **Figure 2–38**). You can use built-in filename templates and create your own. The provided Lightroom filename templates use various combinations of custom text (which you type in yourself), dates, and sequence numbers. These three elements are the most important and commonly used components of good filenames. To modify a template or make a new one, select Edit from the menu. This opens the Filename Template Editor (which can also be accessed from the Library module).

INTRODUCTION TO THE FILENAME TEMPLATE EDITOR

Using the Filename Template Editor you can create and modify templates for renaming files (see **Figure 2–39**). A filename template is made of tokens, which are variable placeholders that can be used to insert dynamic data into the name. For example, you can insert a date token that will automatically insert the photo's capture date into part of the filename. Or you can use a token for custom text, which will let you type your own text to be used in the names. Using the built-in templates as a starting point, customize your template to fit your desired naming conventions. The Filename Template Editor is covered in detail in Chapter 3.

PANEL TEXT FIELDS

Depending on the template you choose, other fields may become available in the panel where you can enter custom text. Fields can be provided for Shoot Name, which is most often used during tethered capture, and Start Number, which sets the first number to be used in a sequence.

Figure 2-37

Figure 2-38

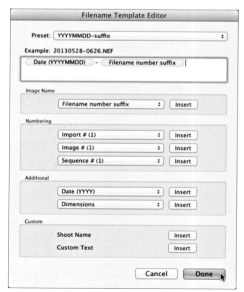

Figure 2-39

EXTENSIONS

You can also choose whether to use lowercase or uppercase for your file type extensions (see Figure 2–37).

FILENAME PREVIEW

At the bottom of the File Renaming panel a line of text displays a sample of how the current file naming options will form the final filenames (see Figure 2–37).

GUIDELINES FOR FILE AND FOLDER NAMING

Even in this age of metadata, when software can perform all kinds of functions using information embedded inside image files, the names you give your files and folders is still very important. The main reason careful naming is important is the frequent need to find, open, and save files using your computer's file system. Navigating through dialog boxes, copying files between media and sending images as email attachments are commonplace

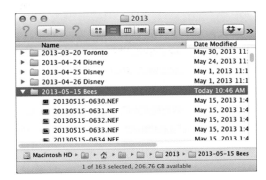

Figure 2-40

activities. Using well-conceived names will make these tasks much easier. The most important thing is that you consistently use a convention that makes sense to you. Following are suggested guidelines for naming your files and folders (see **Figure 2–40**).

1. Your default filename template should contain a timestamp for when the photo was taken, the subject or location of the photograph, or an identifier such as the client name, and a unique sequence number.

2. Use as few characters as necessary to provide all the pertinent information about the contents of the file or folder. Ideally, try to keep your base filename short, because as you create new master and derivative files from the original, their names will become longer with the addition of codes or special designations.

3. Use Internet-friendly names. When it's time to share files, having used Internet-friendly names from the start is a big time-saver. Most importantly, don't use spaces in names; use dashes or underscores to separate words instead. Don't use special characters like "/", "$", "@", "%", and don't use punctuation—in general, avoid parentheses and apostrophes.

Example: *04/18/13 dsc_0651.tiff* could become 20130418_0651.tif

4. Use the same base filename for all the images from a single shoot. Differentiate them with a serial number and/or usage code at the end of each filename.

5. The names of your folders should be consistent with the names of the files they contain.

02

6. You can include your name, part of your name, or your initials in your filenames. (I only do this for files going out for distribution; see example below.)

7. For derivative filenames, keep the base filename the same, and simply append a code indicating the purpose or specifications of the file. I use M for Master files (which include composite images such as HDR and panos); P for print files (with print size); and pixel dimensions and/or color space for files going to the web.

EXAMPLE FOLDER AND FILENAMES

yyyymmdd_location_sequence
Imported Photos > 2013 > 20130317_moab
20130317_moab_001.cr2
20130317_moab_002.cr2
20130317_moab_003.cr2
20130317_moab_003.cr2
…

clientname_yymmdd_sequence
Imported_Photos > 2013 > jones_130204
jones_130204_001.dng
jones_130204_002_500px_rsylvan.jpg
jones_130204_002_M.tif
jones_130204_002_P_16x24.tif
jones_130204_002.dng
jones_130204_003.dng
jones_130204_004.dng
…

Apply During Import

On this panel you can apply various types of metadata to the files as they are imported (see **Figure 2–41**). Remember that metadata is just text and numeric data, containing information about (or instructions for processing) each file. When you apply metadata during an import, that metadata is linked to the file record in the catalog. This metadata can be further modified later.

Figure 2-41

DEVELOP SETTINGS

Develop presets allow you to apply adjustments to photos as they are imported. This gives you control over the initial image settings used at the outset of the workflow and can save processing time later. Use the Develop Settings menu (see **Figure 2–42**) to choose a preset to be applied to the files during import. Keep in mind that Lightroom will always apply a default set of processing settings to raw

Figure 2-42

photos, but does not apply any settings to non-raw photos and videos. Develop presets selected on import are applied to all files imported at that time. In the case of raw photos the preset is applied on top of the default raw settings.

Of course, a Develop preset applied on import is usually not the final stage of Develop processing. You can always modify Develop adjustments and apply additional presets later. I don't usually apply a Develop preset on import, but it's a nice feature to have. Note, if you find you are applying the same settings over and over again you might consider using those settings to create a custom default for Develop, which I show you how to do in Chapter 4.

You can't create new Develop presets from the Import window; you must do it in the Develop module ahead of time. You can learn to do this in Chapter 4.

METADATA

Using a metadata template, you can embed your copyright notice, contact information, and all kinds of other textual information into the file metadata during the import. This saves a lot of time by reducing the need to manually apply metadata later.

Select a preset from the Metadata pop-up menu in the Apply During Import panel (see **Figure 2–43**). If the menu is empty, you can create and modify presets by selecting Edit…, which opens the Edit Metadata Presets window (see **Figure 2–44**). Enter values for the fields you want contained in the preset, and be sure to save the preset when you're done using the menu at the top of the window. You can learn a lot more about using the Metadata Preset Editor in Chapter 3.

Figure 2-43

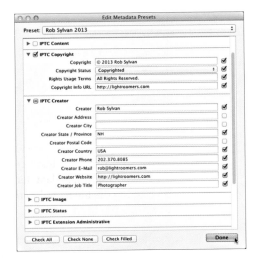

Figure 2-44

 Always include a copyright notice
At minimum, be sure to add a metadata copyright notice containing your name and the year the photo was made. Doing this at the time of import ensures your files will have your copyright notice attached from the very beginning of the workflow.

 When importing existing files from disk, be careful applying metadata
The import screen doesn't indicate whether or not any metadata has already been applied to the files being imported. In general, you shouldn't apply custom metadata when you're importing existing files from your hard drives, because those files might already contain metadata, which could result in conflicts. In these cases, it's safer to

02

apply additional metadata after the import, where you can first review the files in Library to see what metadata is already applied and then modify the metadata where appropriate. (See Chapter 3 for more on working with metadata in Library.) But if you're sure no custom metadata has been already applied to the files—or you're OK with overwriting/modifying it—you can apply your metadata during these import. Just be careful with this.

KEYWORDS

You can type text in the box to apply descriptive words and phrases for the images being imported (see **Figure 2–45**). These keywords will need to universally apply to all the photos in the current import. Separate individual keywords with commas. You can also use keyword phrases containing multiple words. To use keyword hierarchies in the text field, use < or > between parent/child entries, so that the "less than" side points to the child keyword; for example Venice < Italy < Europe. Keyword hierarchies and many other keywording strategies are covered in Chapter 3. I prefer to do more intensive keywording after import, and add only one or two high-level (and relevant) keywords at import just to help me locate these again later.

Figure 2-45

Destination

Like the Files section of the Source panel, the Destination panel (see **Figure 2–46**) displays a list of all connected media containing a computer file system. (In addition to hard disks and network drives, CDs/DVDs, and USB flash drives may be listed here, but you may not be able to use them as destinations for file copies.) The folders targeted in the Destination panel will be indexed in the catalog and shown under the Folders panel in the Library module.

When you're copying or moving files using a Lightroom import, the settings on the Destination panel can be of critical importance. (With the Add method, the Destination panel is hidden and files are added to the catalog using their current location on disk.)

Incorrect copy destinations create massive difficulty and confusion for many photographers using Lightroom! Always remember that when using the copy or move import methods, Lightroom must place the files into a folder somewhere on a hard drive. And if you don't specify this folder prior to starting the import, Lightroom will choose for you.

By default, Lightroom copies photos and videos into the Pictures folder under your user account on the system hard drive, using subfolders sorted and named by capture date. Photos from each single day are copied into a separate folder, underneath a parent folder named by year (see **Figure 2–47**).

Figure 2-46

Figure 2-47

Sometimes this default setup might be OK, and it's certainly easy to just let Lightroom choose destination folders for you. If you're taking responsibility for the organization and management of the files in your photo library, you should carefully specify the folders where new files are copied. At the very least, you should always ensure that the Destination is on the correct hard drive.

Figure 2-48

 Check Destination settings carefully

If you use the default settings, or make a mistake, you can later move or copy files from within the Library module. However, this requires that you realize a mistake was made and are able to locate the copied files immediately after the import completes. If you don't, your problems will be compounded greatly as you continue to work with the files in a folder location you're unaware of.

USING THE TO MENU TO CHOOSE A FOLDER

As mentioned earlier in this chapter, the most direct way to specify the destination for copied files is to click the TO button at the top right of the Import window and choose Other Destination… from the pop-up menu (see **Figure 2–48**). In the resulting dialog box, you can navigate to the hard drive and folder where you want to place the copied files. You can also create a new subfolder from within this dialog box, named appropriately for the current batch of photos as explained earlier. When you choose the folder using this method, the Destination panel list will update to reflect your choice.

Figure 2-49

SELECTED DESTINATION FOLDER

In the Destination panel, the parent folder chosen for the import is clearly highlighted (see **Figure 2–49**). If you don't specify another subfolder, all the photos will be copied directly into this one folder. If you used the TO button to create a new folder, you'll see it highlighted here.

INTO SUBFOLDER

This section of the Destination panel allows you to specify a new subfolder to be created using the provided criteria (see **Figure 2–50**). First, check the box to tell Lightroom to create a new folder for the copied files. When the box is checked, a text field appears (showing "Enter name") where you can type in the name for the new subfolder.

Figure 2-50

ORGANIZE

Use the options on the Organize menu to specify how folders and subfolders will be handled:

- **By date:** This is the Lightroom default described earlier. With this option selected, Lightroom will create a new folder for files from each capture date, and if it doesn't already exist, a parent-level folder, named for the year, to contain the day-based folders. Use the Date Format menu to choose how the folders will be named and organized.

- **Into one folder:** Places all the copied files directly into the destination folder, with no additional subfolders created underneath.

Important: One of the Organize options will be used whether or not Into Subfolder is checked. However, if you don't enter a new folder name, all the files will be copied loose into the selected parent folder. **Pay careful attention to this setting each time.**

OTHER WAYS OF CREATING FOLDERS

Click the + button on the Destination panel header to open a menu with options for creating folders and manipulating the folder view. You can also right-click or Ctrl+click on a folder in the Destination panel to open a pop-up menu with similar options.

DESTINATION FOLDER PREVIEWS

The contents of the folder list in the Destination panel are updated to reflect the current settings. The main parent folder for the destination is highlighted (see Figure 2–49). Folders that already exist on the hard drive are shown in regular white type. Folders that will be created during the import are shown in gray italic type with a + symbol on the folder icon (see Figure 2–50).

With these previews, you can clearly see the folder structure that will result from the current settings. Also, the Destination Folders organization can be previewed in the main preview area, as was illustrated previously with Figure 2-25. **Always be sure to carefully check these previews before starting an import using Copy or Move!**

Import Presets

You can save Import Presets for quick retrieval of frequently used settings. To save a preset, first make sure all the current settings are those you want to save—you can't choose which settings to include. At the bottom center of the Import window, click the pop-up menu to open it (see **Figure 2–51**). Select Save Current Settings as New Preset... Using the menu, you can also load saved presets and delete or rename presets. To set the Import options back to the original state, choose Restore Default Presets.

Figure 2-51

When using a preset, be sure the volume is mounted
If you save a preset that includes a hard drive destination and later attempt an import
when that destination is unavailable, the import will fail.

Show fewer options: the Compact Import Window

After you've done a bunch of imports, you'll find times when
you don't need to see all the options or previews in the Import
window in order to do your importing. This is especially true
when doing automated batch importing from a card. If you've

Figure 2-52

set up your storage
systems, file
naming templates
and Destination
defaults with
batch processing
in mind, you can
do your imports
with just a single
click of the Import
button.

Figure 2-53

At the bottom
left of the Import
screen is a large
triangle button
that toggles

Figure 2-54

between Show more options and Show fewer options
(see **Figure 2–52**). More options is the default; showing
fewer options compacts the Import screen to show only
the essential elements based on the import method (see
Figures 2–53 and **2–54**).

Import from Another Catalog

In addition to importing photo and video files, you can
also import from another catalog using this command
under the File menu (see **Figure 2–55**). This transfers the
data from the other catalog into the current catalog. All
the Lightroom adjustments you've applied to photos and
videos, plus collections, virtual copies, and other catalog-
specific data, are transferred between catalogs. You have
the option to also copy the files referenced by the catalog
being imported. Chapter 11 contains detailed instructions
for working with multiple catalogs, including Import from
Another Catalog.

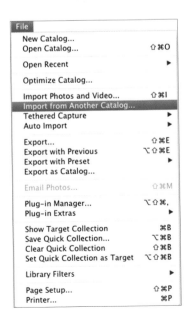

Figure 2-55

Tethered Capture

Tethered capture with Lightroom provides automated transfer of image files directly from your camera to your computer and to the catalog as they are captured. Shooting tethered requires an active connection between your camera and the computer, so it's most commonly used in studio environments. Typically, you connect your camera to the computer using a USB or FireWire cable; some new camera systems also allow wireless transfer, eliminating the need to connect with a cord.

The main advantage of tethered capture is you can review your photos on a larger and more accurate display than the camera LCD screen.

Tethered capture bypasses the main Import window and performs the file transfers, importing, and processing in the background as you continue shooting. Just press the shutter button, and in a few seconds, each capture appears in the Lightroom catalog with all the settings you've applied in the setup. Note, with Canon cameras the photo is also stored on the camera's memory card, but with Nikon the photo is only transferred to the computer.

CANON, NIKON, AND LEICA ONLY

Tethered capture support is dependent on many factors, from camera make and model to your computer operating system. Lightroom's built-in tethered capture is currently available only using Canon, Nikon, and limited Leica cameras, and even with these brands not all models are supported. (And even if your camera is technically supported, your operating system may not be.)

Tethered capture camera support in Lightroom 5 is the same as Lightroom 4.4. Not all features are available with all cameras. See the Appendix for links to more information.

If your camera or computer is not supported by Lightroom's tethered capture, you may be able to use Auto Import (discussed later in this chapter) along with your camera's provided software to accomplish similar results.

⚙ Tethered Capture Setup

Here are the steps for tethered capture:

Step 1. Connect your camera to your computer using a cable or a wireless system. (The first time you do this, your computer might need to install a device driver and/or open the Auto Play window to ask you what you want to do with the camera. If so, you can just close these windows; there's nothing you need to set here.)

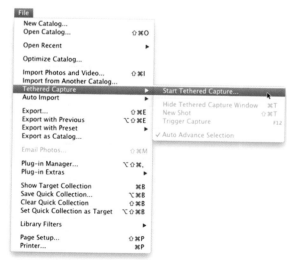

Figure 2-56

Step 2. In Lightroom, select File→ Tethered Capture→Start Tethered Capture (see **Figure 2–56**). **New in Lightroom 5:** You can press F12 to start tethered capture.

Step 3. In the Tethered Capture Settings window (see **Figure 2–57**), configure the batch settings for this capture session. In the top part of the window, give this session a name, which is used to create a subfolder on your hard disk where the captures will be copied.

Optionally, check the box for Segment Photos by Shots. When this is checked, Lightroom will place the photos from each shot into its own subfolder (using names you specify), located underneath the main folder set in the Destination section below. For example, if you're shooting a session with three different models, each model could have her own shots named for the model, and the resulting photos will be grouped together in separate folders. Or, if you're doing product photography, each product could have its own shot. Of course, what exactly comprises a shot grouping is entirely up to you.

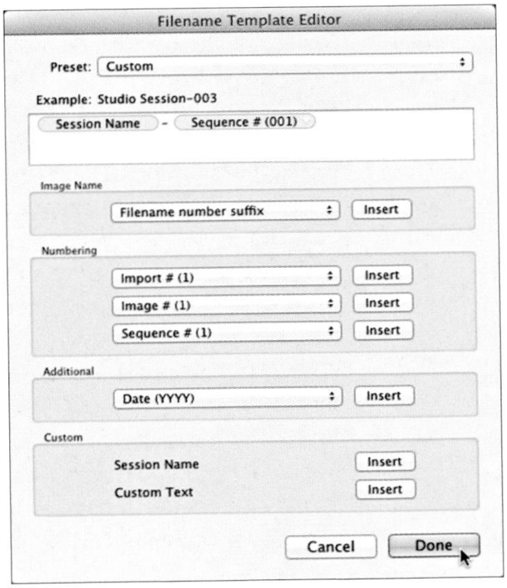

Step 4. From the menu in the Naming section, choose a File Naming Template or create a new template by clicking the Edit command at the bottom of the menu. This opens the Filename Template Editor that is slightly different (due to the limitations of tethered capture there are no tokens that pull from the photo's own metadata) than the full version accessed from elsewhere (see **Figure 2–58**). Using file naming templates is discussed earlier in this chapter and in Chapter 3.

Step 5. In the Destination section, specify the hard disk and folder where the files for this session will be copied as they are transferred from the camera. (You can create a new folder from this dialog box, too, but remember that the Session Name will also generate a new folder.)

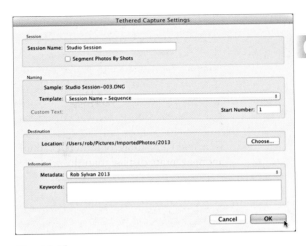

Figure 2-57

Figure 2-58

Step 6. In the Information section, apply your metadata template and optional keywords as appropriate for the session.

Step 7. When you're finished configuring your tethered capture settings, click OK. (If Segment Photos By Shots is selected, a dialog comes up asking for the Initial Shot Name.) When you click OK, the session folder is created on your hard drive and immediately appears in the Folders panel in Library. If you change your mind and didn't import anything, just remove this folder from within the Folders panel and it will be deleted from the hard disk.

Step 8. Lightroom displays the Tethered Capture Window (see **Figure 2–59**). If Lightroom connects to your camera, its name is shown at the left of the Tethered Capture Window. If Lightroom can't connect to your camera, the text displays No Camera Detected. With a successful connection, the capture window also shows the current EXIF settings on the camera, including shutter speed, aperture, ISO, and white balance. (You can't change settings here; you must do it on the camera.) You can move the controls to a different place on your screen if you wish: place your cursor over it, and when it changes to a hand, click and drag.

Figure 2-59

Step 9. If you need to change the file copy settings for this session, you can click the tiny gear icon at the right end of the capture control strip (see **Figure 2–60**). This reopens the Tethered Capture Settings window. To cancel the session, press the small X in the top right corner, above the gear icon.

Figure 2-60

Step 10. You can apply Develop presets to the captures as they are imported to the catalog; click the Develop Settings pop-up menu to the left of the shutter button to select a previously saved preset. (Creating and saving Develop presets is covered at length in Chapter 4.)

Step 11. The large round button is a shutter control. You can click it to activate the shutter, or shoot as you normally would from behind the camera.

 For full functionality, use the camera's shutter button
Lightroom's shutter button does not replicate the full functionality of the camera's shutter button. You can't capture in burst mode—holding down Lightroom's shutter button for an extended period of time still captures only a single shot. Also, the Lightroom shutter button may not trigger if your camera's mirror lockup is enabled.

WHAT HAPPENS DURING THE TETHERED CAPTURE SESSION

While the tethered capture session is active, you can access additional options under the File→Tethered Capture menu (see **Figure 2–61**). In particular, you'll probably want the Auto Advance Selection option enabled; otherwise, the preview will remain on the current capture even as additional photos are imported. This menu also provides options to Stop Tethered Capture, start a New Shot if segmenting photos by shot and to hide or show the Tethered Capture Window. (You can also start a new Shot by clicking on the Shot Name in the Tethered Capture Window.)

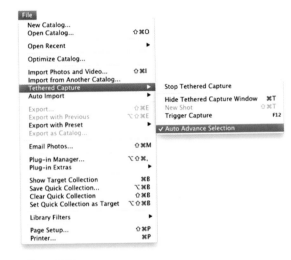

To collapse and expand the tether bar press Option or Alt and click the X close button at the top right.

As the camera captures images, they are automatically downloaded to the specified folder on your hard drive. The files are imported to the current catalog and processed according to your Session settings. Each new photo is shown in

Figure 2-61

Library as it is imported; you can hide panels and switch to Loupe for full screen previews or use Grid view for thumbnails. (You can learn all about Library views in Chapter 3.)

While each photo is being downloaded and processed, the main progress indicator shows in the left of the top panel. Another small, circular progress indicator appears next to the shutter release to show a file is being transferred and processed (see **Figure 2–62**).

Figure 2-62

Use the Layout Overlay for Tethered Capture

In the Library module there's a feature called Layout Overlay, which allows you to place an image that you select into the Loupe preview. The selected image overlays the current preview, providing a straightforward way to see how your captures will look when placed within a specified layout. This feature is particularly well-suited for studio photographers shooting images designed to later be placed into layouts such as magazine covers or advertisements. Since it's enabled and used within the Library module, the Layout Overlay is discussed in detail in Chapter 3, but I thought I'd mention it here, too, as it can be really useful with Tethered Capture.

FINISHING THE SESSION

When you're done with the tethered capture session, click the X at the top right of the window or use the Stop Tethered Shooting menu command.

When you come back later for another session, you'll find that Lightroom keeps track of cameras you've used for tethered capture and you can select a different camera from the menu at the left of the Tethered Capture Window. The Develop preset menu also retains the most recent settings used.

Auto Import

With Auto Import, you can have Lightroom perform automatic imports as new files are detected in a watched folder. As mentioned in the previous sections, you can often use Auto Import in conjunction with the software provided with your camera to do tethered capture. You can also use Auto Import in any scenario in which you are generating new photo or video files from another source, whether it's from another software program; a scanner, camera, or other imaging device; or a network or cloud storage folder.

When new files are found in the watched folder, they are automatically imported using the Move method (described earlier in this chapter) in which files are first copied to a new folder destination and then removed from the original source.

AUTO IMPORT SETTINGS

To set up Auto Import, select File➔Auto Import ➔Auto Import Settings. This opens a dialog box (see **Figure 2–63**).

Figure 2-63

Enable Auto Import

Check the box to turn on Auto Import. This does the same thing as the command on the Auto Import menu.

Watched Folder

Click the Choose... button and navigate to the folder on your hard drive that you want Lightroom to watch. This can be on a local or network drive. The folder must be empty when you first specify it as the Watched Folder.

Destination

Click the Choose... button to navigate to a folder on your hard drive or network drive where you want the imported files to be copied. You must specify also a Subfolder name.

File Naming

From the menu, select a file naming template to use, or create a new one using the Edit... option. Filenaming templates are discussed earlier in this chapter and in Chapter 3.

Information

Apply your Develop Settings, Metadata, and Keywords, as appropriate for Auto Import, and specify the Initial Previews to be generated during the import.

When you're finished configuring the Auto Import settings, click OK.

02

Lightroom continually scans the watched folder, and when new files are detected they are processed and imported according to your Auto Import Settings. Each new photo appears in the Library module as it's imported.

To use Auto Import for tethered capture, connect your camera to your computer using the specified cables. Configure the utility software that came with your camera to auto-transfer new captures from the camera into the watched folder you specified in Lightroom. As you capture images with your camera, they are automatically transferred to your watched folder and subsequently imported using the Auto Import settings.

 Import Preferences

There are several preferences and catalog settings that affect Lightroom's import behavior; these are highlighted in **Figure 2–64**. See the Appendix for more about Lightroom Preferences and Chapter 11 for Catalog Settings.

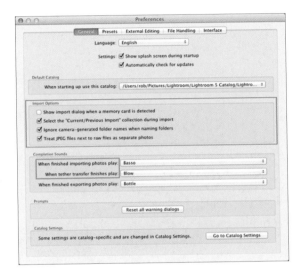

Figure 2-64

Next steps

Importing is one of the most common tasks you'll do with Lightroom. At first, it may seem daunting, and you're bound to make some mistakes. Don't worry! With practice, you'll gain control over the process, and that's when your workflow in Lightroom will really start to take off.

For each import you do, verify (and adjust as necessary) the Source, import method, and Destination settings in the Import window. Carefully confirm your import settings every time! Go through the controls in the import screen methodically—from top to bottom, left to right, and back again—to apply the settings appropriate for the photos and videos that will be affected by the current import. Be sure you've correctly configured all the options in the Import window before initiating the import. Save your most commonly used Import setups as presets to use in the future.

If you run into problems with importing, the most important thing is to immediately stop what you're doing, take a deep breath, and relax. You can do this! If you feel like you're in a hurry, or frustrated, it's better to come back to finish your imports later. You don't want to risk losing anything, and if you're not careful, you might.

If you run into files that Lightroom can't read for any reason, slow down and take the time to read the messages provided. They are essential to working through the difficulty.

When you're finished importing some photos and videos, you can move on to Chapter 3, where you'll begin working with your photos in Lightroom's Library module.

CHAPTER 03
Library

03

LIBRARY: Managing your photos with Lightroom

Once you've imported photos and videos into the catalog, the next tasks are to get everything organized and to separate the best from the rest. The Library module is your command center for managing all your photo and video files, both within the catalog and on the hard drive.

During the import, Lightroom indexed your files with the catalog. Remember that what you're seeing in Library are previews of Lightroom's processing of the files, which are referenced on disk. (So don't think now that your photos are "in the catalog" you can delete them from the hard drive!)

What's New in Library

- **DNG validation**
- **New smart collection criteria**
- **New metadata search filter criteria**
- **Manage smart previews**
- **New Loupe Overlay options**

That said, you can work with your photos and videos in Lightroom *as if* you were working directly with the files on disk. All the work you do in Lightroom is automatically saved in the catalog and you can also save that metadata to the hard drive. (Whenever you're working on photos in Lightroom, you're working with metadata; this is covered extensively throughout this chapter.)

HOW LIBRARY INTERACTS WITH YOUR COMPUTER'S FILE SYSTEM

Although Lightroom is referencing the files and rendering previews as you work, when you make changes to the file system from within Lightroom, those changes also happen on disk. For example, if you rename a photo from within the catalog, that file is renamed on the hard drive. If you move a folder in Lightroom, the folder gets moved on the hard drive. If you delete photos from the catalog, you have the choice of whether or not to also delete them from disk. As I've repeatedly mentioned elsewhere in this book, once photos have been imported to a catalog, you should *always* do any reorganizing from within Lightroom, and Library is where this happens.

MULTIPLE WAYS OF ORGANIZING

Aside from the folder systems where you store your photos on the hard drive, the greatest advantage of working in the Lightroom catalog is that you can also use many other organizational methods to sort, group, and find your photos and videos. Collections, filters, and keywords are among the many ways you can view your digital media within the catalog. You will likely use one fixed folder structure on your hard disk and an unlimited number of other— and more flexible—organizational structures within the catalog (see **Figure 3–1**).

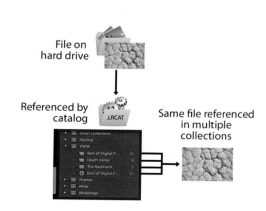

File on hard drive

Referenced by catalog

Same file referenced in multiple collections

Figure 3-1

 **Download all figures**
All figures in this book are available for download at:
www.lightroomers.com/lightroom5book

THE LIBRARY WORKSPACE

Generally speaking, the panels on the left side of the Library module are used for organizing your photos and videos, while the right-side panels are used to apply metadata and Develop adjustments to selected photos and videos (see **Figure 3–2**). You'll use multiple methods (called view modes) of viewing your photos and videos, and you have many, many options available for sorting and arranging photos any way you want to.

The sections of this chapter are sequenced to generally correspond with the way the Library module is laid out and the order in which you see things as you look around the window. However, this does not necessarily correspond with the steps in the workflow you may use. For example, the Metadata panel is at the bottom of the right panel group, which might lead you to assume that it's the least important thing. This couldn't be further from the truth; in fact, working on the Metadata panel is something that you'll do with increasing regularity as you master Lightroom. In some cases, for clarity, we'll need to jump around a bit.

Note: Where I refer to "photos," in most cases I also mean videos.

Figure 3-2

03

ABOUT PHOTO EDITING

Editing photos is an iterative process: you'll review your photos in multiple sequential passes until they are distilled down to the final selects (see **Figure 3–3**). The goal is to go from the many images captured during a session to only your best photos—those chosen to continue through the processing pipeline. You will always start out with many photos that may not survive the editing process; even for many professional photographers, a ratio of 1:100 keepers vs. cuts is common! During each round of editing, decide whether each image stays or goes. "Maybes" stay—at least for the current round.

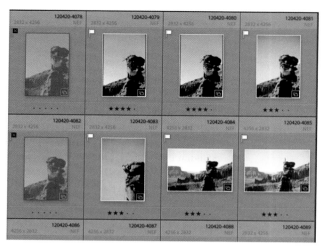

Figure 3-3

As you go through your edit, you can switch between the four view modes (Grid, Loupe, Compare, and Survey) to evaluate larger previews or compare multiple images. We'll look at all of these in a bit. Also, sometimes you'll want to do some processing to make a better decision about how to rate an image; you can do this in Library's Quick Develop. (But don't get too mired in processing during the early stages of editing; just concentrate on picking your favorites.) Once you've identified your best work from each batch of photos, you'll move on to enhance them in Develop.

Edit a shoot

Following is a simplified editing workflow that you can use to quickly edit a photo shoot down to your final selects. This workflow is not perfect for every photographer or every situation, but it will get you headed in the right direction. All the steps and controls are explained in detail throughout the remainder of this chapter.

Step 1. In the Folders panel, select the folder of photos and videos to work with.

Step 2. Select all the photos. From the Metadata panel, apply your metadata preset (if you didn't do this during import).

Step 3. With all the photos still selected, apply a few general keywords common to all items. If you wish, you can also apply other general IPTC metadata (such as Location) at this time.

Step 4. Review the photos one by one, and for your initial selects, apply a Pick flag (P key) to the keepers or a Reject flag (X key) to the clunkers.

If you want to adjust photos at this point to help you decide about the keepers, you can apply some basic processing using the controls on the Quick Develop panel.

Step 5. Enable a filter to show only the photos without any flag, which is the default state. (The filters are accessed from the right side of the Filmstrip or the Filter Bar at the top of the Grid.)

Step 6. Viewing only the unflagged photos, go through them a second time. Be more critical on this cut—you need to start eliminating shots that don't make the grade. Assign a Pick flag or Reject flag to every one of the remaining photos.

Step 7. Enable a filter to show only the photos with a Reject flag. Give it a quick look over to make sure none were flagged by mistake. You can delete them now, or just leave them flagged and take care of them later.

Step 8. Put the Pick flagged photos in a collection. You can do this at any point in the workflow; I prefer to add only my final selects, but I know other photographers who put the entire folder contents into a collection and do all the editing from within the collection instead of the folder. Whichever approach you choose, as you move forward in the workflow, you should be spending less time working in folder views and more time working in collections. (Using collections is discussed at length later in this chapter.)

Here are a few tips to keep in mind while you're editing:

- **Undo/redo:** Remember that you can always undo and redo steps using ⌘-Z or Ctrl+Z. Lightroom keeps track of everything you do while in Lightroom, so in a given work session you can undo your way all the back to the first thing you did that session.

- **Save your work frequently (Optional):** After each round of editing (but before filtering) select all your images and Save Metadata to File by pressing ⌘-S or Ctrl+S. This ensures that your ratings and any Quick Develop adjustments you've applied during editing are saved to each photo's XMP metadata on disk, in addition to the Lightroom catalog. You can learn more about Save Metadata to File later in this chapter.

- **Rename photos:** Even if you didn't rename your photos during the import, you can do so at any time. If you're going to delete photos, it might be best to rename files after the deletions, so you won't have breaks in the sequence numbering. This comes down to personal preference but, at some point, it's a good idea to rename your files to something useful. You'll learn more about this later in the chapter.

- **Add more keywords as you go:** During editing, you should gradually apply more keywords to photos that make it through the current round. At the end, your final selects will ideally contain a complete, unique set of keywords specific to each individual photo.

Refrain from immediately deleting photos during editing
It slows the workflow; worse yet, you might make a mistake. If you want to delete images, you can often make better decisions with some time gone by. Plus, in Lightroom it's easy enough to simply hide the photos you don't want to see. Learn from your rejected photos by going back to study them later—you can sometimes learn much more from your failures than your successes!

Working in Library

Here are the basic tasks you should consider for your typical work sessions in Library, in general order of importance and sequence in the workflow:

1. Keep your files organized within your disk-based folder architecture, including naming/renaming, etc.

2. Apply standard metadata, including your name and copyright notice, etc., to everything in your catalog.

3. Preview individual photos and groups of photos using different view modes.

4. Identify the best pictures and isolate them from the others.

5. Group photos into logical sets based on your needs and usage (mainly using collections).

6. Use keywords and filters to find and sort photos.

7. Quick Develop photos as a starting point for more enhancement in the Develop module.

8. Edit video clips.

You can do these things in any order you prefer, but you'll soon discover that some tasks are much easier to accomplish if they're done before or after other tasks. As I frequently remind you: try to get in the habit of thinking several steps ahead.

IMAGE SOURCES

You'll do all your organizing and editing in Library while previewing various image sources. You use these sources to determine which previews are shown as you work with your files. In Library, the panels and controls where you can access image sources include:

- **Catalog panel:** Built-in sources based on predetermined criteria.

- **Folders panel:** A direct connection to the actual folders on your hard drive.

- **Collections panel:** Virtual groups of photos within the Lightroom catalog.

03

- **Keywords panel:** If a photo has keywords applied, they can be used to define or refine other sources.

- **Filter Bar:** Filters are used to refine the other image sources and help generate new ones.

- **Publish Services panel:** Similar to collections in that they are virtual groupings of photos, with the difference being that each group is connected to a specific output location (more on Publish Services in Chapter 5).

These sources are discussed in detail throughout this chapter.

CURRENT AND RECENT SOURCES

The Source Indicator is shown in text along the top of the Filmstrip (see **Figure 3–4**). This shows the location of the current source, as well as the filename or number of selected items. Clicking anywhere on the current source indicator opens the Recent Sources menu—you can use this to jump to any of the 12 most recently used sources, plus the built-in Catalog sources and Favorite Sources (see **Figure 3–5**). You can clear the Recent Sources list whenever you like. Favorite Sources remain even after clearing the Recent Sources.

Figure 3-4

 Combining sources
When you use ⌘+Click or Ctrl+click you can combine multiple sources, even from multiple panels. This can help create the exact selection of photographs you want to work on.

FORWARD/BACK BUTTONS

At the left of the top part of the Filmstrip are buttons to go forward and back (see **Figure 3–6**). These function very much like forward/back buttons on a web browser. During the current work session, Lightroom keeps track of your location so you can go forward and back between image sources as well as switching modules using these buttons.

Figure 3-5

Figure 3-6

Catalog panel

The Catalog panel, at the top left of the Library module, lists several built-in image sources (see **Figure 3–7**). The core criteria used for these Catalog sources can't be changed, but filters can be applied to refine them, as discussed later in this chapter.

Figure 3-7

- **All Photographs:** Shows all the photos in the catalog.

- **Quick Collection:** Shows all the photos in the Quick Collection.

- **Current/Previous Import:** Shows all the photos added to the catalog during the most recent import. It shows as Current Import during the import process, and after the import process is complete it changes to Previous Import.

- **Other sources on the Catalog panel (sometimes):** Depending on the state of your catalog and the work you've done, sometimes Lightroom shows additional sources on the Catalog panel, including Missing Photographs or Photos Missing from *[folder name]*; Error Photos; Added by Previous Export; Previous Export as Catalog; etc. Though these temporary sources come and go automatically, if you want to remove any one of these from the Catalog panel, right-click its name and from the pop-up menu choose Remove this temporary collection.

 Don't use the Previous Import source for editing

Following an import, switch to the Folder source (the easiest method is to right-click or Ctrl+click a photo and choose Go to Folder in Library from contextual menu) or make a collection before starting to edit the photos. The Previous Import source doesn't provide the full set of options that a folder or collection does, which leads to confusion later in the workflow. It's important that you fully understand where your photos are stored in the Folders panel, and how to find them.

Library previews

Library previews are great for evaluating photos and making editing decisions. In some cases, you may see differences in how a photo looks in Library versus how it looks in Develop. (In these situations, the Develop preview, viewed at 1:1, should be your ultimate guide as it's always the highest quality preview available based on your current settings.) Previews are also introduced in Chapters 1 and 2; for your review, the sizes and quality that Lightroom renders previews are:

- **Minimal:** Small thumbnails, relatively low quality.

- **Standard:** The larger preview used for Loupe, Compare, and Survey views (as well as all other modules except Develop). The size and quality of the Standard previews is set in Catalog Settings > File Handling.

03

- **1:1:** Full-resolution previews rendered from the actual pixel data of the photo. When you zoom in to magnification levels greater than 1:1, you're still always seeing the 1:1 preview, which is the highest resolution possible.

The time it takes Lightroom to render a preview is dependent on the size of the file, your computer system hardware, and the size and quality level specified in Catalog Settings.

RENDER PREVIEWS MENU

At any time, you can have Lightroom rebuild previews. Go to Library→Previews and choose an option from the menu (see **Figure 3–8**).

New in Lightroom 5: You can also choose to render smart previews from this menu at any time. Just select the photos in Grid view and choose Render Smart Previews from the menu. (You were introduced to smart previews in Chapter 1, and learned that they could be rendered as part of the import process in Chapter 2.) If you want to recover space on your drive currently taken up by smart previews, or simply don't need to keep a certain set of smart previews any longer, you can delete smart previews by selecting the photos in Grid view and choosing the Discard Smart Previews… option on the menu.

Figure 3-8

Navigator

As explained in Chapter 1, the Navigator panel provides controls for zooming in and out of the main preview, as well as an additional preview (see **Figure 3–9**).

ZOOM RATIOS

Unlike other programs that specify the magnification level using a percentage, Lightroom's zoom levels are based on the ratio of image pixels to screen pixels. 1:2 is one screen pixel to two image pixels. 4:1 is four screen pixels to one image pixel, and so on. The available zoom ratios are:

- **Fit:** Fits the entire photo into the preview area.

Figure 3-9

- **Fill:** Expands the photo so that the entire preview area is filled. The ends of the photo may not be visible.

- **1:1:** Maps one image pixel to one screen pixel.

- **User-selected setting:** The fourth zoom ratio uses the most recent custom zoom ratio you selected. Clicking this opens a pop-up menu for you to choose the custom zoom ratio.

You'll most often use the Navigator panel to set the user zoom level, rather than actually zooming in and out using these controls (there are better ways). Zooming in and out of previews is discussed in the section on the Loupe view mode.

Library View Modes

Library provides four view modes, each offering a different method of previewing photos and videos:

- Grid view

- Loupe view

- Compare view

- Survey view

You can switch between view modes using the buttons at the left side of the Toolbar (see **Figure 3–10**) or with the shortcuts.

Figure 3-10

Grid view

You will do much of your work in Library using thumbnails of your photos. In Library, the Grid view (see **Figure 3–11**) shows thumbnails inside cells arranged in rows and columns. There are two parts of the thumbnail: the image preview itself and the cell (the gray area surrounding the image). They behave differently and provide different options. Thumbnails are useful for seeing groups of photos together and contemplating their relationships to one another, and when applying settings to multiple photos. Lightroom provides lots of control over the presentation and functionality of thumbnails. You can jump to Library's Grid view from anywhere in Lightroom by pressing the G key.

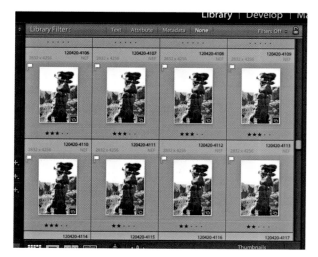

Figure 3-11

 **Use thumbnails for editing**
Your initial rounds of editing can primarily be done using thumbnails; they are good
indicators of strong composition, as you're not distracted by minute detail as with larger
previews.

Use the arrow keys to move from one photo to another
In the Library Grid you can move left, right, up, and down to select images with your
arrow keys. At all other times (and in other modules) use just the left and right arrows to
select the next/previous images shown in the Filmstrip.

NAVIGATING WITHIN THE GRID

When Grid view is active, you have several options for moving around within the rows
and columns of thumbnails:

- **Scroll bar:** At the right side of the main preview area.

- **Panning:** Position your mouse on the border between thumbnails—the cursor turns
  into a hand and you can scroll the Grid up and down. The scroll wheel on your
  mouse or scroll gesture on your trackpad and tablet does this, too.

- **Page Up and Page Down:** To jump between full-screen sets of thumbnails use the
  Page Up and Page Down keys.

- **Arrow keys:** When you use
  the arrow keys to select photos,
  pressing the down arrow scrolls
  the entire Grid view as you move
  down past the lowest visible row.

GRID VIEW STYLE

There are two main styles of Grid
thumbnails: Compact and Expanded
(see **Figure 3–12**). Both can be
customized using View Options (see

Figure 3-12

Figure 3–16). (There are actually two subtypes of Compact cells; one that doesn't show
any extras whatsoever, and one with the settings configured in View Options.) Press
the J key to cycle through the Grid view styles. I almost always work in Grid view using
Expanded Cells, set up to show a lot of information about the photos.

GRID TOOLBAR

Each view mode has its own Toolbar;
the Grid Toolbar is different from that
in Loupe view (see **Figure 3–13**).
You can add and remove items from
the Toolbar using the pop-up menu
accessed with the triangle button at the

Figure 3-13

right of the Toolbar. I like to keep just the Painter and Sort tools visible; I use keyboard shortcuts for everything else shown in the menu. However, you may find it beneficial to also keep the Thumbnail Size slider visible, along with the View Modes buttons. You can hide (and show) the entire Toolbar in any module by pressing the T key.

CHANGING THUMBNAIL SIZE

You can change the thumbnail size by dragging the slider on the Toolbar (see **Figure 3–14**) or using the – key to make them smaller and the = key to make them larger (think of it as the + key, but you don't need to hold the Shift key).

Figure 3-14

 Smaller thumbnails in Filmstrip
Like the other panels, you can resize the Filmstrip by dragging its (top) edge. This changes the size of thumbnails in the Filmstrip. I usually keep the Filmstrip thumbnails pretty small, since I use the Grid view to get more info and don't need the Filmstrip thumbnails to show much detail. The Filmstrip remembers the two most recently used sizes; you can double-click the top edge to toggle back and forth.

SORT ORDER: VIEW YOUR PHOTOS IN A DIFFERENT SEQUENCE

When working in most image sources you can change the sort order in which the thumbnails are shown. The Library Grid Toolbar contains a menu for selecting the sort order (see **Figure 3–15**). The button to the left (labeled AZ or ZA) reverses sort direction.

Figure 3-15

USER ORDER

This is a special sort order you can use to rearrange the thumbnails however you want; click and drag with your mouse to rearrange the thumbnails in the Grid. This automatically sets the Sort Order menu to User Order. **User sort order is not available in smart collections, filtered views, when you have multiple sources selected, and Catalog panel sources other than Quick Collection.**

 Drag using the center of the thumbnail image
When selecting or dragging photos, always click on and drag from the image part of the thumbnail (not the background of the outer cell area). Otherwise, you'll only change the target photo selection. Don't worry about getting fingerprints on the photo!

CONFUSING SORT ORDER

Image files that get added to the catalog during editing or synchronizing may appear in the Grid in an order that can be confusing. If you look for a photo thumbnail in a certain place in the order and it's not there, look at the end of the sort order. Newly added photos (usually with varying file types) often end up there. Once you find the new photos at the end, you can modify the sort order and/or tag photos differently to control where they appear in the sort order. Keeping the sort order to File Name or Capture Time will keep original and derivative photos next to each other.

GRID VIEW OPTIONS

This window, accessed under View→View Options (or the contextual menu), configures the display of the thumbnails in Grid view (see **Figure 3–16**). Click the tabs at the top to switch between Grid and Loupe Views. When you're done changing the settings, close the window. The information you choose to show depends on personal preferences and needs; experiment to find what you like best.

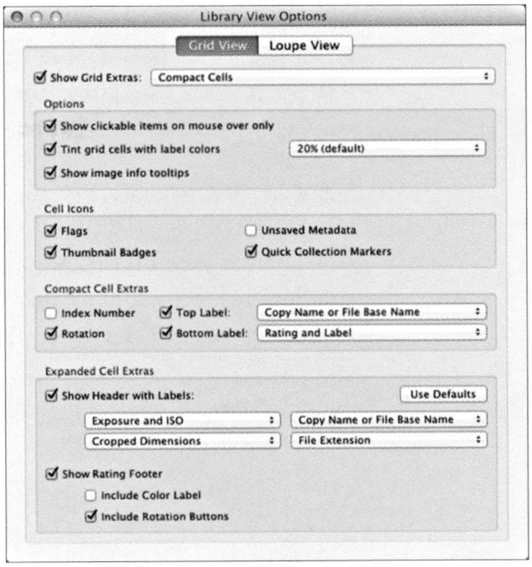

THUMBNAIL BADGES

In Grid view, the default thumbnails show one or more small badges when any metadata (keywords, cropping, adjustments, etc.) has been applied to that image, or if the photo is in a collection (see **Figure 3–17**). Click any badge to jump to that respective toolset or to choose a different collection.

Figure 3-16

Badges in the Filmstrip

The icons in the Filmstrip can show badges, too. Configure this in Preferences→Interface. (Note that some Filmstrip badges won't show if the thumbnails are very small.) I find the combination of small filmstrip and clickable badges a recipe for jumping to the wrong place when you try to select a thumbnail, so I tend to disable badges from showing in the Filmstrip.

Figure 3-17

Selections: Choosing the photos to work with

Most operations in Lightroom require one or more files to be selected. The most obvious way to select files is to click them, but there are other methods. You can select a single file, multiple files, or all files in the current source. You can also select None (no files selected). It's important to understand that most of the time there is at least one photo or video file selected—if only by default—unless you deselect everything.

The Grid and Filmstrip show the same selections. Selected files are highlighted in light gray to stand out against the other unselected files (see **Figure 3–18**). This means that you can select files in the Grid, and then see and work with those selections using the Filmstrip in other modules. The Source Indicator also shows how many files are selected.

Figure 3-18

⚠ Always know what's selected

Keep track of your selections at all times. When you're scrolling in the Grid or Filmstrip, it's possible to have files selected, but not visible in the preview area. This can cause trouble—you could easily apply changes to files that you didn't mean to. Pay careful attention to which files are selected at all times, and be deliberate in selecting and deselecting items. The source indicator or breadcrumb bar in the bottom panel above the Filmstrip is extremely helpful for identifying your current source, how many files are selected, and the filename of the active file.

THE TARGET FILE (ACTIVE FILE)

When multiple photos and videos are selected, the first one you selected is the "most selected" and referred to variously as the *target* or *active file*. The target file is highlighted a little brighter than the others (see **Figure 3–19**) and has unique properties within the selection. The target file also is used for the histogram, is processed in Develop, and contains settings that can be synced (or copied and pasted) to other files.

Figure 3-19

The order in which multiple files are selected is important, because it determines the target file. By default, when you switch between file sources, the first file in the source becomes active. With multiple files selected, the first one selected becomes the target file.

SELECT ALL

There are many situations where you will want to select all the files in the current source, such as when adding to a collection, modifying keywords, and Saving Metadata to File. Use the Select All command under the Edit menu, or use the ⌘+A or Ctrl+A shortcut. All files in the current source become selected (see **Figure 3–20**). If you had a file selected before running the Select All command, it becomes the target file. If no file was previously selected, the first image in the sort order becomes the target file.

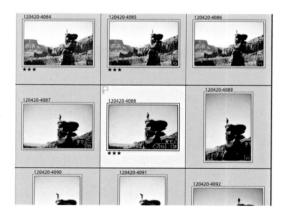

Figure 3-20

SELECT NONE

This is one of the most important commands used throughout the editing workflow. It's a very good habit to deselect any previously selected images before moving on to work on others. Otherwise, you might accidentally apply adjustments or other changes to a photo without intending to!

If the Grid shows some empty space with no thumbnails at the end, you can click there to Select None (see **Figure 3–21**). Otherwise, use the menu command or ⌘+D or Ctrl+D shortcut.

SELECTING AND DESELECTING MULTIPLE PHOTOS

To add to or subtract from a noncontiguous selection, hold the ⌘ or Ctrl key and click additional thumbnails in either the Grid or Filmstrip (see **Figure 3–22**). To add a contiguous range of photos to a selection, with one image selected, hold the Shift key on your keyboard and click another thumbnail. All the images between the two will become selected.

When you have multiple photos selected, you can click a photo's grid cell (not the thumbnail preview) to deselect all the others while keeping that one selected, or press Shift+⌘+D or Shift+Ctrl+D to do the same.

With multiple photos selected, to make one the target photo, click its thumbnail preview (or use the shortcuts).

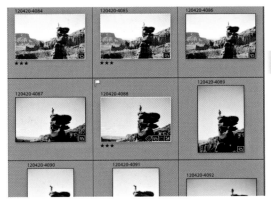

Figure 3-21

Figure 3-22

 Select contiguous images using the keyboard

In the Library Grid you can quickly select images using the arrow keys on your keyboard—left, right, up, down. Or, in all the modules, you can use just the left and right arrow keys to move through images horizontally in the Filmstrip. Hold Shift while pressing the arrow keys to select multiple contiguous images (those next to each other in the sort order).

SELECT BY FLAG, RATING, COLOR LABEL

Within the current image source, you can use these commands under the Edit menu to make specialized selections based on file attributes. (Attributes are covered later in this chapter.)

INVERT SELECTION

These selection commands will invert the selection status of the any photos already selected: selected images become deselected; deselected images become selected.

ADD, SUBTRACT, INTERSECT

These specialized selection commands allow you to make complex photo selections quickly based on several criteria. These selections commands are Boolean; think of them in terms of yes/no, on/off, or active/inactive. You can start with one selection and then modify it to include only the images you want.

Rotating and flipping photos

You can rotate and flip images when viewing either Grid thumbnails or Loupe previews. Remember that this affects only the previews in Lightroom; the original file on disk is not altered. However, when you save metadata to the file, the rotation will be visible in other programs supporting XMP, and when you export new files from photos rotated in Lightroom, the exported images will be rotated.

ROTATING PHOTOS

In Grid, the thumbnails can show arrows for rotation (see **Figure 3–23**). (View Options lets you configure this to show the rotation arrows all the time, or just when your cursor is over a thumbnail.) Click the arrows to rotate the photo(s) by 90-degree increments. If you have multiple photos selected, you can rotate them all at once. (To rotate an image by an amount other than 90 degrees, use the Crop/Straighten Tool in Develop; see Chapter 4.)

Figure 3-23

Select all photos of a specific orientation

You can use filters to select all the photos of either a Landscape or Portrait orientation. (In the filters, it's referred to as *aspect ratio*, though this is a bit of a misnomer.) Library filters are discussed later in this chapter.

FLIPPING PHOTOS

Photos can be flipped around their horizontal and vertical axes. To flip images in Library, select the photos to be flipped, and choose the menu command Photo→Flip Horizontal or Photo→Flip Vertical.

ENABLE MIRROR IMAGE MODE

Under the View menu is an option for Enable Mirror Image Mode. This is a global setting affecting all previews in the catalog. When it's enabled, all the previews are mirrored horizontally. This might be useful for some presentation setups, or when you're showing people portraits of themselves (since we're used to seeing ourselves in a mirror), or possibly when working with flipped scans or photos taken in a mirror. (My guess is that you'll rarely—if ever—use this feature.)

Stacks: Grouping items together

Think of stacks like sets of film slides: you can stack photos "underneath" each other, so that only the "top" photo is visible in the Grid. Stacks save space in the Grid, and can be useful when you've shot a sequence of similar images and want to group them together. Stacking photos of related subject or composition can save time during editing.

Many landscape photographers often capture a sequence of photos, all with the same composition, with only the light in the scene changing over time. Or a portrait photographer might have a series of shots that all have very minor differences in the pose of the subject. By stacking these kinds of shots together you can simplify the Grid view, significantly reducing distractions during editing. Later, when you're ready to choose the champion shot (the winner between several competing images) you can expand the stack to finish editing those photos. Then, when you're done choosing the final selects, you can unstack the photos, or move the champion to the top of the stack and collapse it again.

There are a couple of important limitations to stacking. Stacks are not available in Catalog panel sources, smart collections, or filtered views, and a single photo can be a member of only one stack. If you try to make a stack and it doesn't work, it's likely because the current source doesn't allow stacking, or because one or more of the selected photos already belongs to another stack.

A stack can be collapsed, which will then only show the thumbnail for the top photo, or expanded to show all the photos in the stack (see **Figures 3–24** and **3–25**). You should expand a stack when you want to perform an action or adjustment on all of the photos in the stack, or else only the top photo will be affected.

Figure 3-24

STACK PHOTOS AND VIDEOS
Choose Library➔Photo menu➔Stacking➔ Group into Stack, or use the shortcut (visible in the menu) . The target photo will go at the top of the stack by default, but you can change the stacking order at any time afterward. The top image in a stack shows the photo count for the stack in the upper left corner of the thumbnail. Click this to expand and collapse the stack. Right-click or Ctrl+click on the stack photo count badge to open the stack contextual menu.

Figure 3-25

 Filters and stacks
When filters are applied (see later in this chapter), any photo or video that doesn't match the filter criteria within a stack might be hidden, which can cause confusion. To avoid this, make sure all the photos in a stack are marked with the same attributes (discussed later in this chapter).

CHANGING THE ORDER OF IMAGES WITHIN THE STACK
To change the order of images within the stack you must first expand it. Click the photo count badge or the two thin lines at the right edge of the top image in the stack. Select

the image you want to reposition and use the stack contextual menu commands (or the keyboard shortcuts, not shown) to move the image within the stack.

AUTO STACK BY CAPTURE TIME

First, choose a folder, then right-click or Ctrl+click on one of the thumbnails. From the contextual menu, choose Stacking→Auto Stack by Capture Time. Set your desired time interval by adjusting the slider; the number of stacks that will be created will show underneath. Press Return or Enter. Lightroom will create stacks in the current source for all photos matching the given criteria. Set the interval to 0 seconds to stack all photos taken in the same second.

Loupe view

Loupe view displays a single, large photo (see **Figure 3–26**). You can zoom in and out of the Loupe preview using preset zoom levels based on ratios of image pixels to screen pixels. When the image is magnified you can pan the image to examine different parts of it more closely. You

Figure 3-26

can jump to Library's Loupe view from anywhere in Lightroom by pressing the E key.

The full screen image shown in Loupe view uses the Standard preview size (note that Lightroom will automatically render a larger size if needed). If you zoom in to 1:1 or greater, Lightroom will load the 1:1 preview. When you first enter Loupe view or zoom in close to a photo, Lightroom may need to build the preview. If this is the case, you'll see a message at the bottom of the image that says Loading…. This takes varying amounts of time depending on the size of the preview being built.

ZOOMING IN AND OUT

Lightroom gives you several ways to zoom in and out of images. Each method has its own usefulness; in some situations, one way is easier or faster than the others, so it's worthwhile to learn all the methods for zooming.

To show an image full size in Loupe view, double-click a thumbnail, or press E or Return/Enter. To go back to Grid view, double-click again, or press G. When starting in Grid, pressing Return/Enter cycles through Fit/Fill, most recent zoom, and then back to Grid.

To zoom in closer, use the Navigator panel zoom selectors, the Toolbar slider, or the keyboard shortcuts. A press of the Z key or Spacebar will zoom in and out, or you can just press and hold the Z key to zoom in and then have it zoom back out on release. Using the shortcut ⌘+=/⌘+− or Ctrl+=/Ctrl+− zooms in and out based on the four zoom levels shown on the Navigator, discussed earlier in this chapter and in Chapter 1.

03

Click-release versus click-hold

You've probably already figured out that you can click the Loupe preview to zoom in and out with each click. Try this, too: click *and hold* the mouse button to zoom in, and *without letting go*, drag the hand tool to move around the preview. Then release the mouse button to zoom back out to the previous view. For better access to the entire photo do the same thing inside the Navigator panel.

Zoom clicked point to center

There is a preference setting that recenters zoomed images around the clicked zoom point. Go to Preferences➔Interface➔Tweaks.

PANNING A PHOTO'S LOUPE PREVIEW

When you're in any zoom ratio except Fit, you can pan around the image by clicking and dragging with the hand cursor (see **Figure 3–27**).

Figure 3-27

SCROLLING THE LOUPE PREVIEWS WITH PAGE UP AND PAGE DOWN

Tapping Page Up and Page Down on your keyboard (on some keyboards you might need to hold the fn key in conjunction with the Up/Down arrow keys) allows you to "scroll" over a Loupe preview in equal "columns" whose widths are determined by the zoom ratio and the width of the Loupe preview. When zoomed in to 1:1, press the Home key to start at the top left of the image, and press Page Down repeatedly. When you've reached the bottom of the photo and you press Page Down again, Lightroom jumps the preview to the top of the next column to the right. This is very useful when checking photos for artifacts and doing retouching such as removing dust spots, as it ensures you can see every part of the photo, which can be uncertain using only manual panning. If you have the Caps Lock key active on your keyboard, the scrolling goes horizontally.

LOUPE INFO

Lightroom provides optional text overlays that show the specs of the image file, capture settings, and other useful information (see **Figure 3–28**). Press I to cycle through the overlays. Using View Options (under the View menu in the main menu bar), you can configure the elements making up the info overlays.

Figure 3-28

LOUPE TOOLBAR

The Loupe view mode has a separate Toolbar from the

Figure 3-29

Grid view (see **Figure 3–29**). You can add and remove items from the Toolbar using the pop-up menu accessed with the triangle button at the right of the Toolbar. For the Loupe Toolbar I keep the Attributes visible (Flagging, Rating, and Color Labels) so I can easily see what's applied without switching to another view mode. The Zoom slider can come in handy, too, but I usually use the keyboard shortcuts to zoom in and out of the Loupe preview. **Note:** All the items on the Toolbar might not be visible if the preview area is very small.

LOUPE VIEW OPTIONS

This window, accessed under View→View Options, configures the display of the Info Overlays in Loupe view (see **Figure 3–30**). Click the tabs at the top to switch between Grid and Loupe Views. Use the provided options to set up the info overlays with the elements you prefer. When you're done changing the settings, close the window.

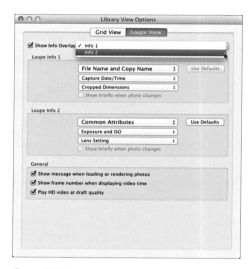

Figure 3-30

LOUPE BACKGROUND COLOR

You can change the color of the background area surrounding the standard Loupe preview. Right-click or Ctrl+click in the background area (you have to be zoomed out for this) and choose a color from the pop-up menu.

LOUPE OVERLAYS

New in Lightroom 5: There are two new types of overlays–Grid and Guides–in addition to the existing Layout Image (previously named Layout Overlay) that first appeared in Lightroom 4. All three overlay types can be used alone or in conjunction with each other, and they also can be used in Develop and when shooting tethered. The purpose of each overlay type is to help you better visualize aspects of your photos in different ways. You can enable and disable each overlay type from the View→Loupe Overlay menu (see **Figure 3–31**).

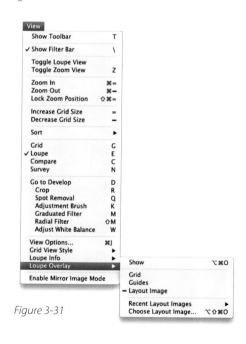

Figure 3-31

USING THE GRID

The Grid overlay can be useful for confirming the vertical and horizontal lines in your subject matter (such as horizons or buildings), or in placing subjects while shooting tethered. With the Grid visible, press the ⌘ or Ctrl key to display the controls for adjusting its size and opacity, and then hover your cursor over the desired control and click-drag left to decrease or right to increase (see **Figure 3–32**). I think I need to straighten that birdhouse.

PLACING A GUIDE

If you shoot tethered (covered in Chapter 2) and need to ensure a subject remains in the same location throughout all photos you'll really appreciate the new Guide overlay. When enabled, a vertical and a horizontal line converge at a point within your photo. You can hold the ⌘ or Ctrl key and click and drag that point to any place within your photo that you want to mark (see **Figure 3–33**). As each photo appears after being transferred from your camera you can easily confirm your subject has remained on the mark. Hold the ⌘ or Ctrl key and double-click a guide to recenter that line over your photo.

VISUALIZE WITH THE LAYOUT IMAGE

The Layout Image overlay allows you to place a PNG file from your hard drive into the Loupe preview (see **Figure 3–34**). This feature is designed to help you visualize how a photo will look when placed into a specified layout—for example, a magazine cover or wedding book layout. I used it when trying to choose potential photos for the cover of this book. You can bring in a PNG file containing transparency, and it shows "on top" of the photo, allowing you to confirm position of elements in your composition. To choose the Layout Image, go to View➔Loupe Overlay➔Choose Layout Image (see Figure 3–31). Select the

Figure 3-32

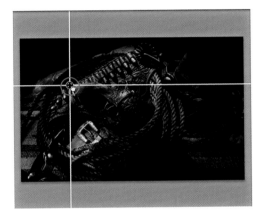

Figure 3-33

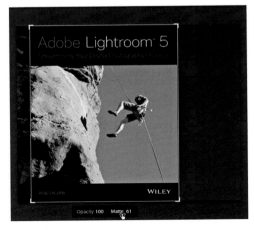

Figure 3-34

image file from your hard drive and click Choose. The Layout Image will appear in the Loupe view.

You can hold the ⌘ or Ctrl key to manipulate the overlay. With the ⌘ or Ctrl key held down, click and drag to move the overlay where you want it. Click and drag the corners of the overlay to resize it. When holding the ⌘ or Ctrl key, controls appear at the bottom of the overlay for Opacity and Matte (see Figure 3–34). Opacity controls the transparency of the overlay itself; matte darkens the preview around the outside of the overlay. Click and drag horizontally over each control to change its value.

You can show and hide the overlay using the command under the Loupe Layout menu. To use another image, just choose the new one from your hard drive. Lightroom remembers the location of the file you selected; if you want to remove it entirely, move, delete, or rename the PNG file. When Lightroom can't find the file, it will be automatically removed from memory.

⇨ Choosing a file for the Layout Image

You first need to make a graphic file in Photoshop or another similar program. The file must be saved as a PNG; other formats are not supported. PNG files can contain transparency, so if you use layers and transparent elements in your layout, they will be preserved in the PNG . (For this to happen, you must save the file in PNG-24 format; you can do this with Save for Web & Devices in Photoshop.)

Compare view

Compare view lets you evaluate two images side by side (see **Figure 3–35**). Select two photos and click the Compare button on the Toolbar, or press C. The target photo becomes the select and the second image becomes the candidate. When you enter Compare view, first take a look at the Toolbar; you'll notice some added controls

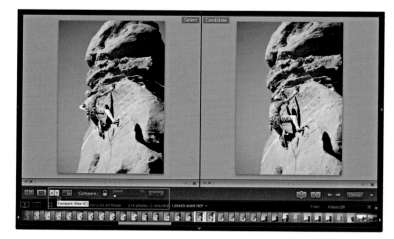

Figure 3-35

for working in Compare. In Compare (and Survey) view it's helpful to hide the panels to allow maximum room for the images. Also, you can use Lights Out to dim or black out the entire screen except for the images.

CHANGING PHOTOS IN THE SELECT AND CANDIDATE POSITIONS

The Toolbar in Compare view contains buttons for switching or swapping photos in both select and candidate positions (see **Figure 3–36**). Hover over each button to see its tool tip.

Figure 3-36

03

LEFT AND RIGHT ARROW KEYS

With two images loaded in Compare view, use the left and right arrow keys to load the next photo in the current source or selection into the Candidate position (see Figure 3–36). Tapping the up arrow promotes a candidate photo to the Select, simultaneously making it the target photo.

LINK FOCUS

With Link Focus, you can zoom into the exact same place on both images to check for critical focus, examine small details, etc. Make sure the Toolbar is visible, and click the lock icon to enable Link Focus (see **Figure 3–37**). You can then zoom in and out and pan both images at the same time.

Survey view

Survey view is for comparing more than

Figure 3-37

two images. All the selected images are scaled automatically to fit into the Survey window (see **Figure 3–38**). (For typical display sizes, I think Survey is most useful with a maximum of 8 to 10 images; with more than that, you're probably better off using the Grid with a large thumbnail size and the panels hidden.)

To enter Survey view, select multiple images from the Grid or Filmstrip and click the Survey button on the Toolbar, or press N. Note that the photos you see in Survey are all selected, so as when working with any group of multiple photo selections, it's important to keep track of the target photo. In Survey, the active ("most selected") photo is indicated by a white outline. Clicking a photo makes it the target photo.

Once in Survey view, you can add, remove, or rearrange the previews (you can only rearrange if you are working in a source that supports user order). Drag a preview to put it in a different position; this also changes the Grid and Filmstrip sort orders. Remove a photo from Survey by clicking the X in the bottom right corner of the photo (you must

03

put your cursor over the images to see the controls). Add photos to the view by selecting them from the Filmstrip while holding the ⌘ or control key. Press / (forward slash) to remove a selected photo from the Survey selection.

 Hide the Toolbar for more room
Press T to hide and show the Toolbar. I usually hide the Toolbar in Survey view, but there are times when the Toolbar is helpful, or even necessary, to perform certain tasks. In all modules, don't forget to frequently check

Figure 3-38

the Toolbar visibility. You can either make more room for photos by hiding it, or show it to provide access to more controls—some of which are not found anywhere else in Lightroom. For more space, press Shift+Tab to hide both side panels, as well as the top and bottom panels, all at once (press Shift+Tab again to bring them back).

Using the Secondary Display with Library

As introduced in Chapter 1, Lightroom offers support for a secondary display that can be configured separately from the main window. The second window can be used to show full-screen Loupe images while you choose from thumbnails in your main window, or vice versa.

You can also use the second window for Compare and Survey views, while keeping your main window in another view. (With this setup, if you have a large enough display, you can benefit from the second window, even using it on a single screen.)

To open the secondary display, click the button on the top left of the Filmstrip (see **Figure 3–39**). At the top left of the second window are the same view modes as the main window: Grid, Loupe, Compare, and Survey (see **Figure 3–40**).

Figure 3-39

LIVE LOUPE

At the top left of the second window, choose Loupe. At the top right, choose Live (see Figure 3–40). Move your cursor over the thumbnails in the main window, and the second window will instantly show each photo under the cursor.

LOCKED

Locked mode retains the same image until you explicitly choose to update it. This can be helpful in client reviews, as you can push images to the second display only when you intend to. At the top left of the secondary display window, choose Loupe. At the top right, choose Locked (see **Figure 3–40**). Right-click or Ctrl+click on a thumbnail for the contextual menu and choose Lock to Second Window.

Figure 3-40

Folders panel: Work directly with folders on your hard drives

The Folders panel (see **Figure 3–41**) shows the hard disk and directory structures for all the photos that have been imported into Lightroom. Folders are the essential system for organizing your photos on the hard disk; when you import a photo into Lightroom, the folder containing that photo will also be added to the Folders list. (By default, parent folders *above* the added folder are not shown, so you don't always see the complete directory structure, but you can change this.)

Figure 3-41

Once photos have been imported, it's best to manage them entirely from within Lightroom. This ensures that Lightroom can keep track of the files. You can directly manipulate the folders on disk from within the Folders panel. For example, if you move or rename folders in the Folders panel, those changes will also be made to the folders on disk.

Unlike the windows and folder views in Mac Finder and Windows Explorer, the Folders panel does *not* show image files. As you select folders by clicking on them, their contents are shown in the view mode previews and in the Filmstrip.

 Resize the panels
Drag the edge of the left panel set to make it wider; this will show longer folder names. On Mac, hold the Option key when dragging the panel edges to make them much wider (see **Figure 3–42**).

Figure 3-42

03

HARD DISK DRIVES AND VOLUMES

At the top level of the folder/file hierarchy is the volume. A volume is usually an individual hard disk drive, but could also be a partition on a single disk or a multiple-disk array.

Figure 3-43

Volumes (and folders) shown in Lightroom correspond directly to the drive volumes on your computer's file system (Mac OS X Finder or Windows Explorer). Volumes are listed in the Folders panel with their folders underneath (see **Figure 3-43**). I imported photos on a second drive (named External) to show that multiple drives can be displayed in the Folders panel.

A single Lightroom catalog can contain images from any number of volumes. As you import images from folders on different drives, each volume also automatically gets added to the list in the Folders panel. Each volume has its own Volume Browser listing, which shows the status of the volume and optional statistics. Click the volume name to hide and show its folder contents.

VOLUME BROWSER INFORMATION

By default, the Volume Browser also shows the available free space and the volume size. This can be changed. Normally there's a green "light" at the left of the Volume Browser indicating the volume is online with available free space. If the light is yellow or red, free space on the volume is low. If a volume is dimmed (gray), that volume is offline. To change the Volume Browser display options, or to show the volume in the Finder or Explorer, right-click or Ctrl+click on the Volume Browser header (see **Figure 3-44**) and choose the information you'd like to show.

Figure 3-44

ROOT FOLDER DISPLAY OPTIONS

To change the details shown on the root folder, click the + button at the right of the Folders panel header (see **Figure 3-45**). From the menu, choose the options you prefer.

OFFLINE/ONLINE

Figure 3-45

A disk volume that is connected and available to the computer is online. A volume that is not available to the computer is offline. You can't work on images from offline volumes in Develop, and a few other controls become unavailable (unless you had rendered smart previews for the photos on that volume before it went offline). This is because when processing an image, Lightroom renders new previews after each change is made, which requires rereading the data from the file on disk. (However, in many cases you can work in a limited capacity with photos that don't have smart previews from offline volumes in Library and the output modules, where Lightroom will use rendered previews if they are available.)

Offline volumes are dimmed in the Folders panel. You can still navigate within their folder structures, although all the folders and photos will show as missing (offline photos that have a smart preview will display a Smart Preview icon, which is covered later in this chapter).

 Volumes not listed in the Folders panel
Lightroom will not show or provide access to a volume until you import photos from that drive. If a drive is connected to your computer but its volume is not listed in the Folders panel, it's because no photos from it have been imported into the current catalog. (This is one easy way to verify you're working in the correct catalog.)

FILE COUNTS

At the right of each folder name a number is displayed showing how many items from that folder have been imported into the catalog (see **Figure 3–46**). If you've imported everything from the folder, this file count should be identical to what you'd see in Mac Finder or Windows Explorer. If a folder in the list contains no photos indexed by the catalog, this will display 0.

Figure 3-46

SHOW PHOTOS IN SUBFOLDERS

When the Show Photos in Subfolders menu option is active, selecting a folder in the Folders panel will show its contents and **also the contents of any subfolders it contains** (see **Figure 3–47**).

Though this is the default condition, depending on your folder structure, this may be neither necessary nor desirable. With photos in subfolders shown, it can be difficult to determine exactly which folder contains the selected photos—the photos will be shown when you select the parent, even though they are actually contained in a different folder underneath (see Figure 3–46). Also, showing all the contents of subfolders can slow Lightroom's performance as it reads and makes previews for the many files in the subfolders. Usually, I think it makes more sense to just load the photos actually contained within the single folder I selected.

You can enable or disable this option from the menu that appears when you click the + button on the panel header. With the Show Photos in Subfolders option turned off, if you select a parent folder with no photos contained within it, by default you will see the message, "No photos in selected Folder. Subfolders not shown." Selecting a folder from the panel will only display the contents of that folder and **not of any subfolders**

Figure 3-47

03

(see **Figure 3–48**). This gives you a much more accurate view of the exact contents of each individual folder and can speed up previewing when switching between folders. A potential drawback to doing this is that the file counts of parent folders are also affected (see Figure 3–48).

Figure 3-48

I normally work with Show Photos in Subfolders turned off, and only turn it on temporarily as needed.

FINDING A FOLDER ON YOUR HARD DRIVE

Depending on what you've imported, the contents of the Folders panel may or may not clearly reveal the complete directory path where the folder is located. If you ever have a question about where the folder resides on disk, or need to quickly go to it in the Mac Finder or Windows Explorer, you can easily locate a folder anywhere on your hard disk: right-click or Ctrl+click on the folder name; from the contextual menu choose Show in Finder or Show in Explorer. This will locate the folder and select it in the file system (see **Figure 3–49**). Note that when you run this command with multiple folders selected, the uppermost folder in the list is the one that will be shown in your file system.

Figure 3-49

RENAMING FOLDERS

Renaming a folder from Lightroom also renames the folder on disk. Right-click or Ctrl+click on the folder name, then choose Rename… from the contextual menu (see **Figure 3–50**). Type the new name and press Return or Enter.

MOVING FOLDERS

You can drag and drop to move folders in the Folders panel. When you move a folder from within Lightroom, it gets moved on the hard drive. Click and drag a folder from one location to another and a dialog box appears for confirmation (see **Figure 3–51**). You can hold the ⌘ or Ctrl key to select multiple folders, and then release the key and drag them all at once.

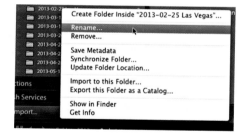

Figure 3-50

Figure 3-51

MOVING FOLDERS FROM ONE HARD DRIVE TO ANOTHER

When you move folders between volumes, Lightroom performs a file copy in the background, and once the copy from one drive to the other is complete, the folders and files are deleted from the first drive.

03

ADDING SUBFOLDERS

When you create a new subfolder from within Lightroom, it is also created on your hard disk. To add a subfolder, right-click or Ctrl+click on a folder in the list and select Create Folder Inside… (see **Figure 3–52**) or click the + button on the Folders panel header and choose Add Subfolder… (see **Figure 3–53**). Type the folder name for the new folder and press Return or Enter. The new, empty subfolder will be placed inside the folder currently selected in the Folders panel.

Figure 3-52

ADDING FOLDERS

When you add an existing folder from your hard drive, you are taken to the Import window set to the Add import method (see Chapter 2 for details on this). To add a folder, click the + button on the Folders panel header, and then choose Add Folder (see Figure 3–53). Complete the import from within the Import window, as described in Chapter 2.

Figure 3-53

REMOVING FOLDERS

When removing a folder from Lightroom, if it contains photos, the folder will be removed from the catalog but will remain on the hard drive with all its contents intact. When you remove an empty folder from the catalog, it's sent to your system trash immediately, without confirmation. Removing parent folders also removes any subfolders contained within it. To remove a folder, right-click or Ctrl+click on the folder name and choose Remove Folder from the contextual menu, or click the – button on the panel header. Press Return or Enter to confirm the removal.

 Removing folders deletes catalog data
When you remove a folder from the catalog, all the information about the contents of that folder—including Develop adjustments, virtual copies, and any other information—is also immediately removed from the catalog. If you make a mistake, you can usually Undo this with the command under the Edit menu.

However, if you quit Lightroom, when you come back later the removed data will not be recoverable.

MISSING FOLDERS AND WHAT TO DO ABOUT THEM

If a folder name contains a question mark (see **Figure 3–54**) it means the folder (and its contents) cannot be

Figure 3-54

located by Lightroom. If you know for sure that you don't need that folder, you can simply remove it from the catalog using the methods described previously. However, if you want to keep the files, and Develop or Export any of the contents of a missing folder, you will first need to locate it.

If you know the location of the missing folder, right-click or Ctrl+click on the folder name and choose Find Missing Folder… from the contextual menu (see **Figure 3–55**). Navigate through the system dialog boxes to find the missing folder and click Select Folder to finish. Lightroom will update the links in its catalog.

Figure 3-55

If you don't know the location, you can't relink the folder. It's possible the folders were imported from a hard drive that is not currently attached to the computer; verify the drive is attached.

Be careful when removing folders, especially those that show as Missing—make sure you have figured out why they're showing as missing before you remove them.

COMMANDS FOR MANAGING FOLDERS IN THE PANEL

There are numerous commands that will help you manage the contents of the Folders panel. Right-click or Ctrl+click on a folder, and choose an option from the pop-up menu (see **Figure 3–56**). (Many of these commands are explained in task-based context throughout the preceding sections.)

- **Move Selected Photo to this Folder:** If you have one or more photos selected, this command appears, allowing you to move those files from their current folder to the folder you right-clicked on. This does the same thing as drag and drop.

- **Create Folder Inside…:** Creates an empty subfolder under the selected folder.

- **Rename…:** Allows you to rename the selected folder.

- **Remove…:** Removes the selected folder (and all its contents) from the Lightroom catalog (see explanations in previous section).

Figure 3-56

- **Hide this Parent:** Use this command to remove a parent folder from the catalog; the subfolders will remain. (This option will be visible only if you right-click or Ctrl+click a top-level parent folder.)

Be careful hiding parent folders
When you hide parent folders, if they contain photos, those photos are immediately removed from the catalog, and all the data about them is deleted. To get them back you'd need to reimport them.

- **Show Parent Folder:** To add the parent folder of an existing top-level parent folder to the Folders panel, right-click or Ctrl+click the folder name, and then choose Show Parent Folder. The parent folder containing the selected folder will be added to the folders panel. However, if that folder contains photos, they are not automatically imported.

- **Save Metadata:** Saves the Lightroom metadata to disk for all the files contained in the selected folder.

- **Synchronize Folder…:** Opens the Synchronize Folder dialog box, which allows you to sync the contents of the Lightroom catalog with the contents of the folder on the hard drive. Synchronize Folder is explained in detail later in this chapter.

- **Update Folder Location…:** Allows you to point Lightroom to a different source folder on a hard disk. This is useful if you've copied files in the exact same folder structure and need Lightroom to use the new location, even though the existing catalog links are not broken. This is handy when replacing an old drive with a new one.

- **Import to this Folder…:** Provides a quick way to import photos into a specific folder. Right-click or Ctrl+click on a folder and select the command from the menu. The Import window opens with the chosen folder as the destination.

- **Export this Folder as a Catalog…:** Creates a new catalog, using the contents of the folder, and saves the files to your hard drive. Exporting as catalog is covered in Chapter 11.

- **Show in Finder (or Show in Explorer):** Selects the folder in your computer file system.

- **Get Info (or Properties):** Opens the system dialog box to display information about the folder on disk.

Managing photos and video files in Library

After photos and videos have been imported into a Lightroom catalog, those image files need to remain accessible to Lightroom for you to do most of the work with them. For example, you can't do any Develop edits without having the actual files or smart previews accessible by Lightroom. You can do metadata edits like keywording, rating, etc. without access to the source files or smart previews, though. When you have access to the actual files, renaming or moving photos in Lightroom also makes those changes to the files on disk (you cannot move or rename offline photos even if they have smart previews).

FINDING A PHOTO IN THE LIGHTROOM FOLDERS LIST

Occasionally, when working in a source other than a folder you may need to find the folder that contains the file within the catalog. Right-click or Ctrl+click on the photo, and from the contextual menu choose Go to Folder in Library (see **Figure 3–57**).

Figure 3-57

FINDING A PHOTO ON YOUR HARD DRIVE

From within the Lightroom catalog, you can easily locate an image file anywhere on your hard disk. Right-click or Ctrl+click on the photo. From the contextual menu choose Show in Finder or Show in Explorer; this will locate the image within your hard drive's file system. Note that when multiple photos are selected this menu option is unavailable.

MOVING PHOTOS

To move photos and videos from one folder to another, simply select their thumbnails and move them from one folder to the other using drag and drop (or use the pop-up menu command on the destination folder). Be sure to click and drag from the central thumbnail portion of the preview, not the outer cell area, or you'll just change the target photo selection. You'll receive a confirmation dialog box reminding you that you're actually moving the files on disk.

 Splitting folders

If you want to separate the contents of one folder into separate folders, simply create the new subfolders in the list at the location where you want them, and move the photos into those new folders using one of the methods described previously.

RENAMING PHOTOS

One of Lightroom's most useful batch processing capabilities is renaming files. Renaming photos in Lightroom also renames the image files on disk. Renaming files is something you should consider carefully and do early in the workflow.

To rename a single file, you can simply change the name in the File Name field on the Metadata panel. To rename a batch of files, use the Rename Files menu command, or the shortcut F2, to open the Rename Files dialog box (see **Figure 3–58**). From here, you can simply select one of the filenaming templates for more control over the names.

Figure 3-58

Filenaming templates

Using filenaming templates, you can set up filenames using whatever conventions you prefer. The templates can then be used to rename files in the Library module as well as during imports and exports. To access the Filename Template Editor (see **Figure 3–59**), choose Edit from the File Naming menu on the Rename Photos dialog box. (You can also access the filename template editor from the import window; see Chapter 2.)

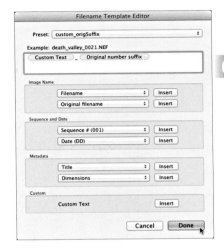

The Filename Template Editor provides controls to set up your template. Your template can contain a combination of set text and tokens—a token is a preformatted container for automatically inserting different types of information, such as date, sequence number, etc. You can type directly in the text box and/or click the Insert buttons to put tokens in the name. Choose the tokens and text you want to form your new naming template, referring to the preview of the name above the box. When it's the way you want it, save the template from the Preset menu at the top.

Figure 3-59

 Rename a batch of images after editing the shoot
If you do your filenaming in Library, rename the photos after you remove any rejects—this will keep your numbering sequence unbroken.

DELETING PHOTOS AND VIDEOS

You can remove images from Lightroom without affecting them on the hard disk, or you can use Lightroom to actually delete files from the disk. Select the image(s) and press Delete. A dialog box appears giving you three options (see **Figure 3–60**):

- **Delete from Disk:** Remove the photo(s) from the Lightroom catalog and put the image file(s) in the system trash.

- **Cancel** and do nothing.

Figure 3-60

- **Remove:** Remove the photo(s) from the Lightroom catalog but leave the image(s) on the disk. (You won't be able to work with the photo in Lightroom anymore, unless it's reimported later.)

 Be very careful when deleting photos
When you remove photos from Lightroom, any edits or adjustments you made to those photos in Lightroom will also be removed. If you haven't saved out the metadata, that work will be lost. (You could reimport the files, but your Lightroom changes will not be restored.) If you make a mistake when removing photos, you can immediately Undo the deletion(s) using the command under the Edit menu (unless you used Delete from Disk).

Delete Rejected Photos

If you use Reject Flags, you can use Photo→Delete Rejected Photos to quickly remove all the rejects from the current source. Flags are discussed later in this chapter.

Extract previews

If you've deleted photos from disk and they are unrecoverable (and not backed up), as a workaround you can extract Lightroom's previews to create new files. This will depend entirely on the size and quality of the previews that were in existence prior to the time the photos were deleted, but in most all cases the extracted previews will be nowhere near the size or quality of the original photos. But in an emergency, having the extracted previews might be better than nothing at all! To extract the Lightroom previews you could try an Extract Previews utility designed by Adobe for this purpose (helpx.adobe.com/lightroom/kb/extract-previews-lightroom-4.html), or if you had previously rendered smart previews for the affected photos you could export them as DNG (keep in mind the reduced pixel dimensions and lossy compression used on smart previews to bring down file size).

MISSING PHOTOS AND WHAT TO DO ABOUT THEM

Remember that the names and locations of your image files are recorded in the catalog during import. This means if you move anything in your file system outside of Lightroom the catalog will not automatically update and the files will show as missing. Photos will show as missing if they've been moved, deleted, or renamed outside Lightroom or if their folder has been moved, deleted, or renamed—you will need to relink the files from within the catalog. Photos will also show as missing if the drive is turned off or disconnected. Whatever the reason, if Lightroom can't locate a file or folder, you'll receive various types of notifications about this, such as exclamation points on the thumbnails and error messages in Develop. (Note that previous versions of Lightroom displayed a question mark on the thumbnails of offline files). The most common causes and solutions for broken links include:

- **The file or folder was moved or renamed outside Lightroom:** Relocate the files from within Lightroom or put things back the way they were.

- **The volume is offline:** Connect the hard drive(s) to the computer (note, Windows users should also see the discussion of Windows drive letters a little further on in this chapter).

LOCATING MISSING PHOTOS

If a thumbnail shows an exclamation point (see **Figure 3–61**), it means Lightroom can't find the image file on disk and you cannot process it in Develop. If the file doesn't show a preview, it's because the previews were not built before the file went missing. In many cases, you will see a preview even though there's also an exclamation point. Click the exclamation point on a thumbnail to open a dialog box that can help you reconnect the catalog to your file (see **Figure 3–62**).

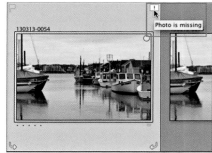

Figure 3-61

An important piece of information in this dialog box is the Previous location, which is the path to that photo stored inside the catalog. This is the last place Lightroom knew that photo to exist and it may clue you in to what happened to that file. **From this point on Lightroom relies entirely on you to find the missing file(s).** To proceed, click the Locate button and navigate to where that

Figure 3-62

03

file is stored and select it. You need to know that location before you proceed, so if you are not sure you'll need to put on your detective hat and figure it out before you can reconnect the catalog.

If you no longer want the missing photo(s) in the catalog, remove them using the methods described earlier in this chapter. Just remember you'll be deleting all the Lightroom information for these files as well.

LOCATING MISSING PHOTOS THAT HAVE SMART PREVIEWS

If a photo is offline, but has a smart preview you'll see a Smart Preview icon in the upper-right corner of the thumbnail (see **Figure 3–63**). While you can still work with that

offline file in all the ways we've discussed regarding smart previews, you may also need to reconnect the catalog to the source photo. Just like when a file is offline, without a smart preview you need to know where the source file is located. When you do, click the Smart Preview icon to open the dialog box with the Previous location and the Locate button. Click the Locate button and select the source file to reconnect. Once the source file is back online the Smart Preview icon will go away.

Figure 3-63

 Windows drive letters

In some situations, it's possible that the files haven't actually been moved, but Lightroom has lost track of them. This can happen when using an external drive on Windows, where the drive is assigned a drive letter each time it's turned on. It's possible that the same drive will be assigned a different drive letter each time it's connected. In these cases, Lightroom won't be able to find the files, because the drive letter is part of the file path stored in the catalog. There are several ways to permanently set drive letters on Windows; search online to find the best option for you. Once you manually restore the drive letter to what Lightroom expects (based on that Previous location path stored in the catalog) your photos will be found automatically.

FIND ALL MISSING PHOTOS

This command, under the Library menu, identifies missing photos in your catalog by putting them in a special temporary collection in the Catalog panel, and filters the Library view to show them. You can then determine whether to relink, remove, or ignore them.

Stay in charge of your files

If you have missing folders or photos showing in your catalog, you should either relink them (if you need to work on them) or remove them (if they are no longer needed). You can certainly ignore them if they are intentionally offline (such as an offline drive), but the key is that you need to make intentional decisions about your files and always know where they are outside of Lightroom. The majority of Lightroom-related problems I help people solve are related to a lack of awareness of the relationship between the catalog and their files on disk. As long as you know where all your files are located you can make the right decision about how to handle and work with offline files.

VALIDATE DNG FILES

New in Lightroom 5: Lightroom 5 offers the ability to check your DNG files for corruption. When photos are converted to DNG a special validation hash or checksum is added to the DNG file. This checksum should not change under normal circumstances, and so a change would signal file corruption. You can select a source containing DNG files and go to Library→Validate DNG Files to have Lightroom compare the current state of the file against the original checksum. If no corruption is found Lightroom will display a pop-up dialog indicating all DNG files in the selected source are valid. If any file corruption is detected Lightroom will display a bad DNG files message and a show button that will create a special collection of just those DNG files when clicked. File corruption is not something that can be fixed, but you can restore the affected files from your backup. You can learn more about DNG in the Appendix.

Synchronize Folder

The Synchronize Folder command compares what's in the catalog with the contents of the folder on disk and allows you to update the catalog accordingly. This is something you should get in the habit of doing every now and then.

Whenever you've made changes to the contents of a folder *outside* Lightroom, such as adding or removing images, renaming files, etc., you should synchronize the folder. For example, if you use Adobe Bridge, Adobe Camera Raw, Photoshop, or Elements to edit photos, you'll often need to synchronize them in Lightroom when you're done, otherwise Lightroom won't know what happened.

Right-click or Ctrl+click on the folder name, and then choose "Synchronize Folder…" from the contextual menu. A dialog box appears (see **Figure 3–64**) with the following options:

- **Import new photos:** If files are found in the folder on disk that are not in the catalog, the number of those files is shown. If you want to have Lightroom import these new photos, check the box. They will be imported using the Add method; see Chapter 2 for more on this. If no new files are found, (0) is shown and this section is dimmed and unavailable.

Figure 3-64

- **Show import dialog before importing:** If new files are found, this option becomes available. Check this box to open the Import window prior to performing the sync. This allows you to verify the images being added and check for any metadata that may be applied during the import. If you're sure that no settings conflicts exist, go ahead and do the sync without checking the Import window.

⚠ **Be careful skipping the Import window**
This is extremely important: the Import window retains all the settings from your most recent import. If you sync a folder and skip opening the Import window, any metadata presets used for the previous import will also be applied to the files in this sync. This means that you could easily—and inadvertently—apply a metadata preset and/or Develop settings to the files being added. For this reason, I almost always show the Import dialog before importing and verify the settings before executing the sync.

- **Remove missing photos from catalog:** Check this box if you want to get rid of any files with broken links. Do this with care, because in some cases you might want to relink them instead. Remember that when you remove items from the catalog, all their processing data goes, too. (You can preview the missing photos first; see the following bulleted list.)

- **Scan for metadata updates:** Tick the box to enable the option for Lightroom to check that the metadata contained in the catalog is up-to-date with what's contained in the file on the disk. (Metadata status is a very important topic, and you can learn a lot more about it later in this chapter.) I usually leave this unchecked because I manage my metadata status manually.

Once you've chosen the options you want to perform for this Synchronize Folder operation, you have several buttons to consider, across the bottom of the dialog box:

- **Show Missing Photos:** If Lightroom detects there are missing photos in the selected folder(s), you can click this button to see them in the main preview area. **Note:** Doing this effectively ends the current sync operation; you'd need to restart it when you're ready to actually sync the folder.

- **Cancel:** Closes the dialog box without performing the sync.

- **Synchronize:** If you have the option enabled to show the Import dialog before importing, clicking the Synchronize button will open the Import window. In this case, work through the Import window just as you normally would (and as covered in Chapter 2) and click the Import button to initiate the sync. If the Import dialog option is disabled, when you click this button Lightroom immediately begins the sync.

 Sync top-level folders periodically
Syncing parent folders also syncs subfolders. Every so often, run a sync on your upper-level parent folders, just to make sure everything's up-to-date in the catalog.

03

Collections: Organize things however you like

Like filters (covered later), collections are one of Lightroom's great strengths. Think of collections like virtual folders: these groupings of images exist only within the Lightroom database. You can make collections for any purpose, subject, or topic and you can use as many collections as you want. A single photo or virtual copy can belong to any number of collections, without requiring additional copies of the file on disk. Adding or removing a photo from one collection doesn't necessarily affect it in others.

I've set up numerous collections to hold client work, portfolios, exhibition entries, magazine submissions, Web galleries, etc. I have collections for work-in-progress, and collections for uncategorized images waiting to be put in a more permanent place in the catalog. Because I add photos to collections after the initial edits, using collections— instead of working in the original folders—reminds and assures me that my editing for those photo shoots was completed and I'm now seeing only the final selects.

 Use collections more than folders

As you move through the workflow, I strongly recommend that you end up working much more from collections than you do folders. The flexibility offered by collections is one of the key advantages of using a database-driven system.

Collections panel

You create and manage collections with the Collections panel, near the bottom of the left panel set (see **Figure 3–65**). The Collections panel is persistent in all modules—unlike Folders, you can access your collections from anywhere in Lightroom (another advantage of using Collections over Folders).

There are three main types of collections: regular collections, smart collections, and output module collections. You can group your collections together in collection sets.

Figure 3-65

COLLECTIONS BADGE

When a photo is in a collection, Lightroom shows a collection badge on the Grid thumbnail (see Figure 3–17). Collections badges only show in folders and sources other than the currently selected collection, though if the photo is also a member of other collections, it will be displayed. Click the badge to go to the photo in that collection.

MAKE A COLLECTION AND ADD PHOTOS TO IT

Regular collections are those you create manually. These "dumb" collections aren't based on any predefined criteria; you can create collections yourself for whatever purpose you choose, and add photos to them however you see fit.

Click the + button on the Collections panel header (see Figure 3–65) and choose Create Collection... Type a name for the collection and configure the other options to your liking. For example, if you have images selected, you can automatically add them to the new collection. Press Return or Enter to create the collection.

To add photos to a collection later, drag their image thumbnails onto the collection name in the panel, or use the Target Collection option discussed in a following section.

Can't add to a collection?

If you try to add a photo to a collection and you're not able to, it's because the photo is already in that collection. If it's not visible within the collection view, check the filter status. Also, make sure you click and drag from the center of the photo and not its border.

Drag and drop a folder to make a new collection

You can drag a folder from the Folders panel onto the Collections panel to create a new collection using all the contents of that folder.

MULTIPLE INSTANCES OF A SINGLE PHOTO ON DISK

When you put a photo into a collection, Lightroom simply keeps track of that in the catalog. The photo is not duplicated on your disk. Lightroom is still referencing the original file on disk, and by default, the settings for the new instance are linked to the settings of the original—changing one will change the other. For example, if you add a photo to a collection and then convert it to black and white from within the collection, the original file in the folder source will also show those changes, and vice versa.

However, when adding photos to a collection it is also possible to create a new virtual copy of the file in that collection. A virtual copy is a special instance made from the original. When you make a virtual copy Lightroom is still referencing the original file on disk; it just creates a second set of instructions for how to process this new instance. Changing settings on a virtual copy does not affect the original, or vice versa. Virtual copies are discussed further in Chapter 4.

When creating a collection from selected photos or adding photos to an existing collection you have the option to make a new virtual copy. I usually leave this option unchecked because I want the photo to be the same in all the sources from which I might access it.

REMOVING PHOTOS FROM A COLLECTION

To take one or more photos out of a collection, select the photo from within the collection and press Delete. This immediately removes the file(s) from a collection without presenting a confirmation dialog box. (This is undoable; just be sure to undo the removal before going on to other work.) Removing a photo from a collection doesn't affect instances of that photo in other collections, or the original file on disk.

MOVING AND COPYING PHOTOS BETWEEN COLLECTIONS

You can add a photo to as many collections as you would like. However, there's no straightforward way to move a photo from one collection to another. You need to add the photo to the new collection and then remove it from the first.

Go to Collection

Right-click or Ctrl+click on a photo; if the photo is in any collections (not smart collections), they will be listed in the pop-up menu under Go to Collection. Choose from one in the list to select the photo in that collection (see **Figure 3–66**).

Figure 3-66

SET AS TARGET COLLECTION

You can set any regular collection as the target collection. Right-click or Ctrl+click the name of the collection and choose Set as Target Collection from the contextual menu (see **Figure 3–67**). A plus symbol next to the collection indicates it is targeted. Photos in the Target Collection show a gray dot on the top right corner of the thumbnail (see **Figure 3–68**). Clicking the dot or pressing the B key will add and remove photos to and from the target collection. To reset the targeting, uncheck the option from the menu and the Quick Collection will again become the target collection.

Figure 3-67

New in Lightroom 5: When you create a new regular collection there is now a Set as target collection check box in the Create Collection dialog box, which is a handy way to get started.

Figure 3-68

 Duplicating collections

To copy one or more collections, hold Option or Alt while dragging in the Collections panel. If you drag to a different collection set (see next section) the collection is copied using the same name. If you drag to the same location Lightroom copies the collection and appends "Copy" to the end of the original name.

Quick Collection

The Quick Collection is a built-in collection that is best used as a temporary holding place during editing or organizing. It's a useful tool for combining search results and filtered views. For example, during editing, you could add photos to the Quick Collection as an intermediate step to getting them all into one permanent collection later. There is only one Quick Collection available in each catalog. Access the Quick Collection in the Catalog panel (see Figure 3–68). Photos in the Quick Collection (when it's the Target Collection) show a gray dot on the top right of the thumbnail image (see Figure 3–68). To remove a photo from the Quick Collection, click the dot or press B.

To add or remove photos from the Quick Collection, press the B key if it's the target collection (see above), or hover your cursor over a thumbnail and click the gray circle in the top right corner. The target collection can also be applied via the Painter tool, which is covered later in this chapter.

03

Smart Collections

Smart collections are like a saved search, and as such are automatically populated with photos that match the provided criteria. You can set up smart collections to show photos from anywhere in the catalog. As you work with photos and their settings are changed, Lightroom dynamically adds or removes them from the smart collections. The only way to remove a file from a smart collection is to change something about it so that it no longer matches the provided criteria, or change the criteria used to create the smart collection.

You could make smart collections for files made in the last 30 days, photos that need keywords, photos to prepare for a client, photos to be sent to a lab for printing, etc. All these smart collections would be based on file metadata, but you can use other criteria as well.

New in Lightroom 5: The available criteria for smart collections has been upgraded, and now includes criteria for size, color profile, bit depth, color mode, PNG format, and the existence of smart previews.

MAKE A NEW SMART COLLECTION

On the Collections panel, click the + button and choose Create Smart Collection (see Figure 3–65). In the dialog box, type a name for the collection, and then add the desired criteria. By default, a new smart collection just contains one rule. Use the plus or minus buttons to add or remove additional rules (see **Figure 3–69**). When you're done, press Return or Enter to create the smart collection.

Figure 3-69

 More options for rules
Hold option or Alt when creating rules; this provides additional, "advanced" options.

A few notes about smart collections:

- Since smart collections work automatically from photo metadata in the catalog, you can't directly add or remove images from smart collections by dragging and dropping them.

- Smart collections cannot use custom (user) sort orders (create a new regular collection from the smart collection files if a custom sort order is needed).

03

- You can modify the rules used for a smart collection by selecting Edit Smart Collection from the pop-up menu.

IMPORT AND EXPORT SMART COLLECTIONS

You can transfer your smart collections between catalogs. Right-click or Ctrl+click on the smart collection name and from the contextual menu choose Import Smart Collection Settings or Export Smart Collection Settings.

Output Module Collections

Each of the output modules—Book, Slideshow, Print, and Web—can create a special type of collection (see Figure 3–65). Although they appear in the Collections panel and can be managed along with other types of collections, it's important to understand that the creations saved from these modules contain much more data than the image references alone. For example, a saved Book has all the settings used for the creation of the Book, in addition to the instances of the actual photos referenced by the Book. In the Library module, these look and feel like regular collections.

From the Collections panel in Library (and Develop), you can double-click on a saved Book, Slideshow, Print layout, or Web gallery or click the arrow to the right of the collection name. This takes you to the corresponding module and loads that creation using the included photos. (From within the output modules, a single click does the same thing.) The chapters discussing each of the output modules explain how to save those items and manage them in the Collections panel.

Output module data is not stored in regular collections. Also important to note is that output module collections can be made as children of regular collections when they're being saved, or later using drag and drop.

Collection Sets

Like a folder can contain subfolders, a collection set can contain collections and other collection sets. A collection set is designated in the Collections panel list by a special icon (see Figure 3–64). Collection sets are a great way to keep your collections organized into larger categories. To make a new collection set, click the + button on the collections panel header and select Create Collection Set. To rename a collection set, right-click or Ctrl+click on its name and select Rename from the pop-up menu.

Managing the Collections panel

Items in the Collections panel can be sorted by category ("kind"), and then alphabetically by name. By default, collection sets always show in a group at the top of the list, with individual collections listed below. You can change the way the collections are sorted: click the + button and choose an option from the pop-up menu (see Figure 3–65). Within a set, the collections and subsets are always sorted alphabetically.

 Use leading numerals

To force collections or sets to different positions in the list, I often use numeric characters in front of the main part of the name.

MODIFYING COLLECTIONS IN THE LIST

To delete a collection or set, select it in the list, and then either click the minus button on the panel header (which appears only when an item is selected in the list; see **Figure 3–70**) or right-click/ Ctrl+click the collection name and select Delete from the pop-up menu. Deleting a collection will not affect any original photos in disk, or instances of photos that might also be in other collections. Deleting a collection set will also delete all the collections—and other sets—contained within it.

Figure 3-70

Introduction to Publish Services

Lightroom has the ability to "publish" photos to hard drives and websites directly from the Library module. This provides great capability for integrating Lightroom with outside services such as social media and photo-sharing websites in addition to networked folders used by workgroups. With websites that support user comments and feedback (e.g. the Facebook "Like" button), Lightroom can automatically sync those comments into your catalog; that's what the Comments panel on the right is for. Since publish services are a sophisticated form of export, you can learn about them in Chapter 5.

 Smart collections connection with publish services
Publish services are similar to smart collections in many ways. In fact, you can import smart collection settings into publish services. Using this method allows you to dynamically generate collections of photos and videos that can be easily synchronized with websites and shared folders.

Attributes: Tag photos with identifying marks

When you assign attributes to photos you can quickly and easily find and sort them. Lightroom's attributes are Star ratings, Color labels, and Flags. With just these three sets of attributes you can differentiate between your photos in many ways.

There are several ways to apply or remove attributes on photos. Attribute controls are available on the Toolbar, but they are not all visible by default. Click the triangle button at the right side of the Toolbar to enable or disable items in the Toolbar (see Figure 3–29).

 Use a consistent meaning
Whatever labeling system you prefer, do your best to use a consistent system of identifying your photos. For example, all images with one star ideally should have the same significance in your catalog, such as indicating a first round select.

 Disappearing thumbnails
During an edit, if you change any of the attributes of a photo and it disappears from view, it's most likely because filters are enabled. Change or disable the filter set (discussed in the next section). It could also be because you are working from a smart collection, so always check your source.

FLAGS

Pick flags and their opposites, reject flags, may be the simplest form of editing decision—yes or no. You can apply a pick flag by clicking the flag icon that appears in the top left of the photo's thumbnail when you hover your cursor over it (see **Figure 3–71**) or you can use the keyboard shortcuts—P for Pick flag, X for Reject flag, and U for Unflag (the default state).

Figure 3-71

⚠ **Flag status is not written to XMP metadata**

Pick flags are specific only to the current catalog. When you save XMP metadata to disk, pick flag status is not recorded. If you apply flags in one catalog, save out the metadata, and then import those into another catalog, the pick flag status will be reset. For this reason, you may prefer to use stars for editing because those ratings are saved out to the files and can also be read by other software.

MARKING REJECTED PHOTOS

Using the reject flag helps hide unwanted photos and speeds their removal from your catalog. When they're unselected, thumbnails for rejected photos are dimmed in the Grid View (see **Figure 3–72**).

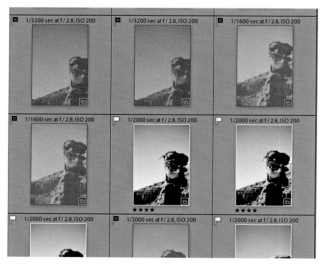

DELETE REJECTED PHOTOS

After marking photos as rejected, press ⌘+Delete or Ctrl+Backspace to filter the rejected photos. A dialog box appears allowing you to remove the photos from the catalog or delete them from disk.

REFINE PHOTOS

Figure 3-72

If you use flags, Refine Photos helps facilitate automated mass-deletion of photos from your Library. When you run Refine Photos, images that had Pick Flags will be set to Unflagged, and previously Unflagged photos will get a Rejected flag. Usually, you'd use this in conjunction with Delete Rejected Photos.

RATINGS

Star ratings (see **Figure 3–73**) are a very common method of ranking photos and other digital media. They are primarily meant to be used as a heuristic ranking model, e.g. five stars are better than one. By default, photos come into the database with no stars, unless they had stars applied in another program.

Like many photographers, I begin rating with one star, going up to two, three, etc. to a maximum of 5. But some people start at 3 and go up or down from there. You can use whatever system you choose, but it's practical to use an ascending order of ratings. In all cases, using a standard system can speed up your workflow and ease decision-making.

Figure 3-73

Apply a star rating to one or more selected photos by clicking the stars in the Toolbar or the expanded thumbnails (see Figure 3–73), or by using the shortcuts. Clicking on the current rating or pressing 0 resets the photo to unrated.

Pondering the meaning of stars

A rating system is most effective when the attributes always have the same meaning, regardless of context. For example, multiple photos with two stars should always have the same significance regardless of the folder, collection, or other sources they might be contained in. This is more difficult than it sounds.

Consider that when you're editing a batch of photos, the ratings necessary to complete that round of editing may differ from one shoot to the next. With some shoots, you might only need to use one or two stars to identify the keepers. Other times, you may need more stars to further refine the selects from rejects. I suggest applying a Pick flag to all of the keepers as a way to identify them in all settings regardless of the rating (or lack thereof). This is one of the challenges of using a heuristic model in varying sources.

COLOR LABELS

You can apply a color label to a photo to indicate a specific meaning (see **Figure 3–74**). In Lightroom, color labels correspond with accompanying text values. The defaults are Red, Yellow, Green, Blue, and Purple. You can apply standard color labels by clicking the color label swatch on the Toolbar or expanded thumbnails, by typing text into the Metadata panel, the Painter tool, or with the shortcuts.

Figure 3-74

The key to using labels effectively is using them consistently in the same way. For example, a photographer might apply a green label to mark portfolio images. Or you could label a set of images blue to indicate they are to be stitched into a panorama, or label photos purple to indicate they had been reviewed by a client, etc. I don't often use color labels; if I need to differentiate between photos with the same rating, I usually use keywords or titles and captions. However, I've known many photographers for whom using color labels is an essential part of a highly evolved workflow. This is one example of how workflows can be personalized based on your own preferences.

COLOR LABEL SETS

You can make multiple Color Label Sets that have different definitions for the colors. Choose Metadata→Color Label Set to edit the current set or make new ones (see **Figure 3–75**). If you have used Adobe Bridge to apply color labels, be aware that the names of the default color labels differ in Lightroom and Bridge. (Lightroom offers a built-in color label set that matches that of Bridge but it's not the default.)

Figure 3-75

CUSTOM LABEL NAMES

On the Metadata panel, you can type any text into the Label field (see **Figure 3–76**), but the five standard colors are the only ones that will actually show a color on the thumbnail. The Label field itself is simply editable text (whereas flags and stars are invariable), so you can enter anything you want for the label definition. If the text does not match a label in the current color set, the color used for the thumbnail will be white.

Note: Custom is an available option in the attribute filters; see the next section for more on this.

AUTO ADVANCE

With Auto Advance enabled, as you apply any attributes to images in Library (flags, stars, etc.) Lightroom automatically selects the next image in the current source. Select Photo→Auto Advance to toggle the control on and off (or toggle on and off with the Caps Lock key). This is an extremely useful feature and can add a real speed boost to your initial round of editing. With Auto Advance enabled you can use flags or star ratings to quickly move through an entire shoot just by using keyboard shortcuts to apply the criteria to trigger Lightroom to advance you to the next photo in the shoot (refer to the Edit a Shoot workflow at the beginning of this chapter).

Figure 3-76

Filters: Show photos and videos based on criteria

This is one of the most powerful and important features for organizing and sorting your photos in Lightroom: applying filters determines which photos will be shown in the preview area and Filmstrip.

03

Filters are configured from the top right section of the Filmstrip (see **Figure 3–77**) and with the Filter Bar at the top of the main preview area (see **Figure 3–78**). Lightroom comes with some built-in filter sets, including Flagged, Rated, etc. Load filter sets using the pop-up menu on either the Filter Bar or the Filmstrip.

Figure 3-77

Figure 3-78

Filters can be used to search your catalog for specific images using any criteria. After you've created a filtered view, you can save a filter preset and/or add those photos to a new collection for quick access later. Typically, you will start by previewing photos in any image source, such as All Photographs, or a folder or collection, and then apply filters to see only the photographs you want from within that source. In this way, filters are used to refine the other sources.

 Filter by location
When photos have GPS data available, you can use a Metadata filter to find them by location. (You can use the Map module to add location data to photos.)

FILTER LOCK
By default, filters are specific to the folder or collection source to which they are applied, and are removed when you leave that source. However, filter settings can be locked so the filter's criteria persist when switching between sources. Click the lock icon on the Filter Bar to lock the filter in place (see the lock icon at the far-right end of the Filter bar in Figure 3–78). After you enable the filter lock you can go to File→Library Filter, and select Remember Each Source's Filter Separately to apply a different (yet persistent) filter in each source.

FILTERS ON FILMSTRIP
At the right side of the Filmstrip is a set of filter controls (see Figure 3–77). If they're not visible, click the word *Filter:* to expand/contract the filters section. These controls are persistent in all the modules and all view modes, so they're the easiest to access. They provide essentially the same functionality as the filter bar (discussed in a following section), and you can select saved filter presets, but you can't configure complex metadata filters here.

THE FILTER SWITCH
The filters section on the Filmstrip includes a switch that disables or enables the current filter (see Figure 3–77). This can produce a result similar to clicking None on the Filter Bar (discussed in a following section), but will only turn off filters based on Attributes. To turn everything off, use None on the Filter Bar, or the shortcut.

Don't modify filters just to disable them

If you want to temporarily show photos that don't match the current filter set, you don't need to modify the filters, just turn them off. For example, if you have a filter enabled to show only picks and need to see the unflagged photos also, don't remove the pick flag from the filter; turn the filter off using None or the Filmstrip switch. This allows you to keep filter sets intact for later use.

FILTER BAR (GRID VIEW ONLY)

The Filter Bar is available in Grid view mode (see Figure 3–78). If it's not visible, make sure you're in Grid view and use the shortcut \ (back slash) or the option under the View menu to show the Filter Bar. Using the Filter Bar, you can set up your own filters based on an unlimited range of criteria, including image file properties and metadata such as keywords and attributes. Filters can be combined to create any kind of file selections and can be saved as presets for later use.

 Showing the whole Filter Bar

If the Lightroom application window and main preview area are not wide enough, the right side of the Filter Bar will not be visible (see **Figure 3–79**). Make the window larger and the panels narrower, or hide unused panels, to see the entire Filter Bar.

Figure 3-79

 # Example Filter workflows

Following are several examples of creating filters. You can work through these steps to get an idea of what's possible with filters, but of course, this is only scratching the surface. The main point to understand is that any time you want to isolate some photos from anywhere in the catalog—even from all the photos in the catalog— filters are the best way to do it.

APPLY A TEXT FILTER

The Text filter is essentially a text search engine. It's most useful for searching for keywords, filenames, and any other text that may be associated with image files or virtual copies. The text filter can find a string of text contained—or not contained—anywhere in the file data.

Step 1. Select the image source you'll be filtering. If you want to search the entire catalog, use the All Photographs catalog source. Otherwise, choose a folder or collection to start with.

Figure 3-80

Step 2. With the Filter Bar visible, click on the Text filter (see **Figure 3–80**). The text filter options become visible below.

03

Step 3. Use the menus to set up your search criteria (see Figure 3–80). The first menu default is "Any searchable field," which looks for the text string anywhere in the files. To narrow the criteria, open the menu and choose from the other options, which include Filename, Title, Keywords, etc.

Step 4. Set how the filter will search using the text (see **Figure 3–81**). The options are Contains, Contains All, Contains Words, Doesn't Contain, Starts With, and Ends With (note that some options may not appear for all types of criteria).

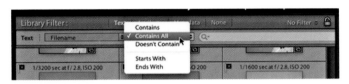

Figure 3-81

Step 5. Type in the text to search for (see **Figure 3–82**). As you type, Lightroom dynamically updates the filtered view to show only the files matching the criteria you've selected.

Figure 3-82

To start over and reset the text search to show all the unfiltered photos in the source, click the X at the right of the text search field (see Figure 3–82).

 Special text search characters
Add ! (exclamation mark) in front of a word to exclude it from the search results. + before a word activates the "Starts With" criteria for that word. + at the end of a word activates the "Ends With" criteria for that word.

If you're searching on filenames and they contain hyphens or underscores, you don't need to include them in the text search field; Lightroom will find the whole words with or without the separating punctuation.

 Tooltips
Remember that when you hover with your cursor over an item for a few seconds, for most objects in the interface, a tooltip appears. This is a great way to learn and memorize what the buttons do.

APPLY AN ATTRIBUTE FILTER
This is the core set of filters used for the Lightroom editing sequence outlined at the beginning of this chapter: ratings, flags, and labels. With the Attribute filter you can also filter by Kind: Master Photos, Virtual Copies, and Videos. (This is often faster than using a Metadata filter, which is covered next.)

Step 1. As before, Select the image source you'll be filtering: if you want to filter the entire catalog, use the All Photographs catalog source. Otherwise, choose a folder or collection to start with.

Step 2. In the Filter Bar, click Attribute to enable the filter (see **Figure 3–83**).

Figure 3-83

Step 3. Click the buttons in the Filter Bar to set what attributes will be used for the filter (see Figure 3–83). The main options are Flag, Rating, Color, and Kind.

- **Flag:** Filter based on flag status—unflagged, picks, or rejects. You can click multiple flags to refine the criteria; click a flag again to remove it from the filter criteria.

- **Rating:** Filter based on the number of stars applied. Between the word *Rating* and the first star is a menu option to choose Rating is greater than or equal to, Rating is less than or equal to, or Rating is equal to. Click a star to set the desired rating level for the filter.

- **Color:** Filter based on a color label, unlabeled, or a custom label. Click multiple colors to create an aggregate filter of labels. Click a label to remove it from the filter.

- **Kind:** Filter based on "Master" (an actual file on disk), virtual copies, or videos. Click to add multiple kinds to the filter, if you like.

⇨ Select by attribute

A cool tip I learned from my friend Mark Sirota (also the fantastic tech editor of this book) is that you can select files based on their attributes (flag, rating, and color label) by holding the ⌘ or Ctrl key and clicking on the desired attribute in the Filter bar. For example, to select all photos with a 3-star rating in my current source I would hold the ⌘ or Ctrl key and click the third star in the Filter bar (this works in the Filter above the Filmstrip, too).

APPLY A METADATA FILTER

You can create image filters based on any file metadata, including EXIF information such as exposure setting, lens used, capture date, flash on or off, etc. (see **Figure 3–84**). You can click and drag the bottom edge of the metadata filter section to expand and compress

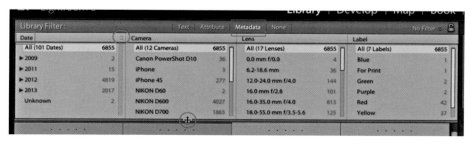

Figure 3-84

the filter bar. If the contents of the columns are too long to show their entire contents, use the scroll bars at the right of each column to scroll up and down.

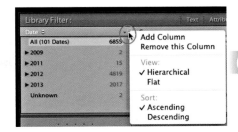

Step 1. Select the image source you're filtering.

Figure 3-85

Step 2. Click the Metadata button on the Filter Bar. The default Metadata filter loads, with four sets of criteria: Date, Camera, Lens, and Label (see Figure 3–84).

Step 3. (Optional) To add or remove columns from the metadata filter, place your cursor over the column header and a small icon appears at the right (see **Figure 3–85**). Click here and use the menu to add or remove the column.

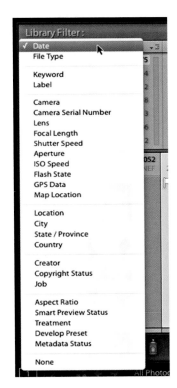

Step 4. To change the metadata being used in a filter column, click the column header to select a type from the pop-up menu (see **Figure 3–86**).

Step 5. From within each column, continue to select the metadata values to use for the filter. As you select criteria, the values in the other columns change to reflect the filtered results.

 Selecting multiple values
You can select multiple criteria within the metadata columns. Hold Shift to select a contiguous range of options. ⌘ or Ctrl selects individual, noncontiguous criteria (see **Figure 3–87**).

RESET FILTERS TO NONE
Clicking None on the Filter Bar (to the right of the main filter type selectors) deactivates the current filter set. The previous filter settings remain intact; they are just disabled.

Figure 3-86

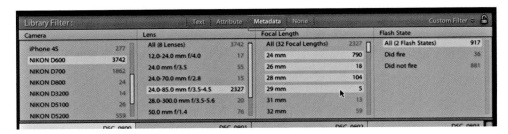

Figure 3-87

03

COMBINING MULTIPLE FILTER TYPES

You can click multiple filter names to add controls for multiple filter types at the same time. For example, you could use a Text filter with Attributes added, or Text with Metadata, etc. A highlighted label indicates that filter is active (see **Figure 3–88**). Click the name of the filter to enable or disable it in the current filter set. (If you spend time configuring a complex filter set, you should consider saving a preset to use again later.)

Figure 3-88

FILTER PRESETS

To save a filter preset, get the filter set up the way you want, and then click the menu at the right side of either the top Filter Bar or the filters section on the Filmstrip (see Figure 3–88). From the menu, select Save Current Settings as New Preset. Give your preset a meaningful name; it will then be listed in the filters menu. You can access your saved filter presets from both the Filmstrip and Filter Bar.

Quick Develop

The Quick Develop panel in the Library module contains a limited subset of the image adjustment controls available in the Develop module (see **Figure 3–89**). (It's a good idea to learn a bit about Develop adjustments before doing a whole lot in this panel.) Click the black triangles to expand all the sections on the Quick Develop panel.

One of the main advantages of Quick Develop is you can apply adjustments to multiple photos at once. Because of the relative nature of Quick Develop, each photo can be processed differently, depending on their previous settings. To apply Quick Develop settings to multiple photos, work in Grid view. (If you're previewing a single photo in Loupe view, Quick Develop adjustments will be applied to only that image).

With one or more photos selected, click the buttons in the Quick Develop panel to adjust the settings. Right-facing arrows increase the value for each setting; left arrows decrease that value. Single arrows increase or decrease by small values; double arrows increase the adjustments in larger increments (see Figure 3–89). Hold your cursor over each setting to see its tool tip.

Develop adjustments are described in much more detail in Chapter 4.

Figure 3-89

Press Option or Alt
This toggles Clarity/Sharpening and Vibrance/Saturation on the Quick Develop panel.

THE PRESET MENU ON THE QUICK DEVELOP PANEL
You can apply saved Develop presets to photos using the Quick Develop Panel. Note that, in contrast to the Quick Develop controls, when you apply a Develop preset, the applied values are still absolute.

 Crop presets in Quick Develop
Using the Crop Ratio menu in Quick Develop, you can quickly and easily crop multiple photos in Library by applying the same crop ratio to them all at once. (To use custom crop presets you'll need to create them first; see Chapter 4 for more on this.)

RESET ALL
This button on the Quick Develop panel (see Figure 3–89) resets the selected photo(s) to the default settings. This applies to all photos selected when in Grid view, or a single photo when in Loupe view. All other metadata (keywords, copyright, title/caption, etc.) are not modified.

UNDERSTANDING ABSOLUTE AND RELATIVE ADJUSTMENTS
Lightroom provides two places for you to apply adjustments directly to photos—Library and Develop—but in each module, the changes are applied differently. Using the Quick Develop panel is very different from using the full Develop module. Though the names of the adjustments are the same, and those adjustments produce the same visual changes in the individual photo(s), how the adjustments are applied makes all the difference.

In Library's Quick Develop panel, all the adjustments are relative: the changes you make are applied **on top of any existing adjustments.** For example, if you start with a Saturation setting of +6 and click a single-arrow button to apply a +5 Saturation increase, the resulting value will be +11. The effects are cumulative. So if you have two photos with different Saturation values, let's say +6 for one and +10 for the other, and you apply a Quick Develop Saturation increase of +5 to both of them, you'll end up with values of +11 and +15, respectively.

Conversely, when you set an adjustment in the Develop module, the slider value—or the number you type—is absolute. That means that the numeric value applies precisely that amount of adjustment, even when dragging the sliders. In the Develop module, if you repeatedly change an adjustment for a photo, the effects of two sequential adjustments are not cumulative. These adjustments are absolute and the numeric value shows exactly what it is. If you start with a Saturation value of +6 and change it to +11, it's really +11, not +17.

INTRODUCTION TO PROCESS VERSIONS
The settings available in Lightroom's Quick Develop panel are dependent upon the Process Version applied to the selected photo(s). By default all newly imported photos are set to Process Version 2012 (PV2012). If you're just starting with Lightroom and

03

haven't imported any pictures from earlier versions, you don't need to worry too much about Process Versions at this point. But if, on the other hand, you have worked on pictures in Lightroom 3 or earlier (Process Version 2012 was introduced in Lightroom 4), and you now want to use the new Quick Develop tools, there are a few things you need to understand.

The available settings are different depending on the process version. Photos newly imported to Lightroom 5 will use PV2012 and will show the new controls in Quick Develop (see Figure 3–89). Those developed with earlier process versions will still show the old controls (see **Figure 3–90**). This means you could end up using one set of Quick Develop controls for photos with PV2012 and another for older versions.

More importantly, the adjustments used by the older process versions (2003 and 2010) do not map directly to the new controls. If you convert photos using older process versions to PV2012, odd shifts will likely occur, requiring you to reprocess those photos one by one. Unless you want to reprocess your photos, I wouldn't recommend you convert them to the new process version.

Figure 3-90

Process Version is covered in much more detail in Chapter 4.

SYNC SETTINGS

You can synchronize Develop settings between multiple photos. When you use Sync Settings, the settings from the target photo are applied to the other selected photos. First, select the photo from which you want to copy the settings, and then select the other photos to have the new settings synced to. Click the Sync Settings button (see **Figure 3–91**). A dialog box opens, allowing you to choose what settings will be synced (see **Figure 3–92**). These are Develop adjustments only—not keywords or any other metadata. (To sync metadata, use the Sync Metadata button instead.)

Figure 3-91

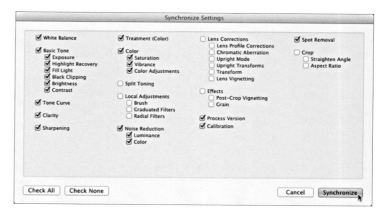

Figure 3-92

03

COPY/PASTE SETTINGS

You can copy Develop adjustments from one photo and paste them to other photos. Copy/Paste is similar to Sync Settings. However, there's one major difference: when you copy settings, they are stored in memory and can be pasted to other photos later. Conversely, Sync Settings happens just the once; these synced settings are not saved anywhere. Otherwise, the Copy Settings dialog box is identical to Sync Settings in appearance and function.

To copy/paste settings, first select an image, then use the Settings→Copy Settings command or shortcut. This opens the Copy Settings dialog box. Choose what Develop settings to copy from the selected photo. Then select one or more photos that will receive the pasted settings. Pressing the Paste shortcut (or using the Settings→Paste Settings menu command) applies the copied settings to all the selected photos. All settings that are different will be pasted.

Keywords: Tag your photos for search

Keywords (also often called *tags*) are words and short phrases used to describe the content, theme, and subject of a photo. In addition to literal descriptions, keywords can be used to describe metaphors, abstract concepts, and graphical elements of the composition. If a photo has keywords applied, a badge shows on the thumbnail (see **Figure 3–93**). (Clicking a Grid thumbnail badge opens the Keywording panel.)

Figure 3-93

WHY USE KEYWORDS?

For most photographers, keywords are essential metadata that should be applied to every photo, especially those that will be posted online. Search engines read keywords embedded in image files and display search results based on the contents of this metadata. Keywords also have many potential uses within your local Lightroom catalogs—you can use keywords to find and organize photos in your archives, even if those keywords are never shown to the public.

OVERVIEW OF THE KEYWORDING WORKFLOW

You can apply keywords in the Import window, and then enhance them in Library, where you work with the Keywording and Keyword List panels. Start adding keywords near the beginning of the workflow, and continue adding and refining your keywords for selects as you move them through the pipeline.

When you apply keywords to photos they are stored in the current catalog. You can import and export keyword lists. You should budget time for managing your keyword list independently from your other photo editing work.

Figure 3-94

Apply keywords to as many photos as possible at one time

As you go through your editing workflow, apply keywords in progressively finer detail. Start with the most generic terms that apply to the most photos, and gradually add more specific keywords to smaller groups and individual photos.

KEYWORD FORMATTING

Within a photo's metadata, keywords are separated by commas and, optionally, spaces as well. You can use single or multiple words. I recommend using specific, distinct phrases as keywords. For example, if I shoot in Rocky Mountain National Park, I will use the phrase "Rocky Mountain National Park" as a keyword, because it's a name, and not "Rocky, Mountain, National, Park". However, depending on the photo, I might also include the word "Mountains" as a separate keyword.

In the sections that follow, you'll read about using the Keywording and Keyword list panels, working with keyword hierarchies, finding photos using keywords, and my thoughts on general keywording strategies.

The Keywording panel

The Keywording panel shows the keywords applied to the selected photo(s) (see **Figure 3–94**). You can edit Keyword Tags in the text field and/or click to apply keywords from the Keyword Suggestions and Keyword Sets.

Click the small black disclosure triangles to expand all the sections of the Keywording panel (see Figure 3–94).

KEYWORD TAGS

With one or more photos selected, type your keywords into this text box to apply them to the selected photo(s) (see Figure 3–94). The pop-up menu at the top of the panel allows you to choose how keywords are shown in this section of the panel:

- **Enter Keywords:** In this mode, all the keywords applied to a photo are shown in the large text box in the top portion of the Keywording panel. **This is the only mode that allows you to edit keywords in this panel.** Click in the text box to add, change, or delete keywords from the selected photo(s). Lightroom's Auto Complete feature helps finish words for you as you type (this behavior is controlled by the option in Catalog Settings→Metadata). Press Return or Enter when you're done working in the text field.

When multiple photos are selected, keywords showing an asterisk (*) are only applied to some of the selected images. In other words, if a keyword does not have an asterisk, it is applied to all the selected photos. To quickly apply a keyword to all the selected photos, simply delete the asterisk. (However, adding an asterisk doesn't work the same way; to remove selected keywords from some photos use the other methods described below.)

- **Keywords and Containing Keywords:** This mode displays the keywords applied to the selected photo(s) along with their hierarchies, which is discussed below.

- **Will Export:** This mode displays the keywords that will be applied to the photos when you export them or generate creations in the output modules. Depending on how you've set up your keyword list, some keywords may not export. This is covered in the next section.

ADD KEYWORDS

If you only want to add keywords to selected photos—not change or remove them—use the Add Keywords field. In the Keywording panel, where it says, "Click Here to Add Keywords" (see Figure 3–94), type the new keywords to be added. When you're done typing, press Return or Enter to apply the keywords to the selected photos.

 Return/Enter or Esc
Always press Return or Enter when you're done typing text into any field in Lightroom. Or, press Esc to leave that text entry field without committing the changes. If you don't do this, and you use keyboard shortcuts, it's quite likely that you will inadvertently type text into a field when you didn't mean to.

 Keyword Entry Preferences
In Lightroom Preferences→Interface there are options controlling the behavior of keywording as you type: you can choose a different keyword separator (I recommend commas) and turn Auto-complete on and off.

KEYWORD SUGGESTIONS

As you keyword photos, Lightroom keeps track of other images to which you've applied similar keywords and, based on capture times, provides Keyword Suggestions (see Figure 3–94). There are up to nine keyword suggestions available at any given time; all the suggested keywords must already exist in the current catalog. The suggestions are constantly updated so when you apply a new keyword, the suggestions may change. Click a suggested keyword to apply it to the selected photo(s).

KEYWORD SET

Keyword Sets are designed to speed up your work when adding keywords to photos with similar subjects or themes (see Figure 3–94). You can make Keyword Sets using any criteria you like. Each Keyword Set contains up to nine keywords. Lightroom comes with several built-in keyword sets: Outdoor Photography, Portrait Photography, and Wedding Photography. There is also a selection for Recent Keywords.

Select a set from the pop-up menu to load that set of keywords. The keywords contained in that set are then shown in the panel. Click the keywords to add them to selected photo(s) or use the keyboard shortcuts for Set Keyword (see below). A keyword will be highlighted if it's already applied to the photo; click the keyword again to remove it from the photo.

You can modify these sets and create your own sets. To edit a keyword set, open the pop-up menu and select Edit Set… The resulting dialog box (see **Figure 3–95**) lets you add, change, or remove keywords from that set. You can enter any keywords you like in this box; if they don't already exist in the catalog, they will be

Figure 3-95

added to the Keyword List the next time they are used. If you make changes to a keyword set, the set will be listed as (edited). Open the menu again and select Update Preset or Save Current Settings to New Preset to save the changes.

KEYWORD SET SHORTCUTS

This is very different than Keyword Sets; it's a shortcut. The nine most Recent Keywords, or those from the current Keyword Set, can be applied to selected photos using keyboard shortcuts or with the Photo→Set Keyword menu command. If you're keywording photos and consistently using the same keywords, Set Keyword can save lots of time. Press Option or Alt to show the numeric keyboard shortcuts in the Keyword Set section of the panel (see **Figure 3–96**).

Figure 3-96

Keyword List

The Keyword List panel (see **Figure 3–97**) shows a list of all the keywords in the currently open catalog. As you add new keywords to photos using the various methods, they are automatically added to the Keyword List. You can use the Keyword List to add and remove keywords to/from photos and to modify the keywords themselves.

The Keyword List is sorted alphabetically; you can't change the sort order of keywords in the list, but you can group keywords together in hierarchies or add numbers or special characters to keywords to control where they show in the list (non-alphanumerical characters appear at the top of the sort order; see Figure 3-97).

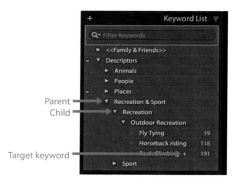

Figure 3-97

 Maximum number of keywords visible in the list
It's been reported that in Windows, the Keyword List will not show all the keywords actually contained in the catalog. A recent test on Lightroom running on Windows 7 indicates 3,271 as the possible maximum number of keywords shown in the list. (I don't know of any limit on OS X.) Using a keyword hierarchy so you can collapse the list is a good workaround.

KEYWORD LIST ICONS

When images are selected, the Keyword List panel shows which keywords are applied to the selected photo(s). A check box to the left of each keyword indicates whether or not it's applied to the photo (see **Figure 3–98**). A check mark indicates all selected photos contain that keyword(s); a dash indicates the keyword is applied to only some of the selected photos (like the asterisk in the Keyword Tags field), or that a single selected photo contains only some of the keywords within a hierarchy.

Figure 3-98

USING THE KEYWORD LIST TO APPLY AND REMOVE KEYWORDS

With one or more photos selected, you can add or remove keywords to or from a photo by clicking the check box to the left of the keyword. You can also add keywords by dragging and dropping them from the list onto the photo, or vice versa. To remove a keyword from a photo, you can uncheck it from the list or use the controls in the Keywording panel. You can also add and remove keywords by right-clicking or Ctrl+clicking on the keyword, and then selecting the appropriate command from the pop-up contextual menu (see **Figure 3–99**).

Figure 3-99

THE TARGET KEYWORD

You can select the pop-up menu option to "Use this as keyword shortcut," which allows you to apply that target keyword using the Shift+K keyboard shortcut. When this option is enabled, a + symbol shows next to the target keyword in the list (see Figure 3–97).

CREATING KEYWORDS IN THE LIST

Create new keywords in the list by clicking the + button at the top of the Keyword List panel. This opens the Create Keyword Tag dialog box (see **Figure 3–100**). In the Keyword Name field, enter the name for the keyword. Explanations of the other options follow.

In both of the aforementioned dialog boxes you have several options for controlling the behavior of the keyword being edited:

Figure 3-100

- **Keyword Name:** This is the keyword itself. If you've made a typo or spelling error, you can correct it here.

- **Synonyms:** When you create a new keyword or edit an existing one, you have the option to include synonyms for the word. Synonyms are words that mean the same thing as the main keyword. On a case-by-case basis, you'll have to decide whether it's better to add a synonym or make a separate keyword. For example, the keyword "Autumn" could have the synonym "Fall." This is likely more efficient than setting up "Fall" as its own keyword. "Vacation" could have the synonym "Holiday," and so on. (Of course, you could also have a second entry for Holiday in a different, more generic context.) Lightroom uses synonyms when generating suggestion lists.

- **Include on Export:** Keywords that have this box checked will become embedded in all photos it's applied to when those photos are exported (unless suppressed by the options in the Export and Publish Services dialogs). This includes Web galleries and files made with the Print to JPEG command in the Print module.

If this box is not checked, the keyword will not be included when the photo is exported. This feature is very useful when you're using keyword hierarchies for internal organization but don't want certain keywords to be exported (see below). For example, I have a keyword called "Geographic Locations," under which are nested keywords for many specific regions and countries around the world. I want the specific place names to be included on export, but not the "Geographic Locations" tag.

- **Export containing keywords:** If a keyword is nested in a hierarchy, this option determines whether or not the parent (upper-level) keywords will be included on export.

- **Export synonyms:** Determines whether or not a keyword's synonyms will be included on export.

- **Add to Selected Photos:** Does just that; if photos are selected, they will instantly have the keyword applied when it is created or edited.

- **Put inside:** if you had a keyword selected when you opened the Create Keyword Tag dialog box, this option allows you to make the new keyword a child of the previously selected keyword.

EDIT KEYWORD TAG

Edit a keyword by double-clicking it to open the Edit Keyword Tag dialog box, which functions identically to the Create Keyword box (see Figure 3–100).

KEYWORD HIERARCHIES

In the Keyword List panel you can create keyword hierarchies, which are multi-level groupings constructed of parent and child keywords (see Figure 3–97). Think of keyword hierarchies like folders and subfolders in a file system where you have one top-level folder, with multiple subfolders underneath. A similar model applies to hierarchies in the Keyword List.

In the Keyword List, hierarchies are indicated by a triangle arrow at the left. Click the arrow to expand or contract the hierarchy.

BENEFITS OF USING KEYWORD HIERARCHIES

Keyword hierarchies provide several significant benefits. For one, hierarchies allow you to keep your keyword list clean and orderly by grouping keywords into larger categories. Using hierarchies also greatly speeds the application of groups of common keywords to photos, all at one time. When you drag-and-drop a lower-level child keyword onto a photo (or multiple photos), all the keywords above it in the hierarchy will also be applied.

You can also set the options differently for each keyword within a hierarchy. For example, within a single hierarchy, you could have some keywords that won't be included on export. This approach provides infinite possibilities for using keywords as organizational tools.

With hierarchies, you can also have multiple instances of a keyword, grouped depending on syntax. For example, the word "Blue" could be under "Colors" and also under "Emotions." As you're keywording photos, you'll find many words that have different meanings based on the context in which they are used; hierarchies accommodate this easily.

WORKING WITH KEYWORD HIERARCHIES

To make a keyword hierarchy, click and drag a keyword to place it over the keyword that will become the parent. The parent becomes highlighted. Release your mouse button to drop the keyword onto the parent, and the child becomes nested underneath.

You can also make hierarchies using commands from the contextual pop-up menu. Create a child keyword underneath a parent by right-clicking or Ctrl+clicking the keyword, and from the pop-up menu, select "Create Keyword Tag Inside [XYZ]...." The new keyword will automatically be placed under the parent within the hierarchy.

Or, right-click or Ctrl+click on a keyword, and from the menu, choose "Put new keywords inside this keyword." Any new keywords you make using any method will be automatically added as children of this keyword until you disable the option.

Use drag-and-drop when you want to move a keyword out of a hierarchy. Simply click on the affected keyword, and drag it to a new position outside the parent (see **Figure 3–101**).

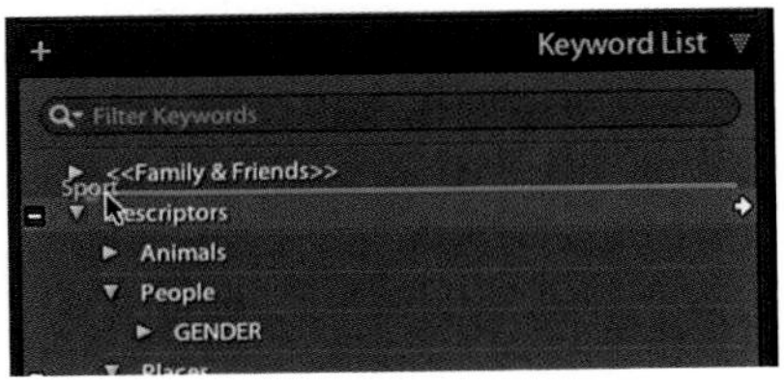

Figure 3-101

ADDING HIERARCHIES DURING IMPORT

In text-entry keyword fields, such as the Keywording panel and Import window, you can manually add hierarchies or specify existing hierarchies. The keywording entry in the Import window works just like Enter Keywords in Library; it shows suggestions as you

03

type. When you enter a nested keyword (if Auto-complete is turned on in Preferences), the rest is added automatically using the < or > symbol to denote the levels in the hierarchy. For example: London < England < United Kingdom < Europe.

New in Lightroom 5: When using the < (less than) or > (greater than) symbol, keep in mind that the word on the less than side of the symbol becomes the child and the word on the greater than side of the symbol becomes the parent. For example, Parent > Child gives the same result as Child < Parent.

MANAGING YOUR KEYWORD LIST

The keywords stored in your Lightroom catalog have a unique, important place in the workflow and deserve regular attention all their own. It's a good idea to do the bulk of your keywording work separately from other photo editing tasks. Periodically update your Keyword List: check for typos and spelling errors, create or fix parent/child hierarchies, update keyword sets and synonyms, and purge unused keywords.

Remember that when you change any keyword in the list, Lightroom automatically updates all the photos containing that keyword.

FINDING KEYWORDS IN THE LIST

At the top of the Keyword List panel is a text search box you can use for finding keywords within the list (see Figure 3–97). By default, the search box says "Filter Keywords." As you type in the field, the keyword list dynamically updates to show only those keywords containing that string of text. To remove the filter, click the X at the right side of the box.

RENAMING KEYWORDS

To change a keyword, double-click it. This opens the Edit box with the name highlighted. Type in the new name for the keyword, and when you're done, press Return or Enter. All photos containing that keyword will be updated.

DELETING KEYWORDS

Deleting a keyword from the catalog also removes it from any photos to which it was applied. Right-click or Ctrl+click on the keyword, and select Delete… from the pop-up menu. Lightroom will prompt you with a warning. Click Delete to accept.

PURGING UNUSED KEYWORDS

This command allows you to remove all the keywords from the catalog that are not applied to any photos. Library module➜Metadata menu➜Purge Unused Keywords. Only do this if you are sure you want to delete all unused keywords!

IMPORT/EXPORT KEYWORDS

You can import and export lists of keywords to and from Lightroom. A standard keyword list is just a simple text file with a .txt extension; the Lightroom hierarchies are determined by tab levels. You can use Import and Export keywords to share keywords with other photographers and, more importantly, keep your Keyword Lists synced between multiple catalogs. Use the menu commands Metadata→Import Keywords and Metadata→Export Keywords. (There are structured keyword lists available for purchase and many photographers are sharing their own; there's a list of keywording resources in the Appendix.)

Using a text editor or spreadsheet to edit keyword lists
You can open keyword lists in a text editor or spreadsheet program to view and edit their contents prior to importing them into Lightroom. In many cases this saves lots of time— you can edit your keywords and set up your hierarchies using simple word processing controls, instead of doing everything in Lightroom's Keyword List panel.

About importing keywords
When you import keywords into your catalog, all your previously existing keywords remain intact. In the case of any conflicts, your original catalog keywords will take precedence. This means that if you've already got an extensive keyword list, any time you're importing more keywords, it's likely that some of those keywords and/or hierarchies in the list being imported won't be added to the catalog. Matching items will be ignored if they are in the same hierarchy order. It's a good idea to evaluate both your list and the list being imported to determine any conflicts so you can resolve them before or after the keyword import.

USING KEYWORDS TO FIND PHOTOS

As you move your cursor over keywords in the Keyword List panel, note the white arrow that appears to the right of the keyword (see Figure 3–98). Clicking an arrow activates a Metadata Filter using that keyword as search criteria, applied to the All Photographs source. With the filter active, you can refine the filter settings or choose a different image source (lock the filter first). In the filter bar, you can hold ⌘ or Ctrl to select multiple keywords in the list. (If necessary, refer to the section about filters earlier in this chapter.)

Don't use keywords instead of collections
Finding photos by keywords is usually most effective as a method of refining another source or searching your entire catalog. To gather sets of photos for longer term storage and retrieval, it's better to use collections. (And you can use smart collections based on keywords!)

Working with metadata

Metadata is one of the most useful, important properties of any digital image. Literally, it means "data about data." Metadata is plain text information embedded in a special section of the image file's program code. Metadata can describe all kinds of things about an image file and is used in a variety of ways by a computer system processing that file.

Because metadata is stored in a different part of the file than the pixel data, it can be created and manipulated independently from the pixel data. Image capture devices, such as digital cameras, write metadata into image files as they are created (EXIF metadata). Imaging software, such as Lightroom and Photoshop, can write metadata into files and can also modify that metadata later.

03

Probably the most well-known types of metadata are keywords, titles, captions, and attributes. Search engines look for keywords and display results containing them; photo sharing websites can display embedded captions and titles for images; even your computer operating system will recognize and display star ratings for photos that have them applied.

Lightroom also uses metadata to make image adjustments. For example, when you change the exposure, sharpening, or white balance settings, those adjustments are stored as metadata in the catalog, and can also be saved onto your hard disk as XMP data, and the original pixel data in the file on disk is never altered.

When you're working with your photos, don't skimp on metadata. **Start applying metadata to your photos during import and continually add and refine metadata throughout editing and processing—especially on your final selects.**

Keep in mind that much of the work you do with metadata today will save significant time and effort later, and will make it much easier for you (and other people) to find your photos far into the future. **Make it a habit to constantly enhance the quality and quantity of metadata in your photos.**

ABOUT VIDEO FILE METADATA

The use of metadata for video files is nowhere near as well-developed as is metadata for still images. When working with video in Lightroom, you can use most of the same metadata controls as you would for photos, including keywords, title, captions, etc. and, of course, attributes. Video format can also be used as a file type criterion for filters and smart collections. The updated Metadata panel also provides an array of fields to enter metadata about video clips.

However, when you export video files from Lightroom, most of that metadata will not be included. This is partly because Lightroom's use of video metadata is in its early stages of development, and also because most video file formats do not provide a dedicated section for metadata the way a still image file does.

So, though you can use metadata controls when working on video clips within the catalog, you won't get much metadata in or out with those clips. All in all, standardization of metadata for video files still has a long way to go.

The Metadata panel

Lightroom's Metadata panel, on the right panel group in the Library module (see **Figure 3–102**), contains information about the digital image file, such as name, location on disk, capture settings, etc. as well as any custom metadata you add to the photo.

Figure 3-102

You can change the types of metadata shown on the panel by choosing from the pop-up menu in the panel header (see Figure 3–102).

SHOW METADATA FOR TARGET PHOTO ONLY

This command, under the Metadata menu (see **Figure 3–103**), controls the behavior of the Metadata panel to only show the metadata for the active (most selected) photo. This option is off by default—when you select multiple photos, the Metadata panel will reflect the fact that multiple photos are selected and will only show specific metadata when all the selected items share the same value.

METADATA PANEL ACTIONS

The buttons to the right of many of the items in the Metadata panel provide shortcuts to a range of editing and updating features. To see the function of

Figure 3-103

a button, place your cursor over it without clicking and wait a few seconds for a tool tip to appear (see Figure 3–102). Pay special attention to right-facing arrows: these provide time-saving shortcuts to useful functions.

TITLE AND CAPTION

Metadata titles and captions (also shown as Description in some views) are useful in many ways, and can be applied in the Metadata panel (see Figure 3–102). Most of all, they help other people find your photos and learn more about them. An image title should usually be a name or short phrase. Captions are often several sentences, describing who, what, where, when, why, etc. about the photo. Depending on the subject of the photo, the caption is usually journalistic, describing a person, place, or event.

Titles and captions are especially beneficial when presenting your work using the output modules, as they can be configured to display along with the photos. For example, you will likely use titles and captions extensively when making books. In Web galleries, title and caption contribute significantly to search engine indexing and phrase-based relevancy of your images on the web. In addition to keywords, search engines often read the contents of the Title and Caption fields and use those fields in their ranking algorithms.

For these reasons, I recommend adding titles and captions to all your best images, especially if you're planning to present them to other people. In many cases, you can simplify and speed up this process using batch processing: select a group of images and enter a title or caption in the metadata panel; all the selected photos will have the new metadata applied.

03

EXIF

The camera writes EXIF metadata into the image file when you take the picture. EXIF includes all the camera settings at the time of capture. Most EXIF metadata cannot be edited in Lightroom but it can be useful when making processing decisions. Examples of some EXIF metadata shown in the Metadata panel are:

- Dimensions—resolution in pixels

- Exposure

- Exposure Bias

- Flash

- Exposure Program

- Metering Mode

- ISO Speed Rating

- Focal Length

- Lens

- Subject Distance

- Date/time (Date Time Original, Date Time Digitized, and Date Time)

- Camera make, model, and serial number

- Artist

- and possibly others, depending on your camera model

 Assigning your name to the Artist field

You can use the utility software that comes with your camera (or the camera's own menu) to enter the name that appears in the Artist field. All the photos digitized with the camera will then have your name embedded in them. **Note:** If you buy a used camera or sell your camera to someone else, this should be updated immediately.

GPS

If a photo has GPS coordinates applied, Lightroom will display it here. Click the arrow at the right to go to the Map module with that location selected.

AUDIO FILES

If you recorded voice notes with your image files, Lightroom will show and allow you to play them on the Metadata panel. A few cameras support audio recordings; otherwise, you can pair a separately recorded audio file. The base filename of the audio clip must exactly match that of the image file for Lightroom to find it. Click the button next to the audio clip filename to play the file. If no audio sidecar file exists for a photo, the field doesn't show in the Metadata panel.

EDIT CAPTURE TIME

If the clock on your camera was incorrect at the time of capture or your image file does not have a date embedded, you can change the image capture time in Lightroom. In the Metadata panel, click the square button next to the capture time, or choose the menu command Metadata→Edit Capture Time (see **Figure 3–104**). You can adjust to

a specified date and time, shift by set number of hours (time zone adjust), or change to file's creation date, if different than the other dates. The dialog box states that the operation cannot be undone, but you could always change the time again to correct any errors. You can do this for a single photo, but more commonly you would select all affected photos and use this function to shift them all by the same amount.

Figure 3-104

 Filter by date
In the Metadata panel, click the arrow button next to the Date to show photos taken on that date.

IPTC METADATA

IPTC metadata is comprised of a wide range of standardized categories for information about images. The most important fields—author, creator, copyright notice, contact information, and keywords—are but a few of the many types of IPTC metadata available. You can view and edit metadata on the Metadata panel (see **Figure 3–105**). To add, change, or remove metadata from any of the fields in the panel, click to activate the field, and then type or delete the text. Be sure to press Return or Enter when you're done in each field.

You can apply the same metadata to many photos selected at once. If you find you're entering the same metadata over and over, you should set up a metadata preset, which is discussed in the next section.

Figure 3-105

APPLY AND JUMP TO NEXT PHOTO

When you need to apply one type of metadata to different photos using different values, try this: instead of pressing enter after typing in your metadata, press ⌘+right arrow, or Ctrl+right arrow. This applies the typed text to the current image and jumps to the next image with the same metadata field highlighted.

CONTACT

Use this section to enter your address, phone number, website, email address, etc.

CONTENT

The Content fields are mainly used by news agencies and image archiving services.

IMAGE

The most important image metadata fields are City, State/Province, Country, and ISO Country Code. These fields are often referenced by search engines. If you're dedicated to adding location metadata for people to find to your photos based on where they were taken, be sure to fill these in manually or by using the Map module.

STATUS

Like content, the Status fields are most commonly used within agencies and service bureaus. You can use these fields to help track jobs within a workgroup.

COPYRIGHT

This is the most important kind of metadata: that which identifies you as the creator and copyright holder for the photo. Even if you don't use any other metadata or keywords, this is the one section you really must complete to protect your rights. I strongly recommend you apply copyright metadata to all your photos.

- **Copyright Status:** For setting the copyright status of your own work; in nearly all cases you'd choose "Copyrighted." "Public Domain" and "Unknown" are also provided.

- **Copyright:** Type your copyright text here, i.e. © 2013 Rob Sylvan. On Mac, press Option+G for the copyright symbol. On Windows, type Alt+0169 on the numeric keypad. If you have trouble entering the copyright symbol directly, you can copy and paste it from a text editor.

- **Rights Usage Terms:** Enter "All Rights Reserved" or "No use without written permission," etc. (If you're concerned about using precise legal terms, search for more information online or consult with a legal advisor.)

IPTC EXTENSION

Lightroom includes an expanded set of IPTC metadata called IPTC Extension. This schema provides additional types of information that can be embedded in image files, and together with IPTC Core is referred to as the IPTC Photo Metadata standard.

Metadata presets

As with all presets in Lightroom, metadata presets can save you huge amounts of time. In addition to working with metadata presets in the Import screen, you can create and modify them using the menu on the Metadata panel (see **Figure 3–106**).

Figure 3-106

SETTING UP STANDARDIZED METADATA PRESETS

Like the other parts of the workflow, you should establish and use a consistent system for your metadata presets. Use the same diligence in maintaining your presets and templates as you do with your file and folder systems. You create and edit metadata presets using the Metadata Preset Editor (see **Figure 3–107**).

The contents of a preset should include items that you'd expect to apply to many images at once. Contact information, copyright notice, etc. make good candidates for presets. (Keywords don't, since they are very image-specific.)

Figure 3-107

Give your presets clear, consistent names. I've seen people use their initials at the beginning of all their custom presets and templates so they are grouped together in alphabetical lists and they can find them easily.

Typically, my presets vary only in the year of copyright. All the other information, such as my address, phone number, and website remain consistent. This means that when entering a new year, all I need to do is make a new preset with a copyright change for that year.

 Blank fields in a metadata template

If you create a metadata preset that includes blank fields, and then apply that preset to photos that previously had data in those fields, the blank fields will clear the existing metadata. Though in some cases this might be a good way to clean up unwanted metadata, normally you want to avoid it. I often import stock photos that already have keywords applied to them, so I use a metadata preset that wipes the keyword field to keep those words from polluting my keyword list. Carefully choose the fields you include in your presets, and uncheck any blank fields to prevent them from being included (see Figure 3–107).

To see all the Lightroom presets saved on your computer, choose Preferences➜Presets

…and then click the button "Show Lightroom Presets Folder." This opens the presets folder in Finder or Explorer. To remove presets from Lightroom, you can delete them from their folders. (Do this with Lightroom closed; the changes will be visible when you restart the program.)

SYNC METADATA

With multiple photos selected, the Sync button at the bottom of the right panel set (see **Figure 3–108**) and its corresponding menu command synchronizes file metadata (but not Develop settings) between multiple photos. The settings from the target photo will be applied to the rest of the selected photos. In the Synchronize Metadata window (very similar to the Metadata template editor), tick the boxes for the metadata to be synced. Anything that remains unchecked will not be modified in the target photos.

Figure 3-108

AUTO SYNC

When you are in Loupe, Compare, or Survey, and have multiple photos selected, you can use Auto Sync. As you make changes to the active photo, the other selected photos are changed at the same time. To do this, use the Metadata➜Enable Auto Sync control or click the switch to turn it on (see **Figure 3–109**). Auto Sync is effectively always on in Grid view.

Figure 3-109

COPY/PASTE METADATA

You can copy and paste metadata from one photo to others. First, select the photo whose metadata will be copied and make sure everything is how you want it. Select the menu option for Metadata➜Copy Metadata; a window appears, similar in appearance to the Metadata Preset Editor, where you can choose which metadata to be copied by checking/unchecking the boxes (and modifying the text entries, if desired). When you're done, click the Copy button. Then select the other photos for which you want to paste the metadata and use the Metadata➜Paste Metadata command.

Metadata Status

As previews are being displayed, Lightroom compares the catalog metadata with the actual file on disk. While Lightroom is comparing metadata you'll see three dots in the top right corner of the thumbnail (see **Figure 3–110**). If a conflict is detected,

Lightroom displays a status indicator in the Metadata panel and, optionally, on the thumbnail (see **Figure 3–111**). Sometimes changes have been made that Lightroom is not yet aware of; if Lightroom hasn't yet checked the status of the file's metadata, you may not see an indicator right away.

SHOW UNSAVED METADATA CELL ICON
Press ⌘+J or Ctrl+J to show View Options and click the check box to enable Show Unsaved Metadata (see **Figure 3–112**). When there's a metadata status conflict, an icon will appear on the top right of the thumbnail. If no conflict is detected, the icon does not appear. I always leave this option enabled.

Figure 3-110

KEEPING METADATA IN SYNC
If you're going back and forth between Lightroom and another application (such as Bridge), Lightroom's metadata (including Develop adjustments) will need to be kept in sync with the files on disk. When editing raw and DNG files, Lightroom uses XMP metadata to help ensure that other Adobe software recognizes the editing data and will show the same results.

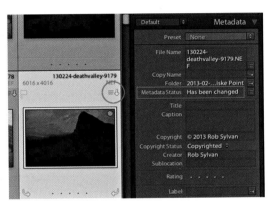

Figure 3-111

For example, if you have a photo in your Lightroom catalog that you've changed in Adobe Camera Raw or Bridge, Lightroom will detect the change but will not automatically update the catalog. In this case, you'd use Read Metadata from Files to bring the changes into the catalog. As another example, if you have a photo in the catalog to which you've applied new keywords, and you want to see those keywords in Bridge, you'd need to Save Metadata from Files from within Lightroom in order for Bridge to reflect the updates. The same applies to rendered files (TIFF, PSD, etc.) that have been edited outside Lightroom: for the catalog to show the edited version, you'd need to Read Metadata from Files.

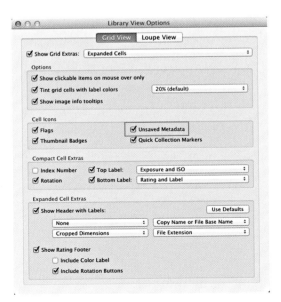

Figure 3-112

Depending on the status of the metadata for the photos being previewed, the Metadata panel and thumbnail status indicator will show one of the following conditions:

- **Up to Date:** No conflict detected; all is in sync. Metadata in the file on disk matches the metadata in the catalog.

- **Has Been Changed:** The metadata in Lightroom is out of sync with the metadata in the file. This can mean either that Lightroom data is newer, or the file's data is newer. Text in the Metadata panel will display Has Been Changed (see Figure 3–111). On the thumbnail icon, when Lightroom's metadata is newer, a down arrow is shown, indicating you should Save Metadata to Files (see Figure 3–111). When the file on disk's metadata is newer, the Metadata panel reads Changed on Disk and an up arrow is shown, indicating you should Read Metadata from Files (see **Figure 3–113**).

Figure 3-113

- **Conflict Detected:** This condition occurs when the file on disk contains different metadata than what's in the catalog record. It usually means there is metadata in the file that is not present in the catalog—not just that the values have changed, such as keywords or IPTC metadata added in another program. This warning can also indicate that the file has potentially been changed both in the catalog and on disk, resulting in mismatched metadata. The thumbnail icon displays a warning (see **Figure 3–114**); you will need to determine which version of the file is newer to resolve the conflict.

When Lightroom indicates there is a metadata conflict, take the necessary time to understand what's happened and, if necessary, click the thumbnail icon or run the for Read Metadata from File or Save Metadata to File command, after which this indicator will show Up to Date.

Figure 3-114

 Two-pass metadata checks

Lightroom makes two passes when checking metadata status. During the first pass, Lightroom simply checks the modification dates for the files on disk and compares them with the files in the catalog. If no file modification date changes are detected, the metadata check stops there. If differences are found, Lightroom performs a second pass, during which all the metadata is compared. For these reasons, sometimes Lightroom will indicate a status conflict at first, and then as files are reread the status will be changed to Up to Date.

ABOUT CAMERA RAW FILES AND XMP SIDECARS

Because Lightroom doesn't directly modify raw files straight from the camera, any metadata applied to the files that you want to save on disk must be stored in sidecar files using the XMP (Extensible Metadata Platform) format. When you run the Save Metadata to File command, if no sidecars exist, they will be created. Each sidecar file is associated with a specific image file, and contains all the metadata changes you've made to the raw file. This sidecar file must always accompany the raw file in order for those metadata changes to be preserved. This is one reason I recommend using DNG for your raw originals instead of native camera raw files—you can save XMP metadata directly into DNG files. You can learn more about DNG in the Appendix.

 XMP sidecars are listed on Metadata panel
In conjunction with the conflict status icon, the Metadata panel shows when a raw file has a sidecar saved with it. Look below the File Name field.

 What's the correct version?
Whenever you're changing file metadata, it's important to understand exactly which version is most current before proceeding. Other software can change your image file metadata even if you don't actually open the file using that software. Bridge is one such application; building previews for image files in Bridge often will alter file metadata, resulting in an apparent conflict with Lightroom. If you know the metadata in Lightroom is the most current, save it out to the files. Otherwise, check the files in question to figure out when and how the metadata was changed before reading metadata into Lightroom. (Of course, if you only use Lightroom for processing your photos, you won't need to worry about this.)

 Metadata Status as a criterion
You can create filters and smart collections based on Metadata Status. This makes it easy to identify photos with out-of-sync metadata.

SAVING METADATA TO FILES

To save all the current Lightroom metadata out to the disk, use the Metadata→Save Metadata to File command or the shortcut, or click the down arrow on the thumbnail. This writes all the Lightroom metadata, including Develop settings and keywords, to the files. If your files are DNG, TIFF, PSD, or JPEG, the metadata is written directly into the image files. Raw files will have XMP sidecar files that store the metadata.

Saving your work is as important in Lightroom as in other software applications, but it's all too easy to work for long periods of time without Lightroom prompting you to save. Though all your changes are automatically saved into the database, they are only in the database until you save the changes out to the files and/or export new files. So save often!

 After import, save metadata to files
If you've applied any metadata during import, save it out to the files immediately after the import is done. I use Select All, and then Save Metadata to Files, via the keyboard shortcuts.

AUTOMATICALLY WRITE CHANGES TO XMP

The Catalog Settings→Metadata dialog box provides this option to automatically save your metadata to the files as you work. I generally don't recommend this, for several reasons. First, some computers may experience a decrease in performance with this option enabled. Second, even on a fast machine, I don't want Lightroom accessing my files that frequently. Lightroom will save out the metadata after every change made to any setting. Third, and

03

maybe most importantly, if Lightroom is always saving out metadata as you work, you won't be able to use the Read Metadata from File command to go back to a previous version. Usually it's best to just regularly save out the metadata yourself. (A notable exception might be when managing photos in workgroup environments.)

READING METADATA FROM FILES

If you've edited your files outside Lightroom (such as in Bridge, Adobe Camera Raw, Photoshop, etc.) and want to update Lightroom to show the latest changes, you can read in the file metadata with the command under Metadata menu, or by clicking the up arrow on the thumbnail. This will update the photo's metadata in the Lightroom catalog. Be careful using the Read Metadata from Files command; it can overwrite all your current Lightroom metadata for selected images.

METADATA STATUS AND SYNCHRONIZE FOLDER

When you run the Synchronize Folder command (discussed earlier in this chapter), you have the option to Scan for Metadata Updates. When you do this, Lightroom will automatically Read Metadata from Files when a conflict is detected.

Using the Painter

The Painter tool provides a powerful way to quickly modify many photo settings while working in Grid view (only). With it you can add, remove, or change all kinds of metadata and Develop adjustments with a single click. To use the Painter, first be sure the Toolbar is showing (T). Click the Painter icon to activate the tool (see **Figure 3–115**). Then, from the Paint: pop-up menu, choose what kind of settings you want to modify (see **Figure 3–116**); the Painter cursor changes to reflect your selection. Next, configure the options for the changes you'll be applying with the additional controls to the right. Then simply click on thumbnails in the Grid to apply the Painter settings (or click and drag across multiple photos to "spray" them all). Note that any keyword listed in the Painter will become the Target Keyword, and multiple keywords (separated by comma) can be entered, too.

To use the Painter to remove some types of metadata, such as keywords, hold the Option or Alt key. The Painter icon changes to indicate you're in erase mode. Click on photos to remove the specified metadata or adjustments from them.

Figure 3-115

When you're done, click the button in the Toolbar or press Esc to turn off the Painter tool.

 Paint Target Collection
Using the Painter you can add or remove photos in the Target Collection. This can be much faster and easier than dragging and dropping or using the contextual menus (but I still usually prefer the keyboard shortcut).

Figure 3-116

Working with video in Lightroom

The Library Loupe view provides essential video editing controls such as high-definition playback (with no rendering required), trimming controls (setting in and out points), extracting JPEG images from video clips, and the ability to apply Quick Develop adjustments and presets. You can export edited videos from Lightroom, and you can also use all of Lightroom's metadata with video clips (although that metadata is not exported).

VIDEO FORMAT COMPATIBILITY

You can import, play, and edit videos from a wide range of devices, from smartphones to DSLRs and compact cameras, including Sony AVCHD files. Although Lightroom now natively supports internal playback of most formats, some video codecs are not supported directly and you may need to install Apple QuickTime for playback capabilities. (Lightroom will notify you if this is the case.)

Generally speaking, if you can import a video clip, the chances are good that you'll be able to work with it using all the controls described in the following sections. However, understand that video editing is still new to Lightroom and can't compete with dedicated video editing software such as Adobe Premiere. The video capabilities offered by Lightroom are designed to serve the basic needs of photographers capturing video along with their still images and isn't meant to be a full-fledged video editing suite.

Working directly with video clips is currently limited to Library and Slideshow modules only. Video playback is color-managed in Lightroom.

Example video workflow

The Lightroom video editing workflow is very simple and straightforward; there really aren't many options to configure. Following is an example:

Step 1. Trim the video. Use the controller to set new in and out points of the clip.

Step 2. Set Poster Frame. Choose the frame used for the Library and Filmstrip previews.

Step 3. Capture Frame. Extract a single frame as a JPEG (useful for applying Develop adjustments).

Step 4. (Optional) Apply adjustments to the proxy JPEG in Develop and save a preset.

Step 5. (Optional) Back in Library Quick Develop, apply the new preset to the video clip.

Step 6. Apply and refine adjustments using the Quick Develop panel.

Step 7. Export the finished video or publish it to Facebook or Flickr.

Note: See the upcoming section on using the JPEG as a proxy in Develop for an alternative workflow.

PLAYBACK AND PREVIEWING

Video clips appear in the Library view modes in basically the same way as still images, with a few important differences. In Grid view, the thumbnails display the duration of each clip (see **Figure 3–117**). You can move your mouse cursor horizontally across the thumbnail to scrub through the video preview. (The first time you do this there might be a short delay as Lightroom retrieves all the frames from the clip.)

PREVIEW VIDEO IN LOUPE

Double-click a video thumbnail, or press the E key, to open a selected video in Loupe view. A large preview loads, with a control bezel below (see **Figure 3–118**). Press the space bar, or click the play/pause button in the controller, to play and pause the video playback. You can also drag the playback head to advance the video, or scrub your cursor side-to-side over the time display. The controller is resizable—click and drag either end to expand or compress it.

Figure 3-117

VIEW OPTIONS FOR VIDEO

In the View Options dialog box for Loupe view (accessed under the View menu) there are options affecting video previews (see **Figure 3–119**). You can **show the frame number when displaying video time.** Most video clips you'll work with use 29 or 30 frames per second and showing the frame number allows much greater precision than time in seconds when trimming videos or extracting frames.

Figure 3-118

Play HD video at draft quality can help previews load faster for high resolution clips. Enabling this option sets the playback to 1/4 resolution MPEG rendering to provide faster frame rates. If you've got a computer with plenty of power (processor speed, RAM, and video memory) you can probably disable this option to see better previews. (When draft quality is enabled and you pause a video, the current frame is rendered at full quality, at which time you may notice a slight change in appearance and overall quality. When draft mode is disabled the previews should appear identical whether the video is playing or not.)

Video Cache settings

Lightroom's Preference dialog box has an option for the Video Cache. The default is 3GB and this is Adobe's recommended size. Setting a larger maximum cache size can provide smoother playback using saved preview data. To force Lightroom to rebuild all the video previews, you can click the Purge Cache button.

 Using the secondary display for video

The video controller is not available in the secondary window, so you can't play videos

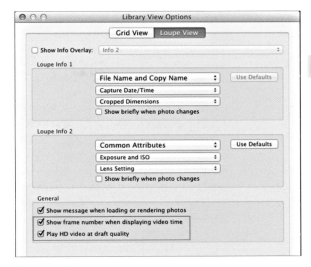

Figure 3-119

there. However, you can set up the second window to show another view mode and play the video in the main window.

TRIMMING

Click the gear icon in the bottom right corner of the controller (see **Figure 3–120**). This expands the controller to show the timeline (individual frame previews) with

Figure 3-120

trim controls at both ends. You can step forward or back one frame at a time using the arrow buttons to the left and right of the main play button. A vertical orange line above the playback head indicates the current position in the timeline; the current frame number is shown at the bottom left of the controller.

To set new in and out points for a video clip, drag the trim controls from either end (see Figure 3–120), or use the keyboard shortcuts to set the in or out point to the current playback head position: Shift+I sets the in point and Shift+O sets the out point. You can do this while the video is playing.

The trim controls will not go past the playback head. As you get close to the playback head, the trim controls snap to the playback head. This can make it easier to set the in and out point very precisely. Use the single frame advance buttons to step exactly to the frame where you want to set the trim point, and then drag the trim control to snap to that point.

SET POSTER FRAME

The Poster Frame is the preview image that shows in the Grid, Filmstrip, and elsewhere. By default, the first frame of the clip shows as the preview, but you can change this. Since a video contains a sequence of unique frames, it's important that you can choose the frame that best represents the content of the clip. To Set the Poster Frame, click the rectangular button near the bottom right of the controller and select the menu option (see **Figure 3–121**).

Figure 3-121

CAPTURE FRAME

The Capture Frame command extracts a single frame from the video clip. Click the rectangular button at the bottom right of the controller and select the menu option to capture the current frame (see Figure 3–121). The frame at the current playback head position is rendered as a high quality JPEG and saved to disk in the same folder as the video clip, and then added to the catalog and stacked with the clip from which it was made. You can capture any number of frames from a single video clip; each of the JPEG file(s) are saved to disk using the filename from the original clip plus a sequence number automatically appended to the end of the filename.

QUICK DEVELOP VIDEO CLIPS

Videos can be adjusted using a limited subset of the same Develop controls you use for still images. (To learn about these adjustments read Chapter 4.) Using Process Version 2012, the available adjustments for video in the Quick Develop panel are:

- Treatment (Color or Black & White, including Auto B/W Mix)

- Auto White Balance

- White Balance (JPEG Equivalent)

- Auto Tone

- Exposure

- Contrast

- Whites

- Blacks

- Vibrance

- Saturation

Applying any of these adjustments will affect the entire video and can take a while to process. Note that Develop History is not saved for videos—you can use Undo or Reset All in the Quick Develop panel to revert your adjustments.

03

USE THE JPEG AS A PROXY IN DEVELOP

As noted earlier, you can't process a video in the Develop module. However, you can Develop the JPEG generated by Capture Frame as a proxy for the video. When you're done adjusting the JPEG in Develop, save a preset and apply it in Quick Develop, or use Sync Settings or copy/paste to transfer the settings to the video clip.

In the Develop module you can apply changes on the Tone Curve, Color Treatment, Split Toning, and Camera Calibration panels, which can then be synced back to the video clip.

 Auto-sync works too!
Try this: after you use Capture Frame, in Library select both the JPEG proxy file and the video clip. Make sure the JPEG is the target photo. Then go to Develop. Turn Auto-sync on, using the switch at the bottom of the right panels. Work on your JPEG file, applying whatever Develop settings you want. The adjustments are simultaneously applied to the video clip! There's one caveat here: only the adjustments in the above list will be used on the video—and any other Develop adjustments that you make to the JPEG will not be applied to the video.

EXPORTING VIDEO

You can export your edited video clips from Lightroom; all your trimming and adjustments will be used to create the exported file. Using publish services, you can also upload videos directly to social media sites like Facebook and Flickr. Exporting is covered in Chapter 5.

 Back up and optimize your catalog
After you've done any significant amount of work in Library, you should back up your catalog. You can use Lightroom's built-in backup feature for this. You can learn all about working with catalogs, including backing up, testing, and optimizing, in Chapter 11.

Next steps

Organizing your files in Library is one of the major pieces in the Lightroom workflow puzzle. Once you've isolated your favorite photos and put them into meaningful collections, you can confidently move on to enhancing them using the adjustments in the Develop module.

As time goes on, do your best to keep your catalog neat and tidy. Occasionally you'll need to spend some time performing maintenance tasks like reorganizing collections, deleting unused presets, and cleaning up your Keyword List.

CHAPTER 04
Develop

04

DEVELOP: Making your photos look their best

After you've edited the shoot, identified your selects, and put them into collections, it's time to make each photo look as good as it can. The Develop module is where you enhance, optimize, and perfect individual photos and you can also very easily sync settings between many photos at one time.

Along with the organizational power in Library, the processing capabilities of the Develop module are among Lightroom's key strengths. Master the Develop controls and you may find that you can complete all of your photo processing entirely within Lightroom.

There are many possible ways to approach your work in Develop; there is no set order of operations. You can apply your adjustments in any sequence and Lightroom will provide the optimal rendering for the best quality during output. As a parametric (or parameter-based) editor, Lightroom uses instructions based on the changes you make to render the previews you see on the screen; all your edits are truly non-destructive. Always remember that your original pixel data in the files on disk is never changed, no matter what formats the original files are in. So you're free to experiment to your heart's content because you can always go back!

That said, with most photos you'll want to tackle the biggest problems first and work your way to the finer details. Processing individual images involves many variables, and what works in one instance won't necessarily work in another. Some photos will require very little adjustment, and others more. Even with the greatest care taken at the time of capture, every digital photo has the chance of being improved—often significantly—during post-processing.

What's New in Develop

- **Performance improvements**
- **Radial filter**
- **Easy duplication of local adjustments**
- **Non-circular healing with Spot Removal tool**
- **Visualize spots**
- **Edit offline photos with smart preview**
- **Aspect ratio crop overlays**
- **Loupe Overlays**
- **Upright perspective correction**
- **Lens correction improvements**
- **LAB readout in histogram**

How this chapter is organized

Writing this chapter, in particular, presented some unique challenges. I could present the material in the order I think you should do the workflow steps, but then you'd be jumping around the screen—the most important tools are all over the place. And when I present the steps in the order they appear on the screen, you'll inevitably need to skip around in the book as you do the tasks in order of workflow.

Ultimately, I've chosen to sequence most of the content based on how the interface presents the tools, with some exceptions where it makes more sense in another order. We'll start with an overview of the general workflow and best practices you'll use, followed by in-depth explanations of the right-side panels, then the Tool Strip, then the left panels. In this chapter we'll cover all the individual adjustments you can make, and you'll learn how to dramatically speed up your workflow using Develop presets. Aside from the occasional detour, I hope you'll find this approach straightforward and easy to follow.

Figure 4-1

 ## Example Develop workflow

To consistently get the best results with the least amount of effort, you should try to follow a consistent series of steps for your work in Develop. Let's outline the general order of the Develop adjustments you'll use to process most of your photos.

Start your photo processing by doing the global adjustments—those that affect the entire image—and progressively work toward fine-tuning the details (local adjustments). For example, do your retouching after adjusting tone and color. Following is an example of a typical Develop workflow (use **Figure 4–1** to follow along with the steps).

 Download all figures
All figures in this book are available for download at:
www.lightroomers.com/lightroom5book

Step 1. Apply a preset, custom default settings, or Auto settings. Your work will go faster when you start with a set of baseline settings tailored to your preferences and the equipment used to capture the original images. Lightroom starts with a preprogrammed set of default settings for your raw photos (no settings are applied to non-raw photos), but you can customize these default settings to fit your needs and taste (we cover this later in the chapter). In addition, you can apply a Develop preset in the Import window or select one from the Presets panel in the Develop module to apply a specific set of adjustments on top of the current defaults.

Step 2. (Optional) Crop/straighten. Cropping a photo changes its composition, affects the histogram display, and determines the work to be done in the rest of the workflow. Many photos may not need cropping; for those that do, it makes sense to crop early in

04

the workflow. (And you can always come back later to refine the crop.) Use the Crop Overlay tool for this.

Step 3. White balance. In some cases the in-camera white balance setting may be optimal; in all other cases where white balance can be improved, try to do it before moving on to other tasks. This is done in the Basic panel.

Step 4. Tone adjustments. For most photos, adjusting tone is the most important part of post-processing. Always enhance tone before moving on to fine-tune color. These adjustments are mainly done in the Basic panel.

Step 5. (Optional) Color adjustments. You can adjust individual colors in the photo based on their hues. Use the HSL panel for global color adjustments using defined color ranges.

Step 6. Noise reduction. Most digital images can benefit from some amount of noise reduction. Most of the time it's best to handle noise reduction before moving on to sharpening. Zoom in close (1:1) to check for noise and use the Detail panel sliders for Noise Reduction.

Step 7. Sharpening. The controls in Develop's Detail panel provide a great amount of control over capture sharpening. The settings you use for sharpening should be based on the characteristics of the photo.

Step 8. Spot Removal. It's a good time to remove dust spots, dead pixels, and other artifacts in your photos while you're zoomed in close for noise reduction and sharpening. The Spot Removal tool is in the Tool Strip. The addition of non-circular healing to the Spot Removal tool has increased its usefulness in removing more than just sensor spots. Note that performing spot removal with lens corrections enabled can slow down performance and accuracy of the Spot Removal tool due to the distortions applied to the photo by the lens correction, so if lens corrections are included in your preset or custom defaults you may want to disable it while doing spot removal, and then re-enable after the work is complete.

Step 9. Apply Lens Corrections. Most photos can be improved by correcting problems caused by the lens. Since this is a global adjustment that can significantly improve image quality, use the Lens Corrections panel controls for this. (Lens Corrections can be included in your standard presets and custom default settings, too.)

Step 10. Local adjustments. Most images look their best when you apply some local adjustments, such as dodging and burning, localized sharpening or smoothing, and local color adjustments. Graduated Filters, Radial Filters, and Adjustment Brushes, found in the Tool Strip, provide enormous amounts of control over the styling of your photos.

You'll find that the majority of your photos will benefit from applying all or most of these standard adjustments, so we'll examine each of these in detail. We'll also take a look at some of the possibilities for special creative effects that you can achieve within the Develop module.

DEVELOPING WITH SMART PREVIEWS

Smart previews were introduced in Chapter 1, where I mentioned that the main benefit of using smart previews is that it allows you to work on your photos in Develop even if the source files are currently offline (such as being stored on a disconnected external drive). A secondary benefit is that photos with smart previews load a little faster into Develop. Smart previews are an incredibly powerful addition to Lightroom 5 that is sure to change the workflow for many people. In Lightroom 4 and below, if you selected an offline photo and switched to Develop you would get a message sprawled across the photo saying that your photo was offline or missing—all of the Develop controls would become inaccessible and work would stop until you brought that photo back online. Now in Lightroom 5, if you had rendered smart previews before the photo was offline you are able to complete the entire series of workflow steps mentioned previously. However, there are a few caveats to keep in mind:

- The reduced pixel dimensions of the smart preview (2540 pixels maximum) means that when you zoom 1:1 you are seeing 1:1 view of a (most likely) smaller image.

- Adjustments best made at close zoom levels (such as sharpening and noise reduction) should be left until the original source photo is back online and you can evaluate at true 1:1 of the source photo.

- The Edit In menu options are grayed out until the original photo is back online.

In Chapter 2 you learned that smart previews can be rendered as part of the import process, and in Chapter 3 we discussed how to render them after import. Under the Histogram in Develop (and in the Library module) Lightroom displays the status of whether a selected photo has a smart preview or not, and is offline or online. In the example shown in **Figure 4-2** the selected photo is online and it has a smart preview. The possibilities are as follows:

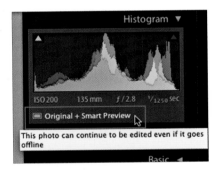

Figure 4-2

- **Original:** The photo is online, but does not have a smart preview. All editing options are available.

- **Original + Smart Preview:** The photo is online and has a smart preview. All editing options are available, and photo displays in Develop a little faster.

- **Smart Preview:** The photo is offline, but it has a smart preview. All editing options are available with caveats mentioned above.

- **Photo is missing:** The photo is offline and it does not have a smart preview. No editing is possible (see Chapter 3 to learn how to bring photos online again).

I am still adapting to using smart previews in my workflow, but I am most excited about using them in a travel workflow when my catalog is stored on my internal drive, but the source photos are left on an external drive. In this scenario I can work with my photos that have smart previews whether the external drive is connected or not (see Chapter 11 to learn more about this option). That said, if you are using a camera with a very high pixel count (such as a D800 or medium format back) or just have older computer hardware (or both) you would get a slight performance boost in Develop by using smart previews for the online photos you are processing in Develop. For the remainder of this chapter I worked with online photos (that may or may not have smart previews) to take full advantage of all zoom levels and the Edit In options to send to an external editor.

Process as far as you can in Lightroom

Many photographers who have been using Photoshop, or other image processing software, for a long time have an inclination to do a minimal amount of work in Lightroom, wanting to switch to the other program as soon as possible to finish the photo. If this describes you, I believe you're cheating yourself! Practice processing the image as far as you possibly can, using Lightroom alone, before switching to another program…you won't regret it! When you've mastered the Develop controls in Lightroom you won't need to spend nearly as much time using other software.

Make a plan for processing

Before starting work in Develop, take a few minutes to evaluate the photo and make a quick plan for the work you're going to do. (You could also do this in Library, as the last step of editing.) It might help to jot down some notes to help visualize the sequence of steps you will take. This doesn't need to be complicated; just take a few moments to envision the desired result.

As every image is unique, each will benefit from different enhancements to make the photograph look its best. These decisions are highly subjective; the choices you make will reflect your creative vision of how the image should look. (Of course, if you're working for a client, their vision might guide the creative process, too.)

There are some common criteria you can use when determining the appropriate improvements to a photo. Some enhancements, like noise reduction and sharpening, are quite objective, as there are established standards of technical and aesthetic quality to consider. For example, in most cases, we would agree that digital noise is undesirable and should be minimized, or, many people would agree when a photo looks crooked or blurry. Of course, there are exceptions to every rule.

Keep in mind that every step of the workflow affects and is affected by every other step. For example, sharpening the image may increase the visibility of existing noise. Adjusting color may affect apparent contrast, etc. Though it may be necessary to go back and forth between steps to perfect the image, following the same general sequence of steps will help you work more efficiently, more effectively, and with greater creative freedom.

MAINTAINING MAXIMUM QUALITY

One of the primary goals of digital image processing is to retain as much data as possible from the original capture throughout the imaging pipeline. Regardless of the types of adjustments you make or special effects that you apply in Lightroom (or any other software) it's usually best to process your images as minimally as you can. This requires you to plan several steps ahead as you adjust images and, in general, to perform your processing tasks in a consistent sequence. Go through your processing methodically, taking the time to finish each step before moving onto the next. In some cases, batches of images can be developed the same way; Lightroom accommodates this with ease.

The order of tasks

You can adjust Lightroom's Develop controls in any sequence you like. You can go back and forth between panels and settings to progressively refine your images and Lightroom will apply the adjustments to the final image in the ideal way to maintain the most possible data. Lightroom's rendering stack combines and recombines your adjustments as you work in order to provide the optimal final results. However, the order in which you perform your image editing tasks can be important, for several reasons:

- **Different adjustment controls affect image data in similar ways.** For example, increasing the Exposure value and adjusting the Tone Curve can produce similar changes in the appearance of the photo.

- **Some adjustments affect others.** Continuing the example above, increasing the Exposure value and decreasing the corresponding areas of the Tone Curve would produce counteracting adjustments and decreased quality.

- **Tone and color should be evaluated and adjusted independently.** You'll often find that once you get the tones right, the colors will also fall into place. For this reason, it's best to do as much tone correction as possible before moving on to adjust color, with the possible exception of white balance.

- **Work gets done faster if you do it the same way every time.** Though some images will require more work and additional processing steps than others, following a consistent sequence of steps allows you to be more efficient through repetition. This allows you to spend more time on the photographs that really benefit from additional attention.

UNDO/REDO

Unlimited undo (⌘+Z or Ctrl+Z) and redo (⌘+Shift+Z or Ctrl+Y) removes the fear of experimentation. In Develop you can't irreparably harm an image (but you can certainly make it look bad!) Lightroom maintains an unlimited history (in the History panel) of all the processing work you do on an image from the import forward. So feel free to play!

Don't use undo/redo like Before/After
Lightroom offers other controls for seeing the image with and without the current adjustments. Before/After is covered later in this chapter.

The Develop workspace

The right panel set provides all the adjustment controls and tools you'll use to Develop your photos (see Figure 4–1). Similar to Library, the left panel set in Develop is mainly used for organization and batch processing. (I usually work with the left panels hidden to give the photo as much room as possible in the preview area and just open the left panels as necessary.) If you keep the Filmstrip open you can easily switch between photos without needing to go back to the Library module.

Make the panels wider

Depending on the size and resolution of your display, you can make the right panels wider to provide more refinement for the Develop sliders. Position your cursor over the edge of the panel, and you'll see the cursor turns into a double arrow. Click and drag outward to expand the panels to the maximum width (see **Figure 4–3**). Tip for Mac users, you can hold the Option key and expand the panels even wider.

Figure 4-3

Solo mode

I almost always work with the Develop panels in Solo Mode. This avoids the need to scroll over the right panel track, which can get quite long. Right-click or Ctrl+click on any panel header to enable Solo Mode from the pop-up menu. An added benefit of Solo mode in Develop is that Lightroom doesn't load panels that are closed, which can speed up performance.

TOOL STRIP

The Develop Tool Strip contains tools for specialized purposes: Crop Overlay, Spot Removal, Red-Eye Correction, Graduated Filter, Radial Filter, and Adjustment Brush (see **Figure 4–4**). Unlike the sliders, which you modify from within the panels, you'll use these tools to edit the photo directly in the main preview area.

Figure 4-4

TOOLBAR

The contents of the Toolbar in the Develop module change depending on the tool selected (see **Figure 4–5**). As you're working in Develop, remember to frequently check the Toolbar for more options. Press T to hide/show the Toolbar. Click the downward facing arrow on the right side to show/hide individual options from the Toolbar.

Figure 4-5

PANEL HEADER SWITCHES

Most of the panels in the Develop module include a small button that acts like a switch to enable and disable the effects of that panel's adjustments (see **Figure 4–6**). Like a light switch, up is on and down is off. Rather than Before and After or Undo/Redo, you can use this to show all the effects of a single panel. Turning on and off a panel's adjustments is tracked in History, is undoable, and can be saved as part of a preset. (The Basic panel doesn't have a switch.)

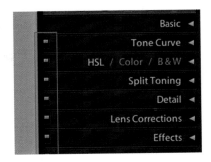

Figure 4-6

DEVELOP PREVIEWS

The Develop module has its own previews, and these are the highest quality, most accurate previews available in Lightroom. As you work, the Develop previews are constantly rendered according to the current adjustments. For this reason, there may be the occasional hiccup in performance, during which time Lightroom is not as responsive as you'd like. Lightroom 5's processing makes improvements in this area, but even on the fastest systems, don't expect Lightroom to be flawless in rendering performance. There's a lot of processing going on behind the scenes.

 Calibrate your display

Lightroom is color-managed internally; its previews are typically extremely accurate for most images. But if you're not working on a properly calibrated and profiled display, it won't matter. In order for you to be able to trust what you see on screen, you must use a hardware calibration device to create a custom profile for your display. I use and highly recommend the products from X-Rite far beyond all others available on the market. The Appendix has links to more information about color management solutions.

Understanding the Process Version

Lightroom 4 introduced a new process version called Process Version 2012 (PV2012). The process version is the core set of programming routines used to develop your photos and videos. The process version has the most impact on the rendering of raw files (including DNG) but also has implications for rendered files like JPEG, PSD, PNG, and TIFF.

The choice of process version also determines the adjustment controls available on the panels, and Process Version 2012 offers different controls than previous process versions.

Newly imported photos will use PV2012 by default (unless you specifically override this). If you are upgrading from Lightroom 4 you are already familiar with this process version. If you are upgrading from Lightroom 3 or earlier you need to know that files already in your catalog will retain their settings using the earlier process version. (If you've never used Lightroom prior to version 4, you don't need to be too concerned with the rest of this section.)

04

What changed with PV2012

Put simply, PV2012 provides dramatically improved image quality than earlier versions. PV2012 introduced an all-new set of tone mapping techniques and corresponding controls, which offer much better highlight and shadow recovery, better contrast, and smoother transitions with reduced hue shifts and other digital artifacts.

The new adjustments for PV2012 are mainly found in the Basic panel, as well as a few other locations in the Develop module, including the local adjustments (graduated filters, radial filters, and adjustment brushes).

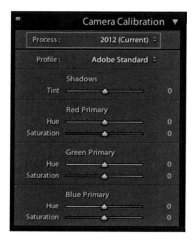

Figure 4-7

What stays the same

Photos in your catalog that were imported with previous versions of Lightroom will have older process version(s) applied. In these cases, your photos will look exactly like they did before; Lightroom 5 is not going to change them automatically. The previous program code for earlier process versions—and the older controls—remain in Lightroom 5.

How to tell which process version is in use

You can see which process version is applied to the selected photo in the Process Version menu in the Camera Calibration panel (see **Figure 4–7**). **New in Lightroom 5:** Photos using an older process version will display a lightning bolt icon under the Histogram (see **Figure 4–8**). Photos using PV2012 will not display the icon. If you hover your cursor over the icon it will display the process version being used by that photo.

Figure 4-8

UPGRADING TO PV2012

To convert the processing on a photo to PV2012, click the notification icon described above, or use the Settings →Update to Current Process menu command. If you use the icon, a dialog box opens to explain what will happen if you proceed (see **Figure 4–9**), along with options to see Before/After previews of the change and an option to Update All Filmstrip Photos. If you use the menu command, no confirmation is presented and all the photo's settings are converted to PV2012.

When you click the warning icon or use the Upgrade to Current Version menu command, Lightroom

Figure 4-9

attempts to make the best possible conversion from your earlier settings to the PV2012 settings. Depending on the adjustments applied using the earlier process version, you may see more or less of a visual change when converting to the new process version. Adobe engineers created mappings of the adjustments from earlier versions to the current version, but some old controls don't translate directly to the new ones. In most cases, after converting to the newer process version, you'll want to fine-tune the adjustments.

 Before/After
You can use the Before/After feature to compare a photo using different process versions. Before/After is discussed later in this chapter.

You can also change process version with the menu on the Camera Calibration panel (see Figure 4–7). Selecting the process version in the pop-up menu on the Camera Calibration panel allows you to switch between different process versions without losing data. Old process version settings are retained in memory, so you can switch back later; however, this only applies to adjustments made with the old sliders—adjustment sliders present in both process versions will always use the new code.

Like everything else you do in Develop, changing process version is tracked as a History state so you can always go back.

 Be cautious about batch converting to PV2012
Because some settings will not translate directly to the new process version, it can be risky to convert large batches of photos to PV2012 unless you plan to go through them one by one to fine-tune their settings later.

For your prized selects, you should seriously consider changing them to PV2012 one at a time, because it's very likely you can make those photos look even better than they did before. In general, I think converting the process version for photos you've previously developed should most often be done on a per-photo basis until you become comfortable with the effects of the PV2012 settings.

Using presets with old process versions
When you apply old presets (or copy/paste adjustments) using earlier process versions to a photo using PV2012, Lightroom will try to convert the old adjustments to the PV2012 settings, as long as the preset doesn't contain the setting for process version, and provided none of the PV2012 settings have already been modified. When applying settings from old process versions, any current settings using PV2012 always take precedence and applying the old settings has no effect.

 Reset applies PV2012
When you Reset a photo, regardless of the process version currently in use, PV2012 will be applied unless you've previously overridden the Adobe Default Settings.

04

Default and Auto settings

In order for you to see a photo on the screen, Lightroom must build a preview; to build a preview it must use some kind of settings. Lightroom will process photos and render their previews using the Adobe Default Settings, unless you override this. You can also apply Auto settings in several panels in the Develop module.

ADOBE DEFAULT SETTINGS

There are always at least two sets of Adobe Default Settings in effect: one for raw images and another for rendered files such as JPEG, TIFF, PNG, and, PSD. For raw images (including DNGs made from raw) Lightroom uses a common set of adjustments to render the raw image data and build the previews. This means that every raw capture imported to your catalog is undergoing some kind of processing, even if you don't apply any adjustments yourself.

By default, TIFF, PSD, PNG, and JPEG files are not adjusted when they come into Lightroom. No processing is done to pre-rendered images and the preview shows the photo with no adjustments applied.

When you click the Reset button, or use the menu commands to Reset the Develop settings, you're applying the current Default settings, whether they're Adobe Default Settings or your own.

 Using your own default settings

Sometimes the Lightroom defaults might render your photos with less than optimal quality, skewing your perception of what needs to be done during processing. However, you can override the Adobe Default Settings with your own. Instructions for setting your own default are provided toward the end of this chapter, after the Develop Presets section.

INTRO TO AUTO ADJUSTMENT SETTINGS

Auto settings are different from the default settings: they are applied on an image-by-image basis in an attempt to create the best rendering for each individual photo. Several Develop panels provide Auto settings, including Auto Tone, Auto WB, and Auto Black & White Mix. Applying Auto settings can be a good starting point for your Develop work. Auto settings are explained in the context of their associated panels, later in this chapter.

Histogram

The Histogram panel (see **Figure 4–10**) is a bar graph representing the distribution of tonal values in the photo. The black point is at the left side; the white point is at the right; midtones are at the middle of the horizontal scale. The vertical bars show how many pixels there are at each

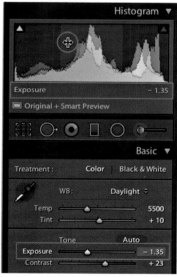

Figure 4-10

04

luminance level. The colors in the Histogram represent pixel values for each of the individual red, green, and blue channels (represented by their respective colors), and areas where two channels overlap (yellow where red and green overlap, magenta where red and blue overlap, and cyan where green and blue overlap). The gray areas indicate the same pixel values present in all three channels.

At the bottom of the Histogram is an information display. As you move your cursor over the photo the readout changes to show the values for each channel, in percentages. Pure white is 100% and pure black is 0%. (When your cursor is not over the preview, this area shows key settings of the photo.)

Working RGB Space

The RGB percentages displayed under the Histogram are derived from using Lightroom's internal working RGB space, which cannot be changed. Lightroom uses a version of 16-bit ProPhoto RGB (named Melissa RGB) that is unique to Lightroom and not representative of the values you would see on eventual output. It uses this very large color space to allow us to work with all of the data contained in our raw photos. We can make adjustment decisions based on output-specific color profiles during soft proofing, which is covered later in this chapter.

Histogram relation to Tone sliders

As you move your cursor across the Histogram, the defined tonal ranges are illuminated, corresponding with the Tone sliders in the Basic panel which also become illuminated, and vice versa (see Figure 4–10). You can click and drag in the Histogram to adjust the sliders in the Tone section of the Basic panel.

Reading the Histogram

There is no such thing as a correct Histogram. As every image is different, every Histogram is unique. However, the shape of the Histogram can help you make decisions about how to process the tones in an image. Usually, the width of the data shown in the Histogram is more important than the height; the Histogram for an image with a wide tonal range will show data distributed over the length of the horizontal axis, whereas a photo with limited dynamic range will show all the data clustered in one area of the Histogram.

The Histogram in Lightroom is animated; as you switch from one photo to another in Develop or Library, the Histogram dynamically updates as the photo is loaded. This helps evaluate minor differences in Histogram data between photos whose previews appear very similar.

HIGHLIGHT AND SHADOW CLIPPING

Clipped highlights are pure white; clipped shadows are solid black. Both result in a loss of detail, so clipping should be identified and dealt with appropriately on each image. On the Histogram, clipping is shown by tall spikes at either end; the triangle warnings also become highlighted (see **Figure 4–11**). The color of the warning triangles indicate which channels are being clipped (see Figure 4-10).

04

Clipping previews

The triangles at the top of each end of the Histogram activate clipping warning indicators overlaid on the image preview. Place your cursor over a clipping indicator to temporarily see the clipping preview. Click an indicator to toggle it on and off. Pressing the J key will also toggle the clipping warnings on/off. In the preview, blue indicates black point clipping; red shows white point clipping (see **Figure 4–12**). The overlays both indicate luminance (brightness) clipping. Clipping warnings appear even when clipping is only present in one channel. (To see clipping in individual channels, use the Option/Alt method in the Basic panel, discussed later in this chapter.) To adjust or eliminate clipping, you can use the Tone sliders, as appropriate for each photo.

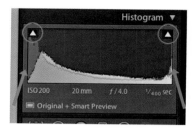

Figure 4-11

Figure 4-12

 Keep checking for clipping and noise throughout processing
While processing your photos in Develop, periodically check for clipping and other artifacts, and as necessary, apply adjustments to remove them.

Lab color readouts

New in Lightroom 5: Lightroom 5 has the ability to display color readouts in the Lab (or L*a*b*) color space instead of RGB. This was mainly added to help people (such as scientists) who need color value numbers from a device-independent color space to aid them in their work. You can enable Lab readouts by right-clicking or Ctrl+clicking the Histogram and choosing Show Lab Color Values from the contextual menu. **This does not convert the color space of the photo.** Once enabled you will see Lab values appear under the Histogram as you hover your cursor over the photo (see **Figure 4-13**). If you are not familiar with the Lab color space then this feature was not added for you. However, if you'd like to learn more about how you could use this feature in your Lightroom workflow I highly recommend you check out the video tutorial on skin tone color correction by Andrew Rodney at http://bit.ly/andrewrodney. I kept mine set to RGB for the remainder of this chapter.

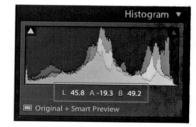

Figure 4-13

The Basic panel: Essential adjustments for every photo

Figure 4-14

The Basic panel contains the most important adjustments for working with all your photos. The Basic panel is separated into four sections: Treatment, White Balance, Tone, and Presence (see **Figure 4–14**). Each section provides adjustments that do very different things, but they're all important.

TREATMENT: COLOR/BLACK & WHITE

At the top of the Basic panel are two text buttons you can use to switch between Color and Black & White. (Keep in mind that a Black & White image in Lightroom is still using RGB color behind the scenes.) Click the buttons to switch modes. By default, clicking the Black & White button applies an Auto Black & White Mix and is the same as pressing the V key, which is discussed later in this chapter. You can use the buttons or shortcut to toggle between color and black & white at any time.

Preferences→Presets→Apply auto mix when first converting to black & white
Lightroom has a global preference setting to automatically apply Auto Mix adjustments when first converting to black & white and it is enabled by default. Uncheck that option if you don't want to use Auto Mix as your starting point. There is more on black & white conversions at the end of this chapter.

WB: WHITE BALANCE

We're surrounded by light sources of widely varying colors. Your eyes and brain constantly compensate for the color of light you see, so white objects always look white. However, a camera records the color of light literally, which can result in apparent color shifts in your photos. For example, you've likely seen photos shot indoors under standard tungsten light bulbs that appear orangey. This is because the white balance used for the capture was intended for daylight, which has a much cooler color. (Yellows and oranges are warm colors; blues and purples are cool colors.)

The White Balance settings in Lightroom (and on your camera) allow you to compensate for color shifts resulting from shooting under different light sources, using adjustments for color temperature and tint. Color temperature is measured in degrees Kelvin, and refers to the color of light sources. For example, bright sunlight at midday is approximately 5000k, open shade is around 6500k (cool), and tungsten light bulbs are about 2800k (warm).

Evaluating white balance

Does your photo appear to have a color cast that may be affecting color accuracy? Many photographers strive to achieve neutral white balance, where the colors in the

04

photo appear as they would to the unaided human eye. But keep in mind that, like all other adjustments, white balance is quite subjective. For many photos, you may not need to worry too much about whether the white balance is numerically "correct"—what matters most is that you like the way the picture looks (see **Figure 4–15**, which shows the Daylight setting on the left and Cloudy setting on the right).

Figure 4-15

Adjusting white balance

You can adjust the white balance to remove any apparent color cast and fine-tune the rendering of color in the image. You can also use white balance to creatively warm or cool the colors in the photo. After the process version and camera profile, the white balance adjustment will have the largest effect on the overall rendering of the image. In Lightroom, even black & white images are affected by the white balance settings. Lightroom's white balance settings are assigned to a photo using the controls near the top of the Basic panel (see **Figure 4–16**).

Figure 4-16

White Balance Tool: Click to sample an area in the photo; this will be used to set the global white balance for the entire photo.

WB Presets: The pop-up menu to the right of the panel contains standardized white balance values.

Temperature and Tint sliders: Drag the sliders or enter a numeric value to set the white balance.

Resetting WB

When using any of these methods, you can always reset the white balance back to its original captured value by choosing As Shot from the pop-up menu. You can reset the white balance to the Default settings by double-clicking the WB: text in the panel.

Another reason to capture raw

You have a lot more latitude for adjusting white balance with excellent results when you're working with a raw capture rather than a non-raw image (JPEG, TIFF, PNG, and PSD). White balance on a raw capture is only a metadata value so you can apply any numeric settings you want in Lightroom with no data loss. You can adjust white balance on non-raw files, but the adjustment shifts the RGB values from the "baked in" values the image came into Lightroom with as opposed to setting an absolute value for the first time with a raw photo. This is why you'll see the Temp and Tint sliders shift from a number on the Kelvin scale with a raw photo selected to plus or minus values when a non-raw photo is selected.

WHITE BALANCE TOOL

To activate the White Balance Tool, click the eyedropper icon near the top left the Basic panel (see Figure 4–16) or use the shortcut W (this works from anywhere in the Library or Develop modules). Move the cursor around the image and the White Balance Loupe appears, depicting the pixels under the cursor in a magnified view (see **Figure 4–17**). If the Navigator panel

Figure 4-17

is visible, it will show a dynamic preview of the white balance that would result from clicking in a particular spot. Click on an area of the image that you want to be neutral and the white balance settings will be adjusted to neutralize that area; all colors in the image will be adjusted accordingly.

▷ **Use zoom level to your advantage**

The White Balance Tool's sample area is dependent on the zoom level you're working at. The pixel values on the WB Loupe are based on monitor pixels, not image pixels, so for photos with a lot of noise you can zoom out and sample a wider area to get a more accurate reading.

White Balance Tool Options

With the White Balance (WB) Tool active and the Toolbar visible you can change the following options (see Figure 4–17):

- **Auto Dismiss:** When checked, this deactivates the WB tool as soon as you click a spot in the photo.

- **Show Loupe:** This check box determines whether or not the WB Loupe is shown to help you pick a location in the photo for WB.

- **Scale:** When the Loupe is enabled, you can change the scale of the WB Loupe. You can also change the sample size using a mouse wheel.

- **Done:** Clicking this button at the right of the Toolbar does the same thing as pressing the W key, the esc key, or clicking in the WB Tool area on the Basic panel; it deactivates the tool.

04

> **Other settings affecting the White Balance Tool readings**
> The results of the White Balance Tool are affected by the camera profile in use (in the Camera Calibration panel), because white balance comes after the profile in the rendering sequence. You may also get different results with the Tool depending on whether or not you're sampling an area where you'd also applied spot removal.

> **When white balance is critical**
> In situations where you need to precisely reproduce color, such as wedding, portrait, product, or fashion photography, you must photograph a reference target under the same light as your subject to properly neutralize the white balance. Capture an image that includes the reference card, and then use Lightroom's White Balance Tool to set the white balance. You can then sync the white balance to all the other photos from the shoot under those same lighting conditions. See the Appendix for recommendations on reference targets.

White balance preset menu
The fastest, easiest way to apply standard white balance values is to select from the preset values in the pop-up menu (see **Figure 4–18**). While doing so, pay attention to each preset's effect on the slider settings. This is a good way to learn the numeric values for specific lighting conditions. After choosing the preset closest to your desired look, you can fine-tune the white balance using the sliders and/or numeric entry. Note, with a non-raw file selected you will only see presets for As Shot, Auto, and Custom due to the difference between raw and non-raw I mentioned previously.

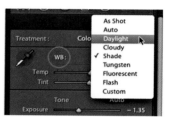

Figure 4-18

 Lightroom vs. camera settings
The exact numeric values for Lightroom's white balance presets may often be different than your camera's corresponding settings. For example, the Daylight setting on a Canon 5D Mark II uses a temperature of +4850 and a tint of +1, whereas Daylight in Lightroom is +5500 and +10. The WB value is not stored as degrees Kelvin by the camera (it is stored as coordinates in a proprietary color space), so the actual numbers may be interpreted differently by Lightroom than by the camera makers—but neutral is still neutral, and how the photo looks is what matters most. Don't get hung up on numbers, just get the photo looking the way you want it.

Temp and Tint sliders
The Temp slider adjusts how warm or cool the photo is, with blue at the left and yellow at the right. The Temp slider is the main White Balance control affecting the overall appearance of colors in the photo. After setting Temp, you can fine-tune the White Balance using Tint, which controls the green/magenta color balance. Both sliders show their effect on color when moving them a certain direction (see Figure 4–16). I usually use the sliders to fine-tune white balance on individual photos. I've found that when I make major changes to White Balance using Temp and Tint, it's a good idea to come back later to look at the photo with fresh eyes and confirm the settings.

TONE

Following white balance, the next Develop tasks to perform are tone adjustments. Tone refers to the range of dark to light values in the image, without regard to color. Though some photos ultimately contain a wider range of tones than others, the goal in post-processing is to optimize the tones to meet your vision of what the final photograph should look like. More than any other aspect, tone sets the mood of the photograph. For most photos, you should finish working with tone before moving on to color.

04

Using PV2012, the Basic panel provides logical Tone controls that also wield a lot more processing power than previous process versions (see **Figure 4–19**). Exposure in PV2012 is the main control for setting the overall brightness of the photo. The other tone mapping controls in PV2012 are Highlights, Shadows, Whites, and Blacks (PV2010 and 2003 included sliders for Recovery, Brightness, and Fill Light that do not exist in PV2012, and a Blacks adjustment that performed differently). The PV2012 adjustments offer much improved control over the entire tonal range, with fewer overlapping effects. They are designed to optimize all the tonal data and extract the full dynamic range of each photo. You may find that with these controls there is much less need for adjustments using the Tone Curve.

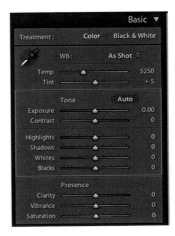

Figure 4-19

The functionality of the PV2012 tone adjustments is also much more intuitive than its predecessors: in all the Tone controls, dragging the slider to the left makes the image darker, and to the right makes it brighter. All the controls have a default of 0 and a range of -100 to +100, so negative amounts are possible on all the Tone controls.

Evaluating the tone in a photo

The available tonal data is dependent on the exposure of the original capture. Is the photograph underexposed or overexposed? Is it too dark, or too light, overall? Evaluate the tones of elements in the photo relative to one another and decide what should be brighter, what should be darker, and where all the tones should fall in between. Especially when working with a raw capture, you may be surprised at how much tonal data you can extract, even from what originally appears as an improperly exposed or low-contrast image. With just a few adjustments you can maximize a photo's dynamic range and increase contrast, often with dramatic results.

Work from top to bottom in the Tone controls

The tone controls are organized in order of importance and relative impact on the processing of the photo. The most important controls are at the top. With just Exposure and Contrast you can optimize the tones in most of your photos. The additional sliders below are for fine-tuning specific tonal regions. Highlights and Shadows are used to compress and expand dynamic range—especially in raw captures—using a process called

04

adaptive tone mapping. These controls can perform differently depending on the data found in the original capture, so the best result can be obtained for each photo. Whites and Blacks set the clipping and roll-off points at either end of the tonal scale.

For the most natural appearance, start with Exposure and Contrast and adjust the other sliders only as necessary to refine specific parts of the tonal range. As you're getting accustomed to the sliders, it might help to work with them in pairs. Do as much as you can with Exposure and Contrast, and then, if necessary, apply Highlights and Shadows. Lastly—and only on photos that need it—use Whites and Blacks.

 Try not to compare the new Tone controls to the old ones
If you've used previous versions of Lightroom, you've probably become familiar and comfortable with the old Tone controls. The new controls are very different and very much improved. If you were used to the old controls in earlier process versions, the new Tone controls can take some getting used to. However, once you get comfortable with the new methods, you won't want to go back!

Here's a tip from Victoria Bampton for those of you coming from pre-PV2012 versions of Lightroom: try using just the Exposure and Contrast sliders to get the photo looking good in the Navigator panel view of the photo (not the main image area), and then move on to adjusting Highlights and Shadows, Whites, and Blacks later on the large view of the photo.

Auto
The Auto Tone button is at the top right of the Tone section (see Figure 4–19). When you click this button, Lightroom evaluates your photo and attempts to intelligently apply the appropriate adjustments based on the characteristics of the image data. The Auto Tone result is affected by the current White Balance setting, as well as the Camera Profile used, but no other adjustments should affect it. In many cases, applying Auto Tone can provide a great starting point for your processing. If nothing else, it's a good way to learn how the new sliders affect your photos.

 Auto Tone in presets
If you like the results of Auto Tone, you can include it in your Develop presets, which can really speed up your workflow when you apply that preset during import.

Preferences→Presets→Apply auto tone adjustments
Lightroom has a global preference setting to automatically apply Auto Tone adjustments.

Exposure
Exposure is the main control affecting the majority of tones in the photo. Regardless of the content and original exposure characteristics of each image, you should start by adjusting Exposure first. It has the strongest effect near the midtones but also affects a broader tone range, especially highlights. The Exposure adjustment uses linear scaling for most of the tone range, but rolls off smoothly as it approaches the highlights. In PV2012, Exposure behaves more like the exposure setting on your camera. Start by using Exposure to set the overall tone range where you want it and then adjust Contrast.

Contrast

Contrast stretches the tonal values, making the highlights lighter and the shadows darker. If you've used Photoshop's Curves, the Contrast slider is similar to applying an S-curve. To make your photo really pop, use higher amounts of Contrast.

Soft contrast

Some photos look best with low contrast. Always make your processing decisions based on the theme, subject, and mood that you want to portray with the photo.

The most important step in successfully processing your photos

Spend a few minutes working both the Exposure and Contrast sliders before moving on. These two sliders make the biggest difference in the overall rendering of the image. In particular, Exposure and Contrast control which tones are affected by the other sliders (Highlights/Shadows and Whites/Blacks)—so, it's important to get Exposure and Contrast right before applying the rest.

Highlights

Use the Highlights slider to refine the tones in the bright parts of the photo and recover highlight detail. The Highlight slider implements updated color rendering and recovery logic, and tries to preserve local contrast while enhancing lighter details in the photo. It's got a broad shoulder for the range of tones it influences, designed to replicate some of the characteristics of film. The Highlights slider doesn't affect the white point. You'll get the most natural looking results using Highlights settings of between -50 to +50; more extreme amounts can be used for special effects.

A note about highlight recovery

In PV2012, the highlight recovery processing is always active, even when you don't adjust any sliders. These built-in highlight recovery routines are connected mainly to Exposure and then, to a lesser degree, Highlights.

Shadows

Use Shadows to "open up" dark areas and reveal more detail. Higher values make the shadows lighter, which may remind you of how the old Fill Light control worked. The Shadows adjustment uses the same adaptive logic as Highlights. It doesn't affect the black point.

Faux HDR

If you're a fan of the so-called "faux-HDR" look achieved with extreme tone mapping adjustments applied to a single raw capture, you'll love what you can do with the Highlight and Shadow controls. (Try reversing their values to make Highlights darker and Shadows lighter, using large amounts.)

Whites

In general, you should adjust the Whites slider to fine-tune the very brightest parts of the photo after setting the Exposure and Highlights adjustments. The Whites slider sets the limit for the very brightest pixels in the image. Using the Whites slider is somewhat akin

04

to dragging the white point in a tone curve: it can compress or expand the entire tonal range with minimal compression of data in the highlights, which maintains separation between the tonal values at the brightest end of the histogram.

Blacks

The Blacks slider sets the limit for the value of the darkest pixels in the image. It's calculated automatically for each photo. In PV2012, there's a much wider range of adjustment possible with the Blacks slider, so it's usually possible to crush the blacks even with very low-contrast images. Adjust the Blacks level to fine-tune the very darkest parts of the photo after making the other adjustments. With photos that are very underexposed, lightening the Blacks level can work wonders when combined with the Exposure and Shadows adjustment.

Hold Option or Alt while dragging the sliders

While adjusting the Tone controls (except Contrast), holding the Option or Alt key displays where clipping is present in individual channels. For example, in **Figure 4–20** I have an overexposed photo selected, and I am holding the Option key (on a Mac) while clicking on the Exposure slider. The black areas are not clipped (have detail), while the areas of white represent clipping in all three channels and colored areas represent clipping in only one or two channels (no detail). If I drag to the left to reduce exposure more of the photo becomes black as I recover detail (no longer clipping). Using this technique on Exposure, Highlights, and Whites reveals highlight clipping (with the rest of the photo in black), while using this with Shadows and Blacks reveals shadow clipping (with the rest of the photo in white).

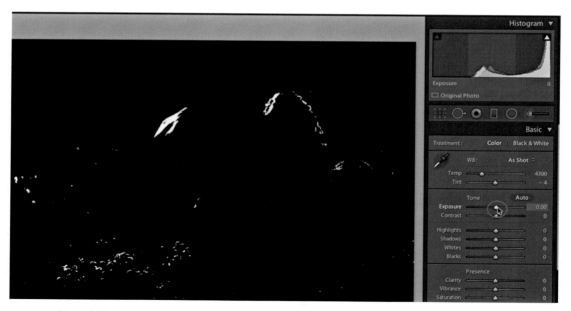

Figure 4-20

Double-click to reset sliders
If you change your mind after adjusting a slider, double-click its name or the slider handle itself to reset it to its default value. To reset all the sliders in a section to their default values, either double-click the name of the section, or hold the Option or Alt key and the name of the panel section changes to Reset. Click to reset all the adjustments in that section.

 Keep working the Basic adjustments
Get as close as you can to your desired result with the controls on the Basic panel before moving on to settings in the other panels.

Figure 4–21 illustrates a photo before and after Tone adjustments only, along with the settings I used.

PRESENCE

The Presence section of the Basic panel contains adjustments for Clarity, Vibrance, and Saturation (see Figure 4–14). (Vibrance and Saturation are disabled for photos using Black & White treatment.)

Clarity

Clarity is all about increasing (or decreasing in negative amounts) local midtone contrast. Increasing the Clarity value can enhance local contrast and the appearance of sharpness and edge definition, while negative amounts create a lower local contrast, softer look. Some images benefit greatly by increasing the Clarity slider; others, not as much. Photos with strong edges and details containing relatively high contrast, such as buildings and architecture, are good

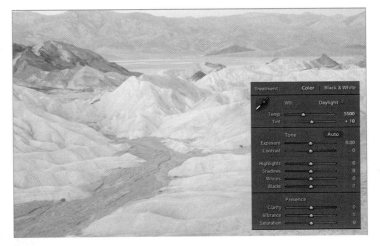

Figure 4-21

04

candidates for increased Clarity amounts (see **Figure 4–22**). Negative Clarity values create a softening effect that is beautiful for some images—portraits, in particular, can benefit from negative Clarity (see **Figure 4–23**), especially when it's applied locally. I particularly like to use negative Clarity on black and white photos.

Figure 4-22

The Clarity adjustment was vastly improved with PV2012; it produces much cleaner results with fewer haloes due to its edge-preserving characteristics. The effect of Clarity is much stronger in PV2012 than previous process versions and is integrated with Highlights and Shadows, so in some cases you might see an overall lightening of the image when using positive amounts of Clarity. You'll likely use lower amounts of positive Clarity than you would have in the past. The effects of negative Clarity are essentially unchanged in PV2012.

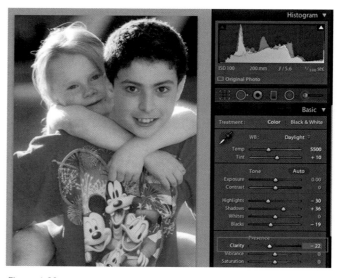

Figure 4-23

Saturation

Saturation refers to how vivid and pure a color is, as opposed to neutral gray. A photo that appears very bright and colorful could be called highly saturated. Some images benefit from increasing the saturation; others may look better with decreased saturation. In the Basic panel, drag the Saturation slider to the left for less saturation, and to the right for more, to see its effect on the photo.

Vibrance

The Vibrance control in Lightroom works similarly to Saturation, in that it makes colors more or less vivid, with a couple of important differences. First, Vibrance will not affect colors that are already highly saturated. This non-linear behavior helps avoid an oversaturated, neon effect when Saturation is pushed too far. Second, the Vibrance control is designed to not affect skin tones—peachy, orangey, or tan shades will not receive the increased saturation. For example, if you're processing a photo of a group of people in a park on a sunny day, increasing Vibrance will help push more color into the blue sky and green grass, without turning the people's faces pumpkin orange. Try Vibrance on a range of photos and you'll quickly get to know its personality. Drag the slider to the right to increase Vibrance; drag left to decrease.

See **Figure 4–24** for examples of the effect of Vibrance and Saturation. The top photo is with both set to 0, the middle photo is Vibrance +50 and Saturation 0, and the bottom photo is Vibrance 0 and Saturation +50. Note the effect on the already-saturated colors and on the skin tones. I used higher than normal settings to illustrate the difference.

Don't overdo it

Because Vibrance and Saturation are applied globally, it's easy to overdo them. (Set the Saturation and Vibrance sliders all the way to the right to see what I mean.) I recommend that as you're mastering Lightroom, and processing larger numbers of your own photos, you apply Saturation and Vibrance with a certain measure of restraint. Like all digital image processes, color saturation is a tool that must be wielded wisely. If you find that you're pushing Saturation or Vibrance over values of +20 or so, stop and think more about it. Unless you're looking for a certain effect, +20 is usually the maximum amount you should need. Choosing a different Camera Profile might be a better way to go.

Figure 4-24

Tone Curve: Modify tones based on ranges of luminance

After adjusting the settings on the Basic panel, you can further refine the photo's contrast by manipulating specific tone ranges with the Tone Curve panel (see **Figure 4–25**). If you've used curves in Photoshop or other software, the Tone Curve panel may seem familiar to you. The horizontal axis represents the original, unaltered values in the image, with the black point at the left and the white point at the right. The vertical axis represents the adjustments you make. The background of the curve box shows a histogram and a highlighted area indicating the minimum and maximum range of curve adjustment possible, based on the split controls in effect (see below).

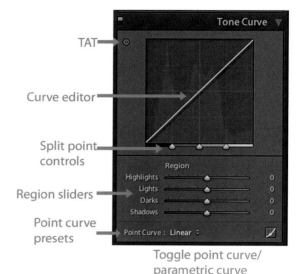

Figure 4-25

Most photos probably won't need the Tone Curve

You should usually focus the majority of your tone adjustment work on the Basic panel instead of the Tone Curve, which is becoming outdated in the era of parametric processing. The processing algorithms used for Basic panel sliders are provide more sophisticated processing routines than a curve. Especially with PV2012, you may find you can make your photos look just how you want without ever touching the Tone Curve panel. Don't be fooled into thinking that just because it's there that you need to use it for every photo! However, when you need very precise control, nothing works like the Tone curve; other practical uses are advanced color correction and creative effects using the individual channel curve capabilities.

PARAMETRIC CURVE

Lightroom's default Tone Curve is parametric: it adjusts sections of the tone scale, rather than from individual points. This provides smooth transitions between tone ranges and reduces the possibility of introducing undesirable hue shifts and posterization (banding).

Adjust the curve to increase or decrease contrast in specific areas of the tonal range. Positive values lighten tones and negative values darken them. The steeper the curve (or section of the curve), the higher the contrast. The flatter the curve, the lower the contrast. A typical example of this is the application of an "S" shaped curve, which increases contrast in the photo by lightening highlights and darkening shadows. Thus, the midtone section of the curve displays a steeper slope than before the adjustment (see **Figure 4–26**).

04

Figure 4-26

04

You can adjust the Tone Curve in the following ways:

- **The Targeted Adjustment Tool (TAT):** Click the bull's-eye to activate the TAT, and then either click and drag up or down in the image, or use the up and down arrow keys. See the next section for more information about the Targeted Adjustment Tool.

- **In the parametric curve, drag the sliders to adjust the four tone ranges independently:** Highlights, Lights, Darks, and Shadows. The curve will be adjusted accordingly. Using these sliders is the easiest way to adjust the curve.

- **Click and drag on the curve:** Up to lighten, down to darken. In the point curve, click to place points on the curve. Drag the points to change the tone values. In the Point Curve mode, the numeric values of point adjustments are shown at top left of the Tone Curve.

- **Select a preset from the Point Curve menu:** Linear, Medium Contrast, or Strong Contrast.

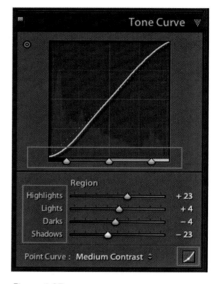

Figure 4-27

REGION SLIDERS

The split point controls on the bottom axis of the curve box define the range of adjustment for each of the four regions (see **Figure 4–27**). As you drag the split controls, the slider background adjusts to display the range of tones available for each region. Using the split controls you can achieve precise control over the curve adjustment.

POINT CURVE

Click on the Point Curve button in the bottom right corner (see Figure 4–27) to switch from the parametric curve to the point curve (see **Figure 4–28**). The two curves are separate, and their effect on the photo is combined. Lightroom's point curve editor provides more precise control than the parametric curve, and is similar to point curves in Photoshop and Adobe Camera Raw, with a couple of differences.

- No Input and Output text boxes (no numeric entry of point values).

- Percentages instead of 0-255 values.

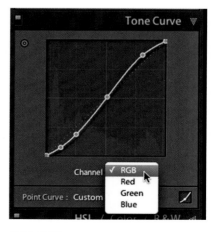

Figure 4-28

04

- Does not retain focus on a point after it's been edited (point does not stay selected).

- You can delete a control point with right-click or double-click, or by dragging it out of the curve box.

- Ctrl+click or right-click in the area around the curve and choose Flatten Curve from the contextual menu to remove all points.

- Holding option/alt requires more mouse movement and provides finer control.

Point curve presets

You can save point curve settings (as XMP files) in the Curves folder (which is shared with ACR curves) by clicking the Point Curve drop-down menu, and then choosing Save from the menu (this only appears after you have adjusted a point curve). When saving Develop presets including the Tone Curve settings, the point curve gets saved along with parametric values in the Tone Curve part of the preset—not independently.

With PV2012, the default Point Curve is Linear, although the default processing applied with Linear is similar to PV2010's Medium Contrast. This is one reason why photos using PV2012 look different even with default settings.

 Inverted curves

Using Lightroom's Point Curve, you can invert a negative image to a positive, and vice versa.

Channel

In PV2012, the Tone Curve panel provides per-channel RGB point curves—you can adjust curves independently for each channel. Should you need it, this is a powerful control for advanced color correction and creative color treatments. You can select an individual channel from the pop-up menu in the middle of the panel (see Figure 4–28).

Targeted Adjustment Tool (TAT)

The Tone Curve, HSL, and Black & White (B&W) panels provide a Targeted Adjustment Tool (TAT) that you can use to edit the image interactively (see **Figure 4–29**). Click the target to activate the tool. Position your cursor in an area of the image that you want to adjust. You can then use your mouse or the keyboard to modify the adjustment directly within the main preview. With the mouse, click and drag up or down to increase or decrease the adjustment (see **Figure 4–30**), or place your cursor on the spot in the preview you want to change and press the up and down arrow keys (my preferred method of using the TAT).

Figure 4-29

04

Figure 4-30

When you're done, click the target again (or press Esc) to deactivate the TAT . When you change to a TAT in a different panel, any TAT that was in use on another panel becomes inactive.

Target Group
When the TAT is active, the Toolbar shows a menu that allows you to choose which types of adjustments to modify. This saves a lot of time over switching to each specific panel.

HSL/Color/B&W: Adjust color by range

With the HSL panel (see **Figure 4–31**) you can adjust colors in the image based on their named color range (orange, purple, aqua, etc.). These colors may seem arbitrary, but quite the opposite is true: Lightroom's color ranges are loosely based on the color wheel and divided into distinct hues that blend together in between. The defined colors are Red, Orange, Yellow, Green, Aqua, Blue, Purple, and Magenta. All the colors in your photos will fall primarily into one of these hue ranges, sometimes with slight overlaps into neighboring colors. Lightroom provides controls for adjusting both specific color hues and blended combinations.

Figure 4-31

HUE
Hue is the named color range. Adjust the sliders to rotate the hue around the color wheel by moving the slider toward either end. The backgrounds of the sliders indicate the effect of moving the slider in each direction (see **Figure 4–32**).

SATURATION

Saturation refers to the purity of the color, as opposed to neutral gray. Adjust the sliders to increase or decrease saturation. Dragging the slider all the way to the left, to a value of -100, removes all the color from the selected hue range.

Figure 4-32

LUMINANCE

The Luminance value represents the brightness of the named color range. Adjust the sliders to lighten or darken. One of the most common applications is darkening blue skies (see **Figure 4-33**).

 Watch for noise
When lowering Luminance values, such as when darkening skies, keep an eye out for the introduction of noise as a result. This can sometimes be corrected in the Detail panel and/or using noise reduction with the adjustment brush.

Figure 4-33

 Targeted adjustments for the HSL panel
You can quickly and easily adjust colors in the photo (including darkening and lightening them) with the TAT, available in each of the HSL panel sections. This is much easier than adjusting sliders directly. More importantly, when you use the TAT in HSL; several sliders are often adjusted at once. This provides much more accurate adjustments and allows you to fine-tune colors by directly manipulating them in the preview.

COLOR ADJUSTMENT PANEL MODES

The HSL panel is itself comprised of three distinct sets of controls. Click the names in the panel header to access the various types of adjustments:

04

HSL

This is the default set of controls in the panel for working on a color photo. The three color components are separated into groups; click each adjustment name to access the sliders for that set of controls. Click All to show all the controls on one (very long) panel.

Color

These controls do the same things as the standard HSL sliders; they're just arranged differently. Adjusting the sliders in the Color mode also adjusts them in the HSL view, and vice versa. Click a color swatch to show all three component sliders for that color (see **Figure 4–34**). Again, click the All button to see all the controls at once.

Black & White

When working on a black and white image you can adjust the brightness of the original color components of the photo here, resulting in different grayscale conversions. Clicking this in the panel header changes the Treatment to Black & White and applies an Auto B&W Mix. See the section toward the end of this chapter for working in Black & White.

Split Toning: Apply creative color treatments

The term *split toning* refers to the application of different color tints to highlights and shadows. For example, you can warm the highlights and cool the shadows, or vice versa. To apply split toning to a photo, open the Split Toning panel and make sure the controls are expanded with the black triangle buttons (see **Figure 4–35**).

HUE AND SATURATION

You can independently adjust the hue and saturation for Highlights and Shadows. You can set the hues using the sliders, or click the color swatches to open the color picker.

➡ **Hold Option or Alt while dragging Hue sliders**
You won't see any effect from changing the Hue sliders until you also change the Saturation sliders, unless you hold Option or Alt while dragging a Hue slider. This provides a live preview of the color overlaid on the image, simulating a Saturation of 100.

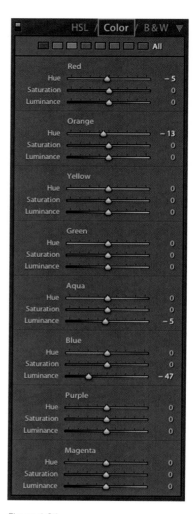

Figure 4-34

Figure 4-35

BALANCE

The Balance slider adjusts the balance between the highlight and shadow tints.

APPLY A SEPIA TONE TREATMENT

To give a photo a uniform color tint (see **Figure 4–36**), first convert it to black and white (you can learn about methods for B&W conversion at the end of this chapter). Then use the Split Tone panel to apply the color. For a uniform color tint, set the Highlights and Shadows sliders to the same values. You might find this serves as a starting point where you can then tweak either the highlights or shadows slightly warmer or more saturated as your tastes dictate.

Figure 4-36

You can use this same method to apply any solid-color tint to a photo or video.

APPLY A CROSS-PROCESS TREATMENT

Cross-processing is a way to create unusual colors in your photos, and originates in processing certain film emulsions in the chemicals for a different type of film (such as processing C-41 color negative film in E-6 color slide processing). Lightroom comes packaged with several cross-process presets to serve as starting points (see **Figure 4–37**). You can increase or decrease the Saturation to suit your taste.

Figure 4-37

 Using split toning on color photos

Split toning isn't just for colorizing black and white photos. You can selectively warm or cool highlights and shadows on color photos, too.

Detail: Fine-tune sharpening and noise reduction

The Detail panel contains Lightroom's controls for Sharpening and Noise Reduction (see **Figure 4–38**).

About Sharpening and Noise Reduction previews

The effects of the Detail panel are visible at all zoom ratios in the main preview, but higher zoom levels are more accurate. The Detail panel also includes a small preview where you can see the effects of adjustments at 1:1 independently from the main Develop preview. If it's not showing, click the black triangle button to expand the preview section of the panel (see Figure 4–38). To choose the area of the photo to use for the preview, click the target button at the upper left of the panel (see Figure 4–38), and then click in the photo. The Detail preview window will then show the area clicked. You can also click and drag to pan in the preview box, or single-click to zoom in and out, just like in the main image preview area.

 Zoom in and out when processing for small details
To effectively apply many of Develop's adjustments requires you to get in closer to really see what's happening, sometimes at very high zoom levels. If working with an offline photo using smart previews you'll want to wait until the source photo is online to be able to zoom to true 1:1 (and not 1:1 of the smart preview).

SHARPENING

The appearance of sharpness in a photo is determined by edge contrast—the amount of contrast between the pixels defining edges and details in the photo. Most digital images can benefit from some kind of sharpening. The ideal sharpening for any image depends on the content of the photo, the resolution of the file and the medium in which it is viewed. Use the sharpening controls on the Detail panel to apply Lightroom's capture sharpening to your photos (see **Figure 4–39**).

 Sharpening doesn't fix blurriness
Is the image in focus? If not, you might well choose to work with another capture. A photo captured out of focus can't be fixed with sharpening in post-processing. However, the appearance of sharpness in a capture that was made in perfect focus can be enhanced dramatically.

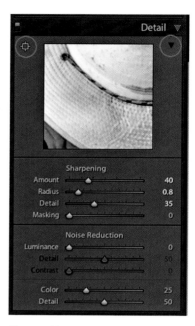

Figure 4-38

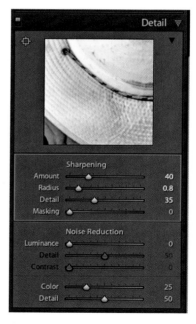

Figure 4-39

Amount

The strength of sharpening to be applied. The default is 25; my typical range is 30-40.

Radius

The width of the edges on which to apply sharpening. Decimals are provided due to the feathered falloff of the sharpening. Recommended range: .8 up to 1.4. As a general rule, to avoid visible halos from sharpening with higher Amounts, use lower radii. The default is 1.0.

Detail

Set this slider value based on the amount of fine detail in the image. I find that nearly all images benefit from some amount of the Detail adjustment. My recommended starting range: 15-35.

Figure 4-40

Masking

You don't normally need to sharpen smooth, solid areas of a photo, such as bare skin or blue sky. Masking provides the ability to restrict the sharpening to only the edges in the image that meet the minimum contrast level defined by the Masking slider. With Masking at 0, sharpening is applied to the entire image uniformly. At higher values, sharpening is only applied to defined edges.

The ideal amount of masking varies by image. To see the effects of Masking, hold the Option or Alt key as you adjust the slider. The grayscale preview shows the areas where masking will be applied: the areas in black will not be sharpened, and the areas in white areas will be sharpened, with gray levels in between producing sharpening of varying amounts (see **Figure 4–40**). I almost always apply some Masking; my default starts at 15. I find Masking is a huge help in preventing the application of sharpening to noise in the background, skies, and other solid areas of color in the photo.

Alternate sharpening previews

As you're adjusting the sliders, Hold Option or Alt while dragging the sliders to see the separate sharpening adjustments displayed as a grayscale preview in the main preview and Detail panel (see **Figure 4–41**). Zoom in to various levels to check for sharpness in key areas and consider whether some parts of the image need more sharpening than others. The suggested values are based on raw capture; if you shoot JPEG then some sharpening is already applied in the camera and the optimal settings would be different.

If you do as much of your work as possible in Lightroom, you may find that you never need to go into Photoshop, especially for sharpening. Though there may be special cases and images that benefit from the pixel-level editing that Photoshop provides, Lightroom's sharpening options, when properly used, may be all you need.

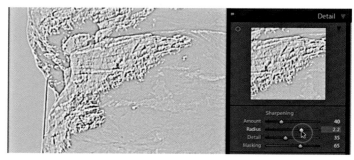

Figure 4-41

SHARPENING FOR CONTENT

The settings you use for sharpening should be based on the characteristics of each photo. Photos with lots of small, fine detail are often called high-frequency images; those with little detail are low-frequency images. As a general guideline, when you use higher Amounts, you'll want to use lower Radius; this applies well to high-frequency images (see **Figure 4–42**). For low-frequency images, use a lower Amount and a higher Radius (see **Figure 4–43**). Lightroom comes with default presets for Sharpen-Faces and Sharpen-Scenic; you can find these in the Lightroom General Presets folder in the Presets panel.

Figure 4-42

Figure 4-43

 Smoothing

If there are areas of the image that show noise or include more sharp detail than is desired, you can smooth these areas using negative Clarity. For example, smoothing is effective for reducing the appearance of wrinkles in human skin. See the section on local adjustments for more about this.

04

ABOUT MULTI-PASS SHARPENING

In today's digital image processing, it's usually better to sharpen an image in several steps rather than all at once. The late Bruce Fraser is credited with greatly advancing the art of digital image sharpening in recent years, and many of the principles he developed have been implemented in Lightroom's sharpening routines. The modern sharpening workflow is comprised of the following stages:

- **Capture sharpening:** When the continuous-tone real world is mapped onto a grid of pixels in a digital image, some softening is introduced. The first pass of gentle sharpening is intended simply to overcome the loss of sharpness resulting from digital capture. The sharpening controls on Lightroom's Detail panel are primarily designed for capture sharpening.

- **Creative sharpening:** Intermediate rounds of sharpening can be applied, as needed, to enhance all or part of an image, based on its characteristics. For example, areas of high-frequency information—those with lots of small, fine detail—require different sharpening treatments than do low-frequency areas with relatively little detail. Creative sharpening is also dependent on subjective considerations, such as the desire to emphasize or de-emphasize parts of the photo. Creative sharpening can be applied using Lightroom's local adjustment brushes (see next section).

- **Output sharpening:** The final application of sharpening is dependent on the size and resolution of the file and the medium for which it is intended. For example, a low resolution image destined for display on a website requires different sharpening than does a high resolution file that's going to be printed. Lightroom's output sharpening is applied either when exporting (see Chapter 5) or printing (see Chapter 9).

 When to turn off Lightroom's sharpening altogether
If you're planning to do all of your sharpening in other software, set the Amount to 0 to turn off sharpening in Lightroom. (And if you're Exporting files for that purpose, make sure you don't apply any sharpening there, either; see Chapter 5.)

NOISE REDUCTION

Digital noise is a common artifact that appears as small dark speckles and/or soft colored blobs in an image (see **Figure 4–44**). Noise is typically introduced at high ISO settings, during long exposures and exposures made in low light and in captures that are underexposed.

Figure 4-44

04

Because other adjustments can affect the appearance of noise, you should check for it at several points during processing. In most cases, noise reduction is best done before sharpening, as any noise present in the image is increased when sharpening is applied. A little noise here and there does not always present a problem; the main issue is whether or not the noise will be visible when the final image is printed or viewed on-screen.

To reduce or remove noise from photos in Lightroom, use the Noise Reduction controls on the Detail panel (see **Figure 4–45**).

Figure 4-45

Luminance NR Sliders

Luminance noise reduction reduces the appearance of gray/black speckles in the image (see **Figure 4–46**). Be conservative applying Luminance noise reduction; at extreme amounts, fine detail can suffer. Applying a value other than 0 enables the Detail and Contrast sliders. After setting the amount for noise reduction, you can use Detail and Contrast to fine-tune its application. Detail helps preserve areas of minute detail in the image; using a higher value will preserve more detail, at the possible expense of also preserving more of the noise. The Contrast slider sets the amount of edge detection used to identify noise in the affected areas.

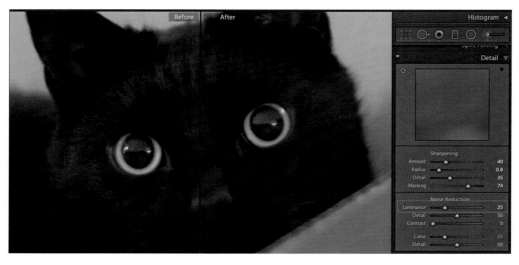

Figure 4-46

Color Noise Reduction Sliders

The Color Noise Reduction (NR) sliders reduce the appearance of color noise, which shows itself as multicolored, soft blobs in the image, especially in shadows and solid-color midtones (see **Figure 4–47**). Color noise reduction also provides a Detail slider (see description above).

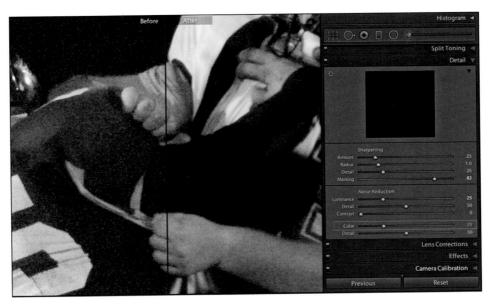

Figure 4-47

The type and amount of noise reduction you'll need is very image-specific; there are no magic formulas for noise reduction. Work with the sliders at various zoom levels to get the appropriate amount of noise reduction for each photo; if you have other photos in the shoot with similar characteristics, noise reduction is a good setting to Sync.

Lens Corrections: Fix image problems caused by the lens

New in Lightroom 5: A number of exciting new tools have been added to the Lens Corrections panel. The Lens Corrections panel allows you to correct lens distortion, perspective distortion, crooked photos, chromatic aberration, and vignetting (see **Figure 4–48**). The Lens Corrections panel now provides four modes of operation: Basic, Profile, Color, and Manual.

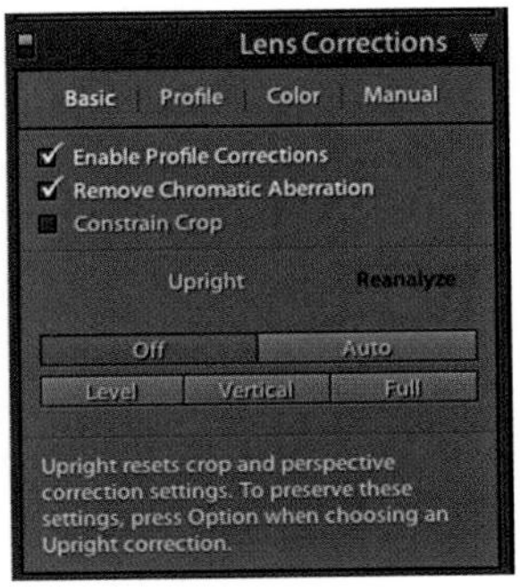

BASIC

New in Lightroom 5: There is a now a Basic tab with a brand new feature called Upright at the bottom, and three check boxes at the top for Enable Profile Corrections, Remove Chromatic Aberration, and Constrain Crop (see Figure 4–48). These check boxes are associated with additional controls on the Profile, Color, and Manual tabs respectively (and I'll discuss them further in the context of each tab), but are grouped on the Basic tab to make is simpler to enable all three before using the new Upright tools because the upright perspective correction tools perform best when Enable Profile Corrections is checked. The Remove Chromatic Aberration and Constrain Crop functions are optional, but you may wish to enable them all from the outset. More on each of those when we discuss their relative sections in the Lens Corrections panel.

Figure 4-48

04

Upright

Within the Upright section of the Basic panel are four buttons designed to automate the application of leveling and perspective corrections, and the Off button for disabling the corrections if you choose:

- **Level:** Performs only a leveling correction. Good for straightening crooked horizons and otherwise tilted images.

- **Vertical:** Performs a leveling correction combined with a vertical perspective correction. Good for fixing keystoning distortion that happens when you stand in front of something tall and tilt your camera upward to include more of it in the frame.

- **Full:** Performs a leveling correction combined with a full vertical and horizontal perspective correction that may even include a large rotation. Good for images with severe perspective distortions.

- **Auto:** Performs a leveling correction combined with a vertical and horizontal perspective correction, but with a more balanced and realistic looking outcome. Good for correcting images with converging vertical and horizontal lines where you want a more natural looking result.

 Remember the Loupe overlays

Back in Chapter 3 I introduced you to the new types of Loupe Overlays added to Lightroom 5 and mentioned that they also work here in the Develop module. If you need to display a grid (very handy when using Upright), guidelines, or even an image over your photo while processing you can enable all three from Loupe Overlay under the View menu.

 Upright resets existing crop and perspective corrections

As is noted under the Upright correction buttons, Lightroom resets any existing crop and manual perspective corrections so that it is best able to analyze the image and perform its own corrections. You can override that reset behavior by holding the Option or Alt key while clicking an Upright button.

The Level adjustment is pretty straightforward and works remarkably well. It essentially automates the same task we can perform manually with the Rotate slider in the Manual tab (though this is often an adjustment performed with the Straighten tool in the Crop Overlay) with a single click.

The Vertical, Full, and Auto corrections are worth looking at a little more closely. Let's compare the results of each correction on the same photo of the Massachusetts State House located in Boston. **Figure 4-49** shows the uncorrected photo with Enable Profile Corrections, Remove Chromatic Aberration, and Constrain Crop unchecked.

Just by checking Enable Profile Corrections we can see an improvement thanks to the lens profile that was automatically applied, which corrected lens distortion and the vignette (see **Figure 4-50**).

Starting with the Vertical correction we can see that the photo was slightly leveled and the vertical perspective distortion was corrected (see **Figure 4-51**). Correcting the distortion in the photo requires distorting the actual photo, which is why we see the empty white areas on the bottom left and right edges of the photo. If Constrain Crop were checked the photo would have been automatically cropped to exclude those areas. You can check that box at any time or manually crop it yourself in the Crop Overlay.

The Vertical correction did a nice job, but let's compare that with Full to include a full 3D correction of the photo (see **Figure 4-52**). The vertical correction remained as it was, but a slight rotation was introduced that, while subtle, was effective.

Figure 4-49

Figure 4-50

Figure 4-51

04

For a more balanced correction we'll compare the results we get from clicking Auto (see **Figure 4-53**). The resulting correction is not quite as severe as Full, but much improved from the starting point. I find the result of Auto to be much less forced and more appealing to my own sense of perspective. Any one of these results can serve as a final result or simply a new starting point for tweaking the adjustments further with the settings on the Manual tab (covered a little further on).

Figure 4-52

 When to Reanalyze
Lightroom caches the results of the Upright correction to make it faster and smoother as you try the various options. If you go back and enable (or disable) profile corrections after applying an Upright correction

Figure 4-53

you'll want to click the Reanalyze button (this is the only time it will become active) to make Lightroom clear the cached result and reanalyze the photo based on the changed setting.

 Upright Copy/Sync/Preset behavior
There are two new Upright-related options—Upright Mode and Upright Transforms—under the Lens Corrections section of the Copy Settings, Synchronize Settings, and Develop Preset dialog boxes to help us transfer settings between photographs. Check Upright Mode when you want to include a setting that tells Lightroom to analyze each photo independently and determine the best result for each one (this is useful when applying to a variety of unrelated photographs). Check Upright Transforms when you want to include the exact transformation settings from the target photo and have it applied the exact same way to all other photos.

PROFILE

In Profile mode, Lightroom first reads the photo's EXIF metadata to identify what lens was used to make the picture. It then loads a corresponding lens profile, if one is available, and uses the profile to make automatic adjustments (see **Figure 4-54**). Lightroom ships with profiles for many popular lenses; if Lightroom can't find a profile for the lens that was used it will display None in the Make field. If you know the lens make and model you can manually select it from the list. Many of the new lens profiles include crop factor metadata for non-full-frame cameras, which can provide better results on photos from those cameras when using lenses designed for full-frame cameras.

Figure 4-54

Enable Profile Corrections

Check the Enable Profile Corrections to apply lens corrections using a profile (this is the same check box that is on the Basic panel). The following controls become available:

- **Setup:** This is a preset menu containing shortcuts to load Default and Auto values, and presets you've saved yourself. Lightroom loads the default Setup based on the chosen profile. The Default applies to each camera and lens combination and also will include the values of the settings below.

- **Lens Profile:** If the EXIF lens data is recognized and Lightroom has a profile available for the lens used to make the photo, those settings will be automatically loaded in the fields for Make, Model, and Profile. You can change these values by choosing a different option from the menus; however, if the correct profile loads you're usually best off using it. If no profile loads, or any of the fields say None, you can manually choose the lens profile to apply. Note that due to the characteristics of different lens designs, using a lens model that seems close to yours may or may not produce an improvement in the image.

▷ **Adding more lens profiles**
Lightroom may not have an exact profile, especially for old lenses. If your lens is not listed, you can make your own, or you may be able to find and load a profile made by someone else. Also, Adobe continues to create and provide new lens profiles, so there's a chance a profile may become available in the future. See the Appendix for more information and links.

- **Amount:** At the bottom of the panel are sliders for Distortion and Vignetting, which allow you to further customize the adjustments beyond what's specified in the lens profile. It might help to think of these like individual volume controls, allowing you to increase or decrease the strength of the adjustment. The default values are 100 and can be adjusted up or down. Setting a slider to 0 turns off that adjustment entirely (I often like to dial back the Vignetting slider to bring back a little of the original lens vignette). Using these adjustments in Profile mode usually produces much less dramatic results than when in Manual mode, discussed after the Color section.

⇨ Include Lens Corrections in your preset or default

Lens Corrections are not enabled by default. I recommend you save your own standard Develop preset and/or set your own Default settings to include the Lens Corrections, in Profile mode, so they're active from the very beginning of your processing. Be warned that if you enable profile corrections in your custom Default settings it can be resource intensive when Lightroom is rendering its initial previews.

COLOR

Chromatic aberration (CA) is caused by the camera lens. Under certain lighting conditions, when the light comes through the lens, the light rays are scattered at the point where they hit the sensor, causing colored edges to appear in the image. There are two types of CA that we can encounter: Lateral CA and Axial CA. Lateral CA is easiest to find near the corners of the image, along edges of high contrast (see **Figure 4–55**), and this is usually corrected by checking the Remove Chromatic Aberration box. Axial CA can appear throughout the photo and presents as out of focus reddish-purple fringe in front of the plane of focus or out of focus greenish fringe behind (see **Figure 4–56**), and is corrected with the Defringe sliders.

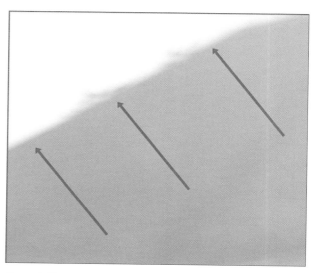

Figure 4-55

Fringing (also called sensor blooming) is different from chromatic aberration; it's an artifact that occurs on the sensor itself. Fringing happens when a high amount of energy hits a photosite and some of its charge spills over onto adjacent photosites. Fringing usually shows as purple outlines around very hot specular highlights, such as sunlight glinting on specular surfaces like water, chrome, etc. (see Figure 4–56), and can also be corrected with the Defringe sliders.

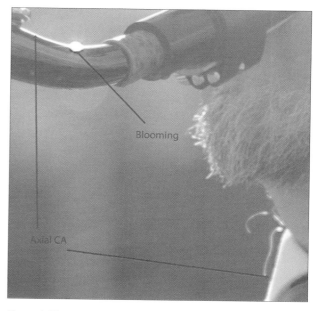

Figure 4-56

The set of tools on the Color tab are designed to aid us in removing both types of issues from our photos (see **Figure 4-57**). It all starts with the Remove Chromatic Aberration check box, which is the exact same check box from the Basic tab. When checked Lightroom automatically attempts to remove any lateral chromatic aberration that exists in the photo, and it does a pretty good job.

The more stubborn type of fringing is handled with the tools in the Defringe section (see Figure 4-57), which consists of a Fringe Color Selector (the eyedropper shaped tool) and two pairs of sliders, one for Purple Amount and Hue, and the other for Green Amount and Hue. The concept behind these sliders

Figure 4-57

is simple: to remove purple-reddish fringing slowly increase the Purple Amount slider until it is gone, and likewise to remove greenish fringing you would increase the Green Amount slider. Note, you're going to want to zoom into 1:1 or greater when making this type of correction. You only want to make as small of an adjustment as is necessary to reduce/remove the fringing because this adjustment can desaturate those same colors that are supposed to be there in other parts of the photo.

Color check

It is great to be able to remove a purple fringe from around a specular highlight, but you don't want to impact the purple flowers that may also be in the image. Hold down the Option or Alt key while moving any Defringe slider to see exactly what colors are being affected by that adjustment.

For example, in **Figure 4-58** I have a photo of a musician that has significant fringing around all of the highlights glinting off his sax, but he is also wearing a necktie with a similar shade of purple. There is also a little bit of greenish fringing along his collar. By combining a conservative increase in the Amount sliders for both purple and green with a shift in the Hue sliders I was able to reduce the fringing to a negligible amount while minimizing the impact on his tie.

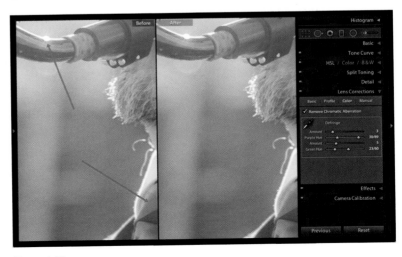

Figure 4-58

Paint it on

For ultimate control over what area of the photo is affected by your Defringe adjustment you can use the Adjustment Brush with a positive Defringe amount and just brush it on the areas of fringe to wipe it away. Alternatively, you can paint with a negative Defringe amount to paint over areas of the photo where you want to reverse the correction and bring back the color (like that necktie).

The intention of the Color Selector Tool is to help you choose the most accurate range of hues contained in the fringe areas and choose the appropriate Amount setting to remove that fringe. I find I always need to manually tweak all of the sliders to get the best results, so I prefer to skip the Selector and just use the sliders alone. That said, to give the Selector tool a spin, zoom in to 1:1 (or more) on the affected area, and then move the Fringe Color Selector tool over the fringe area and click on the spot showing the most color fringing to sample it. As soon as you click, Lightroom analyzes the colors and applies an adjustment by setting the relevant pair of purple or green sliders (depending on the color of the fringe)—after which you can then tweak as needed to refine the correction (press the Escape key to exit the tool).

 Fringe Color Selector tip

Axial CA is translucent in nature, meaning you can see the underlying color of the photo through the fringe. To get a more accurate result with the Fringe Color Selector tool try to click on an area of the fringe that is in front of a more neutral area of the photo, which should minimize the impact of the underlying color.

MANUAL

The Manual tab offers additional control over Lens Corrections, especially distortion. Click the Manual text button at the top of the panel to switch tabs (see **Figure 4-59**).

Transform

This section of the panel provides sliders to adjust for Distortion (pin cushioning and barreling), Vertical and Horizontal warping, Rotation, and Scale.

Figure 4-59

- **Distortion:** Drag this slider to remove pincushion or barrel lens distortion.

- **Vertical:** Drag this slider to correct vertical perspective distortion, such as the converging verticals created when shooting tall vertical objects such as buildings and trees.

- **Horizontal:** Drag this slider to adjust horizontal distortion.

- **Rotate:** Drag the slider to rotate the image. Use this slider in conjunction with perspective adjustments to level the photo as opposed to the Straighten tool in the Crop Overlay.

- **Scale:** This slider is most effective when used in conjunction with the Constrain Crop option; see below.

- **Aspect: New in Lightroom 5:** This slider gives us the ability to squish (drag to the left) or stretch (drag to the right) the photo in small amounts to give a more natural appearance to the distortion correction that was applied.

04

Constrain Crop

Checking the Constrain Crop box forces the crop rectangle inside the edges of any transformations applied. It is the same as the Constrain Crop check box on the Basic tab, and does the same thing as the corresponding Constrain to Warp function enabled in the Crop Overlay settings.

Lens Vignetting

Vignetting is darkening (or lightening) around the corners of an image. A dark vignette can be caused by the camera lens, especially wide angle lenses, particularly with a filter attached. Depending on the photo and your preferences, vignettes can either be pleasing or altogether undesirable; vignetting has historically been considered an unwanted photographic artifact.

The adjustments in the Lens Vignetting section are designed to reduce or remove the effect of vignetting caused by the lens (or add it). It's applied at the corners of the full-frame image, regardless of crop. (Lightroom also offers Post-Crop Vignetting, on the Effects panel, discussed in the next section.)

- **Amount:** The Amount slider controls the strength of the adjustment; you can apply positive amounts to lighten the corners of the image or negative amounts to darken.

- **Midpoint:** The Midpoint slider determines how far from the corners the adjustment is applied. When the Amount is set to 0, this slider is disabled.

Effects: Add vignettes and simulate film grain

Using the controls on the Effects panel, you can apply creative processing effects such as Post-Crop Vignetting and Grain.

POST-CROP VIGNETTING

These adjustments use a slightly different algorithm than the Lens Vignetting in the Manual tab of the Lens Corrections panel and thus produce an effect that looks a bit different. As its name implies, the Post-Crop Vignette is applied to the inside of the crop, not the outer edges of the full image. There are three types of vignettes, accessed from the Style pop-up menu (see **Figure 4–60**).

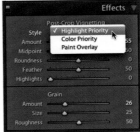

Figure 4-60

Style

This option sets how the vignette is blended with the colors in the photo.

- **Highlight Priority:** The default style and is most similar to the processing in the regular Lens Vignetting adjustments.

- **Color Priority:** Similar to Highlight Priority but also attempts to avoid shifts in hue.

- **Paint Overlay:** Most similar to the Post-crop Vignette from Lightroom 2, where the adjustment applies black or white overlays to achieve the effect.

Amount
The Amount slider determines the overall strength of the effect on the photo.

Midpoint
The Midpoint slider sets how far from the edges the vignette is applied.

Roundness
Roundness makes the vignette more circular or square.

Feather
Feather makes the vignette edges softer or harder.

Highlights
For Highlight and Color Priority, if the amount is set to a negative value (to add vignetting) the Highlights slider becomes active, which applies a different level of processing for lighter areas of the photo.

 Zero Feather
You can get a good feel for what the other sliders do by setting Amount to a large non-zero number and Feather to zero, and then play with the other sliders to see how each affects the vignette.

GRAIN
To apply a simulated film grain effect to the photo, first set an amount other than 0. You can then adjust the Size and Roughness of the grain (see Figure 4–60). Zoom in to 1:1 to accurately see the effect.

Amount
The Amount slider sets the overall strength of the grain effect on the photo.

Size
The Size slider sets the size of the grain. With larger sizes, the grain edges become softer and less pronounced.

Roughness
The Roughness slider sets the frequency of the grain effect (coarse or fine).

Camera Calibration: Precisely control raw image rendering

The settings on the Camera Calibration panel affect the baseline rendering of photos. The panel is split into sections for Process Version, Camera Profile, and Calibration sliders (see **Figure 4–61**).

The processing for these controls is applied near the start of the rendering pipeline. It's a good idea to establish your own standard settings for the Camera Calibration panel and use those as the starting point for all the processing for photos from a specific camera. To do this, you can apply a Develop preset during import, or override the Adobe Default Settings to use your own. Otherwise, Lightroom will default to PV2012 and the Adobe Standard Profile.

Figure 4-61

PROCESS

You can use the pop-up menu to choose the Process Version used for the selected photo(s). See the section earlier in this chapter for more information about process version. The default for Lightroom 5 is Process Version 2012.

PROFILE

In addition to Process Version, another important starting point for establishing the best possible default rendering for your photos is to apply a camera profile (see **Figure 4–62**). Camera profiles can only be applied to camera raw and DNG images. Other file types will show "Embedded" (though you can still modify the slider adjustments below).

Adobe profiles in the menu

With the current camera profiles installed, Lightroom will show only the profiles applicable for the camera used to make the capture. The default is Adobe Standard, and for some camera models that may be the only profile available.

Figure 4-62

If you are using an older camera model, you may also see several older versions of Adobe Camera Raw (ACR) profiles in the menu. The numbers indicate during what version(s) of Adobe Camera Raw the original profile was created. If there is more than one listed, this indicates the profile for that camera was updated in newer versions of ACR. For camera models released after ACR 5.2 in 2008, the profile menu will not list any ACR profiles.

The newer Adobe Standard profile replaces all of the older ACR profiles.

Other camera style profiles listed

In addition to the Adobe Standard and ACR profiles, depending on your camera make and model, you will also very likely see camera-specific profiles listed. These are designed to replicate the picture styles in the camera and the camera-maker's dedicated software. Some images might look better with one profile or another; you can try each of the various profiles until you get the best results. Sometimes choosing a different profile can dramatically improve the baseline rendering of your captures.

Comparing profile results

To see how different camera profiles affect a photo, you can make multiple virtual copies from a photo, apply different camera profiles to each of them and then preview them all in Survey view in Library. (Working with virtual copies is covered later in this chapter.)

Adding and removing camera profiles

Adobe's camera profiles are automatically loaded when you install recent versions of Lightroom, DNG Converter, or Adobe Camera Raw. If you installed earlier versions of these products you might also still have the old profiles on your system. These can be removed by deleting them from the folder (however, be aware that any presets you made using those profiles will no longer function correctly). The default locations of the camera profiles are:

Mac OS X: Macintosh HD/Library/Application Support/Adobe/CameraRaw/ CameraProfiles

Windows: C:\ProgramData\Adobe\CameraRaw\CameraProfiles

Making custom camera profiles

Though the Adobe profiles can often get very close to the optimal rendering on many images, you will usually achieve the best results by profiling your own camera. The most popular method for creating custom camera profiles is the use of the X-Rite ColorChecker Passport system. You can also make profiles using Adobe's free DNG Profile Editor, but you'll need to purchase the Color Checker target separately. See the Appendix for links.

Camera Calibration sliders

Prior to the introduction of camera profiles, the Camera Calibration slider adjustments were commonly used to apply baseline rendering values stored in Develop defaults. Camera profiles have made the Camera Calibration slider adjustments obsolete, and I generally recommend you don't make adjustments to these sliders or use them in presets. However, due to the fact that many Lightroom users have processed photos and created presets using these sliders in the past, it's likely that they will remain in the panel.

Before/After

In Develop you can see left/right or top/bottom comparisons of the before and after states of the photo. You can also toggle the main Develop preview to show Before/After. To see the Before/After previews, click the button on the Toolbar (see **Figure 4–63**) or use

the \ keyboard shortcut to
quickly switch between the
current state and the before.
The triangle button next
to the Before/After button
opens a pop-up menu with

Figure 4-63

options for changing the layout of the before and after views. The Before state shows
either the image as it came into the catalog during import, including any Develop presets
that were applied on import; or a Before state that you have applied yourself. The After
state always shows the image with all current settings applied.

Progressively developing a photo using Before/After

When you get to a point in processing where you want to take all the current settings
and apply those to the Before preview, simply drag and drop any step from the History
panel (discussed later in this chapter) onto the Before preview. You can then continue
processing, using the newly created Before state as your reference. Alternatively, you can
Ctrl+click or right-click any Snapshot (discussed later in the chapter) and choose to set
that Snapshot as the Before state.

Come back later

Sometimes it's helpful to work an image up to the point where you can't seem to make
it any better and then stop. Come back later, with fresh eyes, to confirm your previous
processing decisions and make additional changes if needed.

Changing Before/After settings

When the Before/After preview is active, you can use the buttons on the Toolbar (see
Figure 4–63) to copy settings between the Before and After states, or use the shortcuts.
You can Copy Before's Settings to After, Copy After's Settings to Before, or Swap Before
and After Settings. (Hover your cursor over the buttons to see tooltips.) I usually don't
mess with these buttons—things can quickly get confusing. If you want to copy settings,
you're probably better off using one of the many other methods.

Crop Overlay: Cropping and straightening your photos

As the first step in evaluating each image, carefully consider whether it could be made
stronger with different cropping. Since cropping removes parts of the photo—and thus
changes the composition—this can be the most significant modification you make to an
image. Before you go much further into processing, take a few moments to crop and/or
straighten the photo as necessary. (Note that because all digital images are rectangular,
straightening a photo in Lightroom always involves cropping.) Be willing to crop photos
in Lightroom whenever it makes an improvement.

Crop does not resize in Lightroom

Lightroom always applies the crop using the full resolution of each file. There are no
resizing/resampling controls directly within Lightroom; to resize an image you must
Export it, which is covered in Chapter 5. Don't be concerned with the size or resolution
of the image when you're working in Develop.

04

Crop in-camera

It's always best if you don't have to crop or rotate in post-processing; in both cases, you'll lose resolution. While shooting, whenever possible, slow down and take your time to perfect your compositions.

CROP GUIDE OVERLAY

Lightroom's crop and straighten tools are in the Tool Strip on Develop's right panel set, just below the Histogram (see **Figure 4-64**). Click the Crop Overlay to activate it, or press the R key from anywhere in Lightroom. Activating the Crop Overlay also opens the tool drawer underneath the Tool Strip. (The tool drawer contains controls for all of the tools in the Tool Strip.) When the crop overlay is active, additional crop settings are also available on the Toolbar.

Figure 4-64

Adjusting the crop

The Crop Overlay is displayed over the main preview. Drag the corners or the sides of the overlay to adjust the crop (see Figure 4–64). The crop overlay always remains straight and centered in the image preview area; the photo moves underneath it. Drag the photo to reposition it under the crop overlay. Hold Option or Alt to crop from the center of the current crop.

Applying the crop

To apply the crop when you're done adjusting, press Enter or R, or the Done button in the Toolbar, or the Close button in the tray. Alternatively, to cancel cropping without applying the changes press Esc.

Choosing a different overlay

Lightroom's crop tool provides a variety of overlays: Rule of Thirds, Golden Ratio, Diagonal Lines, Triangles, Golden Mean, Grid, and Aspect Ratios. To cycle through all the overlays, press the O key. Press Shift-O to flip the overlays.

New in Lightroom 5: If there are crop guide overlays that you don't want to use you can go to Tools➔Crop Guide Overlay➔Choose Overlays to Cycle to open the Cycled Overlays dialog box (see **Figure 4-65**) and uncheck the boxes for any overlays you don't want to see cycled through when you press O.

Aspect ratio overlays

New in Lightroom 5: Lightroom 5 has an aspect ratio overlay to help you visualize how a crop will impact other standard print (and screen) aspect ratios. For example, say you have a typical 2x3 aspect

Figure 4-65

ratio photo and you want to see how you might accommodate a potential 5x7 and 8x10 aspect ratio crop. Enable the overlay as described above and cycle to the Aspect Ratios overlay, then go to Tools➔Crop Guide Overlay➔Choose Aspect Ratios and check the boxes for just the aspect ratios you want included in the overlay (see **Figure 4-66**). The overlay will update to include guides that show exactly how

Figure 4-66

the other aspect ratios would look to help you make your cropping decision.

➧ **Use standard aspect ratios when possible**

In Lightroom you can crop a photo any way you like, with or without using a specific aspect ratio. I think it's always best to let the composition of the image dictate the best crop. However, your plans for printing and framing the photo may introduce other constraints. For example, using a 4x5 aspect ratio will allow an 8x10 print in a 16x20 frame. Envision how you will finish the photo, and when appropriate use a standard aspect ratio.

➧ **Try Lights Out when cropping**

Press L once or twice to darken or black out everything on your screen but the image—it's much easier to see how the cropped image will look. (Lights Out is discussed in more detail in Chapter 1.)

CROP FRAME TOOL

With the Crop Frame Tool (see **Figure 4-67**), you can draw a freehand crop in either portrait or landscape orientation. When using the Crop Frame Tool, the aspect ratio controls apply in the same way as when manipulating the crop overlay directly.

ASPECT

The aspect ratio of an image refers to its length and width, expressed as a ratio. For example, 2:3 (sometimes shown as 2x3) means that the photo's short side is 2 units and the long side is 3 units. These units can later be translated into real world measurements, such as size in inches for printing.

Figure 4-67

When cropping in Lightroom, you can constrain the crop to a precise aspect ratio or apply a free-form crop that is not locked to any aspect ratio. The padlock button (see Figure 4–67) toggles whether or not the aspect ratio is constrained. Next to it, a pop-up menu allows you to choose a standard ratio or to create your own custom aspect ratios, which are then listed in the menu (see **Figure 4–68**).

Figure 4-68

The built-in aspect ratios also include common screen aspect ratios: 4x3, 16x9, and 16x10. In addition, the fields for entering values for custom ratios can accommodate numbers up to 9999.99 so you can use screen resolution in pixels to create ratios. It's crucial to understand that these are only ratios of the two edges, not actual dimensions.

When you bring a photo into the Crop Overlay it will always display its current aspect ratio, which for most photos starts as Original (for dSLR cameras the original aspect ratio is 2x3). Some cameras allow you to choose an aspect ratio in-camera that is applied to the raw photo even though the full sensor area is included in the capture, in which case Lightroom will display that as As Shot, but you can regain the full image by choosing Original from the drop-down menu. I often get asked how to set a default crop ratio so that all photos start at some given aspect ratio (i.e. 8x10), but that is not possible. Lightroom has to always start by displaying the current aspect ratio of the photo, and then you can change it from there. See the tip below on using the Quick Develop panel in Library to batch apply a crop-ratio to multiple photos before moving to the Crop Overlay.

 Staying centered
New in Lightroom 5: When you change aspect ratios the new aspect ratio crop remains centered on the part of the photo you were cropping instead of resetting to the center of the full-size photo.

 You can apply Crop presets in Library's Quick Develop
To quickly Crop one or more photos, select them, and choose the desired preset, or custom option, from the Crop Ratio menu in the Quick Develop panel in Library. Note that the applied crop will be centered on all the images; you can then go into Develop to adjust crops for individual photos as necessary. This is a really fast way to set a large number of photos to a specific crop ratio, and then press the R key to jump to the Crop Overlay where you can tweak the each photo's crop for composition.

ANGLE

You can rotate your photo to make it appear more level or you can use rotation as a creative effect. The easiest way to arbitrarily rotate the photo is to place your cursor outside the crop overlay; the cursor turns into a curved double-arrow. Click and drag to rotate the photo under the crop overlay (see **Figure 4–69**). You can double-click on either the Angle label or its slider to reset it.

Changing orientation

You can use the crop tool to turn a landscape-oriented image to a portrait and vice versa. Press the X key; it toggles the crop overlay between portrait and landscape orientation. Alternatively you can click Rotate Crop Aspect under the Settings menu, but the keyboard shortcut is easier to remember.

Figure 4-69

04

STRAIGHTEN TOOL

In addition to rotating in the preview, you can use the Straighten Tool to click and drag a line that you want to make straight (see **Figure 4–70**), drag the Angle slider to change it, or enter a numeric value in degrees. Note, holding the ⌘ or Ctrl key automatically switches to the Straighten Tool for an easy click and drag along a line.

 Use overlays to assist with rotation

If you want to straighten a horizon or other prominent line in the photo, use the grid overlays to help line things up.

Figure 4-70

CONSTRAIN TO WARP

This check box works in conjunction with Lens Corrections, forcing the crop within the boundaries of the Transform controls. If no Transform adjustments are applied, this check box has no effect on the crop (see Figure 4–70).

RESET

To reset the crop overlay to its original settings, click the Reset button in the tool drawer or use the shortcut. (**Note:** Both crop and rotation will be reset.)

CLOSE

Click the Close button to apply the current crop and hide the tool options. This does the same as pressing Enter, or R.

Spot Removal: Retouching photos in Lightroom

Are there elements in the image you'd like to remove or otherwise clean up? Typical retouching tasks include removing dust spots, smoothing or removing wrinkles and blemishes from skin, and generally eliminating distracting elements from the composition. Determine what elements you want to remove from the photo, and reassess the need for retouching after completing all the other steps—as you work on the image you're likely to discover artifacts and other flaws you didn't notice earlier and/or find that the processing has reduced the need for retouching or eliminated it altogether.

➲ Do your retouching late in the workflow

Most often, it's best to wait until the end of the workflow to do your retouching—you might save lots of time. You will often find that other processing reduces the need for retouching. For example, you wouldn't want to spend time retouching the edge of the image and then crop it. Bearing in mind the principle of working from large to small, global to local, it stands to reason that retouching is best done after the other stages of the Develop workflow.

New in Lightroom 5: The Spot Removal tool has received a fantastic upgrade in the form of non-circular healing. It can still take good care of sensor spots and other isolated blemishes, but now can also be used for more ambitious removal jobs as well. Essentially the Spot Removal tool now has two types of spots:

- **Circle Spots:** This is the single-click circular spot removal functionality that has always existed in Lightroom. Simply click a spot and Lightroom attempts to remove it from the photo.

- **Brush Spots:** This is the new functionality that allows you to paint over an area (such as power lines and other small but unwanted distractions) and Lightroom will attempt to remove that from the photo.

New in Lightroom 5: A Visualize Spots check box appears in the Toolbar when the Spot Removal tool is active. When checked, a grayscale mask appears over your photo to help you quickly see where all the dust spots are located.

USING CIRCLE SPOTS

Lightroom's Spot Removal tool is primarily used for getting rid of small- to medium-sized imperfections in the photo. There are two modes available: Heal and Clone. Each has its own strengths and best uses.

Heal dust spots

Following are steps to remove dust spots, using Heal mode:

Step 1. To activate the Spot Removal tool, click its icon in the Tool Strip under the Histogram (see **Figure 4–71**) or use the shortcut Q. This enables the tool overlay, which shows any previous applications of the Spot Removal tool on the photo, and reveals the controls in the tool drawer, which contains the most recently used settings.

Step 2. Set the tool options. First, select Heal mode by clicking the text button to the right. Heal works best for retouching areas of solid color or smooth gradients, like sky and skin.

Figure 4-71

Step 3. In the Toolbar, check Visualize Spots in the Toolbar (or press the A key) to see where the spots are located in your photo (see **Figure 4-72**). Adjust the spot visualization threshold slider to make the spots easier to see.

Step 4. Set the size of the spot. As with the other sliders in Lightroom, there are several ways to adjust the size using the slider or shortcuts (if you're using a mouse with a wheel, that's the easiest way). The Spot Removal tool works best when the size of the brush is just larger than the spot to be removed (see **Figure 4–73**). (Optional) You can also adjust the opacity of each instance of the Spot Removal tool, though I usually work with opacity set to 100.

Figure 4-72

Step 5. To remove spots, click once on each element to be retouched and Lightroom will automatically designate a nearby source to sample for the new pixels, or hold the ⌘ or Ctrl key and click and drag to manually designate the source. Heal mode smoothly blends the sample into the spot. Each time you click, two circles are added to the overlay, connected by a line with an arrow at one end. The arrow shows the direction from the sample to the spot being retouched (see **Figure 4–74**).

Figure 4-73

You can come back later to change all these settings after applying the Spot Removal tool.

Figure 4-74

Some tips for using the spot removal tool:

- **Hide the overlay:** Like the other tools, you can press the H key to hide the spot removal overlay while you work. I find this really makes retouching easier.

- **Zoom in:** It's difficult to accurately retouch a photo viewing the full image; zoom in to various magnification levels while doing your retouching.

- **Use Page Up and Page Down:** You can scroll the image in precise vertical columns. As you reach the end of each column, the preview resets at the top of the next column. This ensures you cover the entire image.

- **Space bar:** Press the spacebar to temporarily enable the hand tool. You can then click and drag to pan the image in any direction.

MODIFYING CIRCLE SPOT SETTINGS

After applying Circle Spots, you can adjust each instance of it in the tool overlay. Start by clicking any circle to select it. The active circle has a heavier outline than the other (see Figure 4–74). With any instance of the Spot Removal tool selected, you can modify it in several ways:

- Click and drag the edge of the circle to change its size;

- Click and drag the center of the target circle to reposition it (this can be used to move the target circle to better cover the target area);

- Switch between Clone and Heal;

- Click and drag the center of the source circle to move it to a different location (this can be used to move the source circle to a different point for better sampling); or

- Delete it.

AUTO-SPOTTING

To easily apply spot removal to multiple photos containing the same spots, just spot the first photo, making sure not to move any of the source circles. If you allow Lightroom to determine the source spots, you can then Sync that photo with others, and Lightroom will automatically clean up spots in those photos too, even if they have different compositions. This doesn't always work perfectly, but is a huge time-saver when you've got lots of photos to clean up. You can then go back and fine tune spotting in individual photos. See the information about Syncing settings toward the end of this chapter.

USING BRUSH SPOTS

The new Brush Spots function of the Spot Removal tool takes everything that was good in the original Circle Spots function and transforms it into a freeform healing brush that can be used to remove all manner of irregularly shaped objects from your photos. Granted, the key to using this tool still remains that you need to have a good clean source of pixels that matches the area you want to remove. For example, I liked the symmetry of the slope and line of trees in **Figure 4-75** except for the fact that there is a dead tree smack in the middle of the scene. Thanks to the new Brush Spots capability in Lightroom 5 I can skip the trip to Photoshop and simply grab the Spot Removal tool and brush right over the dead tree. Lightroom does the rest (see **Figure 4-76**). While Lightroom does automatically select a source of pixels for the removal I can still reposition it just the same as with Circle Spots.

Brushing in a straight line
Hold the Shift key while dragging
the brush to constrain it to a
horizontal or vertical line. Click at
one end of a line, then hold Shift
and click again at the other end to
connect the dots and paint a Brush
Spot along that line.

04

MODIFYING BRUSH SPOT SETTINGS

Brush Spots can be modified in
the same ways as Circle Spots with
the exception of size. If you need
to change the size of a Brush Spot
it is best to delete the existing
adjustment and apply a new Brush
Spot to the area.

Figure 4-75

 **When to use Photoshop for
retouching**
You can use Lightroom's retouching
tools to remove many unwanted
elements, but Photoshop's
retouching capabilities far surpass
those in Lightroom. One example
is the replacement of any large
section of a photo; Lightroom

Figure 4-76

can't do this. Heavy-duty retouching is best accomplished in Photoshop using the Edit In
Photoshop command, discussed in Chapter 5.

Red Eye Correction

Red eye in photography is a phenomenon caused by light from a flash bouncing off
the inside of a person's eyeball. Usually, it's an undesirable effect. Lightroom's red-eye
removal tool looks for red-colored pixels and changes them to neutral gray or black. Its
application is similar to that of the Spot Removal tool.

To remove red eye from a photo, zoom in close to see the affected eye; work on one at

a time. Click to activate the red
eye tool (there is no keyboard
shortcut). Click and drag to set the
tool to just slightly larger than the
pupil you're working on (or use the
current size). Release the mouse
button to apply, and you're done
(see **Figure 4–77**)!

Figure 4-77

Local Adjustments: Dodging, burning, and so much more

As part of your standard editing workflow, you should evaluate whether or not the photo could be enhanced with local adjustments. These are changes you make to only part of the photo; darkening a stormy sky, sharpening eyes, smoothing skin, changing the color and removing moiré on a shirt, removing noise in a dark shadow... the list goes on and on. You may be surprised how much you can do to improve your photos in Lightroom— if you master Lightroom's local adjustments, you may find you no longer need to use Photoshop or other software for these tasks.

About dodging and burning

Selectively lightening or darkening localized areas in the photo has traditionally been referred to as dodging (lightening) and burning (darkening). Most photos can benefit from some amount of dodging and/or burning. You can use dodging and burning to direct eye movement within the frame, remove distractions, enhance depth and dimension, and increase contrast to make images pop!

INTRODUCTION TO THE GRADUATED FILTER, RADIAL FILTER, AND ADJUSTMENT BRUSH TOOLS

You apply local adjustments with the tools on the Tool Strip (see **Figure 4–78**). **New in Lightroom 5:** A third type of local adjustment called a Radial Filter has been added:

Figure 4-78

- **Graduated filters:** Linear gradients that can be applied anywhere in the image. Click and drag to create a straight mask within which the adjustments will be applied.

- **Radial filters:** Circular gradients that can be applied anywhere in the image. Click and drag to create a radial mask where the adjustments can be applied either inside or outside of the circle.

- **Adjustment brushes:** "Painted-on" adjustments. Select brush options and then paint with the cursor to apply the adjustments wherever you want them.

The choice of which tool to use depends on what you need to accomplish, so this is a good time to sit back, evaluate the image, and envision exactly where you want to take it. In general, the Graduated Filter is best where the adjustment will be applied in a wide swath, across a big section of the photo. The Radial Filter is great when you only want to adjust a limited area within the bounds of the filter or to protect the area within the filter and adjust everything outside of it (or both). The brush is perfect for getting in tight corners and following the contours of random edges.

Save local adjustments in presets

You can store the settings for local adjustments in Develop presets, which are explained in detail toward the end of this chapter. Graduated and Radial Filters are especially useful in presets.

MASK: NEW, EDIT

A mask defines the specific area where the local adjustment will be applied (see **Figure 4–79**). The New and Edit text buttons toggle the mask mode for the panel: you're either going to create a brand new mask using the Graduated Filter, Radial Filter, or Brush or edit an

Figure 4-79

existing mask. You can use as many separate masks as you need. Always keep track of whether you're making a new one or changing an existing one. Only one mask can be selected at any given time. We'll get further into that in just a moment.

With any local adjustment tool active, you can press Return or Enter at any time to create a new mask.

EFFECT

The Effect menu is where you access local adjustment presets (see **Figure 4–80**); these are shared by all three local adjustment tools. Lightroom comes with many useful presets and you can also save your own. The presets store the values for the local adjustment sliders. The Effect menu is used by all three tools.

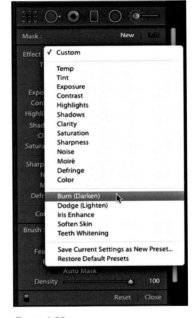

Figure 4-80

You can choose from one of the provided presets to start working with the local adjustments right away. When you've applied settings you want to save for later, you can create your own preset: with the desired settings applied click the Effect: menu and select Save Settings as New Preset.

 Sharpening or smoothing with adjustment brushes
You can use graduated filters, radial filters, or adjustment brushes to sharpen or smooth local areas of the photo. To sharpen, increase the amount of the Sharpness slider. To smooth, use negative amounts of Clarity and Sharpness. These techniques are very handy for portrait retouching.

LOCAL ADJUSTMENT SLIDERS

The graduated filter, radial filter, and local adjustment brush masks apply a common set of adjustments (see **Figure 4–81**). These are a subset of the main controls found on the Basic panel and other Develop panels. The local adjustments with the same names as on the global panels are Temp, Tint, Exposure, Contrast, Highlights, Shadows, Clarity, Saturation, Sharpness, and Noise. (To review how these work, see those sections earlier in this chapter.) Although the way these settings affect the image is generally the same with global and local adjustments, most of the local controls are applied at lower strengths than their equivalent global panel sliders, so you can gradually build up their effects. The local adjustments also provide three additional controls: Moiré, Defringe, and Color.

Figure 4-81

You can use any combination of adjustments on any mask. You can adjust settings before or after creating the mask. The adjustments all default to 0 so they can be adjusted up or down. To reset any slider double-click its name.

You can apply local noise reduction (NR) using graduated filters, radial filters, and brushes. Local NR is somewhat unique among the sliders; it increases or decreases the amount of global NR applied in the Detail panel. Also, it's Luminance NR only; color noise is not affected. Applying local NR is especially useful in areas of the photo where you've applied heavy adjustments to Shadows. Defringe works in a similar fashion in that it applies the Defringe settings you configured in the Color tab of the Lens Corrections panel as I mentioned in the section on that panel.

Settings for New mask or currently selected mask

Note the darkened background around the sliders (see Figure 4–81). This indicates there is no adjustment mask currently selected. If you change settings with no mask active, these settings will be used for any new masks, until you change them again with the mask selected. Each new mask you apply with either tool will use these settings as the starting point. When a mask is selected, you can adjust its settings, in which case the changes apply only to that mask and the background becomes lighter (see **Figure 4–82**).

Moiré

A moiré pattern is an optical effect that happens when patterns overlap, creating interference. You may have seen moiré on the nightly TV news, when the anchor is wearing a blazer with a pattern that seems to ripple, creating concentric rings in a wave-like effect. In a digital capture, moiré occurs when a high-

Figure 4-82

frequency pattern interferes with the pixel grid of the digital image. It shows in a photo as a ringed, rainbow effect and, though it may sound pretty, it's usually quite undesirable. Moiré is often found on photos from cameras without antialiasing filters.

Using the Moiré removal tool, you can paint away the moiré effect. The tool searches the area around the mask for a suitable replacement color, which can include non-contiguous mask areas to find the best match. The slider sets the limit for the distance to search for the replacement color. Using higher amounts for the Moiré slider can produce more pleasing results, but can take a toll on performance, since Lightroom has to sample many pixels to calculate the ideal color to paint with. The Moiré setting is specific to the local adjustments; there is no global equivalent. Erasing from the Moiré mask to carefully control its effect usually creates the best results.

04

Color

You can apply a color to the graduated filter or adjustment brush. For dodging and burning, a little color helps blend the adjustments into the image and makes them appear more natural and realistic. For a big shift in color try setting Saturation to -100 and then choose a highly saturated color to take its place. Note that since the luminance value is preserved you cannot paint white or black, you can only apply a tint to the grayscale pixels after saturation is reduced. (It's not possible to apply local adjustments using a fully opaque, solid color.)

By default, when you apply any of the local adjustments, the color swatch is neutral gray with an X through it (see **Figure 4–83**). To apply a color tint to the adjustment, click the color swatch to open the color picker.

USING THE COLOR PICKER

Figure 4-83

The color picker is used in many panels in modules throughout Lightroom (see **Figure 4–84**). (In particular, the color picker is used extensively in the output modules.) Regardless of where you access the color picker, it functions essentially the same everywhere. Also, using keyboard shortcuts, it's possible to switch between some modules and panels while leaving the color picker open.

Figure 4-84

To choose a color, click in the spectrum, click a swatch, or enter numeric values. When you're done making changes in the color picker, click the X in the upper left corner of the picker or simply press Return/Enter. If you want to cancel any changes you just made in the color picker (except for changing swatches) press Esc.

Note: Many of the figures and descriptions in the following section apply to the color pickers in the output modules, since they have more options. The color picker in the Develop module has fewer controls but essentially works the same way.

Sample a color from anywhere on the screen

From within the color palette, click down with your mouse button, and while holding down, drag the eyedropper anywhere on your screen to sample a color (see **Figure 4–85**). This is very useful for precisely matching colors from any other items visible on your monitor, such as an existing website, logo art, etc.

Figure 4-85

Color swatches

While you're picking colors, notice the small color swatch at the top right of the color picker (see **Figure 4–86**). It constantly updates to show you the currently selected color. Next to it is the previous color; you can click it to reset the color picker to the previous color. To the left of the current and previous color

Figure 4-86

swatches are five additional swatches where you can store colors for later use. These five swatches are shared between all the modules. Click on a swatch to load it as the current color. To save a color swatch, first set the color that you want to save. Then simply click and hold on a swatch to set it to the current color. Setting swatches cannot be undone, so be careful about overwriting swatches you've previously saved, especially if you set those swatches using another module.

Numeric values

Along the bottom of the color picker are readouts of numeric values for the current color (see **Figure 4–87**). The values displayed will change depending on the module you're working in. The default readouts are HSL (Hue, Saturation, and Lightness) and RGB (Red, Green, and Blue). If you have the numeric values

Figure 4-87

for a color you're trying to precisely match, you can double-click to manually enter the numbers, or drag the scrubby sliders right and left to change the values.

Switching between color and grayscale in the output module color picker

In some instances of the color picker, such as the output modules, the color picker layout is a bit different. If the color currently selected is a shade of gray, white, or black, and you want to pick a color, you first need to click somewhere in the vertical saturation slider (called the *elevator*) at the right side of the color picker (see **Figure 4–88**). Then you'll see a full-color spectrum. Click inside the spectrum to choose the hue range you want, then use the saturation elevator to increase or decrease saturation. To change from color to grayscale, drag the elevator all the way down to the bottom. Then you can choose a luminance level from within the gray spectrum.

Hexadecimal colors

In the output module pickers, you can also view and select colors using Hexadecimal (Hex) color values. Hex colors are commonly used for web graphics because their values can be specified to conform to operating

Figure 4-88

system color palettes. Many web designers specify colors as Hex values and there are lots of online resources for color pickers in Hex and other color modes (Adobe's very useful Kuler application, for example). To switch between Hex and RGB values click each respective text button in the palette (see Figure 4–88).

LOCAL ADJUSTMENT OVERLAYS

All the tools in the strip—Crop, Spot Removal, Red-Eye, Graduated Filter, Radial Filter, and Adjustment Brushes—provide a tool overlay when activated. The tool overlays provide controls for manipulating each instance of the tool application or deleting it. The overlays can also be hidden or shown while the tool is active by pressing the H key.

The graduated filters, radial filters, and adjustment brush overlays provide a node pin, used for selecting each individual instance of the tool within the overlay. Graduated filter and radial filter pins can be used to move the mask to a different place in the photo (see **Figure 4–89**). Adjustment brushes have node pins too, but they can't be moved. You can hover your cursor over the brush pin to see the mask, or click and drag your cursor over the node pin to increase or decrease the intensity of the adjustments (see **Figure 4–90**).

Figure 4-89

Figure 4-90

The Toolbar provides a menu for controlling how node pins are displayed, and in the case of adjustment brushes, the visibility of the mask overlay (see **Figure 4–91**).

Show Edit Pins : Always ⬍   ✓ **Show Selected Mask Overlay**   Done

⮕ **Easy duplication of local adjustment pins**

Figure 4-91

You can easily duplicate pins to compound adjustments or perform other creative adjustments. Hold ⌘+Option or Ctrl+Alt and click the adjustment pin you want to duplicate. With Graduated and Radial Filters it helps to make it a click and (slight) drag to position the duplicate pin slightly off of the original pin, which makes it easier to select either pin for modification. With the Adjustment Brush, since you can't reposition a pin you can only click to duplicate it in place (great for compounding effects).

HIDING AND SHOWING LOCAL ADJUSTMENTS

Use the switch at the bottom left of the panel (see **Figure 4–92**) to temporarily disable and re-enable the adjustment from the active local adjustment tool.

Figure 4-92

Working with Graduated Filters

On a camera lens, a graduated neutral density (ND) filter (or split ND) reduces the amount of light entering part of the lens. Graduated filters are normally used to balance the exposure between bright highlights and dark shadows; the most common use is balancing a bright sky with a darker foreground. Similarly, Lightroom's Graduated Filter tool simulates the effect of a split neutral density filter and allows you to apply local adjustments in a smooth, gradual transition. The graduated filter tool is accessed from the Tool Strip (see **Figure 4–93**).

Figure 4-93

The graduated filter creates linear gradients that are applied in a straight line between two points: start and end. The graduated filter smoothly transitions from full effect to no effect (see **Figure 4–94**). Put another way, the strength of the adjustment at the start of the gradient is 100%, and at the end is 0%. The transition between the start and end is always soft, and its strength is determined by the distance between the start and end points coupled with the settings you choose.

Figure 4-94

From each end of the gradient, the strength level of the adjustment continues to all edges of the photo in both directions (see **Figure 4–95**). You can't restrict the effect of the gradient to a specific area (use a local adjustment brush for that; see the next section).

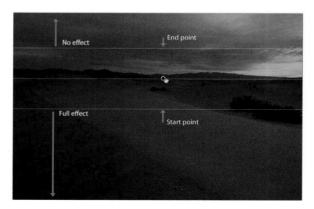

Figure 4-95

Apply a graduated filter

Following are steps to apply a new graduated filter mask; you can use multiple overlapping graduated filters (see **Figure 4–96** for a before and after view of what the Graduated Filter can do):

Step 1. Click the graduated filter tool to activate it (or use the M shortcut).

Step 2. Place your cursor at the spot where you want the gradient to start.

Step 3. Click and drag to the point where you want the gradient to end.

> **Options:** To constrain the gradient to 90 degrees, hold the shift key while dragging. To create the gradient from its center, hold Option or Alt while dragging. (You can also use this with Shift.)

Figure 4-96

Step 4. Use the sliders to set the desired adjustments to be applied by the graduated filter.

MODIFY AN EXISTING GRADUATED FILTER

Click an existing graduated filter's node pin to select it and you can change it in the following ways (see **Figure 4–97**; note that this is a composite figure—you won't see all these cursors at once).

- Click and drag the center node point to move the entire graduated filter.

- Click and drag the start or end points to reposition them.

Figure 4-97

- Click and drag the line extending from the node to rotate the graduated filter.

- Change the adjustments being applied by the active graduated filter.

DELETE A GRADUATED FILTER

If you want to completely remove a graduated filter mask, select its node pin and press Delete. This is undoable within the current session.

Working with Radial Filters

The most basic use of the Radial Filter, nestled in the Tool Strip between the Graduated Filter and the Adjustment Brush, that best illustrates its potential is the creation of highly customizable centered and off-centered vignettes (see **Figure 4-98**), but seeing that its range of settings goes way beyond just darkening edges I expect we'll see an array of creative uses of this new tool.

Figure 4-98

The Radial Filter creates circular gradients that can alternatively affect only the area within the bounding circle or only the area outside of the bounding circle, which is controlled by an Invert Mask check box at the bottom of the Radial Filter tool well (see **Figure 4-99**). The blending of the adjustment between the unaffected and affected areas around the bounding circle is controlled by the Feather slider directly above the Invert Mask check box.

Figure 4-99

 ## Apply a Radial filter

Following are steps to apply a new radial filter mask; you can use multiple overlapping radial filters and even invert them to change the area being affected by the adjustment (see **Figure 4–100**):

Step 1. Click the Radial Filter's icon or press Shift+M to activate the tool.

Step 2. Begin drawing out an ellipse anywhere in the workspace by clicking and dragging from the point you want at the center of the radial filter, or ⌘+double-click or Ctrl+double-click within the image to automatically expand the filter to cover the visible image area.

Option: Hold the Shift key while you drag out the Radial Filter to create a perfect circle.

Step 3. Use the sliders to set the desired adjustments to be applied by the filter.

Step 4. (Optional) Apply additional Radial Filter adjustments as desired.

The adjustment shown in Figure 4-100 consists of five different Radial Filters. One centrally located filter that darkens the edges of the photo as well as

Figure 4-100

decreases sharpness in that same outer area, then over each subject there are two filters that are the inverse of each other that add a slight bump in brightness and decreased clarity on the inside coupled with a slight decrease in exposure on the outside. I moved the duplicated pins slightly off each other to make them easier to see.

MODIFY AN EXISTING GRADUATED FILTER

Click an existing radial filter's node pin to select it and you can change it in the following ways:

- Click and drag the center node point to move the entire radial filter (the bounding circle can extend beyond the edge of the image).

- Click and drag any of the resize handles on the bounding circle to reposition them.

- Click and drag any point on the bounding circle (except the resize handles) to rotate the radial filter.

- Change the adjustments being applied by the active graduated filter.

04

 Duplicate existing adjustment pins

This bears repeating in the context of the Radial Filter as it can create a really powerful effect by using the Invert Mask check box to apply opposing adjustments inside and outside of the bounding circle. Hold ⌘+Option or Ctrl+Alt and click the adjustment pin you want to duplicate. With Radial Filters it helps to make it a click and (slight) drag to position the duplicate pin slightly off of the original pin, which makes it easier to select either pin for modification (and inversion).

DELETE A RADIAL FILTER

If you want to completely remove a radial filter mask, select its node pin and press Delete. This is undoable within the current session.

Figure 4-101

 You can't erase from graduated or radial filters

To remove areas of a graduated or radial filter, you can use an adjustment brush to apply opposite adjustments (see next section).

Working with adjustment brushes

Using Lightroom's local adjustment brushes, you can perform precise dodging and burning, localized sharpening, color tinting and much more. The brushes allow you to "paint" adjustments with varying opacity, feathering, and edge control. On a single photo, you can add as many instances of the brush as you like.

Activate the local adjustment brush tool by clicking it in the Tool Strip (see **Figure 4–101**), or use the shortcut K (works in Develop and Library). When the brush is active its controls are displayed in the tool drawer: the same adjustments as the graduated filter (see previous section) plus brush controls below.

With the brush active, the first thing you will likely want to do is change its size and other options. Click the black triangle button (see Figure 4–101) to adjust its settings at the bottom of the drawer. As with other settings, you can drag the sliders, enter numeric values, or use shortcuts to change the brush settings.

Figure 4-102

BRUSH: A AND B SETTINGS

You can store two brushes, each with different settings (see **Figure 4–102**). Each brush set retains the most recently used settings until you change them. I usually use A for the soft, feathered brush and B for a harder edged brush (see **Figure 4–103**). You could also use one for a large brush and the other for a small brush, one with Auto Mask on and the other off, etc.

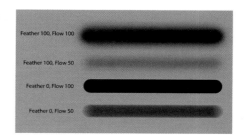

Figure 4-103

Size

Sets the size of the current brush. If you have a mouse with a wheel, you can use it to change brush size without using the slider, or the [and] keys decrease and increase the size of the brush.

Feather

Choose a soft or hard edge for the brush, or somewhere in between. With Feather at 0, you see just a single circle for the brush cursor. Higher amounts of Feather show two circles on the brush, indicating the range of the feathering. Similar to the start/end on the Graduated Filter, the inner brush circle is 100% (full effect) and the outer edge is 0% (no effect). Hold the Shift key while pressing [or] (or rotating the wheel on your mouse) to decrease or increase the feather amount.

Flow

Flow controls how fast the "paint" is applied while clicking and dragging the cursor over the preview. Higher values apply the effect faster. You can "build up" an application of the adjustment brush by using a lesser Flow and gradually painting over the area again and again.

AUTO MASK

When the Auto Mask box is checked, Lightroom will try to find edges in the photo and restrict the edge of the painted mask to those edges (see **Figure 4–104**). Auto Mask can be useful if you need the adjustment to be applied within a specific area, such as whitening teeth in a smile. It works OK, some of the time. For most local adjustments, you'll have much better results (and responsiveness from the tool) if you leave Auto Mask disabled.

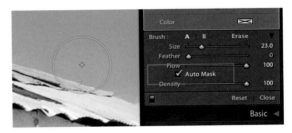

Figure 4-104

 Usually leave Auto Mask off

For general dodging and burning, you should usually leave Auto Mask off. For one thing, dodge and burn effects typically look more natural if they are soft and feathered, rather than hard edged. Also, leaving Auto Mask on, especially when painting over large areas, can significantly degrade performance. If you need very precise masking, you're better off using Photoshop.

DENSITY

This slider sets the opacity (or alternatively, the transparency) for the current mask, and thus effectively limits how strongly the adjustment settings are applied to the masked area. Values less than 100 will result in a corresponding decrease in the strength of any slider active for that particular mask.

ERASE

You can refine brush masks by erasing from them. Like the A and B brushes, the eraser has its own settings. To erase from a mask, first click its node point to activate it. Show the overlay, too—this makes erasing lots easier. Make sure the eraser is active and set the eraser brush settings as necessary (size, feather, etc.) Paint to erase from the selected mask (see **Figure 4–105**). While on the A or B brush, you can hold Option or Alt to temporarily toggle to Erase mode.

Erase with Auto Mask

If brushing with Auto Mask enabled is not working well (spilling into unwanted areas) you can try applying the adjustment over the entire area with Auto Mask unchecked, and then select the Erase mode with Auto Mask checked and try erasing on just the area you don't want affected by the adjustment and to see if Auto Mask does a better job that way.

Figure 4-105

APPLY A LOCAL ADJUSTMENT BRUSH

Using your mouse, click and drag to paint over areas of the image you want to adjust. (Using a tablet and stylus is much easier and produces better results.) As you paint, the mask is applied to the image and the current adjustment settings are applied within the mask. You can set the adjustments before and/or after you paint the mask, but each individual mask uses only one set of adjustments.

The mask node pin is placed where you first started painting. You can see how many brush masks are applied by how many node pins there are in the preview (see **Figure 4–106**).

When you're done, press Enter or Return to apply the current mask, which also makes the panel ready to create a New brush mask. You can create additional masks, and modify or delete existing masks. Make new masks wherever you want different adjustments—each mask can have its own settings.

Figure 4-106

Paint in a straight line
Hold Shift while painting to constrain the brush stroke to a straight vertical or horizontal line. This comes in handy when a graduated filter doesn't properly cover the desired area. A very wide brush with a high feather amount, applied in a straight line, essentially makes a gradient that fades out equally in both directions (see Figure 4–103).

Showing the mask overlay
Hover your cursor over a node pin to temporarily show the mask overlay (see Figure 4–105). To select a brush mask, click its node pin. A solid black center indicates a brush mask node is active; only one can be active at any given time (and it's possible that none are selected). Press O to turn the mask on (or use the control on the Toolbar) or off, and press Shift+O to cycle through the four color options.

 Missing adjustment pins
If you find that your adjustment pins seem to have gone missing it is most likely that you inadvertently hit the H key, which hides and shows the pins. You can also control pin visibility from the Toolbar.

Applying adjustments with the masks
With one mask, the adjustment can be applied in multiple places anywhere in the photo; the painted areas don't need to be connected. Also, a single mask can be created by painting with different brush settings, so some areas of a mask can apply stronger adjustments than others.

To increase or decrease the values of all the adjustments at once, click and drag left/right over the node pin. All adjustments for that mask will be increased or decreased simultaneously, relative to their starting values.

DELETING AN ADJUSTMENT BRUSH
To completely remove a brush adjustment, select its node pin and press Delete.

 Limit the number of brush masks
… but use as many as necessary for the work you need to do. Just as with global adjustments, you should be economical with your application of localized adjustments. For example, if you want to dodge multiple areas of the photo using the same adjustment, use just one mask for all the areas, rather than separate masks for each of them. For dodging and burning, you will need at least two separate masks (one for each).

MODIFYING AND RESETTING LOCAL ADJUSTMENTS
Click the Reset button near the bottom right of the panel (see **Figure 4–107**) to remove all adjustments from the active tool. There are separate Reset buttons each local adjustment tool.

Figure 4-107

APPLY LOCAL ADJUSTMENTS AND DEACTIVATE THE TOOLS

To close the local adjustment panel and turn off the selected tool, click the tool in the Toolstrip or the Close button at the bottom right of the panel, or use the shortcuts. The effects applied by the adjustments remain visible, but the tool overlays and sliders are hidden. You can return to adjust them at any time.

Navigator panel

The Navigator is in the first position of the left panel group in Develop module. As also explained in Chapters 1 and 2, the Navigator panel provides controls for zooming in and out of the main preview, as well as an additional preview. The Navigator shows a preview of the selected photo, or the target photo if multiple photos are selected. The Navigator panel can be used to select zoom ratios, or levels of magnification. Selecting a zoom level in the Navigator enlarges the main preview to that size; as you use other methods to zoom in and out of previews, note the selected zoom ratio displayed on the Navigator.

ZOOM RATIOS

The available zoom levels are:

- **Fit:** Fits the entire photo into the preview area.

- **Fill:** Fills the preview area top-to-bottom with the image. The sides of the photo may not be visible.

- **1:1:** Maps one image pixel to one screen pixel.

- **User-selected setting:** The fourth zoom ratio uses the most recent custom zoom ratio you selected. Clicking this opens a pop-up menu for you to choose the custom zoom ratio.

You'll most often use the Navigator panel to set the user zoom level, rather than actually zooming in and out using these controls (there are better ways). Zooming in and out of previews is discussed in Chapter 3 in the section on using the Loupe view mode.

Move around an enlarged preview with the Navigator.

When zoomed in to a photo, drag the white box in the Navigator preview to change the area shown in the main preview.

Presets: Apply multiple Develop adjustments with one click

The Presets panel lists all the presets currently installed with your copy of Lightroom (see **Figure 4–108**). A Develop preset stores absolute Develop adjustment values. It's a simple text file, containing Develop module settings, saved in the Lightroom configuration files on your hard disk. Develop presets are read in by Lightroom when the application starts. Since each preset is just a standalone text file, presets can be imported, exported, and shared using several methods.

Presets are organized into folder hierarchies (see Figure 4–108). This makes it much easier to navigate the panel and find what you're looking for. You can create your own folders using unique names.

A Develop preset can contain one, many, or all of the Develop settings active at the time it's created. Lightroom comes with many default presets installed and you can create your own at any time. Before you save your own Develop presets, you will probably want to process a few photos and note the common settings you frequently apply to help determine the adjustments to include. Or,

Figure 4-108

if you create a "happy accident," you can save the settings as a preset to quickly retrieve later. You can also install presets made by other people; there are many resources on the web where photographers share presets. (See the Appendix for links.)

Develop presets have another useful function: transferring Develop settings to videos. This is discussed in Chapter 3.

When you find that you are repeatedly applying the same settings to many photos, you should consider saving a Develop preset with those settings. For example, you can save a preset for your preferred sharpening settings, or one for custom Contrast and Highlights adjustments. Or one that applies a point curve. Or, modify all the settings at one time. (In general, it's usually most convenient to save presets with fewer settings, rather than more, but there are exceptions.)

Preview presets in Navigator

In Develop, the Navigator also shows previews of presets. Just hover your cursor over the presets in the list, and Navigator will show you what that preset looks like applied to the selected image. This is an easy way to preview presets without actually needing to apply them (see **Figure 4–109**).

Preset compatibility

If you've used Lightroom 3 or earlier, you need to pay attention when applying presets. It's possible (even likely) that you'll have presets installed from different process versions. Remember that when a preset is saved it can include all the settings in place at the time it's made; this can include the Process Version setting. If you've developed your photos in one process version, then apply a preset using a different process version, your adjustments will change, as will the available controls.

Maybe more importantly, even if the preset you apply does not contain the value for Process Version, it may still contain values

Figure 4-109

for controls from the other process version. As explained earlier in this chapter, some of the controls map quite well to the different process version, others not as much.

Just understand that when you're using different versions of software with presets made at different points in time, applying these presets may produce unexpected results. But if you're careful and observant, this shouldn't pose a real problem.

Migrating presets between process versions

Since the controls offered by each process version are different, it's not likely that you can directly upgrade a preset from one process version to another. Your best option is to apply the preset to a sample photo, refine the adjustments, and then create a new preset.

CREATING A NEW PRESET

To make your own Develop preset, first make sure the active photo has the exact adjustment settings that you want to store. Then click the + button on the Presets panel header (see **Figure 4–110**). A dialog box opens asking you to select the settings that you want to save into the preset (see **Figure 4–111**). The Develop settings shown are very similar to those in Copy/Paste and Sync dialogs.

This choice is important. Remember that Develop settings are absolute. Thus, a preset that contains a value for a given adjustment will override the current setting when the preset is applied. Any adjustment that isn't included in the preset will not be changed when the preset is applied.

For example, if you have a photo with a Contrast setting of +25 and you apply a preset that contains a Contrast setting of +35, the resulting value will be +35 (not +60). But if you apply a preset that doesn't contain a setting for Contrast, it will remain +25, regardless of the other adjustments that are changed.

Since each adjustment checked in the dialog box will be saved into the preset using the current value, you should carefully consider which settings to include, and in most cases, it's best to include as few adjustments as possible within each individual preset so you can apply them progressively.

Figure 4-110

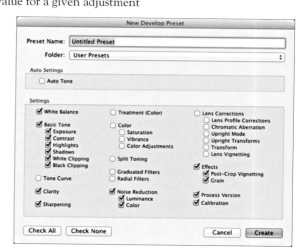

Figure 4-111

Eventually, you'll probably make some presets with lots of settings included, and others that include only a single adjustment. It all depends on the purpose of the preset.

Give your presets meaningful names
Name your presets according to their settings or purpose, for example, "Sharpen–Scenic."

APPLYING PRESETS TO PHOTOS

There are many places in Lightroom where you can apply Develop presets. You can apply multiple presets, one after another, in any order. Just remember that preset values are absolute; if two consecutive applied presets both contain a value for the same adjustment, the latter will override the former.

Develop Presets panel

Click a preset in the list to apply it to the active photo (if you have Auto Sync enabled you can apply a preset to all selected files in the Filmstrip at once). The name of the preset remains highlighted to indicate the current settings exactly match the settings contained in that preset. If you change any settings, the preset is no longer highlighted in the list. You can Undo the application of a Develop preset.

 See what preset you applied
If you need to find out which preset(s) you've applied to a photo, look in the History panel.

Contextual menu

Right-click or Ctrl+click on a photo; you can apply presets using the Settings menu at the top of the pop-up menu (see **Figure 4–112**).

In Library Quick Develop

You can access the same list of presets contained in the Develop Presets panel from the Presets menu in Quick Develop.

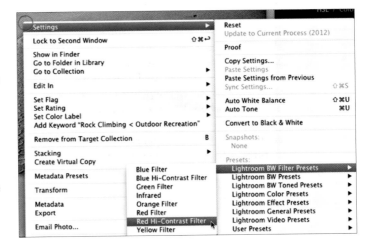

Figure 4-112

During Import

After you've worked with Lightroom a while you will begin to identify settings that you frequently apply as a basis for your starting point in processing. During future imports, apply the preset to photos in the Import window. Your images will come into the catalog looking much closer to the way you like them.

Right-click or Ctrl+click on a preset and from the pop-up menu choose Apply on Import. This sets that preset as the current value in the Develop Settings menu in the Import window.

04

MANAGING DEVELOP PRESETS WITH THE PRESET PANEL

You can update the settings contained in a preset or remove it from the list entirely. Right-click or Ctrl+click on a preset or folder to open the presets contextual menu (see **Figure 4–113**). Then select an option from the menu.

Figure 4-113

Folders and hierarchies

You can organize them as you see fit; right-click or Ctrl+click to open the presets pop-up menu to create a New Folder or rename an existing folder. You can drag and drop to rearrange presets in the list. (In all cases, the default folders and presets cannot be modified.)

 Video presets

Note: Lightroom comes packaged with a set of presets designed for editing videos.

Updating Develop presets

Update with Current Settings: Replaces all the settings in the selected preset with all the current Develop settings you choose. To update a preset's settings, apply it to a photo and then adjust the settings you want to change and add any new settings you want to include. Then right-click or Ctrl+click the preset and choose Update with Current Settings from the contextual menu. This opens the Update Develop Preset dialog box where you need to check all of the settings you want to include in this preset (even settings you did not just update). Make your selections carefully to avoid inadvertently including a setting you did not intend or omitting a setting you want to remain. Then click the Update button. The updated preset will only include the current settings for the boxes you checked.

 Restore default presets

In Preferences→Presets there are buttons to restore most types of default presets. Options for restoring presets can also be found on some menus, such as local adjustments.

Deleting presets

Delete or Delete Folder: Immediately removes the preset from the list and deletes it from the Lightroom presets folder. You can't delete the default Lightroom Presets.

 You'll get no confirmation when deleting presets and preset folders

Be forewarned that when you select Delete or Delete Folder from the presets contextual menu you will not get a confirmation dialog—the preset files will be deleted from disk immediately. They do not go to the trash or recycle bin! (Deleting presets or preset folders is undoable within the current program session, but if you quit Lightroom, those deleted presets will be gone forever.)

Find the presets folder on your hard disk

To show the Lightroom presets folder in Finder or Explorer, go to Preferences→Presets→ Show Lightroom Presets Folder (see **Figure 4–114**).

Save an alias or shortcut to the Lightroom folder on your desktop
If you frequently add, remove, or otherwise maintain presets, you may want to save some shortcuts in your file system to make finding the Lightroom folders easier. This way, you can update Lightroom folder contents without needing to launch the program first. (This tip applies for all types of Lightroom presets and templates; not just Develop presets.)

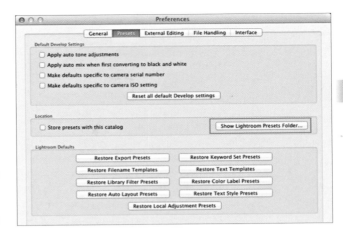

Figure 4-114

04

 See the contents of presets
You can open Lightroom presets in a text editor. This will show you how they are structured. (Just to be safe, I recommend you make a copy of any presets before you open them.)

Using downloaded presets
A good way to learn the effects of the Develop adjustments is to use presets from someone else and then evaluate the results. To use presets from an outside source, you can copy them into the respective presets folder and restart Lightroom, or use the Import command on the pop-up menu and they are added immediately. Any preset with a valid format will then appear in the list. (Note that presets made for earlier versions of Lightroom may produce unexpected results—or may not work at all—in Lightroom 5.) There are some resources for presets in the Appendix; you can also Google "Lightroom presets" for more.

Set Default
As described toward the beginning of this chapter, in addition to presets, you can also use your own Default Settings. Lightroom uses the Adobe Default Settings until you override them. When you do this, your own settings will then be applied to all new raw photos from that camera model added to the catalog. Files already in the catalog won't be affected. If you apply adjustments using presets during import, Lightroom will use those settings on top of the Defaults.

Multiple defaults based on camera EXIF
When you make your own Default Settings, they are specific to each camera model, so you can actually have multiple defaults. (The Adobe Default Settings are the same for all cameras.) You'll need to work with your photos for a while to determine which Develop settings provide the best rendering for photos from each camera. You'll need to have a photo loaded in Develop that contains the settings you want to use for your new Default.

04

Before you change the default, first make sure all the Develop settings are the way you want them—all the settings will be used. (Unlike presets, you can't choose which settings are included.) If you have multiple cameras, you might want to set a new default using a photo from each of them.

How to set the new default

Hold down the Option or Alt key; this changes the Reset button on the bottom right panel to say "Set Default…" (see **Figure 4–115**). Click the button to set the default. Or, select the menu option Develop→Set Default Settings. In the dialog box, choose Update to Current Settings (see **Figure 4–116**). You'll see a message stating that the changes are not undoable; this means just what it says—you won't be able to use Undo to reverse your action here. However, you could always just resave a new default, or revert back to the Adobe defaults. And remember, your existing photos already in the catalog will not be affected by this choice.

Figure 4-115

Figure 4-116

Applying your new Defaults

Going forward, if you don't apply a Develop preset during import, your Default settings will be used for all new photos as they are added to the catalog. Also, when you click the Reset button or reset individual panel adjustments, your Defaults will be applied.

 Default settings by camera or by camera and ISO

When you set a Default, you can use different settings based on camera, serial number, and even ISO in Lightroom preferences (see **Figure 4–117**). This way, you can use a wide range of defaults without needing to apply different presets to every photo from different cameras or

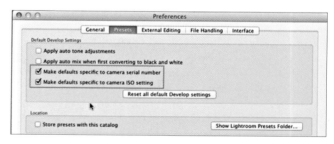

Figure 4-117

ISO settings. For example, this is especially useful when you want to create additional Defaults for a camera with its low-pass filter removed or to automatically handle noise reduction at high ISOs.

Snapshots

Unlike presets, Lightroom snapshots always include all the settings in effect when the snapshot is made—you don't have the option to choose what settings are saved into the snapshot. Snapshots are useful for saving various states of history for a single photo. Use snapshots when you want to store all the photo's current settings to retrieve later; they are stored in the Snapshots panel (see **Figure 4–118**). Click the + button at the right of the panel header to create a new snapshot. When you save a new snapshot, it's given a default name using the date and time. **Snapshots can be stored in a photo's XMP metadata (unlike virtual copies).**

Figure 4-118

 The on/off state of panels is included in Snapshots
If you have panels turned on or off using the switch in the panel header, that condition is also stored in the Snapshot.

Snapshots versus virtual copies
If you want to make different versions of a photo, use virtual copies (VCs) instead of Snapshots. One major advantage of virtual copies is that you can view multiple variations all at once; this is not the case with Snapshots, which you can only view one at a time. VCs are discussed later in this chapter.

RESETTING ADJUSTMENTS

There will be times when you want to reset one or more adjustments from photos. Resetting restores the default settings. There are several options for resetting some or all adjustments applied to a photo:

- Reset a single adjustment slider by double-clicking its name or the slider's handle;

- Reset a group of sliders in a panel by double-clicking the name of the group; or

Figure 4-119

- Reset all adjustments on a photo with the Reset button on the bottom of the right panel group (see **Figure 4–119**). Click the button to reset the photo to the Default settings.

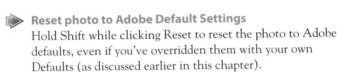 **Reset photo to Adobe Default Settings**
Hold Shift while clicking Reset to reset the photo to Adobe defaults, even if you've overridden them with your own Defaults (as discussed earlier in this chapter).

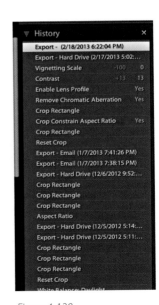

 **Resetting is undoable**
Like most everything else in Lightroom, if you Reset a photo and then change your mind, simply Undo it (⌘+Z or Ctrl+Z).

History: Track changes and go back to any point

Everything you do to a photo in Develop is tracked in the History panel (see **Figure 4–120**). This is one of the great benefits of using the Lightroom catalog to manage your photos. You can go back to any point in time, unless you clear

Figure 4-120

04

the history using the X button at the right of the header. (I don't recommend clearing the history. The textual data being used to store each adjustment hardly takes up any disk space at all, and removing the history does not change the settings applied to the photo—it only prevents you from stepping back through the settings.) You can hover your cursor over any history step to display a preview of that state in the Navigator.

Clicking any step in the History panel will return the image to that state. History is linear, however: if you make further adjustments after going back to that state, all the steps that were after it will be lost. History is most useful for recovering from mistakes or changing your mind. If you want to go back and forth, that's where Snapshots come in. **The individual historical steps in a photo's History cannot be written to its XMP metadata** (only the current settings can be written to its XMP metadata).

Collections

The Collections panel in the Develop module is identical to the panel in the other modules. For more information about Collections, read Chapter 3.

Virtual copies: Create multiple versions of a single photo

While processing your files in Lightroom, you can generate multiple instances of a file in the catalog from a single, original file on disk. This is done using virtual copies (VCs).

A VC is simply an additional set of processing instructions that references the original file on disk. Lightroom can create as many additional sets of processing instructions (or VCs) as your workflow requires. A VC is indicated by a turned-corner icon on the thumbnail (see **Figure 4–121**). VCs exist only within the catalog, but in terms of adjustments, they are treated exactly like originals.

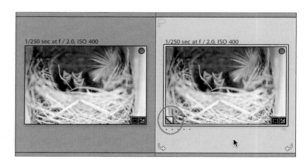

Figure 4-121

CREATING A VIRTUAL COPY

To make a VC , right-click or Ctrl+click on a photo or video, and from the pop-up menu select Create Virtual Copy, or use the ⌘+' or Ctrl+' shortcut. When you make a VC, the current settings on the photo being copied (whether an original or another VC) are used as the base settings for the copy. But this is where the direct connection between settings ends; **further modifying the original will not affect the copy/copies, or vice versa.** (However, you can sync the settings from a copy back to the original.) Resetting a VC will revert its settings back to the default settings. By default, a VC copy is stacked with its original.

You can also make a VC of a VC. With this method, virtual copies can be used to progressively process an image in a variety of ways, producing multiple versions that can then be compared to determine the best one or used for different kinds of output.

Name the VC and find the original
In Library's Metadata panel is a special field, Copy Name, where you can give a VC a unique name. Also, next to that is an action button which, when clicked, will locate and select the original from which the VC was made. See Chapter 3 for more on the Metadata panel and working with VCs in Library.

WORKING WITH VIRTUAL COPIES

VCs can be useful in a number of ways. For example, you could try different crops and compare them side-by-side. Or develop an image in both color and black and white. If you're not sure where you want to go in processing a photo, you might want to work on a VC first, then later sync the settings from the VC to back to the original. There are also some interesting and practical uses for VCs when working in the output modules... the possibilities are virtually endless!

Using VCs with Library View Modes
Use Compare and Survey view modes in Library to evaluate many variations on a photo. This is a much easier and more powerful technique than using Snapshots. You can compare different crops, process versions, special effects, etc., all on one screen.

Transferring Settings from VCs to Master Photos
If you've made a virtual copy and processed it to perfection, you might want to apply those settings back to the original photo. You can do this using the Sync or Copy/Paste functions, covered in the next section.

Set Copy as Master
This command, under the Photo menu in the Library module, changes the virtual copy to become the Master in the catalog and vice versa. To understand how this is possible, remember that everything in the catalog is just a database entry, referencing an original file on the hard disk. Whether something appears as a Master or a VC is simply a matter of changing the marker used to identify the record in the catalog. This might be useful if you want to keep the settings in the VC, but no longer have a need for the settings applied to the Master. Once the VC has been made the new Master, the original Master becomes a VC and can be removed.

 Deleting originals also deletes VCs
Virtual copies exist only in the Lightroom database. If the original file on disk is removed from Lightroom its VCs will also be removed.

Apply settings from one photo to others

Lightroom—a batch processing application at heart—allows you to very easily apply Develop adjustment settings to many photos at one time using a variety of methods. Any Develop setting on one photo can also be applied to other photos; for example, you could replicate your application of Spot Removal or dodging and burning to multiple images.

 Select photos from the Filmstrip or collections
While working in Develop, you don't need to go back to Library to load different images.

04

COPY/PASTE

You can copy and paste Develop adjustment settings from one photo to another. To copy the settings from the active photo, use the command under the Settings menu (see **Figure 4–122**) or the shortcut. A dialog box will be presented for you to choose which settings are being copied (see **Figure 4–123**). Make your selections then click the Copy button.

To paste the copied settings to other photos, select them, and then use the Paste Settings command or shortcut. When you paste, all settings you chose in the copy dialog will be pasted to the selected photo(s).

Figure 4-122

Paste from Previous

This command, also under the Settings menu, will instantly copy and paste all the settings from the previously selected photo to any selected photos.

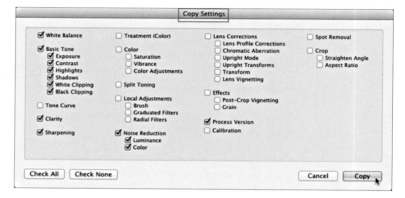

SYNC SETTINGS

Figure 4-123

You can synchronize Develop settings between multiple files in Lightroom. This produces the same results as Copy/Paste—the settings from the active photo will be applied to the other selected photos. It's just another way of applying one batch of settings to multiple photos. You can also sync settings from a VC back to the original. (**Note:** I prefer Sync Settings over Copy/Paste and use it in the vast majority of cases where I need to transfer settings.)

With multiple photos selected (pay attention to which is the target photo), click the Sync… button on the right panel group, or use the shortcut. A window appears allowing you to choose what settings to sync (see **Figure 4–124**).

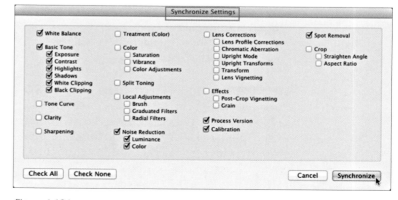

Figure 4-124

 **Sync white balance**

One very useful application of Sync Settings is adjusting white balance. To accurately set white balance for a batch of photos, begin a photo shoot by making an initial capture containing a target reference, such as the X-Rite Passport. In Lightroom, use the reference shot to set the white balance with the eyedropper. Then simply use Sync Settings on the rest of the files to match the white balance from the reference image.

 Copy/paste vs. Sync

The end result of copying/pasting settings and syncing settings is the same. However, when you copy settings, they remain in memory and thus can be pasted to other photos later regardless of what source you might be working from. A sync operation does not store the synced settings anywhere.

AUTO SYNC

Next to the Sync button at the bottom of the right panel group is a switch that toggles between Sync and Auto Sync (see **Figure 4–125**). When active, Auto Sync continually applies any adjustments made to the active image to all the other selected images. When you're finished using Auto Sync, click the switch to turn off Auto Sync and return to the standard Sync button.

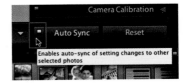

Figure 4-125

 Use Auto Sync when working with video

As described in Chapter 3, you can use Auto Sync when you're developing a proxy JPEG selected with its master video.

MATCH TOTAL EXPOSURES

Use this command to even out the tones for photos that have different exposures. This is useful in a situation where perhaps the light levels fluctuated during a shoot and you want to balance out the exposure between all of the photos in that series. Start by selecting the photo that you believe has the best looking exposure (confirm via the histogram), and then select the rest of the photos in that series and select Match Total Exposures from under the Settings menu. The Match Total Exposures command will balance (not copy) the exposure settings for each photo (exposure setting only) by analyzing the settings used by the camera for each individual photo and factoring in the settings in the active photo (most selected) you designated to come up with an adjustment for each photo.

Soft proofing

Soft proofing is a special preview mode and supporting function that allows you to simulate what a photo will look like when it's output to a specific device. The most common application is printing—you can simulate the printed output on your monitor. (Hence the term *soft proof*, as opposed to a *hard proof*.) You can also use soft proofing for checking photos you're planning to upload to the web or present using a projector.

If you've ever made prints of your photos, or uploaded photos to a website and seen them on someone else's computer, you're well aware of how colors and tonal values can shift. For all these situations, Lightroom's soft proofing allows you to see ahead of time how a photo will look under the specified output conditions and then make any necessary adjustments.

What to do before soft proofing

Before soft proofing a photo, you should have already completed all your Develop work to produce the finished Master file. The Master file contains your final edits, based on how you want the photo to look, and should always remain output-neutral. In other words, the processing applied to your Master file is never dependent on any specific output condition. You'll use soft proofing and virtual copies, as necessary, to create multiple versions of the file, each tailored for a particular output destination.

 Calibrate and profile your display

Soft proofing is useless if you can't trust what you see on your display. It's essential to calibrate your monitor using a hardware system (such as the X-Rite ColorMunki Display and i1 Display Pro) to get the benefits of soft proofing. See the Appendix for recommended color management links.

About printer profiles

Soft proofing uses profiles to simulate the output of different devices. In order to soft proof for printing, you'll first need to have the appropriate profiles installed on your computer. If you're working with a lab, ask them to provide (or recommend) the profiles to use. If you're making your own prints, use the correct profile for your printer and paper combination. You can learn more about printing in Chapter 9.

Soft proofing a photo

Following are the basic steps you'll use to soft proof your photos. This same method can be used to soft proof for any output condition.

Step 1. In the Develop Toolbar, check the box or press S to enable Soft Proofing (see **Figure 4–126**). The preview area background changes to show "paper white," and in

Figure 4-126

the top right corner, Proof Preview is displayed. At any time, you can uncheck the box in the Toolbar or press S again to turn off soft proofing.

Step 2. At the top of the right panel set, the Histogram panel changes to Soft Proofing (see **Figure 4–127**). If the panel is not expanded, it will show the name of the profile being used for proofing. Click the panel header to open it.

Step 3. In the bottom half of the panel, open the Profile menu and select a profile to use for soft proofing (see **Figure 4–128**). sRGB

Figure 4-127

and Adobe RGB are included by default; you can add more profiles to the list later.

Step 4. Use the Intent text buttons to choose Perceptual or Relative (see **Figure 4–129**).

Step 5. Use Before/After to see what your original Master photo looks like compared to the proofed output. On the Toolbar, click the button to enable Before/After (see **Figure 4–130**).

Step 6. (Optional) Usually, the goal is to get the soft proof to match as closely as possible to the unproofed Master. To do this, you can use any of the Develop adjustments; typically you should only need a couple of simple adjustments in the Basic panel. When you first make adjustments, Lightroom will ask if you want to use a virtual copy. More on this is covered below.

Narrow versus wide gamut output

When you're soft proofing, it's important to remember that output devices have varying ability to reproduce specific colors. For example, a print made on a professional inkjet printer using high quality paper can reproduce color much better than lower-grade equipment and materials. You will see the difference when soft proofing.

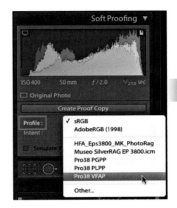

Figure 4-128

Figure 4-129

Figure 4-130

SOFT PROOFING PANEL

When Soft Proofing is enabled, the following controls are available (see **Figure 4–131**). When you're not working with a proof copy, all the controls are global view settings—you can soft proof any of the photos in your catalog and the settings for the photos aren't changed.

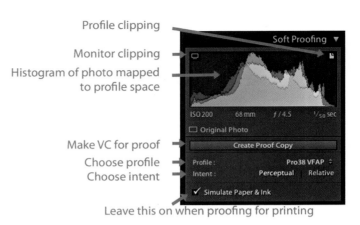

Profile clipping
Monitor clipping
Histogram of photo mapped to profile space

Make VC for proof
Choose profile
Choose intent

Leave this on when proofing for printing

Figure 4-131

Histogram

The histogram shows the tonal values for the image using the selected profile (see Figure 4–131).

RGB values

As you move your cursor over the preview, the numeric values below the histogram show the proofed values in the destination color space (see **Figure 4–132**). The RGB values are shown in the 0-255 level format, which is especially useful when proofing files for the web.

Gamut Warnings

At the top left of the histogram is a button to enable the monitor gamut warning. When enabled, the main preview highlights in blue those areas with color values outside the range of colors that your monitor can display. At the upper right is a button to enable a gamut warning for the destination profile (see Figure 4–131), which is overlaid on the main preview in magenta; use this to see where colors are present in the photo that the target output profile has trouble reproducing (see Figure 4–132). The usefulness of this overlay is somewhat limited, though, because it doesn't differentiate between colors that are far out of gamut and those that are just barely out of gamut. Use it only as a general reference.

Figure 4-132

Create Proof Copy

When you're not already working with a proof copy (a virtual copy of your master file, explained further below), you can click this button to create one.

Profile

From this menu, choose the profile to use for the soft proof. If the profile you want to use isn't listed, go to the bottom of the list and select Other. A dialog box opens, showing a list of all the profiles on your computer (see **Figure 4–133**). This list is shared with the Print module. Check the boxes to add your desired profiles to Lightroom.

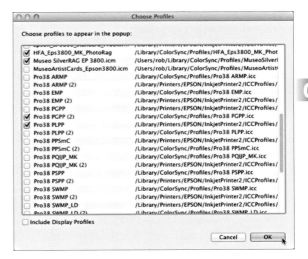

 RGB profiles only
Lightroom cannot load CMYK or grayscale profiles.

Figure 4-133

Intent

These two buttons switch between the two available rendering intents. You can toggle them back and forth to see which you like better. For most photos, Perceptual might provide the most predictable results; it adjusts the colors to preserve their relationships. However, I almost always use Relative, which is numerically more accurate. (Rendering intents are discussed in detail in Chapter 9). When you're using a profile for an RGB working space, such as Adobe RGB, sRGB, ProPhoto, ColorMatch, etc., it doesn't matter which intent you choose. These profiles only contain one rendering intent table (Relative Colorimetric).

Simulate Paper & Ink

When a printer profile is selected, the check box at the lower left is automatically enabled to Simulate Paper & Ink (see Figure 4–131). I recommend you always leave this on; one of the main reasons to soft proof is to see how the brightest whites and darkest blacks will look on the selected paper. This can take some getting used to; just remember that a print can never show whites as bright, and blacks as dark, as your monitor can.

Proof Matte Color

By default, when you enable soft proofing, the background of the main preview area changes to show the paper white. This is derived from the printer profile. When soft proofing for print, this is ideal, but if you're proofing for screen output such as web or projection, you might want to change the background color. Right-click or Ctrl+click on the background and choose a different color from the pop-up menu (see **Figure 4–134**).

Figure 4-134

PREVIEW OPTIONS

When using Soft Proofing there are several ways you can change the previews to help you evaluate color in your photos.

Zoom out and use Lights Out

You can use the zoom levels of 1:8 and 1:16 to see more area around the photo. This can help evaluate the photo in better context of how it will look on the paper. Also, press the L key to toggle between Lights On and Lights Out in soft proof mode (there's no Lights Dim). This fills your screen with the Proof Matte Color.

Detail panel preview

The preview in the Detail panel also shows the soft proof at 1:1 (see **Figure 4–135**).

WORKING WITH PROOFS AND PROOF COPIES

The main advantage of soft proofing is that it allows you to make adjustments specific to the output you're targeting. You can make the adjustments on the Master photo, or use a virtual copy. (It's almost always better to use a copy, unless you're already working with a VC.) It's best to keep your original Master as it was and create copies for different outputs.

Figure 4-135

With soft proofing enabled, drag any Develop slider to make an adjustment. When you attempt to make this first adjustment, a dialog box opens asking you if you want to make a proof copy if you haven't already (see **Figure 4–136**). If you choose the option for Create Proof Copy, a new virtual copy is created and stacked with the Master. The VC is marked as a Proof and loaded in the soft proof preview. The original is deselected and remains unchanged. The VC copy name is set to the name of the profile. If you choose Make This a Proof, the Master photo will be tagged as a Proof. Selecting Undo cancels the adjustment you were making when prompted by the dialog box. You can also make any photo a Proof using the Settings→ Proof menu option.

Figure 4-136

A Proof stores the setting used for profile and rendering intent applied in Soft Proof mode. If you no longer want to store those settings, just uncheck the Proof option in the menu. The photo will no longer store the proof settings, but the most recent proof settings— along with any adjustments you made—will remain applied until you change them.

What adjustments should you make?

Depending on the profile and rendering intent you've chosen, you may need to make different Develop adjustments. Again, the goal is to get the Proof to look as close to the Master as possible. You can use any of the Develop adjustments to finalize your Proof settings, but as with all your Develop work, try to use as few adjustments as possible to get your desired result. Your typical adjustments for printing might include increases in

Exposure, Shadows, and Saturation. For some photos, using the HSL panel might help. You can also use the Quick Develop panel in Library to make relative adjustments to multiple proof copies at once.

Use ColorMatch for CMYK conversions later

If you're planning to have your photos printed in CMYK and you want to soft proof them in Lightroom, use the ColorMatch profile. It's RGB, but has colors that are much closer to CMYK than most other RGB profiles. You'll need to export the photos using ColorMatch, too, and you can then convert the files to CMYK using Photoshop.

Exporting a photo to convert color space

In some cases, you'll get the best color conversions if you export the photo using the destination color space instead of adjusting it with Soft Proofing. This is because when you export a photo, Lightroom automatically converts all the colors in the photo to the destination color space (using Perceptual rendering intent). This can produce better results than trying to selectively adjust individual colors in the photo. Your results may vary; it's worth doing a few tests yourself.

Printing a Proof Copy

When you print a Proof version from the Print module, these settings override the rendering intent settings on the Print Job panel on a per-image basis. This means that you can combine multiple photos, using different rendering intents, onto a single page and each photo will use its own rendering intent settings! If you want to override the previously-stored soft proof settings for the selected photos, you need to uncheck the Proof option in the Settings menu for those photos. The printed photos will then use the rendering intent specified in the Print Job panel.

Check the profile name in Print

When you are ready to print in the Print module, verify the name of the Proof in the Current Source Indicator at the top of the Filmstrip to confirm you're printing the version made for the current printer/paper combination.

USING BEFORE/AFTER WITH SOFT PROOFING

Using Before/After, you can compare the proof copy with any other version of the photo. The best use of this is to refer to your original, output-neutral Master file, but you could also compare to any other proofed version. On the Toolbar, click the button to enable Before/After. By default, the two previews are presented side by side, with the Before showing the Master state on the left (the photo as it looked before you created the saved proof copy) and the Proof Preview on the right (see Figure 4–130). **Note:** This is an improved change in behavior over Lightroom 4 that would show the Before state of the photo at import on the left unless you manually updated the Before state to the level of the current Master.

You can change the Before/After options. With Before/After enabled, click the Before menu to choose what to show in the Before view (see **Figure 4–137**). You can also drag and drop the Master Photo, or a virtual copy of it, onto the left side of the preview to load it as the Before state. Alternatively, press the \ key to toggle between Before and After.

 Name your VCs
The content of this menu is a good example of why it's good practice to give your VCs meaningful names.

Figure 4-137

The Master menu option loads the original output-neutral settings that were in place before the Proof was made. When you're using a copy, Before defaults to the original Master; when you're using a Master as a Proof, Before defaults to the Saved State of the first copy if one exists, or Saved State if there are no VCs of that photo.

 Managing Proofs with smart collections
Smart collections criteria include a rule for "Is Proof," which lets you easily keep track of your Proofs within the catalog. For more about using smart collections, see Chapter 3.

Converting color photos to black and white

If you like black and white photographs, this can be one of the most fun and creatively rewarding aspects of working in Lightroom. Black and white photographs can convey a very artistic impression. Most notably, a black and white photograph inspires the imagination. Whereas a color image is naturally visually stimulating, a black and white photo is also intellectually stimulating, if for no other reason than it's not the way most people see the world.

Starting with a color original, it's possible to produce stunning black and white photos in Lightroom. And, no doubt, some images look better in black and white than in color!

In-camera versus computer processing

Many modern cameras provide options for making black and white images entirely within the camera. Some also offer special color processing effects. However, I strongly recommend that you always capture in straight, neutral color and convert your photos to black and white later during post-processing in the computer.

There are several reasons for this. First, most cameras can only capture JPEG images in black and white mode. In these situations, your camera captures the original raw data in color, converts it to black and white using the camera settings, and then saves the JPEG to the memory card. The raw data is not preserved. You lose lots of quality and lots of options for later processing.

The second reason not to process in-camera is that you might want to produce both color and black and white versions. If you only have the converted version made in the camera, you're out of luck if you want to make a color version later. Some dSLRs do allow you to capture in raw format and apply a black and white conversion in-camera, but the image is still in color and the instructions for the black and white conversion are only stored as metadata. To preserve black and white metadata settings for raw files on the computer you'd need to use the dedicated software that came with the camera; not Lightroom.

You have much more flexibility and choice in how you process your black and white photos if you leave them in color on the camera and use Lightroom for your black and white conversions.

Pre-visualizing tone conversions while shooting

As you set up your shots, look carefully at the objects in your composition. Compare their brightness relative to one another. What's the brightest spot? The darkest? How do the varying levels of brightness relate to the shapes and textures of the objects? Pay special attention to mergers of tone and color. When you convert a photo to black and white, all the elements of a given color range are essentially converted to the same level of gray. Also, two overlapping objects of different colors might be the same tone, in which case the default black and white conversion may merge them into one indistinguishable object. While you're shooting, think about how you will convert the various elements in the compositions to black and white. Based mainly on color, you can decide which elements will become darker or lighter in the conversion.

Mapping color to gray levels in software

Lightroom allows you to map individual colors to specific gray levels. For example, you could choose to have the blue sky rendered as a very dark tone, a light tone, or somewhere in between. If you can separate the colors of elements in the image, you can control how those colors are converted to gray levels. This way, you'll have the most control over the look of the final conversion. For nearly all original color photos, controlling the conversion of color to gray levels produces a much better result than automatic conversion.

MAKING BLACK AND WHITE CONVERSIONS IN LIGHTROOM

There are several ways to turn a color image into black and white in Lightroom. However, this is a case where the fastest method doesn't always produce the best results. Keep in mind that the color components are being turned into gray levels, but Lightroom still always processes them based on their original, named hue values (red, purple, aqua, etc.).

Fastest: Click the Black & White button the Basic panel (see **Figure 4–138**), the HSL / Color / B&W panel header, or the Quick Develop panel in Library, or use the V key shortcut. You can then edit the sliders on the B&W panel to your liking (see **Figure 4–139**). This provides basic control for how the colors in the original photo are mapped to gray values. Drag the sliders to make each color range lighter or darker in the conversion (see **Figure 4–140**).

Figure 4-138

 Use the TAT
When you're fine-tuning your black and white conversions, use the Targeted Adjustment Tool. Click and drag in areas of the photo you want to make darker or lighter. The TAT adjusts the luminance of the color sliders accordingly.

04

Best: Make the conversion by desaturating all the colors, individually, first. In the HSL panel, set all the Saturation values to -100. Then use the Luminance sliders to brighten or darken the converted grays. This gives you the maximum amount of control over the placement of tones in relation to their original color values (see **Figure 4–141**). You can tweak the Hue sliders a bit, too, for the most control over the conversion (see **Figure 4–142**).

 Create a preset
Once you've set all of the Saturation sliders to -100 create a preset containing just those settings to serve as a quick starting point for the future (click Check None to clear the dialog, then check Color Adjustments, which will automatically include Treatment too).

Figure 4-139

 White balance effect on Black and White conversions
Regardless of the method you use to convert your color original to black and white, **try manually adjusting white balance afterward.**

Figure 4-140

As mentioned earlier, white balance has a major effect on the rendering of the base raw capture, resulting in wide variation in the resulting tones. In addition, you can also manipulate the sliders in the Camera Calibration panel for greater color separation and enhance the opportunity for tonal separation in B&W.

 Black and white exports as RGB
In Lightroom, a black and white image remains in RGB mode, even when exported. The colors in the image are simply converted to equal values in all three channels. (This is very different from the Grayscale mode in Photoshop, which contains only one channel.)

Figure 4-141

Soft Proof black and white photos
Soft proofing isn't just for color photos! With a properly calibrated display you will be able to preview onscreen what your B&W prints will look like, too.

Next steps

After you've used Develop to enhance each of your photos to perfection, be sure to save your metadata to disk and update all your backups!

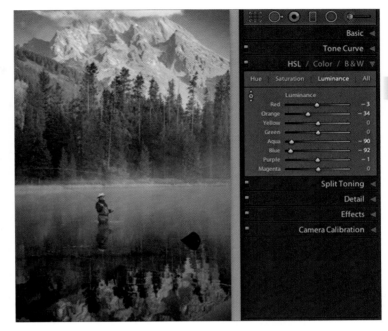

Figure 4-142

Now that you have finished work on your photos, you're ready to share your masterpieces with the world. In the remaining chapters, you'll learn about all the ways you can use Lightroom's output modules to create Books, Slideshows, Prints and Web Galleries.

 When to export or Edit In...
Sometimes, after you've gone as far as you can with your photos in Lightroom, you may want to work on them more in Photoshop or other software. Before proceeding, carefully determine your creative visions for the photos and the next workflow steps that might be required. When you're done in Develop, you can use the Edit In... command to send files to Photoshop or other software, or export new Master files. See Chapter 5 for more information on saving new files from Lightroom.

CHAPTER 05
Export

05

05

EXPORT: Creating new copies from Lightroom

By now you've worked all the way through importing your photos and videos, editing them in Library, and processing them in Develop. So what's next? Maybe you want to email a few pictures to someone, upload photos or videos to Facebook, or burn a DVD for a client to proof. At times, you might also want to use another program to do more processing on your photos; in addition to generating finished files, Lightroom exports can also help you feed your image files into more extended, automated workflows using post-processing actions and plug-ins. When you've gone as far as you can with processing your photos and videos in Lightroom, or you want to share them with other people, it's time to consider some type of export.

Unlike most other programs, Lightroom doesn't have a "Save As..." command. So whether you're distributing finished photos or need to get your files into other imaging software, you will need to export those files with Lightroom. Always keep in mind that the photos and videos aren't actually contained within the catalog—Lightroom is only *referencing* the actual files on the hard drive. So when you do an export, you're using Lightroom to make new copies of the photos and videos, while applying the Lightroom metadata and specified file parameters. When you export, the current adjustments and other metadata are baked in to the resulting files.

Exporting photos and videos from Lightroom *always* generates new files, but depending on the export method, those new files are not always saved to your hard disk after the export is finished. For example, when you burn a DVD, you may not need to also save those files to the hard drive again. But in cases where you do save the newly exported files to your hard drive, you have the option to also add those files automatically to the current Lightroom catalog.

As with many aspects of Lightroom, exports provide powerful batch-processing capabilities. You can export one photo or many photos at the same time: select any number of items, from any image source in your catalog, and a single export can process all the selected files using the same settings.

You'll most often export files from Lightroom using the main Export window. However, this is only one of several ways to save new files with Lightroom. Though it may seem daunting at first, don't be afraid of exporting over and over again—there's no inherent risk in exporting any original file an unlimited number of times. And sometimes the best way to master a process is to play with it for a while! You'll gain more control and confidence with each export you do. In this chapter, we'll look at all your options.

What's New in Export

- **Preserve transparency in TIFF and PSD on export**
- **Publish service connection to Behance**

Basic export workflow

The general workflow for exporting files is simple, but depending on your needs there can be many settings to consider. Here are the basic steps.

Step 1. Select the photos and/or videos to export.

Step 2. In the Export window, configure the settings to be used for the exported files: destination, file format, output size, etc. All the selected photos and videos from the current export will use the same settings.

Step 3. Click the button to start the export. Lightroom processes the export in the background, and you can move on to working on other tasks.

 Multiple simultaneous exports

You can start a new export while a previous export is still in progress (unlike imports, of which you can have only one going at a time). When you queue multiple exports, Lightroom will process them all simultaneously using its multi-threading capabilities. If you have a large number of files to export, rather than exporting them all at once, break your exports up into smaller batches. For example, exporting 4 sets of 25 photos is much faster than exporting 1 set of 100. This can save a lot of time, especially when exporting JPEG files (your mileage may vary based on your hardware).

Export methods

There are four primary methods for exporting files from Lightroom: Email Photos (not shown in Figure), the Export window, Publish Services, and Edit In (see **Figure 5-1**). In general, if you're batch exporting lots of files, using a regular Export or Publish Services is ideal; when you're just working with a single photo and want to continue processing it in another program, Edit In is usually your best option. These methods are all discussed in detail in this chapter.

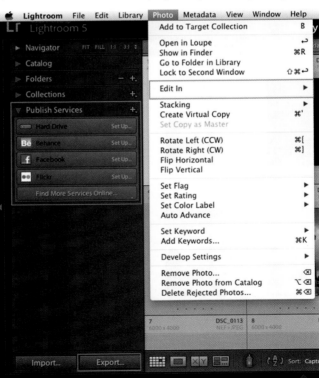

Figure 5-1

05

- **Email Photo(s):** You can send copies of photos by email directly from Lightroom.

- **The Export window:** Use this when you want to save final derivative files to disk or upload directly to a website using export plug-ins (the Web module is another option to consider for uploading to a website and is covered in Chapter 10).

- **Publish Services:** These use the same basic options as the standard export window, with the addition of settings for connecting directly to websites and synced folders. Use these when you want to keep Lightroom collections in sync with galleries on a website, folders on a local disk, or removable devices.

- **Edit In:** This command hands off the exported photos from Lightroom to do more work in another program. The most common example of this is Edit in Photoshop. Usually, if you want to do more work to your photos in other software, you shouldn't export them—instead, use Edit In.

What to do before exporting

Like other stages of the workflow, you'll get better results exporting from Lightroom when you think a few steps ahead. Before starting an export, you should clearly identify the requirements for the files that will be produced—be as specific as you can. Ask yourself:

- How will the files be used?

- Is there a set of specifications to follow?

- How should you name the exported files?

- Will you keep the exported files on your hard drive? If so, where?

- Do you want the new files to be added to the current Lightroom catalog?

- Following the export, what additional tasks might need to be performed on the files?

Spending a few minutes preparing helps ensure you use the correct settings and reduces the potential for needing to do the work again.

ORIGINAL, MASTER, AND DERIVATIVE FILES

From each photo or video you create, you might export multiple additional files, each serving a different purpose. The number of versions you can produce from an original file is unlimited.

As a general rule, you should always retain the original source media in its native, unmodified format (converting to DNG is OK). As you progress through the workflow, you will create derivative files for particular uses. Following are descriptions of the files used in the digital imaging workflow.

Original: The photo or video you downloaded from your camera; or a file generated from a scanner or other digital capture device. These are usually raw (including DNG), JPEG, TIFF, or movie files. Safely archive your originals and protect them long-term! If the worst should happen and all else is lost, you need to be able to go back to these versions if necessary. (In Lightroom, *original* is also a generic term used simply to describe any item used to make copies.)

Master: In a Lightroom workflow, the Original remains the Master as you process it within Lightroom because Lightroom never changes the image data in the Original, and only stores the work you do in Lightroom as processing instructions to be applied to copies created in some form of output. In cases where you extend your photo processing beyond Lightroom to external editors (such as Photoshop), the copy sent to that editor becomes the new Master as it contains all of your original Lightroom work plus the new work from the external editor. These new Master versions are typically PSD or TIFF files (Adobe recommends TIFF).

Derivative: Files saved from the Master and modified for specific purposes, such as printing or Internet distribution. In most cases, these are TIFF or JPEG files. Derivative files are often only used temporarily and deleted when their task is done.

About Lightroom originals

When you export photos from Lightroom, the "original" is the item from which the new files are being made. An original can be any photo, video, or virtual copy in your catalog. In some situations you might have more than one original version of a photo or video in your catalog, even though all were made from a single, original file on the hard disk.

Here are a few examples of original and derivative versions:

- You have a native camera raw file in your catalog that you need to export and send to a print lab in TIFF format. The raw file is the original and the TIFF is the derivative.

- You have a PSD file in your catalog from which you export a JPEG file to email to your client. The PSD is the original; the JPEG is the derivative.

- You use virtual copies (VCs) to produce color and black-and-white versions using different crops, and export them as JPEGs to send to a client. Each VC could be considered an original in the context of the export. The JPEGs are the derivatives.

- You have a layered TIFF file in the catalog that you want to edit in Photoshop. You use the Edit In Photoshop command. In this case, you would choose Edit Original in the options, because you're telling Lightroom to open the actual TIFF file on disk, instead of making a new copy. (We'll talk more about this a bit later.)

Junk files

Because exporting always creates new files, it introduces the likelihood that you will often generate files that will serve no future purpose and only take up unnecessary space on your hard drive. If you're not careful, it's easy to end up with a bunch of useless image files strewn all over your hard drives. You can avoid this by being conscientious and somewhat conservative with your exports. If you're just practicing or testing the export functions, it's best to save the exported files into a temporary folder that you regularly clear out.

Email photos

This function creates a new email message with photos attached. You can email photos from within any of the modules. By default, Lightroom's email functionality uses the program that you've set as the default email program—for example, Apple Mail or Microsoft Outlook. However, you can add other email services, including webmail clients such as Gmail, Yahoo!, AOL, etc. The process of emailing photos from Lightroom using these services is more straightforward than using an email program on your computer. Follow these steps to set up your email client connection and then email photos from Lightroom.

Step 1. Make sure the photo(s) you want to email are selected. (You can't email video clips.)

Step 2. Select File→Email Photo(s), or right-click or Ctrl+click and select Email Photos, or use the shortcut ⌘ +Shift+M or Ctrl+Shift+M. The Email Photos window opens (see **Figure 5–2**). On the From: menu at the middle-right of the window the default email program will be selected, and in the title bar at the top of the window the currently selected email service is shown.

Figure 5-2

Step 3. If you want to use the selected service, leave this menu as-is. (You must already have the email account correctly set up on the selected service.) To use a different email service, click the From: menu and choose one from the list, or select Go To Email Account Manager.

Figure 5-3

Step 4. In the Email Account Manager (see **Figure 5–3**), click the Add button at the bottom left. Choose your service provider from the menu, and enter a descriptive name for this preset. (If you choose Other, and manually enter your account information, Lightroom can send email without using an additional email client.) Click OK.

Step 5. If you selected any email service besides Other, your Outgoing Server Settings should be entered automatically. If they aren't, or they're incorrect, you need to get that information from your email service provider and enter it manually.

Step 6. Enter your email address and password in the Credential Settings panel and click the Validate button. Upon successful validation, your new account will show in the list on the left side of the window, with a green light icon indicating you're good to go (see **Figure 5–4**). If so, click the Done button at the bottom right. If not, you need to reenter the correct server and credential settings to proceed with using this account.

Figure 5-4

Step 7. Back in the main Email Photos window, fill in the fields for the email (see **Figure 5–5**). Depending on the selected email service, you will have different options here. With a webmail service, in addition to the To: and Subject: fields you may have a box where you can enter text for the body of the message. If you're using an email program on your computer, this field will be absent, and you'll complete the message body after Lightroom hands the files off to the email program.

Figure 5-5

05

Step 8. At the bottom of the window are thumbnails for the Attached files (see Figure 5–5). Verify these are the photos you want to send. (If not, click Cancel and start over with another selection.) If your webmail service supports it, and the photos have captions applied (in the captions metadata field), you can check the box to include those captions as description labels. (When using a local mail client this option is unavailable.)

Step 9. You can specify the export options to be used for the photos being sent. The default setting will be preloaded, using 500 pixels on the long edge and medium quality JPEG compression. This setting is fine as a starting point for most emails. To change these settings, choose a different preset from the menu. Or, choose the option Create New Preset (see Figure 5–5). This opens the standard Export window (the controls for which are discussed in detail in the next section of this chapter) where you can configure your own settings for email presets. If you make changes in the Export window or choose a different preset, click the Export button at the bottom right and you'll be returned to the Email Photos window; otherwise, click Cancel.

Step 10. When you're finished setting up the email, click Send. If you're using a webmail client, the export and send will happen in the background; Lightroom's status indicator updates to show what's happening. If you use an email program on your computer, Lightroom will render JPEG files and hand them off to the program as attachments to a new email message, where you finish creating and sending the message from within that program.

Once you've set up your email client(s) the sending of future email is as simple as selecting the photos, choosing Email Photo(s) from the menu, and writing the email.

 Send some test emails
It's a good idea to send a few test emails to yourself or a friend before sending an important email to a client!

LIGHTROOM ADDRESS BOOK

Lightroom has its own address book where you can store email addresses. To access the address book click the Address button at the top right of the Email Photos window (see Figure 5–5). You can create and edit addresses and groups. Currently, there's no built-in functionality to import email addresses from another source. (However, if you are using an email client on your computer, you can wait to select your recipients from there before sending the email.)

Working in the Export window

You can use the main Export window to save new files to a hard disk, burn a CD/DVD, and upload photos and videos to websites (using plug-ins, which is discussed toward the end of this chapter). When you're ready to export photos or videos, you can click the Export button at the bottom of the left panel in Library (see Figure 5–1), or from anywhere in Lightroom—use the File➔Export menu command, or the keyboard shortcut ⌘+Shift+E or Ctrl+Shift+E. You can also export files using the contextual menu, which is discussed a bit later. You'll be presented with the Export window (see **Figure 5–6**).

You can click and drag the bottom right corner to make the window larger.

Carefully enter the settings in each panel; if you use the wrong settings you may have a mess of files to clean up later. Start at the top of the Export window and work your way methodically through the settings, making sure everything is correct before you click the Export button.

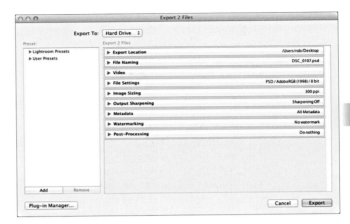

Figure 5-6

05

➧ **Opening and closing panels**

Like panels in the modules, you can close the panels in the Export dialog box when you don't need them. When closed, each panel's header shows a summary of its current settings. Click a panel header to open/close it. (You don't need to click the arrow; just click anywhere on the panel's title bar.)

➧ **Start with a preset**

The easiest way to set up an export is often to select an existing preset and then customize the settings from there. The left side of the Export dialog box lists all the available export presets. Under Lightroom Presets, there are a few built-in presets for some common tasks that can serve as a starting point for customization. (When you're just starting with a new installation of Lightroom, there won't be any User Presets yet.)

➧ **You can work in the Export dialog box without exporting**

You don't necessarily have to complete an export to work in the Export window; you can view and change settings, create and modify presets, etc., and just click Cancel. This closes the window without performing the export. All the work you did in the Export window is retained for later.

Export To:

With the default Lightroom installation, you have several built-in choices for the destination of exported files: Email, Hard Drive, or CD/DVD. When Export plug-ins are installed, more options may show in the menu. The Export To: menu at the top of the window shows the selected option (see **Figure 5–7**).

Figure 5-7

The destination selected in this menu determines what panels and options become available in the rest of the window. The following panel descriptions are with the destination set to Hard Drive.

Export Location

The top panel in the main section of the window is Export Location (see **Figure 5–8**). (This section of the Export window is visible only if the Export To: menu selection above is set to Hard Drive—if it's set to Email or CD/DVD, the files will not be saved on the disk and this panel is hidden.)

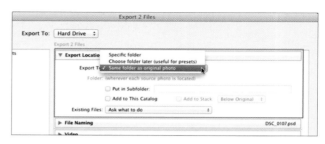

Figure 5-8

These are some of the most important settings in the Export window—where to save the exported file(s) and whether or not to add the new file(s) to the current Lightroom catalog.

EXPORT TO

Use this menu to specify the main folder for the exported files. (If you choose to add the exported files to the catalog, any new folders you've made are also added to the Folders panel in Library.)

Specific folder: If you want to save the exported files in a location other than the original folder, select this option from the menu (see **Figure 5–9**). Then click the Choose button to the right, and navigate to the target folder on your hard drive. During this step, you can also create a new folder for the exported files if you wish.

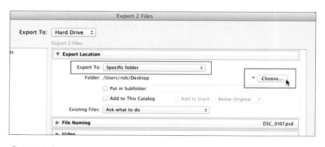

Figure 5-9

Recent folders menu

If you're using Specific Folder, click the small black triangle to the left of the Choose button to select a recently used folder from the pop-up menu (see Figure 5–9).

Choose folder later: Lets you specify the destination after the export begins. The export process will pause at the point where the new folder is being created, allowing you to specify the name and location at that time. This is particularly useful when creating Export presets.

Same folder as original photo: This will save the newly exported files into the same folder as the originals.

Folder: preview text below menu

A line of text shows the destination folder where the files will be saved (see Figure 5–9).

 Choosing the folder

If I'm just going to use the derivatives temporarily and don't plan to keep them, I usually save them in a folder on my desktop and trash the files when I'm done with them. If I'm going to retain the exported files long-term, I save them into the same folder with the originals.

PUT IN SUBFOLDER

By checking the box and entering a folder name in this field, you can create another folder inside the one specified above.

ADD TO THIS CATALOG

Enabling this option automatically imports the newly exported file(s) into the current Lightroom catalog. I always do this for files I intend to keep, and usually don't for files that are only temporary.

ADD TO STACK

If the Export To: destination is set to Same Folder as Original Photo and you also enable Add to This Catalog, you can stack the exported derivatives with the original masters. (Stacks are discussed in Chapter 3.) I usually enable this option; if you export derivatives that you also want to add to the catalog, stacking them with the originals can help keep your Library image sources neatly organized. Use the pop-up menu to choose where in the stack the exported files will be inserted. (You can change the stacking later.)

EXISTING FILES

This setting tells Lightroom what to do if files with the same names are found in the destination folder. I usually keep this on "Ask what to do" unless I'm doing a large batch and want to overwrite everything in the target folder, in which case the other options come in handy.

Choose a new name for the exported file: When Lightroom comes to a file with the same name, a sequence number is automatically added to the end of the new file's name.

Overwrite files WITHOUT WARNING: The older file with the duplicate name is overwritten by the new file. (Be careful with this.)

Skip: The export process ignores the file with the name conflict. The new file is exported and you will not see a warning.

File Naming

Exported files can use the same or different filenames as their originals. Keep in mind that files in each folder must have a unique name, but the names can be differentiated by the file type extension alone. For example, *Moab_03152013_0262.dng* and *Moab_03152013_0262.jpg* are different file names.

Bearing this in mind, you can choose to keep the same base file name as the original or use an entirely different name. For example, exporting *Tetons_072012_1319.dng* could create a derivative file named *Tetons_072012_1319.jpg* or it could become *0234_sylvan_tetons_2012.jpg*.

Carefully consider the names for your exported files. Think of this like a "Save As…" in other programs: you're starting with one file and creating a new file from it. Just as with Save As… you should be deliberate about how you name the new file. As with other stages in the workflow, practical naming of exported derivatives makes your work much easier.

I almost always apply new names to derivative files to indicate their settings and/or what they are to be used for.

RENAME TO

To name the exported files differently from the originals, tick the check box and choose a file naming template from the menu (see **Figure 5–10**). To create a new template, choose Edit…. File naming templates are explained in detail in Chapter 3.

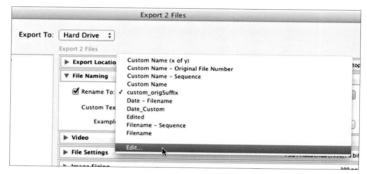

Figure 5-10

If you don't check the box, the exported file will use the same base file name as the original.

Example

An example of how the current file naming template and preferences will affect the names for the files being exported is shown at the bottom of the File Naming panel.

Extensions

Use the pop-up menu to choose the case for the file extensions.

 Naming preferences

An option in Lightroom Preferences→File Handling→File Name Generation controls Lightroom's automated file naming behavior (see **Figure 5–11**). This is intended to assist in ensuring file names are Internet-friendly. The preferences give you options for how to handle "illegal" characters and spaces in the name. They can be replaced with dashes or underscores, or left as is. During an export, if you create a file name that breaks the rules you've set, Lightroom automatically changes the name to reflect your preference settings.

Video

The Export window has a panel with options for exporting video files (see **Figure 5–12**). If no video files are selected for the current export, these options are disabled.

INCLUDE VIDEO FILES

Check the box to export video files along with images. When you check the box to Include Video Files, the additional options below are enabled for you to specify settings for the exported video files.

If you have video files selected when you try to do an export and leave this box unchecked, at the end of the export, the Export Results window will display the message that "Some export operations were not performed," with a list of the video files that were not exported.

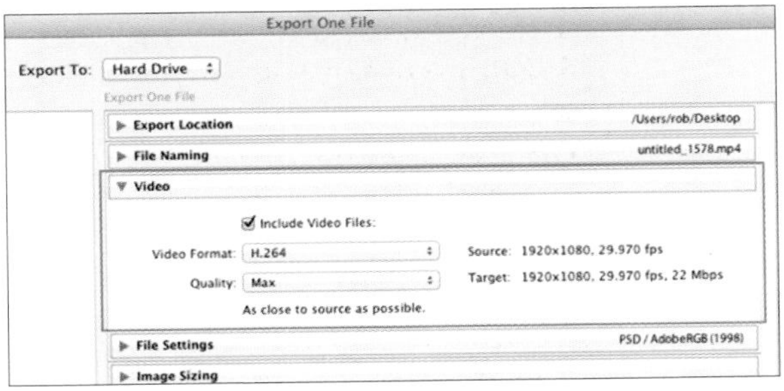

VIDEO FORMAT

Lightroom can export video files in DPX and H.264 (.mp4) format. H.264 is currently the

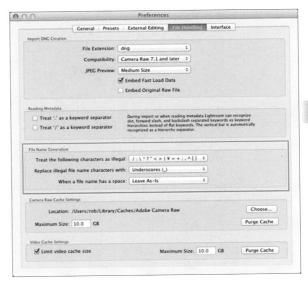

Figure 5-11

Figure 5-12

most common file format for delivering digital video. To export finished, full-motion video clips from Lightroom, you should use H.264. (DPX is used in video production and special effects work. Choosing this option results in each frame being saved as a separate file; you may want to use this if you'll be editing videos in Adobe Premiere.) If you choose Original, unedited file, Lightroom will export the new file using the same format, size, and quality as the original video clip and it won't have any Lightroom adjustments you may have made to the clip.

QUALITY

The quality options available depend on the video format selected. For H.264, the available options are Low, Medium, High, and Max. Each quality setting determines the size and bit rate of the exported video file. The Quality setting is the only place you can change image processing options for the exported videos. (Most of the other Export window panel settings are unavailable or have no effect on video files.)

File Settings

In this section of the export dialog box (see **Figure 5–13**), enter the file settings for the exported photos. If you're doing a batch export, all the files will be exported using the same settings, unless the output file format is set to Original, in which case each exported file uses the same format as the original file from which it was made. (Using Original is the only way to export files with different formats within a single export.)

Figure 5-13

IMAGE FORMAT

First, select the image format for the exported files, each of which will present different options, and then apply the other settings specific to that format. Following are the types and descriptions of the formats available for exporting with Lightroom. (File formats are also discussed in Chapters 1 and 2.)

JPEG (Joint Photographic Experts Group)

Can be used for web, email, and print. Standard JPEG files always use 8-bit data and can use any color space. The file extension is typically displayed as JPG.

Exporting as JPEG requires you to specify a Quality level, using numeric values from 0 to 100 (see Figure 5–13). The Quality setting determines the amount of compression to be applied to exported JPEG files. JPEG compression is always lossy—data is discarded as the file is saved in order to reduce file size. The higher the Quality setting, the larger the file size will be. A higher Quality setting applies less compression, providing better-looking (and larger) files, while with lower Quality settings more compression is applied, potentially resulting in degraded image quality. With JPEG compression, some data is always discarded, even at the maximum Quality setting.

For web use, I usually limit the JPEG Quality to between 50 and 80, unless I need to adhere to provided specifications. If you're exporting JPEG files to send to a lab for printing, you should usually set the Quality at 80, unless instructed otherwise.

 JPEG quality levels in Lightroom and Photoshop
Lightroom's JPEG Quality slider values are different than Photoshop's Save As options for JPEG , where you set the quality level using an integer from 1 to 12. In Lightroom, Quality 100 is equivalent to Photoshop's level 12 quality. Lightroom's Quality setting of 80 is equivalent to Photoshop's level 10.

When Image Format is set to JPEG, you can check this box to have Lightroom attempt to create exported files that fit within the specified size limit. However, be aware that other settings on the Export screen can interfere with this goal, and that this option does slow down the export process. You may need to use the Resize to Fit option (covered further on in this section) to reduce the pixel dimensions enough to help reach your file size goal.

PSD (Photoshop Document)

You can use PSD to work with the exported files in Photoshop or Elements. Exporting as PSD allows you to set the bit depth (see below). PSD files exported from Lightroom are saved with Photoshop's Maximize Compatibility option enabled.

New in Lightroom 5: If you have a single layer TIFF or PSD file selected in Lightroom that contains transparent areas, the exported copy will retain the transparent areas. However, if you have a layered TIFF or PSD source file it will be flattened and you will lose the transparency (you can choose Original image format to preserve layers; see the following Warning).

 Exporting layered originals produces flattened derivatives
Although Lightroom will preserve any layers contained in TIFF and PSD files when they are imported, when you export those layered files, the resulting derivatives are flattened if you choose JPEG, TIFF, or PSD as the Image Format. Lightroom has to flatten the files to apply Lightroom adjustments to the derivative copies. If you want to retain your layers you need to choose Original as the Image Format option. While you do retain original layers in the exported copies when you choose Original no Lightroom adjustments will be applied to them.

TIFF (Tagged Image File Format)

TIFF can be used for virtually any purpose except viewing in a web browser. TIFF is often used as the format for working Master files and derivatives for printing. When exporting TIFFs you can specify bit depth and apply Zip compression (see **Figure 5–14**). Zip compression on TIFF files is lossless—no data is discarded. Compressed TIFF files can be significantly smaller than uncompressed; however, large compressed files can take longer to open and save than uncompressed files. (I prefer to work with uncompressed TIFF files.)

Figure 5-14

New in Lightroom 5: There is a check box labeled Save Transparency when TIFF is selected as the Image Format. If you have a single layer TIFF or PSD file selected in Lightroom that contains transparent areas you can check that box and the resulting exported copy will retain the transparent areas. However, if you have a layered TIFF or PSD source file it will be flattened and you will lose the transparency even if that box is checked (you can choose Original image format to preserve layers as mentioned earlier).

Options for exporting PNG files

While Lightroom has the ability to import PNG files there is no PNG option in the Image Format drop-down menu. If you select a PNG source file for export and want to export a copy in PNG format, you can choose Original and it will create a PNG copy. If you've made adjustments to the PNG file in Lightroom and want to export a copy with those changes and retain transparency in the image choose TIFF (with Save Transparency checked) or PSD.

Bit Depth (TIFF and PSD only)

When exporting TIFF or PSD files you have a choice of 8 bits/component or 16 bits/component (see Figure 5–14). This sets the amount of data used to render the file. Higher bit-depth means more data is being used to describe the pixels in the file. An 8-bit file uses 256 levels of brightness per color channel; a 16-bit file uses 65,536 levels. Most often, more data equates to higher quality, especially if you're doing lots of editing on the file. If you are exporting files to be used as Masters for processing in other software, I recommend you use 16-bit whenever possible. A 16-bit image provides much more processing flexibility than does an 8-bit image—16-bit data can be manipulated much more before the appearance of the image starts to degrade. 16-bit allows smoother transitions between colors and reduces the appearance of posterization where areas of color become solid and transitions become hard-edged.

If you're exporting final files for printing, 8-bit is usually adequate. (However, some printers can take advantage of 16-bit; ask your vendor how they want the files saved.)

DNG (Adobe Digital NeGative) can be used to export files originating in any format. Historically, DNG has most often been used for converting raw captures. However, Adobe has released an updated DNG specification with some great new options that provide significant advantages in also converting original JPEGs to DNG. (In addition to export, you can also convert files to DNG during import and from within the Library module.)

For most conversions to DNG, I recommend using the default settings (see **Figure 5–15**). Of particular importance are the settings to Embed Fast Load Data and Use Lossy Compression, as well as the option to resize exported DNG files.

- **Embed Fast Load Data:** Provides speed gains when working with DNG files in Lightroom, especially DNGs made from raw captures.

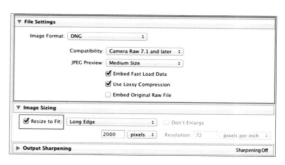

Figure 5-15

- **Use Lossy Compression:** Applies JPEG compression to the linear, demosaicked image data in the DNG. As this creates potentially degraded files and is not reversible, this isn't recommended for archival purposes.

- **Image Sizing:** When Use Lossy Compression is enabled, you can resize exported DNGs (see Figure 5-15).

See the Appendix for more about DNG.

Original
You can export derivative files in the same format as the original. In a batch with multiple file types selected, each derivative will be saved in the same format as its own original. You can't change any file settings when exporting to Original format. No Lightroom adjustments are applied to the pixels of the exported copies, though changes are written into the metadata of the copies.

 Using export to copy files
One of the most basic applications for Lightroom's capabilities is batch-copying files. There are likely to be occasions where you need to export copies of image files and videos in their original pre-import state and file format, but with the Lightroom work written into the file's XMP metadata space; Lightroom exports can be good for this purpose. One example might be if you want to export raw files in their original raw format, but with your Lightroom work included in the metadata for archival purposes. To do this you just need to choose *Original* as the File Format.

COLOR SPACE
Different devices (printers, monitors, projectors, etc.) interpret the colors in your photos in different ways. A color space defines the digital color values of an image or a device, and the range of available colors is called the color *gamut*. A small gamut contains fewer colors and a large gamut has more colors.

Color spaces and their gamuts are described by profiles. When you export from Lightroom (in any format other than Original or DNG) a color space must be selected (see **Figure 5–16**). During the export, Lightroom converts the colors in each photo and embeds the corresponding profile for the specified color space. The default Lightroom color spaces are:

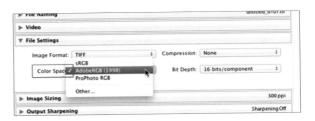

Figure 5-16

- **sRGB:** "Standard RGB" was developed by Microsoft and Hewlett-Packard in the 1990s, and is often referred to as *small* RGB due to its relatively small gamut. Of the three main working spaces, sRGB most closely resembles the output spaces of computer monitors and laser imagers (LightJet, Frontier, and Chromira printers, for example). sRGB excels in producing vivid greens and blues. If you're preparing files for viewing on-screen (e.g. a website) or having prints made at a lab, use sRGB. For our purposes, you can think of sRGB as the "small" color space.

- **Adobe RGB (1998):** Also sometimes referred to as *aRGB* or *RGB98*, this is the most flexible of the export color spaces provided by Lightroom. Adobe RGB can work great for fine art inkjet printing and usually also translates well to CMYK for offset printing. Adobe RGB converts well to sRGB, too. Adobe RGB is capable of reproducing rich reds and oranges while maintaining dense blacks. As a general rule, you should use Adobe RGB if you're preparing the file for printing with ink, and when you're saving Master files and don't yet know the ultimate destination of the image. Think of Adobe RGB as the "medium" color space.

- **ProPhoto RGB:** In Lightroom, this is the "large" color space. While not the largest color space ever invented (look up EktaSpace and Bruce RGB for other examples), ProPhoto is by far the largest of the three standard color spaces included in Lightroom. ProPhoto maintains the most vivid saturation of the three color spaces, particularly super-saturated yellows, oranges, and reds. The ProPhoto color space encompasses all the colors that can be captured by a digital camera. (Use this only with 16-bit files.)

Always choose the color space based on how the exported files will be used. For most exports of final files, this is sRGB. However, if an exported image will be used as a new Master working file, you should usually use Adobe RGB or ProPhoto. (ProPhoto is recommended only for photographers with a good understanding of color management—it contains many colors that are difficult or impossible for output devices to reproduce.)

 Maintaining the most possible data
When exporting new Master files from Lightroom, I always use 16-bit ProPhoto. This ensures the maximum amount of data from the raw capture will be preserved in the rendered file.

Using a custom profile

Select your own color space by choosing *Other...* from the menu (see Figure 5–16). You can load any profile available on your computer. This is especially useful when preparing files for printing by an outside vendor: if your lab provides a custom profile, add it to the list here and you can export files using that color space (if that is what they require). If you used Soft Proofing in Develop, you can load the same profile here.

 Ask vendors for their profiles
When sending an image to a lab or service bureau, you need to know how your file will be reproduced. Ask if they want the file saved in a specific color space.

Image Sizing

Resizing a photographic image involves resampling—pixels must either be created or discarded. For enlargements, new pixels are made (upsampling); for reductions, pixels are eliminated (downsampling). This is done using a process called *interpolation*. You should resample only when necessary, because interpolation always results in some loss of quality.

When you export JPEG, TIFF, PSD, and DNG (with Use Lossy Compression checked) files from Lightroom, you have the option to specify the dimensions for the new files. (You can't resize files being exported as Original.) Lightroom uses an adaptive bicubic resampling algorithm similar to Photoshop's bicubic smoother/bicubic sharper algorithm—but better, as it automatically adjusts according to the dimensions of the original and exported copies.

05

You specify the output size in the Image Sizing panel (see **Figure 5–17**). When you specify a size in anything other than pixels, the resolution setting also becomes important (see the next section).

Figure 5-17

 Resize at the end of the workflow
Always resize your photos after all other post-processing has been completed, and only resize as necessary for the intended purpose. If you're planning to do more processing on the files after the export, you should not resize them at this time.

RESIZE TO FIT

In this section of the export dialog box you can specify the dimensions for the exported files. Check the box to resize all the exported files using the specified measurements; otherwise, the derivatives will be the same size and resolution as the originals. All the numeric entries represent *maximum* constraints: the numbers entered here are always the largest possible size that would result. Regardless of how you specify the output size, no distortion of the exported images will result—the exported images will retain the proportions of the originals.

If you're exporting for screen display, use pixels. If you're exporting for printed output, specify the measurements in inches or centimeters. If you specify a size in inches or centimeters, you should also specify the Resolution using the same unit of measurement (see the next section).

Your choices for resizing are:

- **Width and Height:** Enter the maximum size(s) for width and/or height. (You can leave one or the other blank.) The photo(s) will be scaled so that both dimensions fit within the specified measurements.

- **Dimensions:** The images will be scaled to fit within the specified dimensions without regard to which is width and which is height. The source image orientation is maintained, so a mix of landscape and portrait photos can be exported together.

- **Long edge:** Set the size for the long side of the photo; the short edge will be scaled proportionately.

- **Short edge:** Set the size for the short side of the photo; the long edge will be scaled proportionately.

- **Megapixels:** This will proportionally scale the photo to fit within the target size.

To export a file without resizing/resampling, leave Resize to Fit unchecked.

DON'T ENLARGE

Check the Don't Enlarge box to prevent Lightroom from enlarging any images whose originals are already equal to or smaller than the specified output size. This can be useful when some of the photos you're exporting are already at or under the maximum size limit specified and you don't want them to be upsampled.

RESOLUTION

To specify a resolution for the exported files, enter a value in the text field and choose pixels per inch or pixels per cm from the menu (see **Figure 5–18**).

Figure 5-18

The concept of resolution is difficult for many digital photographers to understand. I think this is because the term is commonly used in two different ways. One meaning refers to the actual pixel dimensions of a file (x pixels by y pixels). A "high resolution" file contains lots of pixels and a "low resolution" file contains relatively fewer pixels. **A pixel does not have a fixed size; it's just a piece of a digital image with a numeric value.**

The second meaning for resolution—and the one used in the Resolution setting in the Lightroom Export window—*refers specifically to printed output.* This resolution, measured in pixels per inch or pixels per cm, determines how the pixels in the image will be "resolved" to the physical measurements of a print. **The resolution setting in Lightroom Export (and its equivalent in Photoshop) is only relevant for printing.**

With printed output, besides the actual pixel count, you have another issue to consider—real world, physical measurements, such as inches or centimeters. On a printed photo, the pixels in the image need to be mapped to these real-world measurements. Which raises the question, "how many pixels in an inch?" That's where the Resolution setting comes in: it determines how the pixels in the image will translate to the printed output. For example, an image set to 240 ppi will print with 240 pixels per inch on the printed output. That same image could be printed at 600 pixels per inch, resulting in a smaller print, or 80 pixels per inch, resulting in a larger print. In this context, resolution determines the amount of detail visible in the print. If the resolution is too low, you'll see the actual pixels in the printed image.

If you are exporting files for printing, set the resolution for the type of print being made. A few examples: For inkjet printing, resolution anywhere between 180 and 480 will work. For offset printing at 150 lpi (lines per inch), 300 ppi is good. For lab prints,

05

300 ppi is also common. Ask your print vendor what resolution they want. If you're printing yourself, 240 ppi is a good default.

If you're exporting files for any kind of screen output, don't worry at all about the Resolution setting: it will have no effect on the final output size of screen-based media. For screen-based media, such as a monitor, projector, etc., the actual pixel dimensions are all that matters. This applies to web browsers, email readers, television, handheld devices, etc.

Output sharpening

In current digital photo workflows, we use three types of sharpening: capture sharpening, creative sharpening, and output sharpening. In Lightroom, the first two are applied in the Develop module. (You can learn more about this in Chapter 4.)

When exporting image files, Lightroom provides the capability to automatically apply output sharpening. The exported files are sharpened at the optimal processing stage and at the proper amount for the image size and intended media.

SHARPEN FOR

To enable output sharpening, tick the Sharpen For: box, and then choose the type of sharpening and the amount to apply (see **Figure 5–19**).

Figure 5-19

- **Screen:** Use this if you're exporting files for display on a computer, television monitor, or mobile device.

- **Matte Paper:** Use this for printing on matte paper, such as cotton rag art papers like Hahnemühle Photo Rag and Epson Somerset Velvet. Sharpening for Matte is stronger than for Glossy.

- **Glossy Paper:** Use this for printing on glossy, luster, and semi-gloss photo papers like Fuji Crystal Archive, Harman Glossy FB AL, Epson Premium Luster, and Ilford Galerie Gold Fibre Silk.

(The sharpening paper types apply to both inkjet prints and lab prints.)

After choosing the type of sharpening, set the amount: Low, Standard, or High. Because sharpening routines are image-specific and dependent on file size, finding the ideal amount may require you to do some testing. Try the standard amount first, evaluate the results, and adjust as needed.

 When to not sharpen
If you're going to use another program (such as Photoshop) to resize, apply noise reduction, and/or sharpen the photo, turn off the sharpening in the Lightroom export settings and do your final sharpening later in the workflow.

Metadata

In this section of the Export window you can set how the metadata is handled during the export (see **Figure 5–20**). Choose an option from the menu to control the types of metadata from the original files that will be copied into the exported files.

Figure 5-20

- **Copyright Only:** When you choose this option, all metadata except the IPTC copyright fields will be omitted from the exported files. Depending on how much other metadata you've applied, this can result in significant savings in file size. If you need to export files at the smallest possible size, enable this option. Just be aware that all other metadata—including keywords—will not carry over to the new files.

- **Copyright & Contact Info Only:** Omits all metadata except IPTC copyright and contact fields.

- **All Except Camera & Camera Raw Info:** Using this option will omit camera EXIF and Adobe raw processing information. This can be useful when you don't want to reveal technical information about the image file, or to ensure adjustment metadata is not included.

- **All Metadata:** When you choose this option, all original EXIF metadata and metadata applied in Lightroom will be copied to the new file(s).

At bare minimum, I think it's usually best to include copyright and contact metadata.

REMOVE LOCATION INFO

Enabling this option instructs Lightroom to omit location information from the exported files—IPTC location fields, geographic coordinates, and Lightroom map data. Use this option if you don't want to reveal where a photo was taken. This option is only available when using All Metadata or All Except Camera & Camera Raw Info.

 Preferences for exporting reverse geocoding suggestions

In Lightroom preferences there's a new option that works in conjunction with the Map module. When you enable "Export reverse geocoding suggestions whenever address fields are empty," reverse geocoding suggestions from the Map module will be written into the corresponding IPTC fields in the exported files. Reverse geocoding uses only geographic coordinates already present (or created by placing an image on the map) to populate the address fields. If Remove Location Info is checked no address data or geographic coordinates are written into the file. With the Export reverse geocoding suggestions checked, it will write those in the metadata when exported. If unchecked, only location data that you enter will get written (by specifically typing in a sublocation, city, state, or country).

WRITE KEYWORDS AS LIGHTROOM HIERARCHY

If you use keyword hierarchies in Lightroom, checking this box will preserve those parent/child relationships when the keywords are written into the exported files. This can be helpful when you're going to import the files into another Lightroom catalog—your keyword list will retain the hierarchies you've previously created. However, this keyword structure may not be recognized by other software. If you leave this option disabled, the keywords in the exported files will be separated by commas, as per the more common standard. (I almost always leave this off.)

Watermarking

A watermark is a text or graphical overlay that appears on your photo(s). On the web, you've probably seen countless photos containing watermarks—they are often used to identify the creator/copyright owner of an image. A watermark is very different from the copyright metadata embedded in a photo: the watermark is visible on the image itself whereas metadata is plain text embedded in the code of the computer file. (Unfortunately, you can't use metadata to automatically create watermarks in Lightroom beyond the Copyright field used by the Simple Copyright Watermark.)

You can access Lightroom's Watermark Editor from the Export window. From within any of the modules, you can also open the Watermark Editor with the Edit Watermarks command under the Lightroom Menu on Mac and the Edit menu on Windows. All modules access the same set of saved watermarks—if you create a custom watermark in any of the modules or via the Export screen, you are able to use it anywhere else within Lightroom.

WATERMARK

To apply a watermark to exported files, first check the box to enable the function (see **Figure 5–21**). Then select a saved watermark from the menu, or, to make a new one, choose Edit Watermarks…. The default is Simple Copyright Watermark, which

Figure 5-21

places a simple line of white text using the contents of the Copyright field in the photo's metadata in the lower left corner. This simple watermark has no controls for sizing, placement, or color. It is simply meant for small web-sized images. To create a more customizable watermark you need to use the Watermark Editor.

Working in the Watermark Editor

Selecting Edit Watermarks… opens the Watermark Editor window (see **Figure 5–22**). You can click and drag the bottom right corner of the window to resize it.

At the top left is a menu to choose a watermark preset; you can also save new presets here. To the right of that menu, above the preview, are left and right arrows. If you have multiple photos selected for the export, these buttons allow you to cycle through them to see how your watermark will look on different photos.

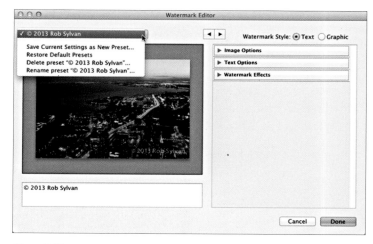

Figure 5-22

WATERMARK STYLE

At the top right of the Watermark Editor window, choose whether to use a text or graphic watermark; you can't use both at once (see **Figure 5–23**). Clicking the Graphic button opens a window where you can choose a file from your hard drive.

Regardless of which watermark style you choose, the panels below are all visible, but with a graphic watermark some controls will be unavailable.

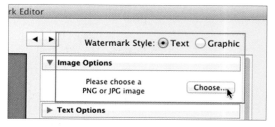

Figure 5-23

IMAGE OPTIONS

Click the Choose… button to load an image from your hard drive; it doesn't need to be in the catalog. Clicking this will switch from Text to Graphic mode in the watermark. As the text below the option explains, this must be a PNG or JPEG image.

Just like identity plates, watermarks made using a PNG file provide support for image transparency.

TEXT OPTIONS

If you're using a text watermark, type the text into the box below the preview (see **Figure 5–24**). Then style the text with the following options. (Unlike identity plates, you can't use multiple font styles within a single watermark.)

Figure 5-24

- **Font:** From the menu, choose one of the fonts installed on your computer.

- **Style:** Depending on the selected font, additional styling may be available. Font styles usually include bold, italic, small caps, etc.

- **Align:** Choose left, center, or right text alignment.

- **Color:** Click the swatch to choose a color for the text.

- **Shadow:** Check the box to turn the text watermark shadow on or off, and then use the controls below to style the shadow.

- **Opacity:** This sets how strongly the shadow appears behind the watermark. At 100%, the shadow is fully solid on the photo. At lower opacity values, the photo shows through. Drag the slider to see the effect.

- **Offset:** This determines how far from the text or graphic element the shadow is placed.

- **Radius:** The width of the shadow.

- **Angle:** Adjusts the direction of the shadow as it falls on the background. Try this in conjunction with the Offset slider.

WATERMARK EFFECTS

The settings in the Watermark Effects section control the placement and appearance of the watermark (see **Figure 5–25**).

Figure 5-25

- **Opacity:** Sets the opacity/ transparency of the watermark as it's overlaid on the photo. Drag the slider or type a number to set the opacity.

- **Size:** Sets the size of the watermark on the photo. Choose between Proportional, Fit, and Fill. If you choose proportional, you can drag the slider or type a number to scale the watermark in the photo.

- **Inset:** Drag the sliders or type numbers to set the spacing between the watermark and the horizontal and vertical edges.

- **Anchor:** Determines the point from which the watermark is placed on the photo. The other controls will work relative to the anchor point, unless it's set to the center.

- **Rotate:** Click the buttons to rotate the watermark clockwise or counterclockwise in 90-degree increments.

SAVE OR CANCEL

When you're done setting up your watermark, click the Save button at the bottom right and give your watermark preset a name, or click Cancel to leave the Watermark Editor without applying your changes. To update an existing watermark with the current settings, choose that option from the menu.

Keyboard shortcut for the copyright symbol
You can copy and paste the copyright symbol into the text field or you can use the keyboard shortcut Option+G on a Mac, or on Windows hold down the Alt key and press 0169 on the numeric keypad (the numbers along the top of the keyboard won't do it) to create the ©.

Post-Processing

Lightroom can integrate export operations with other software via the controls in the Post-Processing panel (see **Figure 5–26**). The other software can be automated scripts such as Photoshop droplets, or programs installed on your computer. When Lightroom is done with the export, the files are handed off to the other program for further processing. (Post-Processing is not available when exporting to email or CD/DVD.)

Figure 5-26

The sequence of operations
If you run a Photoshop droplet on the exported files, all the steps contained in the action—and any resulting changes to the files—will be performed *after* Lightroom's export processing is completed. Keep this in mind when you're planning the export workflow; it has a significant effect on how your steps should be arranged when post-processing is involved.

If the derivative files are added to the catalog during the export, any changes applied during post-processing will also be automatically updated on the files in the catalog.

AFTER EXPORT

The default for this menu is Do nothing, in which case, when the export is complete, nothing further will happen. You can select another item from this menu to hand off the file(s) the selected application, run a Photoshop droplet, etc. Other built-in options include Show in Finder (Mac) or Show in Explorer (Windows) and Open in Photoshop (if it's installed).

Adding your own Export Actions

You can add Photoshop droplets, scripts, and shortcuts to other software programs to the After Export menu. Any item that can be executed on a photo (or batch of photos) can be added as an Export Action.

From the pop-up menu, select "Go to Export Actions Folder Now". This takes you to that folder within the Lightroom presets folder on your computer. Place your droplets in the Export Actions folder, and after restarting Lightroom, they will appear in the After Export menu.

 Aliases and shortcuts

In many cases you can also add Mac aliases or Windows shortcuts in the Export Actions folder.

APPLICATION

If the After Export menu is set to Open in Other Application, you can choose that program here. Click the Choose button and navigate to the program on your hard drive. When you use this post-processing option, after Lightroom is done exporting the files they are opened in the other program. (Of course, this depends on the ability of the other program to actually open the exported files!)

 Use Edit In… for additional processing

The Post-Processing options in the Export window are best suited for automated batch processing using droplets or other scripts. In most cases, if you want to work on your photos yourself, it's better to use the Edit In… command instead of a batch export. (Working with External Editors is covered later in this chapter.)

Export presets

As with most other parts of Lightroom, whenever you customize export settings you should save a preset for later use. First, you need to have your desired settings applied in the Export screen— saving a new preset will store all the current settings. Next, click the Add button at the bottom of the presets list on the left side of the Export window (see **Figure 5–27**). Choose where to store the new preset and give it a name. You can keep your presets in the default locations, or make other folders and use custom naming to group your export presets together for specific purposes. Click Return or Enter to finish saving the preset.

UPDATING AND DELETING PRESETS

You can update presets in the list: right-click or Ctrl+click on a preset, and from the pop-up menu,

Figure 5-27

select Update with Current Settings. Delete presets from the list either by selecting the preset and then clicking the Remove button at the bottom of the preset list, or right-clicking or Ctrl+clicking on the preset and choosing from the options on the pop-up contextual menu.

05

EXPORT WITH PRESET AND EXPORT WITH PREVIOUS

Once you've done a few exports and/or set up export presets, you can begin the export process much faster with the Export With… commands, accessed from the File menu and the contextual menu. When you right-click or Ctrl+click on a photo or video anywhere in Lightroom, the pop-up menu provides shortcuts to export commands (see **Figure 5–28**). Export with Previous uses the settings from the last export you did; Export with Preset uses the settings saved in the selected preset. Both options bypass the Export window altogether and start the export immediately, so you need to have your settings worked out ahead of time.

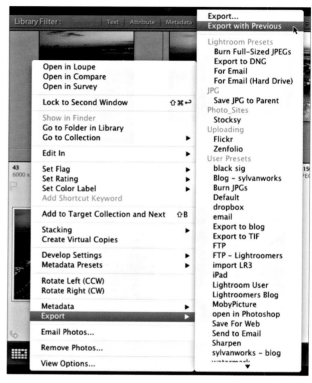

Figure 5-28

 Import and export your Export presets

You can import and export the Export presets. Right-click or Ctrl+click on any preset, and from the pop-up menu choose the applicable option. Importing and exporting presets makes it easy to synchronize presets between machines.

Burn a CD/DVD

You can burn your exported photos to a CD or DVD using Lightroom. During the export operation you can also apply any of the file options, but post-processing options are not available. After Lightroom generates the derivatives, they will be burned to the disc using your operating system's built-in functions. With a few exceptions (based on operating system and disc burner), Lightroom works with your operating system to complete the process.

Step 1. In Library, select all the photos to be exported and open the Export window.

Step 2. Select a disc burning preset from the left pane of the window (see **Figure 5–29**) or choose CD/DVD from the Export To: pop-up menu at the top of the Export window.

Step 3. Configure the settings for the files to be exported/burned, taking even more care than usual—a disc will be burned even if your file settings are incorrect!

Step 4. Click the Export button, or press Return/Enter. If you don't already have a blank, writable CD/DVD in the writer, Lightroom will prompt you when it's time to insert one.

Figure 5-29

Export plug-ins

You can install many specialized export plug-ins. These add-on extensions, created by independent developers, provide enhanced integration and functionality with other software and web services, as well as facilitating some additional functionality within Lightroom itself. Most plug-ins are very inexpensive; many are free.

To find plug-ins, click the Plug-in Manager... button at the bottom left of the Export screen (see **Figure 5–30**). Then, in the Plug-in Manager, click the button for Plug-in Exchange...

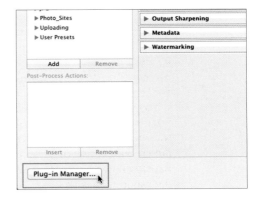

Figure 5-30

(see **Figure 5–31**). This takes you to the Adobe website, where you'll find many Lightroom plug-ins for export as well as other purposes. There are also a few Lightroom plug-ins available that are not listed on the Adobe site; you can Google "Lightroom plug-ins" to find them.

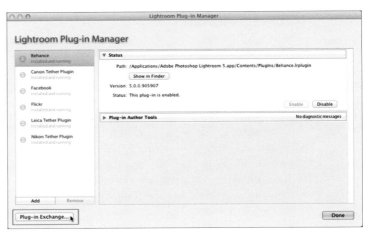

Figure 5-31

After you download the plug-in files, there are several ways to install them. Some come with their own installer. For others, if you copy them to the Lightroom/Modules folder (you may need to manually create that folder if it is not there), they will appear in the

05

Plug-In Manager the next time Lightroom is started. Alternatively, you can simply store the plug-in files in a folder of your choosing and use the Add button in the Plug-in Manager to install them (most plug-in authors favor this option and I recommend it). Once the plug-ins are installed, each offers different settings and controls within the Export screen. You'll need to read the instructions provided for each plug-in.

To remove a plug-in from the Plug-in Manager list, select it and click the Remove button. (You can only do this with third-party plug-ins that were added using the Plug-in Manager—Lightroom default plug-ins, plug-ins placed in the Modules folder, and those added using installers can't be removed from here.)

You can find a list of export plug-in links in the Resources section of the Appendix.

Publish Services: Synchronize your photo collections

Publish services are a special type of export: they essentially combine the functions of Lightroom Collections and Exports, allowing you to keep your collections synchronized with websites, folders, and devices. They are accessed via the Publish Services panel in the Library module (see **Figure 5–32**). Lightroom comes installed with publish services included for Hard Drive, Behance, Facebook, and Flickr. You can also add publish services for export plug-ins connecting to services such as SmugMug, Zenfolio, and other photo-sharing sites.

New in Lightroom 5: The Publish Services plug-in for the Behance network comes preinstalled. Behance is Adobe's online portfolio platform. You can learn more about the platform by clicking the Set Up button on the Behance publish service.

Figure 5-32

Find more services online
Click the button at the bottom of the Publish Services panel and you'll be taken to the Adobe website in your default browser. On the Lightroom Exchange pages you can get more publish service plug-ins.

USING PUBLISH SERVICES
When you "publish" one or more photos, Lightroom can compare the files in the catalog with those on the selected web service (or folder on a hard drive) and automatically perform exports according to the rules and settings you establish. Publish services remember different versions of photos, when they were published, and what's been modified since the last publication, and you can choose whether or not to publish/republish any item. In some cases, a publish service can also *remove* files from the selected destination, providing total synchronization between the contents of your catalog and the selected destination.

Publish services need to be set up before they can be used. When initially configuring a publish service, it doesn't matter if you have any photos selected; you'll add them later. The Publish Services panel functions similarly to the Folders and Collections panels.

When you create publish collections, they are grouped under the appropriate service and you can have multiple publish collections linked to each service.

After you set up the connection options for each service, you can drag and drop photos to your saved publish collections or set them up to be dynamically generated using criteria such as keywords, attributes, or any other metadata. You can even transfer smart collection settings directly to your publish services, and a publish service can also be designated as the Target Collection (which is covered in Chapter 3).

A couple of advantages publish services have over regular exports:

- Publish services show you photos that you've already published and identifies those that have been updated in Lightroom since the last publication. Published photos are automatically separated out in the preview area so you know what's changed.

- In a regular export, if there are file conflicts, you need to specifically permit Lightroom to overwrite those files. But when you republish, changed files are automatically rewritten so everything stays updated to the current version. Files that haven't changed don't need to be reprocessed.

Publish services can be an ideal solution for any situation where you regularly need to synchronize your collections in the catalog with collections of photos and videos outside Lightroom.

Note: To use publish services for websites, you must have an active Internet connection.

Publish to Flickr

Let's look at an example workflow using the publish service for Flickr. (You need to use your own Flickr account for this.) During this process, Lightroom communicates with the Flickr website to provide integrated services. Note, the wording and options vary somewhat between different service providers.

Step 1. In the Publish Sevices panel, click the Set Up… button on the Flickr publish service (see **Figure 5–33**).

Step 2. In the Lightroom Publishing Manager, go to the top panel and give your Flickr publish service a useful name in the Description: field (see **Figure 5–34**).

Figure 5-33

Step 3. Now you need to authorize your account. Click Authorize. A dialog box with a message and instructions appears; click OK. This takes you to the Flickr website for authorization. Follow the instructions on the Flickr pages. When you're done, come back to the Lightroom Publishing Manager and click OK again to finish the authorization.

05

Step 4. On the Flickr Title panel, set the options for how the new files will be named and titled on the Flickr website.

Step 5. Work through the rest of the export settings in the window, just as you do for other exports and as described earlier in this chapter. Some export settings will be disabled, or set to default values, for a particular service; in many cases the service will provide additional panel options.

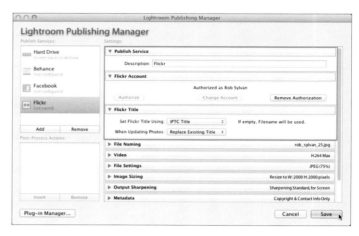

Figure 5-34

Step 6. When you're done with the settings, click Save.

Step 7. Back in the Library, add photos to your published collection by dragging and dropping from any other source. After you've put photos in the publish service collection, make sure to click on its name so you're viewing its contents. You'll see a bar across the top of the photos reading New Photos to Publish (see **Figure 5–35**).

Figure 5-35

Step 8. Click the Publish button at the bottom of the left panel (see Figure 5–35), or you can right-click or Ctrl+Click on the service name and choose Publish Now from the pop-up menu.

Lightroom exports the photos (and videos) and uploads them to Flickr; see the status indicator to verify progress (see **Figure 5–36**). Visit your account on the Flickr site to view your published photos.

Figure 5-36

COMMENTS

Lightroom can also synchronize comments, "Likes," "Favorites," etc. from supported websites, including Facebook and Flickr. Feedback from the website is shown in the Comments field on the right panel in Lightroom's Library module (see **Figure 5–37**).

When comments are synced, selecting an item in your catalog will display the comments found for that item. You can click the button at the left of the panel header to Refresh Comments, and you can even add new comments in the text field at the top of the panel (simply type in your text and press Return or Enter when you're done). The main status indicator (top panel, left side) shows when Lightroom is syncing comments with the Web service.

Publish to Hard Drive

You can use publish services to sync files with a folder on a local or network hard drive. This functionality can be used to share files among a workgroup, make backups, sync files with mobile devices, and much more.

Figure 5-37

Following are instructions for setting up a publish service to export files to a folder I set up to hold photos for my computer's screensaver slideshow. You can use the same setup to publish to any folder.

Step 1. Click the Set Up… button on the Hard Drive publish service (see **Figure 5–38**) to open the Lightroom Publishing Manager, which contains essentially the same controls as the Export screen. In the Publishing Manager window, we'll configure the settings for this Service.

Step 2. In the top panel of the Lightroom Publishing Manager, enter a Description for the new service.

Figure 5-38

Step 3. In the Export Location panel, choose the destination folder where the published files will be exported (see **Figure 5–39**). This cannot be changed after the publish connection is created (but you could always remake it if necessary.)

Step 4. Continue setting all the export options in the rest of the panels, just as you would for regular exports, as described earlier in this chapter. Post-processing is not available.

Figure 5-39

05

Step 5. When you're done configuring the settings for the service, click the Save button at the lower right of the window.

Step 6. Back in the Publish Services panel take a look at what's changed. The Hard Drive service now shows the description you added in the Publishing Manager. (You can rename it later, if you like). Below the Hard Drive service is the new publish collection. Lightroom has established a dynamic link to the new folder. You can right-click on the publish collection and select Go to Published Folder if you want to check your hard drive to confirm the folder has been created; you'll see it's empty. This is because although we've established the connection and the export parameters, we haven't yet published any photos to the folder.

Step 7. Load any image source in your catalog. Select a few photos, and drag and drop them onto the new publish service. The name now shows the number of photos in the published folder.

Step 8. To publish the photos to the folder, click the Publish button (or Publish Selected), or right-click or Ctrl+click on the published folder in the list and from the pop-up menu select Publish Now. While Lightroom is publishing the photos, notice that the main preview updates to show what's been published and what's still waiting to be done. When the process is finished, go back out to your folder to confirm that your photos are now saved there.

Step 9. Now, to see the real advantage of publish services: make a change to one or more of the photos you're viewing in the preview. (For this example, I re-cropped these photos.) The main preview now shows that I have photos waiting to be republished (see **Figure 5–40**). Again, right-click or Ctrl+click on the published folder in the list, and select Publish Now. Lightroom re-exports only the modified photos to the same folder, using the same settings.

Figure 5-40

➤ **Mark as Up-To-Date**

If you've made an accidental or insignificant change to a photo, or if you simply don't want to republish the changed photo, you can right-click or Ctrl+click the photo and choose Mark as Up-To-Date to remove it from the Republish queue.

➤ **Syncing with mobile devices**

If you have an iPad or other mobile device, you probably have some of your favorite photos stored there. I know many photographers who use their tablet or smartphone as a portable, electronic portfolio. You can use Lightroom's publish services to effectively sync your favorite photos in your Lightroom catalog with your mobile device. Set up a hard drive publish service to sync Lightroom with a folder that is also set to sync with your device. Publish the photos to the folder and then sync the device.

Changing Publish Services settings

There may be times when you want to tweak the settings for your publish services and collections. There are several menus containing important options for this.

THE + BUTTON

Click the + button on the right side of the Publish Service panel header (see **Figure 5–41**). The first item is Go to Publishing Manager.... Below that are commands grouped in sections for each installed service. You can also change the sort order and turn on/off the service icons with this menu.

Figure 5-41

MODIFYING PUBLISH SERVICES

Right-click or Ctrl+Click on a publish service in the panel. A pop-up contextual menu opens to provide the following options (see **Figure 5–42**):

- **Edit Settings:** Opens the Lightroom Publishing Manager with the current service loaded so you can make changes.

- **Rename Publish Service:** Opens a dialog box to rename the service.

Figure 5-42

05

- **Delete Publish Service:** Will remove the service after you confirm in the resulting dialog box.

- **Create Collection:** Allows you to make a new published collection using the same settings as the main service. The wording varies based on the service you are connecting to here. (When you select this option on a Web service, it may take a few moments for the window to open as it connects with the service.)

- **Create Smart Collection:** Provides controls like smart collections (see Chapter 3) to add a smart collection to the publish service.

- **Create Another Publish Service via [*publish service name*]:** Makes a new service with initial settings copied from an existing service.

MODIFYING PUBLISHED COLLECTIONS

Right-click or Ctrl+Click on a published item in the panel; a pop-up contextual menu opens containing some of the above options, plus the following (see **Figure 5–43**):

- **Create Photoset:** Creates a new collection under the selected service connection. The available options for the new collection depend on the service.

- **Create Smart Photoset:** Creates a new smart collection under the selected service. The available options for the new collection depend on the service.

- **Set as Target Collection:** Sets the item as the Target Collection (see Chapter 3).

Figure 5-43

- **Edit Collection:** Depending on the service, opens a window where you can rename the collection and/or configure its settings. In cases where the collection can't be changed after the fact, you can create a new one using the settings you want and then delete the previous collection.

- **Rename:** Change the name of the published collection (not all services have this option).

- **Delete:** Remove the published collection from the service (not all services allow this).

- **Add Selected Photo:** Adds the selected photo (or multiple selected items) to the collection (this appears only when you have a photo selected that is not in the current collection).

- **Publish Now:** Updates all items in the collection according to the settings saved in the publish service.

- **Mark to Republish:** Indicates that all items in the published folder need to be republished; this may occur by manually publishing just the collection or when initiating an automatic publish update from the parent service.

- **Show in [*publish service name*]:** Goes to the website and loads the selected album in your browser.

- **Go to Published Folder (Hard Drive services only):** This will show the folder in Finder or Explorer.

- **Import Smart Collection Settings:** Allows you to import settings from a smart collection (see Chapter 3) as the criteria for a smart publish collection.

Edit In other programs

There may be situations in which you have gone as far as you can processing in Lightroom and want to continue working with your photos in another program. In most cases, Lightroom integrates well with other image editing software. You can organize and manage all your files in the Lightroom catalog and do as much work as possible in Develop, and then send photos to another program to do additional processing.

The best way to do this is with the Edit In... command, which instructs Lightroom to open the selected photo(s) in the other program. If you keep Lightroom open, it maintains a dynamic link to the file while you're making changes in the other software and automatically updates the items in the catalog. (This is in contrast to independently editing a photo outside of Lightroom—if you change a photo by opening it directly from the hard drive into the other program, the version stored in the Lightroom catalog will be out of sync with the actual file on disk.) When you come back to Lightroom, the file is in the catalog and up-to-date with the latest version saved by the other program. The process of sending photos from Lightroom to other software and back again is often referred to as *round-trip editing*. Below are a few common scenarios for which you may want to consider using the Edit In... command:

- **HDR (High Dynamic Range) imaging:** You can use Photoshop (or other software) to blend exposures for HDR. To do this in Photoshop, use the menu command in Lightroom: Photo→Edit In...→Merge to HDR Pro in Photoshop. You need to have more than one photo selected to make this option available.

- **Panoramas:** You can use Photoshop, or other specialized software, to stitch exposures together to create panoramic photos. To do this in Photoshop, use the menu command in Lightroom: Photo→Edit In...→Merge to Panorama in Photoshop. You need to have more than one photo selected to make this option available.

05

- **Placing multiple images in Photoshop as layers:** With one or more photos selected in Lightroom, use Photo menu→Edit In…→Open as Layers in Photoshop. Each photo will be opened as a new layer, all in the same document. You need to have more than one photo selected to make this option available.

- **Advanced noise reduction, sharpening, color effects, etc.:** You can specify other stand-alone programs as an external editor to use as needed.

Figure 5-44

When you open the Edit In… menu, Lightroom lists all the external editors you have configured (see **Figure 5–44**). In this example I have set up Snapseed as an additional editor. Select one and, depending on the type of file being opened, Lightroom may provide additional options for rendering the file. When you're ready, click Edit, and Lightroom will hand off the file to the other program using the settings you specified.

Note: Some programs offer different methods of integrating round-trip editing with Lightroom. For example, when you install Photomatix HDR software for Lightroom, you access it from within the File→ Plug-in Extras menu.

Preferences→External Editing

In Lightroom Preferences, you can specify other programs to use as external editors for Lightroom (see **Figure 5–45**). If you have one or more versions of Photoshop installed on your computer, the most recent version will be selected as the primary external editor

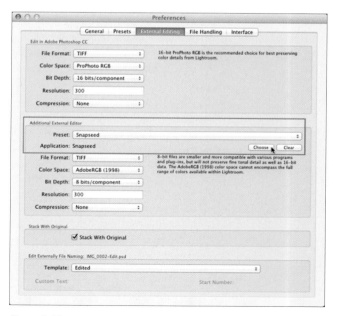

Figure 5-45

by default (and you can't change this). However, you can set any other image editing program as an additional external editor, and can save presets for as many as you need.

File Settings
In addition, Lightroom's External Editing Preferences allow you to specify the settings for the files that will be created when Lightroom hands off a file to another program. The main considerations are File Format, Color Space, Bit Depth, and Resolution. In some cases, you will also have the option to change these settings during an Edit In session.

I recommend always using TIFF for the External Editors file format. For color space, use Adobe RGB (1998) for the most flexibility (not all programs can handle ProPhoto), or ProPhoto to preserve the most color data from the original capture (if you know your destination program can handle 16-bit files saved in ProPhoto RGB). Whenever possible, using external editors, I recommend working in 16-bit or higher. (File formats and color spaces and file formats are covered earlier in this chapter.)

You can also specify the Filename Template to use for files generated with Edit In…

In the External Editor preferences there's an option to Stack with Original. (See Chapter 3 for more about working with stacks.)

 Color consistency with Photoshop
For the most predictable results, be sure that your Photoshop Color Settings are set to use the same Working RGB Space as you set in Lightroom's External Editing preferences.

 ## Edit in Photoshop
As much as Lightroom is capable of, there will be times when you've got to take a file into Photoshop to finish your work. One common example is when you need to combine multiple captures. This is called compositing—you're making a composite image from multiple original photos. Compositing can be done manually, such as stacking multiple layers with masks in Photoshop, or automatically, such as with HDR tone mapping or stitching panoramas.

Another example is heavy retouching, which also could reasonably be considered compositing. If you need to replace a large or complex section of a photo, you'll likely need more retouching power than Lightroom can provide. Or, many photographers like to apply elaborate special effects, like watercolor painting, charcoal, etc., which can be done in Photoshop. Also, there are advanced sharpening and noise reduction packages available that go far beyond what Lightroom can do in these areas, and are often implemented as Photoshop plug-ins. The outcome of all these processes is a final, composite image.

Step 1. With one or more photos selected in Grid or Filmstrip, choose the Photo menu→Edit In Photoshop… command, or use the shortcut or contextual menu. Depending on the version of Photoshop being used and type of original file, one of two things will happen:

Option A. For DNG files, camera raw files and virtual copies, Lightroom will render the file and switch over to Photoshop, where the file is opened in memory. A file on disk has not yet been saved at this stage—the image data has simply been rendered as a new file in Photoshop.

Option B. For all other file types, Lightroom opens a dialog box offering the following options (see **Figure 5–46**):

- **Edit a Copy with Lightroom Adjustments:** Instructs Lightroom to create a new file on disk, using all the current Lightroom adjustments, and open the new file into Photoshop.

- **Edit a Copy:** Lightroom creates a copy of the selected photo, but no Lightroom adjustments are applied to the copy. The resulting copy is then opened in Photoshop. Choose this option if you want to create a copy of the selected photo and maintain any layers in that photo.

Figure 5-46

- **Edit Original:** Opens the actual file on disk without applying any Lightroom adjustments to it. Here, the use of the word *original* can be confusing. What it's really doing is opening the file you have selected in Lightroom, and not rendering a new one. This also applies to a virtual copy (VC), in which case Lightroom will open the original file from which the VC was created. Choose this option if you want to open a TIFF or PSD with layers intact (just as if you opened it from the Open menu inside of Photoshop).

Step 2. In Photoshop (or other external editor) do your necessary work, and when you're done, save the file in that application (don't use Save As). Lightroom will automatically update the catalog to reflect the changes.

Open as Photoshop Smart Objects

To open a photo in Photoshop as a smart object, go to Photo menu➜Edit In…➜Open as Smart Object in Photoshop. This tells Lightroom to embed a copy of the selected photo inside a smart object layer within the copy that is sent to Photoshop. This can provide an additional level of editing flexibility. For example, you could start to process a raw photo in Develop and then open it as a smart object in Photoshop. A copy of the raw photo, plus all the existing processing instructions, will be embedded in the copy sent to Photoshop (there is no further connection between this embedded copy and the original source file). While in Photoshop you can begin editing the new copy and at any time double-click the smart object layer and open the embedded copy of the raw photo into the Camera Raw plug-in and edit it further or even undo the processing you started in Lightroom. When finished editing in Photoshop, use the Save menu (under the File menu) to save your work and have the copy automatically added to the Lightroom catalog.

⚠ **You need the latest version of Photoshop for full functionality with Lightroom**
Depending upon the version of Photoshop you have installed and how recently you've updated its Camera Raw plug-in, you may receive a Lightroom dialog box warning you that you should update Adobe Camera Raw (see **Figure 5–47**) for full compatibility. Lightroom 5 uses the same camera raw engine as Camera Raw version 8, which is compatible with Photoshop CC. Adobe releases updates to Lightroom and the Camera Raw plug-in several times per year to include new camera raw support and bug fixes. I recommend that you install these updates for both Lightroom and Camera Raw as they are released.

Figure 5-47

If you see this dialog box and if you have Photoshop CC installed, you just need to make sure the Camera Raw plug-in is up-to-date and the dialog box will go away. If you have Photoshop CS6 installed you can install the Camera Raw 8.1 plug-in to become compatible with Lightroom 5. The version of Camera Raw 8.1 for CS6 can render the new features in Lightroom 5's Develop module, but it does not expose the controls to change those new adjustments. This is an unusual move for Adobe, but they committed to providing support for the current shipping version of Photoshop (which is CS6 at the time of this writing). Once Photoshop CC begins to ship to customers it is unclear if Adobe will update the Camera Raw plug-in for Photoshop CS6 any further.

If you are unable to update the Camera Raw plug-in in your current version of Photoshop (and you are not upgrading Photoshop to CC), you have two choices: Render using Lightroom or Open Anyway.

If you use Render using Lightroom, a copy is immediately saved to disk and that file is opened in Photoshop. All your Lightroom 5 adjustments will be applied to the new file. This is the recommended option to get all of the new Lightroom 5 features and camera support with any older version of Photoshop. If you use Open Anyway, the Adobe Camera Raw (ACR) plug-in will attempt to render the raw data using the same adjustments currently applied in Lightroom. However, if the version of ACR does not have identical adjustments as the version of Lightroom you're using they will not appear, and if you are using a camera raw format not supported by the older Camera Raw plug-in then nothing will appear.

What to do with original JPEGs

If you have photos in your catalog that were originally captured as JPEG, you need to take special precautions with them. In Lightroom, JPEG files are processed non-destructively, just like all other file types, and you can process them with no loss of quality because the original pixel data is never altered. You can usually export final derivative files from original JPEGs without problems.

However, in Photoshop and other pixel-based imaging programs, you should never use a JPEG as your working Master file! Each time you save over the same JPEG again you will lose image quality. If you need to work on original JPEGs in Photoshop or other imaging software, always save them as TIFFs first, and use the TIFFs as your working Masters. (If you're working on original JPEGs only in Lightroom you can convert them to DNGs first; see the Appendix for more on this.)

Next steps

In many instances, exporting will be your final stage of the workflow. Other times it might be just the beginning! You can use Lightroom exports to copy and back up files, burn discs, send email, and synchronize your collections with websites. Whatever the case, whenever you're planning to make new files with Lightroom, you should take the time to clearly understand the requirements for the exported files and plan out your steps carefully.

 Exporting photos for copyright submission

For most U.S.-based photographers, registering photographs with the Library of Congress is highly recommended. I suggest that at least once per year you export your finished photos from Lightroom for submission to the copyright office. The easiest way to do this is to export medium-sized JPEGs and upload them in large batches to the Copyright.gov website—you can submit an unlimited number of files to the copyright office using a single payment. See the Resources section in the Appendix for link information.

INTRODUCTION TO EXPORT AS CATALOG

In addition to exporting photo and video files, you can create new catalogs from selected files (or from collections) using Export as Catalog. This creates a new catalog file on the hard drive, containing all the data for the selected photos and videos. You also have the option to export copies of the referenced files, whose new locations are updated within the exported catalog. This can be a straightforward way to transfer work between different machines. You can learn all about Export as Catalog in Chapter 11.

CHAPTER 06
Map

06

MAP: Plot your photo locations with GPS coordinates

You can use the Map module to add and view geographic information about your photos. The idea of having your photos tagged with GPS (Global Positioning System) location data opens a world of opportunities. You may remember where all of your photos have been taken now, but as your catalog grows and the years go by, those memories will fade. By tagging your photos soon after they are taken, this location information will be stored with your photos.

06

Being able to view your images on a map can help immensely when planning future trips and shoots, as well as offer the ability to analyze how a certain location affected a shot. And on the Internet, it's easier than ever to share the location where your photos were taken if they have GPS data. Having complete, accurate location metadata in your photos can provide all these benefits and more.

ABOUT GPS AND LIGHTROOM LOCATION DATA

For photographers, GPS data is most commonly recorded using handheld devices. The data is stored in tracklogs as latitude/longitude (lat/long) coordinates along with a timestamp for each recorded point. Unfortunately, today most cameras—including high-end professional dSLRs—don't record GPS data without using optional accessories. But many consumer cameras do, and most recent models of smartphones, such as iPhone and Android devices, also automatically record GPS data as each photo is taken.

Lightroom reads and understands the GPS data from all devices from which it can import photos. You can also use the standard IPTC metadata fields for address, city, state, country, etc. to further enhance the geographic details about each photo. In Lightroom, collectively, all of this data is generally referred to as *location data*.

Adding GPS coordinates to your photos in Lightroom is as easy as finding the location on the map and dragging your photos to mark the spot. Not only will the lat/long coordinates be entered in the metadata, but Lightroom can also use reverse geocoding (if it's enabled) to suggest other location information for the photos. It couldn't be any easier!

Note: By default, video files don't have location data, so in most cases you can't use the map to see where videos were shot.

 Internet access required
The Map module requires Internet access to display map data since it uses Google Maps. Map is Offline will be displayed if there is no connection available. Just like when using your browser, the speed at which the maps are loaded will vary based on your connection speed.

⚠ **Loading may be slow at first**

If you have lots of photos with GPS data, the first time you switch to the Map module with those photos loaded Lightroom will take a while to process all the files. If your photos are in subfolders, it might be best to do one folder at a time, or plan to walk away to let Lightroom do its thing and then come back later. Working in Map gets faster after the location data has been initially processed.

⚠ **Google Maps limit**

Google Maps sets a daily limit of 100k reverse geocoding requests within a 24-hour period. If you attempt to process large numbers of photos in the Map module in a short period of time you might run into this limitation.

➧ **Download all figures**

All figures in this book are available for download at:
www.lightroomers.com/lightroom5book

MAP WORKSPACE

Unlike the other modules, there aren't a lot of options in Map (see **Figure 6-1**). The left panel set contains Navigator, Saved Locations, and Collections. The right panel only contains the Metadata panel. You'll do the majority of your work using the Filmstrip and Toolbar in the main map view.

Figure 6-1

Working with photos that already have GPS data

If you already have photos with GPS coordinates attached, you can use the Map module to see them on a map with varying levels of detail.

Step 1. Select a photo or a group of photos that contain GPS coordinates from a source in Library.

Step 2. In the Map module, a marker will be displayed showing the location of the selected file in the center of the map. The marker for the selected photo(s) is highlighted in yellow. Markers contain a number if there are multiple photos in the Filmstrip taken near or at the same location. (Use the Map Key to help understand what the markers mean.)

Step 3. Click on a marker to open a balloon with a thumbnail of the photo(s). When there are multiple photos, you can click the arrows on the sides of the thumbnail to move through them.

Step 4. Click on another photo in the Filmstrip to change the map view to display its location.

Step 5. Use the Toolbar controls to change the map style and view the location with different levels of detail.

Adding GPS coordinates to photos using the map

The Map module makes it easy to add GPS coordinates and location data to any of your photos. As you're doing these steps, keep an eye on the Metadata panel.

Step 1. In Library, select a photo or a group of photos to which you wish to add GPS coordinates.

Step 2. In the Map module, navigate to the location where the photos were taken. You can search in the Location Filter bar at the top of the map view, or drag in the map to move around.

Step 3. Drag the selected photos from the Filmstrip to the location on the map. Or, right-click or Ctrl+click on the map and select Add GPS Coordinates to Selected Photos. To do this, you need to be zoomed in close enough to have a reasonable level of accuracy. Or, **new in Lightroom 5**: you can drag selected photos from the Filmstrip to a saved location in the Saved Locations panel or drag the saved location to the selected photos to add the photos to that location on the map.

Step 4. (Optional) Enter more location data in the Metadata panel based on the recommendations Lightroom provides or that you already know about that location.

Adding GPS coordinates to photos using a tracklog

GPS coordinates can be added to photos by matching the capture times to a coordinating tracklog created by a GPS device. You need to have the tracklog downloaded to your hard drive to begin the process.

Step 1. In Library, select the photos that were taken within the time frame that the GPS tracklog was created.

Step 2. In the Map module, load the tracklog using the command on the Tracklog menu.

Step 3. (Optional) Adjust the time zone offset, if necessary, using the same menu (it's helpful if the camera and the GPS device used to create the tracklog did not have their clocks synchronized beforehand).

Step 4. With the photos selected in the Filmstrip, choose the Auto-Tag Photos command on the Tracklog menu to add GPS coordinates based on the tracklog data.

Step 5. (Optional) Enter more location data in the Metadata panel based on the recommendations offered or that you already know.

Navigator

The Navigator panel (see **Figure 6-2**) displays the current map view on a small map showing a larger area. The view displayed on the main map can be changed by dragging the box or clicking in the Navigator. Use the mouse wheel to zoom in and out in the Navigator.

Figure 6-2

Saved Locations

Map locations can be saved to make it easy to navigate from one location to another or to view photos from specific areas. Saved locations can also be used as criteria to filter photos in other modules.

The default folder for your saved locations is called My Locations (see **Figure 6-3**). If you haven't yet saved any locations, this folder will be empty. Locations can either be stored in this folder or you can save them in other folders with unique names that you create.

Figure 6-3

ADDING A SAVED LOCATION

To add a location, navigate to the location on the map to be saved. Zoom in or out so that the entire area is visible. Click the + button on the right of the panel header (see Figure 6-3). A circle appears on the map representing the area to be saved and the New Location dialog box opens (see **Figure 6-4**). Enter

Figure 6-4

a Location Name. Select a folder from the drop-down menu or choose New Folder and enter a folder name. The radius of the circle on the map can be adjusted by dragging the slider or by directly entering a number. Checking the Private setting will disable exporting of location data for all photos within the saved location (more on this later). Press Return or Enter to create the saved location.

ADDING/REMOVING A SAVED LOCATION FROM PHOTOS

With photos selected in the Filmstrip, checking or unchecking the box at the left of the saved location name will add or remove those photos from the saved location.

Photo Counts on Saved Locations

The number of images within a location will be displayed to the right of the name (see **Figure 6-5**). The count includes only photos with GPS coordinates in the Filmstrip.

LOADING A SAVED LOCATION IN THE MAP

Click the arrow on the right side of the location name to display it on the map (see Figure 6-5). You can toggle on or off the circle overlay by pressing O.

Figure 6-5

EDITING A SAVED LOCATION

Load the saved location you wish to edit by clicking on the arrow. You can move the location by clicking on the pin in the center of the circle and dragging; change the location radius by dragging the pin on the outside of the circle in or out (see **Figure 6-6**). On the panel, right-click or Ctrl+click on the name and select Location Options from the contextual menu (see **Figure 6-7**) to open the Edit Location dialog box, which allows you to change the name, radius, and privacy settings.

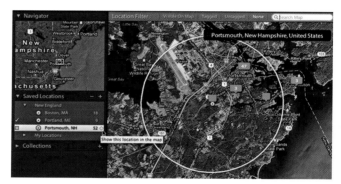

Figure 6-6

RENAMING A SAVED LOCATION

Right-click or Ctrl+click on the name and select Rename from the contextual menu (see Figure 6-7) to open a dialog box. Enter the new name and press Return or Enter.

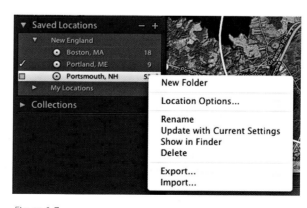

Figure 6-7

DELETING A SAVED LOCATION

Right-click or Ctrl+click on the name and select Delete from the contextual menu (see Figure 6-7). The Saved Location is deleted without any confirmation.

MANAGING SAVED LOCATIONS

To create a new folder, right-click or Ctrl+click on a location or folder name in the list and select New Folder from the contextual menu (see **Figure 6-8**). If you do this on the name of a location rather than a folder, that location will be moved to the new folder after it's created. Locations can also be moved from one folder to another by dragging and dropping.

Figure 6-8

Note: Saved Locations cannot be nested into hierarchies.

 Filter by location
In the Library module you can filter photos by location. Also, in Grid view and the Filmstrip there's a thumbnail badge showing when a photo has GPS location data attached. You can click the GPS badge to jump right to the Map module.

Collections

The Collections panel in Map displays the same list of collections available in all the other modules. Collections and related menu commands are discussed in much more detail in Chapter 3.

Figure 6-9

 **Geographic collections**
The map only displays photos in the Filmstrip, based on the source you have selected and any filters you have applied. However, you can create and manage collections from within the Map module: as you geotag your photos, you may want to consider creating collections based on a geographic area to make it easy to select them for viewing in the Map module later (see **Figure 6-9**). See Chapter 3 for information on working with collections.

Metadata

The Metadata panel is the only panel available in the right panel group of the Map module (see **Figure 6-10**). The content and functionality of this panel is identical to the Metadata panel in Library. In Map, the Location metadata field set is displayed by default, which shows the fields available for adding location data. If you need to see other metadata fields, you can load another set by choosing one from the pop-up menu in the panel header.

06

New in Lightroom 5: An editable Direction field has been added to the Metadata panel. If the GPS information includes compass direction information (North, South, East, West, etc.) it will be displayed in the field, or you can add it in manually. If present in the metadata, compass direction in degrees will display in a tooltip when you hover the cursor over the field (see Figure 6-10).

Reverse geocoding

If reverse geocoding is enabled in Catalog Settings→ Metadata→Reverse Geocoding, the address fields will be populated based on the GPS coordinates entered. The fields will display in light grey text, which means that information has not yet been committed to the photo. This is done so that if you tweak the placement of the location of that photo on the map Lightroom will automatically recheck the reverse geocode results and update location information if necessary. Once you commit the data to those fields you can still tweak the placement of the photo on the map, but Lightroom will not recheck the reverse geocode results (you can always manually enter location information). To accept this location data and commit it to the photo, click on each location field and then click the supplied information for that field, after which it will display in white text (see Figure 6-10).

If there is already data in any of these fields at the time the GPS coordinates are entered, no recommendations will be offered and nothing will be changed. The reverse geocoded fields will be exported as part of the location data, if enabled. With this in mind, you may wish to use the reverse geocoding information as a recommendation and accept it or manually enter it to make sure it is permanent.

Map display

In the center of the window, the map display area shows the location for the currently selected photo (see **Figure 6-11**). If the photo doesn't have any GPS coordinates, the display will default to the most recent location.

MAP INFO

Select View→Show Map Info or press the I key to toggle the display of the current location information in the upper right corner.

Figure 6-10

Figure 6-11

NAVIGATING THE MAP

Click and drag to move the map. Zoom in or out using the mouse wheel, the + and - keys, or the slider in the Toolbar. Double-click on the map to zoom in and center the map. Hold Option or Alt and drag the mouse to quickly zoom in on the selected area. Use the page up and page down keys to shift the map up and down. Use the home and end keys to shift the map left and right. Use the left and right arrow keys to switch between photos in the Filmstrip, which also updates the map display.

MAP KEY

The map key can be enabled by selecting View→Show Map Key (see **Figure 6-12**). Close it by clicking on the X in the upper right corner.

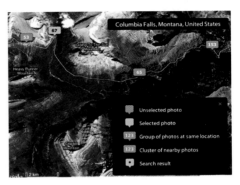

Figure 6-12

Unselected photo: The locations of unselected photos in the Filmstrip are identified with an orange marker.

Selected photo: The marker changes to yellow to identify the location of selected photos.

Group of photos at the same location:
A balloon marker identifies the location of one or more photos with the same GPS location. The number denotes how many.

Cluster of nearby photos: A rectangle marker identifies the general location of a cluster of nearby photos. Zooming in will show the locations of the separate markers.

Search result: Identifies the location of the search result.

WORKING WITH MARKERS

Photos with GPS coordinates in the Filmstrip are identified on the map with markers. There are a number of options available to work with map markers.

Figure 6-13

View photos: Click on a marker to open a balloon with a thumbnail of the photo. If there are multiple photos at the location, click the arrows on the sides of the thumbnail to move through them (see **Figure 6-13**).

Move a photo: Drag a marker on the map and drop it in a new location. (This is disabled if markers are locked.)

Move a group of photos: To move a group of photos that are at the same location, click on the marker to select them all in the Filmstrip and then drag the photos from the Filmstrip to the new location. Resist the urge to drag the marker. It is the photos you need to reposition.

Delete GPS coordinates: Right-click or Ctrl+click on the marker to bring up the contextual menu (see **Figure 6-14**) and select Delete GPS Coordinates. A dialog box will be displayed asking for confirmation.

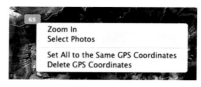

Figure 6-14

06

Set GPS coordinates: If you wish to synchronize the GPS coordinates for a group of photos that are in the same area, select Set All to the Same GPS Coordinates from the contextual menu.

Location Filter

You can use the Map module's Location Filter bar to refine the selection of photos in the Filmstrip and search the map (see **Figure 6-15**). Select View→Show Filter Bar to show or hide the filter bar or use the \ (backslash) keyboard shortcut.

Figure 6-15

MAP FILTERS

Click on the text buttons to change how thumbnails are displayed in the Filmstrip.

Visible on Map: Displays only photos that have GPS data that are in the current map view.

Tagged: Dims all thumbnails except for those that have GPS data.

Untagged: Dims all thumbnails except for those that do not have GPS data.

None: All photos are displayed in the Filmstrip.

 Filter using the Filmstrip
Use the filter options at the right of the Filmstrip to further refine what photos are shown on the map.

SEARCH MAP

Use the Search Map tool on the filter bar to quickly move to an area on the map. Enter a location name, specific address, or GPS coordinates and press Return or Enter. The map view will change to show a yellow search result marker at the chosen location. If there are multiple results for the location name, they are shown in a dropdown menu below the search box.

To remove the marker, click the X next to the search box; the map remains centered on that location.

Map Toolbar

The Map Toolbar (see **Figure 6-16**) controls the map display and provides all the tools needed for working with tracklogs.

Figure 6-16

MAP STYLE

The Map Style menu on the Toolbar lets you choose the amount of detail to display on the map. The maximum amount of zoom available varies with each style, so if you need a closer look try another style. Displaying satellite data may slow down zooming depending on your Internet connection. Click on the pop-up menu to change the style (see **Figure 6-17**) or click on the Map Style text to cycle through them all.

Hybrid: satellite data and roads

Road Map: road map (maximum zoom depth)

Satellite: satellite image only

Terrain: map with elevation representation (minimum zoom depth)

Light: light grayscale map

Dark: dark grayscale map

Figure 6-17

ZOOM

You can change the zoom level for the map by dragging or clicking the slider on the Toolbar, or by clicking on the plus and minus symbols on each end, or using the shortcuts described earlier.

LOCK MARKERS

The padlock on the Toolbar locks or unlocks the markers on the map. If unlocked, individual markers can be moved on the map by dragging and dropping. Group and cluster markers for multiple photos cannot be moved regardless of the lock status.

TRACKLOGS

The Tracklogs menu provides all the options available for working with saved tracklogs. Most of them are unavailable until a tracklog is loaded.

Lightroom can read any tracklog written in GPX format. Many GPS devices natively save the location data in this format. If so, you simply need to get the file off the device and onto your hard drive. For devices that create a different kind of file, the manufacturer often provides software that will get the file from the device and then save it out in GPX format. You may wish to name your tracklog files with a date and location to make it easier to select the proper file in Lightroom.

06

LOAD TRACKLOG

Select Load Tracklog… from the menu (see Figure **6-18**). Find a saved tracklog file on your hard drive and click Open to load it. The view will change to display the latest track on the map (see **Figure 6-19**). If the track was made while moving, it will be represented by a blue line. If the track was made while staying in one location, it will simply be a blue dot. The date of the current track is displayed on the Toolbar (see Figure 6-19).

Figure 6-18

GPS, GPX, and tracklog utilities

There are many software packages available to help manage location data. If your Tracklogs are not recognized by Lightroom, check the list of links in the Appendix for resources.

Tracklogs containing multiple tracks

A tracklog file often contains multiple tracks for different dates and times depending on the frequency the logs on the device are cleared. When the tracklog is loaded into the Map module, each track will be displayed separately. The date of the current track is shown on the Toolbar next to the Tracklogs menu. Click on the date to open a menu that displays all the tracks in the tracklog (see **Figure 6-20**). Select a track from the list to make it current and change the map display accordingly. Clicking on the word Track next to the date will cycle through all of the tracks.

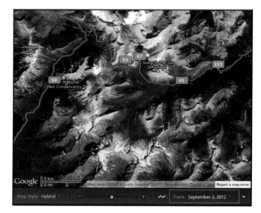

Figure 6-19

RECENT TRACKLOGS

Displays a list of recently loaded tracklogs (see **Figure 6-21**), which provides an easy way to switch back and forth between multiple tracklogs.

Figure 6-20

PREVIOUS TRACK

Move to the previous track in the log file.

NEXT TRACK

Move to the next track in the log file.

SELECT PHOTOS ON TRACKLOG

Use this menu option to select all of the photos in the Filmstrip that are part of the current track.

Figure 6-21

SET TIME ZONE OFFSET...

Use this option to synchronize the times photos were taken with the times that the GPS device recorded in the log. The most common scenario where this is necessary is when the time was not changed on the camera when in a different time zone. The Offset Time

Figure 6-22

Zone dialog box (see **Figure 6-22**) shows the time range for both the selected files and the tracklog that is loaded. If necessary, use the slider to adjust the offset in hourly increments until they are in sync. If only one track in the tracklog needs to be adjusted, tick the box next to "Offset only the selected track." Click OK to continue or Cancel to exit.

AUTO-TAG SELECTED PHOTOS

Select the photos in the Filmstrip and choose this option from the menu (see **Figure 6-23**) to enter GPS coordinates by matching them up with the tracklog. Markers appear on the map identifying the photo locations as the data is loaded and a message will display in the preview indicating the status of the operation (see **Figure 6-24**).

Figure 6-23

 **My photos are in the wrong locations!**
It is possible that auto-tagging will end up putting the wrong GPS coordinates on the photos if the times don't match up correctly with the tracklog. Zoom in and make sure that the photos are in the right locations after performing an auto-tag operation. If they are incorrect, don't worry—use the instructions below to delete the location data and start over with a different time zone offset.

Figure 6-24

TURN OFF TRACKLOG

Stop displaying the tracklog.

 **Deleting Location Data**
There may be times you wish to remove location data from your photos. Maybe you realize that the information is incorrect, or just want to start over fresh with a set of photos. Use Photo→Delete GPS Coordinates to remove just the GPS coordinates. A dialog box will ask for confirmation (see **Figure 6-25**). Use Photo→ Delete All Location Metadata to remove the location data and GPS coordinates. You will be prompted to continue (see **Figure 6-26**).

Figure 6-25

Figure 6-26

06

Sync Metadata

Location data can be copied from one photo to others using the Sync Metadata button at the bottom of the right panel set (see **Figure 6-27**). Select a group of photos and press the button to open the Synchronize Metadata window (see **Figure 6-28**). Tick the boxes for the metadata to be synced. Anything that remains unchecked will not be modified in the target photos. The settings from the target photo will be applied to the rest of the selected photos.

Figure 6-27

Figure 6-28

Keeping your location data private

There may be times when you do not want to share the location data for photos (such as your home or your favorite fishing spot). You can use the provided controls to ensure this metadata will not be embedded in the copies exported out of Lightroom.

PRIVACY SETTINGS FOR SAVED LOCATIONS

Saved Locations have the option to be set as private (see **Figure 6-29**). With this enabled, all location information will be excluded from the metadata of exported copies. This will apply to all photos that have GPS coordinates in the saved location.

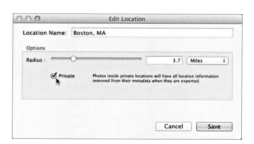

Figure 6-29

REMOVE LOCATION INFO DURING EXPORT

Excluding location data can be done on a per-photo basis during export. Select Remove Location Info in the Metadata section of the Export window. See Chapter 5 for more information on exporting.

Next steps

As the number of photos that have GPS data in them in your catalog increases, you will no doubt find interesting ways to start looking at and organizing them in the Map module. You will probably be eager to start going back through your photo archives and adding location data.

If you are bitten by the geotagging bug, you're certainly not alone. There are numerous online and real-world groups and clubs that share techniques, tips and travel stories. See the Appendix for links.

COLLECTING DATA

If you're like me, you'll immediately wish you had more GPS data for photos in your archives. Although you can certainly start geotagging any and all your photos using the drag-and-drop methods described in this chapter, what's probably more important is that, going forward, you geotag your photos as they're created. Depending on your camera, you may have many options for adding GPS data at the time of capture; the major camera manufacturers are beginning to add GPS capability to many new camera models.

You'll quickly find that the practice of including location data with your photo library is fun and easy, and creates new interest and relevance for your images.

Smartphone GPS apps

If you regularly take photos using your smartphone, make sure the settings are enabled to record location data. There are also rapidly increasing numbers of iOS and Android apps available to record tracklogs with your phone.

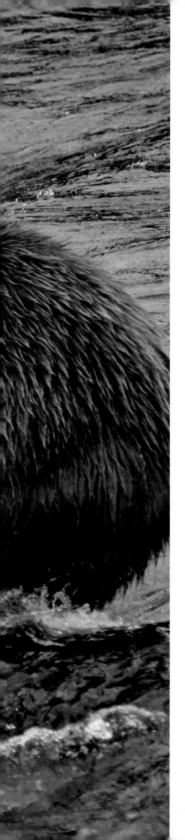

CHAPTER 07
Book

07

07

BOOK: Design and order photo books in Lightroom

Photo books have become enormously popular in recent years. This is primarily due to advances in digital technology that have made print-on-demand practical and economical. As recently as the 1990s, if you wanted to produce a photo book it meant shooting film, producing scans and color separations, and printing with plates made from film negatives. Making a book was a very costly and time-consuming process.

All of this is no longer necessary—you can now capture digital photographs with quality that surpasses the reproduction characteristics of film and immediately have those images printed using a digital press. Digital imaging and printing technology has made high-quality book printing available to the masses.

With the Book module you can design sophisticated books entirely within Lightroom and upload them directly to Blurb or Export as a PDF or series of JPEGs.

What's New in Book

- **Add page numbers to your book**
- **Save custom page layouts for reuse**
- **Improved text options**

Photo books can be used to present any kind of photography. In particular, books are very popular with wedding and event photographers, who frequently produce them for clients. Photojournalists can put together portfolio collections of their documentary work and present them in book format. A sports photographer shooting a little league team can hand out books at the end of the season. During the holidays, photo books make great gifts for friends and family. You'll undoubtedly find unlimited potential uses for your photo books. What's more, seeing entire collections of your best photos in print can be very gratifying. Whatever your intended purpose may be, you can now easily produce books to share your photography with clients, family, and friends without using other software.

 Download all figures

All figures in this book are available for download at: www.lightroomers.com/lightroom5book

Publish a Book

When you load the Book module by clicking in the Module Picker, there's usually a short delay as Lightroom reads the photos in the selected source and prepares the layout using the default settings or the most recently used settings. If you switch to the Book module using a saved Book in the Collections panel, all the settings and photos will be loaded for that book. As described in Chapter 1, the first time you enter a module you'll see the Module Tips. (You can show the tips again at any time using the command under the Help menu.)

WORKSPACE OVERVIEW

The Book module workspace has organizational panels on the left and layout panels on the right (see **Figure 7-1**). Previews for the book pages load in the center of the screen; you can zoom in and out of the previews like in the other modules. When working

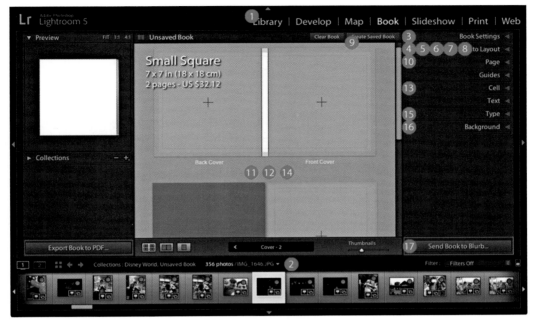

Figure 7-1

in Book, you'll mainly use the right panels, the Toolbar, the Filmstrip, and the main preview area; I usually keep the left panels hidden. The Book module also has its own set of Preferences, which are discussed later in this chapter.

INTRODUCING CELLS

Every page in a book, regardless of the template it's made from, is built using cells. Photos are placed in cells; text is placed in cells; the cells are positioned in the layout based on the chosen template. You can change the content of a cell at any time. The Book module combines the functionality of cells with drag-and-drop controls, resulting in simple yet powerful solutions for laying out pages. Using cell padding to control spacing of elements on the page, you can design book page layouts that you'd previously have to make with InDesign or Illustrator.

BOOK TEMPLATES AND PRESETS

The Book module is template-driven: you can't just drag and drop elements and move them around freely on the pages. This helps reduce the chance for error. But with the provided controls you can create sophisticated book designs using just about any layout you can imagine. And with Auto Layout Presets, you can quickly format an entire book using dynamically generated content based on the templates of your choice.

ITERATIVE WORKFLOW

If you have no prior experience laying out pages for a book, don't worry! Perhaps more than anywhere else in Lightroom, working in the Book module is an *iterative* process. It's unlikely, especially at first, that you'll make a perfect book without needing to make any changes to the layout and settings. Instead, you'll take one or two steps forward, then go back to refine your settings, and continue back and forth until you coax the layout into its final form. This is normal! The Book workflow is very fast and mostly intuitive. After you've made a few books, you will have a clearer idea of your ideal starting point for each set of photos, and you'll be able to better pre-visualize the steps to take and settings to use for the layout you want.

240-PAGE MAXIMUM FOR BLURB BOOKS

The Book module can create Blurb books of up to 240 pages. (If you need more pages than this, you can export PDFs and combine them, if necessary, outside Lightroom.) When you run the Auto Layout function, depending on how many photos are in the current source, you may receive a message stating that you've reached

Figure 7-2

the maximum of 240 pages, and the number of photos not being used, based on the current layout (see **Figure 7-2**). Understand that this is the maximum number of book pages, not the maximum number of photos allowed. There is no set limit to the number of photos you can include (although the maximum number of photo cells available in the built-in templates is 30 per page). Obviously, the more photos you use, the slower the performance will be, based on your computer hardware.

There is no limit to the number of pages you can use for a PDF book.

MAKING A BOOK USING DEFAULT SETTINGS

When you first enter the Book module, a new book may be laid out for you automatically, using the default settings. If you want to use these settings, you might be ready to have your book printed right away! Otherwise, you can tweak the settings, such as page size and layout, and then click the Auto Layout button to rebuild the book. Although this is by far the fastest, simplest way to make a book, you'll probably want a bit more customization. If this is the case, you can use the workflow outlined in the next section to make your first custom book.

Create a new book with a custom layout

Because the new screen interface and the required steps are a bit confusing, creating a brand new book from scratch can be the most difficult part of using the Book module. That said, you can do it quickly and easily using the following steps (use Figure 7-1 to follow along with the steps). All the settings and procedures are described in detail in the remainder of this chapter.

Step 1. In Library, organize the photos you want to use for the book. It's easiest if you put them into a unique collection but you can use filters, too. Also, it helps if your Develop work is finished on your master files at this point, but you can always go back to Develop later if you need to.

Step 2. Go to the Book module and verify that the correct group of photos is showing in the Filmstrip. You will be able to add or remove photos from the book later if necessary.

Note: There is no Use: menu in the Book Toolbar. Also, if you want to reorder the photos in an unsaved book, you need to do it in Library.

Step 3. On the Book Settings panel at the top right, enter the basic settings for the book. The most important setting at this point is the Size—it establishes all the rest of the layout parameters. Any time you change to a size other than the one used by the current layout, you'll see an alert dialog letting you know the layout has to be rebuilt. You can always come back later to change settings on this panel.

Step 4. On the Auto Layout panel, click the Clear Layout button. Unless you want to use the default layout preset (and even when you do) it's usually easiest to start with a clean layout for each new book.

07

Step 5. Also on the Auto Layout panel, click to open the Preset menu to the right and select Edit Auto Layout Preset. This opens the Auto Layout Preset Editor.

Step 6. In the Auto Layout Preset Editor, choose the layout you want to use for left and right pages. Use the controls to set up the starting layout for your new book. You should choose a layout closest to your ideal master layout for the majority of pages, including how many photos per page and whether or not the pages include text. (Later, you can apply any layout you want to any individual page.)

Step 7. When you're done setting up the layout templates to be used for your pages, click the Save button at the bottom right to save a new preset. Be sure to give your preset a meaningful name.

Step 8. Back in the Auto Layout panel, click the Auto Layout button. Lightroom places all the photos from the current image source into cells on the pages in the layout.

Step 9. Now is a good time to save the book if you have any expectation of revisiting it later. At the top right of the main preview, click Create Saved Book. Give your saved Book a useful name, and if you wish, change the options in the Save Book dialog box (keeping the defaults is usually OK). Once you've saved the Book, all the changes you make going forward are automatically saved as you work.

Step 10. (Optional—but Recommended!) If you want to change the layouts of any pages, select them in the preview and then choose another template from the Page panel. You can also use the Page panel to add new pages. (To delete pages, right-click or Ctrl+click on the page(s) in the main preview and select Remove Page from the pop-up menu.)

Step 11. (Optional) If you wish, you can reorder the pages by dragging them around in the preview. Click at the outer edge of any page to select it. As you click and drag, a thin yellow line indicates where the page will be placed when you let go of the mouse button.

Step 12. You'll often want to refine the sequence or placement of the photos after seeing them in the layout cells. You can drag and drop photos from the Filmstrip to place them into specific cells. (If another photo is already in the cell, it will be replaced.) To move a photo from one cell to another, just drag it to the new location. If there's already a photo in the destination cell, the two photos will be swapped. The photo thumbnails in the Filmstrip show a marker indicating the number of times the photo is placed in the current layout.

Step 13. (Optional) Use cell padding (on the Cell panel or by dragging in the layout) to precisely position any element on any page.

Step 14. (Optional) You can fine-tune the position and scaling of each photo within its cell. Click on the photo and drag to reposition it. When a photo is selected in its cell, a zoom slider appears so you can make the photo larger or smaller in its cell. If you want space around a photo, use the padding controls on the Cell panel or by dragging in the layout.

Step 15. (Optional) After you've gotten the pages and photos where you want them, you can add text to any pages that contain text cells. Use the controls on the Type menu and/or the Type TAT to style the text.

Step 16. (Optional) Apply any Background elements you want to include.

Step 17. Preview all the pages of the book to verify everything looks the way you want it. Go back to refine anything, as necessary, using the drag-and-drop functionality or by fine-tuning the settings on the panels. Verify the Book Settings, and when you're ready, upload to Blurb or Export to PDF.

 Undo and Redo

Perhaps nowhere more than in the Book module, the Undo and Redo commands are invaluable! Find them under the Edit menu or use the shortcuts.

Preview panel

The Preview panel shows a preview of the current page, or the cover if you're in Multi-page view (see **Figure 7-3**). At the right of the panel header are text buttons to change the preview zoom level (but it's easier to use the keyboard shortcuts instead). Otherwise, the preview panel has limited usefulness in the Book module; all the layout previews are presented elsewhere.

Figure 7-3

 Hide the left panels

When you're working in Book and you want to make the most of the available screen size, you can hide the left panels by clicking anywhere on the outer left edge of the panel. Right-click or Ctrl+click to change the hiding options. (My preference is to keep the side panels set to Manual visibility.)

Collections: Create and manage Saved Books

The Collections panel in the Book module shows the same list of collections available in all the other modules (see **Figure 7-4**).

Figure 7-4

CLEAR BOOK

If the book has not been saved, you can click the button to Clear Book at the top right of the main preview (see **Figure 7-5**). This removes all the photos and pages from the current working book. The button is not available when you're working within a saved book.

Figure 7-5

SAVING A BOOK

When you save a Book it gets added to the Collections panel with a unique Book collection icon (see Figure 7-4). To save a new Book, click the + button at the right of the Collections panel header menu. This does the same thing as clicking the Create Saved Book button in the bar at the top of the main preview area, discussed later in this chapter. The Saved Book stores the current layout settings and the selection of photos you've included. Clicking the saved Book in the Collections panel list, from anywhere in Lightroom, reloads the saved Book with all the most recent settings.

UNUSED PHOTOS IN BOOKS

Because a saved Book is essentially a type of collection, it can contain photos that are not actually used in the book layout. The inclusion or exclusion of photos in the saved Book is not dependent on whether or not those photos are placed on any of the pages. (The Filmstrip indicates whether or not a photo is used on a page in the book, which we'll look at later in this chapter.)

However, if you're working with an *unsaved* book, and you remove photos from the layout and then save the book for the first time, the photos that are not placed on any pages can be removed and not included in the saved Book. (This setting is the default in the Create Book dialog box.) If you change your mind later and want those photos back, you'll need to find them in another source and put them in the saved Book collection. In any of the other modules, you can drag and drop to add photos to the saved Book. (However, they won't be automatically placed in the layout.)

BOOK CONTEXTUAL MENU

Right-click or Ctrl+click on a Book in the Collections panel to access commands for working with the books in the panel (see **Figure 7-6**). Working with collections and related commands are discussed in detail in Chapter 3.

Combine photos from multiple sources into one book

Once you are familiar with the Book workflow, you can quickly and easily make books using photos from multiple separate sources. Hold Ctrl as you click on Collections (and/or Folders in the Library module). The photos in all the sources will be loaded in an Unsaved Book. When you save the Book, copies of all those photos from different sources will be merged into the one new Book collection.

Import Smart Collection Settings

Saved Books (and saved Slideshows, Prints, and Web Galleries) can use smart collection settings. This allows you to keep your saved books up-to-date as you make changes in the catalog. (But you'll still need to place any new photos added as a result of photos in the catalog matching the criteria.)

Figure 7-6

Book previews

As with all the other modules, you'll preview your work in Book using the main preview in the middle of the window (see **Figure 7-7**). Rather than showing just photos, the Book previews show layouts, as do the other output modules. You can view a single page, two-page spreads, or multi-page views, and you can zoom in as close as you need to make precise changes, such as when editing text. Regardless of the zoom level you're using to preview the pages, the controls all work the same.

Figure 7-7

ZOOM LEVEL

There are several ways to change the preview mode in the Book module. You can use the zoom levels on the Preview panel header to zoom in and out (see Figure 7-3) or use the keyboard shortcuts. You can use the buttons on the Toolbar (discussed next) to change what shows in the main preview.

Working in the main preview

Probably more than any other module, you will work on your book layouts directly within the main preview area. You can click on pages and photo and text cells to manipulate them and their content within the previews.

VIEW MENU

There are commands for manipulating the Book module views under this menu (see **Figure 7-8**). Note the keyboard shortcuts shown in the menu, in particular for changing View modes.

INFO OVERLAY

The Book module has only one info overlay (shown on Figure 7-1). Press the I key to toggle the info overlay on and off. The information is derived from the settings on the Book Settings panel.

PREVIEW BACKGROUND COLOR

You can change the background color used for the main preview area. Right-click or Ctrl+click in the background and select an option from the pop-up menu (see **Figure 7-9**). **Note:** This option changes the preview background in all the modules at once.

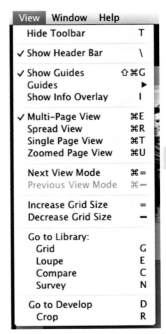

Figure 7-8

Book Toolbar

Like the other modules, Book has its own unique Toolbar (see Figure 7-10). If the Toolbar isn't visible, press the T key to show it.

PAGE VIEWS

At the left of the Toolbar are three buttons you can use to switch between the three main preview modes (see **Figure 7-10**). The first button is for Multi-Page View; use this to see many pages in the preview all at once. When you're viewing these Multi-Page previews, you can use the Thumbnails slider on the right side of the Toolbar to make the page previews larger or smaller (see Figure 7-10). The middle button is for Spread View, and the button at the right is for Single Page View. You can zoom in and out of all these views.

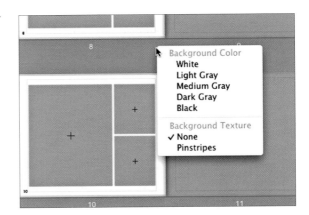

Figure 7-9

Figure 7-10

SCROLLBAR AND PAGE NAVIGATION CONTROLS

Most of the time all the pages are not visible in the main preview area. Regardless of the preview mode you're currently viewing you can use the scrollbar at the right of the main preview (see Figure 7-7), the page up/page down keys, or your mouse wheel to scroll up and down in the main preview.

You can also use the arrow buttons in the middle of the Toolbar to go forward and back in the page sequence, one full screen of previews at a time (see Figure 7-10). The number of pages these buttons advance the preview depends on your zoom level.

GO TO PAGE

In the middle of the Toolbar, the information display indicates which page previews are currently loaded in the preview area (see Figure 7-10). On Mac, you can click to type in a number and then press enter to go to a specific page (see **Figure 7-11**). On Windows, click and you'll see a Go To Page dialog box.

Figure 7-11

Book Filmstrip

The Filmstrip in the Book module is like in all the other modules, with a couple of differences. A numeric marker on each thumbnail indicates whether or not the photo is used in the current book layout, and if so, how many times (see **Figure 7-12**).

Figure 7-12

To add any photo to a layout, drag it from the Filmstrip onto a photo cell.

Custom sort order is available, but only for saved Books—if you try to rearrange the thumbnails in the Filmstrip without first saving the Book, you'll get an error message.

BOOK FILMSTRIP FILTERS

In the Book module you can filter the Filmstrip view to show Used/Unused photos (see **Figure 7-13**).

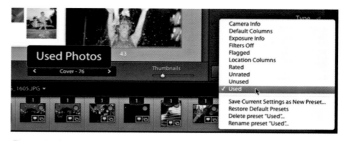

 **Filmstrip sequence and Auto Layout**

When you generate an Auto Layout, the initial sequence

Figure 7-13

of photos on the pages is based on the order they are arranged in the Filmstrip. If you drag thumbnails in the Filmstrip to change how those photos are ordered, you will need to do a new Auto Layout for their positions to change. Once photos are placed on the pages, changing their order in the Filmstrip does nothing. To reorder photos, you can drag them in the layout preview itself, which is discussed later in the chapter.

Book Preferences

Under the Book menu you can access a set of controls that dictate some essential behaviors of the Book module (see **Figure 7-14**).

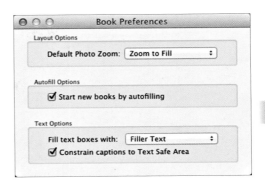

Figure 7-14

LAYOUT OPTIONS

With Default Photo Zoom you can choose between Zoom to Fill or Zoom to Fit. If you choose Zoom to Fill, Lightroom will automatically scale all your photos to the maximum size that will fit in the *shortest* dimension of each cell. This means the longer edge of a photo will be cropped unless it's an exact fit.

Zoom to Fit ensures that photos aren't cropped at all—each will be scaled so that the longest edge fits within the cell. Again, this is just the default setting, and you can always change this on a preset-specific or page-specific basis. For example, maybe you want to use a cover design with square-cropped thumbnails of all the photos inside the book, in which case you'd use Zoom to Fill. On the inside pages, you want to show each photo using its original cropping, in which case you'd use Zoom to Fit.

AUTOFILL OPTIONS

A simple check box presents a yes or no choice: when you first start a new book, do you want the photo cells to be filled with photos automatically? Leaving this box unchecked means that when you make new books you'll be presented with empty pages. If you know you're going to be making your own pages or using Auto Layout with a custom preset, leaving this option turned off can save time and computing overhead.

TEXT OPTIONS

These controls set the default behavior for text cells. If your Book is only photos, these settings won't matter, but when you're using templates that include text these options come in handy. From the menu, you can choose what text to automatically insert when new text cells are created. Your choices are Filler Text, Title Metadata, and Caption Metadata. When you use Filler Text, Lightroom uses placeholder text (similar to Lorem Ipsum) to show you where the text cells are and how the type is currently styled. If you choose photo metadata and none is found, the name of the selected metadata field will be inserted as filler text.

The Constrain captions to Text Safe Area option is the area inside the page margins where you can be reasonably certain your text won't be chopped off when the book is trimmed. Enabling this option sets a constraint whereby you cannot place text cells containing captions outside the safe area, and this applies to Auto Layout as well.

Book Settings

The Book Settings panel, at the top of the right panel set, contains the fundamental settings for the format of the book (see **Figure 7-15**).

Figure 7-15

BOOK

The Book menu currently offers three choices: Blurb, PDF, and JPEG. If you want to make a book and have it printed somewhere other than Blurb, use PDF and send the files to the vendor.

BLURB

Choosing Blurb provides the following panel options: Size, Cover, Paper Type, and Logo Page (see Figure 7-15). If these choices are unfamiliar to you, click the Learn More button to visit the Blurb website for details. The settings you choose will result in an automatically calculated Estimated Price shown below. You can choose another currency from the price menu.

New in Lightroom 5: A cheaper paper type, Standard, was added.

 Language support

Lightroom offers more extensive language support than Blurb. Depending on your operating system, installed language packs, and default language settings, you might experience unexpected behavior in the Book Settings panel if Blurb isn't compatible with your language settings.

PDF

When you choose PDF from the Book menu, the options change to provide controls for the output settings that will be used when you save the PDF file. These settings are discussed toward the end of this chapter in the section on export to PDF workflow; you can also review Chapters 5 and 9.

JPEG

The JPEG option is identical to the PDF option in regard to settings, with the only difference being that the output is a single JPEG image for each page instead of a PDF document of all pages.

 About the Size

The page templates are all based on the common preset sizes shown in the Size menu, so regardless of whether you choose Blurb, PDF, or JPEG you will have the same layout options. Since choosing the size determines all the other layout functions, you should always start your work by deciding on the size of the book you're creating. Changing sizes later can require lots more work. If you need to change a book's size, you're usually better off starting an all new book and using Auto Layout again to regenerate the pages, unless you've already spent a lot of time placing photos and editing text manually.

 About the Cover

The cover of your book is always output as a separate file, regardless of whether you choose Blurb, PDF, or JPEG.

About Book templates

All the page layouts you use in the Book module are driven by a template of one kind or another. Templates are used by the Auto Layout presets; you can also insert new pages using any template or change the template for an existing page using the Page panel, both of which are discussed below.

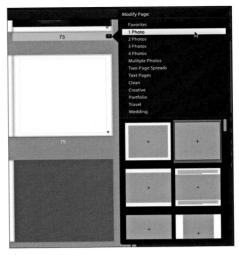

Lightroom comes with over 180 professionally designed book page templates. Each page template is based on a specific type of layout. Templates are grouped into sets of templates for 1, 2, 3, and 4 photos, Multiple Photos, Two-Page Spreads, and Text Pages (see **Figure 7-16**). They're also grouped again by style and suggested usage. (These are the same templates, just different groupings).

Figure 7-16

These templates provide a fantastic starting point for the vast majority of your book projects. You can choose from portrait, landscape, and square orientations; pages with different configurations for the placement of photos; and pages with and without text. As with all the other Lightroom modules, you can create and save your own presets. You can also save your favorite layouts using the Page panel, and even create custom pages, which you'll learn more about later in the chapter.

⇒ Drag and drop content but not cells

Although you can't directly move objects to place them just anywhere on the page, you'll usually find that using the Cell Padding settings can give you all the control you need to precisely position photos and text elements. At first, you may feel constrained by the templates and controls, but the flexibility you want is mostly there—it's just a matter of finding the correct settings.

Auto Layout: Create a book with one click

Using the controls on the Auto Layout panel, you can automate the process of creating new books and update books to use different photos or layouts (see **Figure 7-17**). Auto Layout is the fastest way to take all the photos in the Filmstrip and place them onto pages. The process consists of two main steps: choosing a layout preset and clicking the Auto Layout button.

Figure 7-17

Lightroom comes with three default Auto Layout Presets, shown in the Preset menu (see **Figure 7-18**) and you can make your own presets. Choose a preset from the menu, and

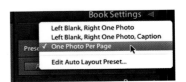

Figure 7-18

then click the Auto Layout button to build the layout using the selected preset. All the pages are automatically created using the same template depending on whether they're left or right pages.

Lightroom will create your book using as many pages as necessary based on the template and the number of photos. When you're starting a new book, this can give you a good idea of how many pages you might ultimately need.

When the Auto Layout is complete, you can individually change the template used for any page, add new pages using any template, and/or modify the individual elements on a page.

Of course, you can skip using Auto Layout altogether and build your book page-by-page yourself, using the Page panel.

CLEAR LAYOUT
You can use the Clear Layout button to delete all pages and photos, essentially starting the layout from scratch. The most recently selected template will remain applied to the layout.

Working in the Auto Layout Preset Editor
To open the Auto Layout Preset Editor, select Edit Auto Layout Preset... from the Preset menu in the Auto Layout panel (see Figure 7-18). When you first open the Auto Layout Preset Editor you'll see the settings for the preset that was selected prior to opening the dialog box. The primary default preset uses a Fixed Layout of 1 Photo on the Right Page, and nothing on the Left Page (see **Figure 7-19**). You can load settings from other saved presets by selecting them in the menu at the top of the window.

The process of defining a template for the Auto Layout preset is a matter of defining some general variables first and then getting more specific, in effect drilling down through the available choices to narrow your options and ultimately find your desired layout style. You need to specify settings for both Left Pages and Right Pages. They can be based on the same template, but usually they will be different.

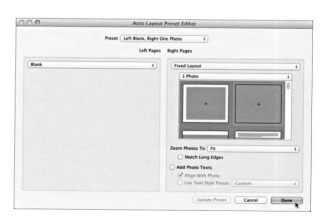

Figure 7-19

To make a new Auto Layout Preset:

Step 1. Choose the type of layout.

Step 2. Choose the template set.

Step 3. Select the specific template in the set.

Step 4. Specify options for photo zooming and photo captions.

Step 5. Save the preset.

CHOOSING THE TEMPLATES

First, use the top menu on each Left and Right page settings to determine the type of layout to use: Fixed Layout, Random from Favorites, Blank, or Same as [other] Side (see **Figure 7-20**). Most of the time you'll use a Fixed Layout, but you can also set up presets to use random layout templates based on your favorites. (You'll need to actually save some favorites first—if no favorites are available and you attempt to build an Auto Layout using Random Favorites, you'll get an error message.) Both sides cannot be Blank or Same as [other] Side.

When you choose Fixed Layout, the next menu below lets you choose from a list of the available template sets (see **Figure 7-21**). The most basic criterion is how many photos you want on each page. Choose a template set from the menu and the available templates in that set will then load in the preview area below.

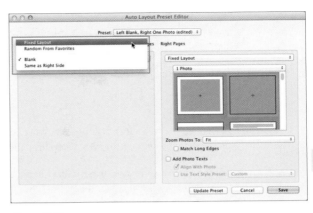

Figure 7-20

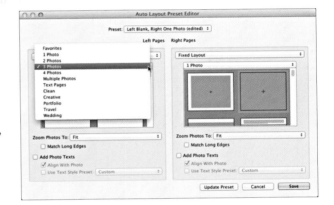

Figure 7-21

The template previews show basic renderings of the placement of photo and text cells on each page. A gray rectangle or square with a black cross in the middle represents a photo; horizontal lines represent text. Scroll through the previews to choose the specific template you want to use (see **Figure 7-22**). If you can't find what you're looking for in the current set, choose a different one from the menu above.

When you're choosing your templates, keep in mind that you will be able to fine-tune the layout using Cell Padding and Offsets. The templates only define the starting page grids for left and right pages.

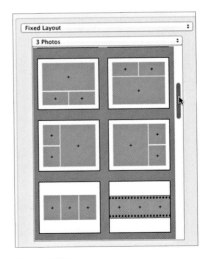

Figure 7-22

SETTING CONTENT OPTIONS

When you've selected a template, the options below the previews provide more control over how your photos and text will be placed into the cells on each page.

ZOOM PHOTOS

Choose from Zoom to Fill or Zoom to Fit. If you choose Zoom to Fill, Lightroom will automatically scale all your photos to the maximum size that will fit in the *shortest* dimension of each cell. Most of the time, this means the longer edge of photo will be cropped, unless it's an exact fit. Zoom to Fit ensures that photos aren't cropped at all— each will be scaled so that the longest edge fits within the cell. This is only the default setting for the preset; you can always change this on a page-specific or cell-specific basis.

ADD PHOTO

Check this option to have the Auto Layout process insert text cells to be used for photo captions. You can also set the default styling of the text cells to Align with Photo and Use Style Preset. Align with Photo will force the text cell to be flush with the edge of the photo it's associated with, regardless of padding; I almost always leave this checked. Use Text Style Preset refers to the saved text style presets in the Type panel. If you've saved your own, they will be listed here, otherwise you can choose from the provided defaults. Both of these options are discussed in context with their associated panels.

 Serif and Sans Serif

The Photo Caption preferences allow you to choose one of the default Text Style Presets:

This is a serif font.

This is a sans serif font.

SAVING THE PRESET

When you're done setting all the options for the preset, click the Save button at the bottom right. A dialog box appears, prompting you to enter a name for the preset. Enter a name for your preset and then click Create.

MODIFYING AN AUTO LAYOUT PRESET

If you want to come back later to modify your preset, after making changes in the Editor, use the Preset menu at the top of the Auto Layout Preset Editor to Update the preset using the current settings (see **Figure 7-23**).

Figure 7-23

Page panel: Add or change pages

You'll probably use the Page panel more than any other panel in the Book module—it presents very simple controls that belie great power and flexibility (see **Figure 7-24**).

PAGE NUMBERS

New in Lightroom 5: There is now an automated way to add page numbers to your book. Check the Page Numbers check box to insert the page numbers, and then click the associated drop-down menu to choose where they will be located on the page (see Figure **7-25**). Page number text attributes are changed via the Type panel, and Apply page number style globally is checked by default under the Edit menu, so any change you make to one page number will be reflected in all page numbers automatically (uncheck it to change page number text on a page-by-page basis).

Figure 7-24

 Choose where to start page number
By default, page numbering starts on the first page after the cover, but you can choose what page starts with numbering by right-clicking or Ctrl+clicking the page number on the desired page and choose Start Page Number from the contextual menu to make that page 1.

TEMPLATE PREVIEW AND SELECTION MENU

In the middle of the Page panel a preview is shown of the currently selected template. As you navigate through the pages of the book, this preview updates to show the template used for the currently selected page. (Covers have their own templates.) Click the black triangle button to the right of the preview (or anywhere in the Page preview) to open a menu from which you can access all the templates (see **Figure 7-26**). This is the same list of templates used by the Auto Layout Preset Editor.

Figure 7-25

MODIFY PAGE

If you have a page selected, choosing a template from the menu will apply that template to the selected page. If no page is selected, you can choose a template from the menu to use for adding new pages. You can also change the template applied to a page by clicking the bottom right corner and selecting another template from the pop-up menu.

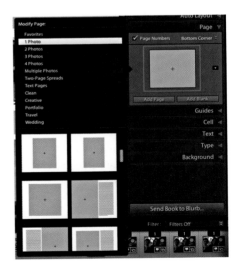

Figure 7-26

FAVORITES

In the Page panel or the flyout menu listing all the templates, right-click or Ctrl+click on a template preview and from the pop-up menu select Add Layout to Favorites, or (**New in Lightroom 5**) click the circular button that appears when you hover your cursor over the layout (see **Figure 7-27**). Favorites are dependent on the book size specified in the Size menu in the Book Settings panel. **Only favorites saved for the current size are available at any given time.** Any templates saved as favorites appear under Favorites in the flyout menu. You can easily remove a favorite by clicking the circular button a second time.

CUSTOM PAGES

New in Lightroom 5: You can save customized page layouts for reuse on other pages and in other books. We'll get into the details of how you can customize and save a page layout shortly, but I mention this exciting new feature now because once you start saving custom pages you will see a Custom Pages menu appear in the flyout menu that contains all of your saved custom templates (see **Figure 7-28**). Note, you can remove custom pages by right-clicking or Ctrl+clicking the unwanted template and choosing Remove from Custom Pages.

ADD PAGE

At any point in your workflow, you can click the Add Page button to insert a new page into the Book layout (see **Figure 7-29**). If one or more pages are selected in the main preview, the new page will be inserted after the current page(s). If no pages are selected the new page is inserted at the end of the book (but always inside the back cover). When necessary, one additional page is inserted to comply with front/back numbering and page count. (There are always full spreads used in the book—you can't use single pages alone.) The new page will use the template currently selected in the Page panel, but you can change it any time afterwards.

 Auto-repagination (aka page shuffle)
When you add an odd number of pages, the layout shifts your page content relative to the left-right page templates in use. Right pages could become left pages, and vice versa. If you've carefully refined the positions of elements based on their placement on a left or right template, you need to add an even number of pages to keep the same layouts on the existing pages.

ADD BLANK

Click this button to insert a blank page (see **Figure 7-30**). This uses the same behaviors for Add Page, described previously.

Figure 7-27

Figure 7-28

Figure 7-29

COPY/PASTE LAYOUT

You can copy the layout from a page and paste it as a new page anywhere in the document. Right-click or Ctrl+click on a page in the main preview area and choose Copy Layout from the pop-up menu (see **Figure 7-31**). Then highlight a page in the preview; right-click or Ctrl+click again and select Paste Layout from the menu. A new page is inserted using the copied layout. (Note that all the other pages will shift; see the previous notes about page shuffle.)

Figure 7-30

REMOVING PAGES

Right-click or Ctrl+click on a page in the main preview and from the pop-up select Remove page (see **Figure 7-32**). When you remove a page the photo remains in the Book Filmstrip. As explained earlier, if you'd previously saved the book, the photo will remain indefinitely; if you save a Book with unplaced photos in the Filmstrip, by default they are removed when the book is saved. (You can change this option in the Create Saved Book dialog box.) Watch out for page shuffle when you remove pages.

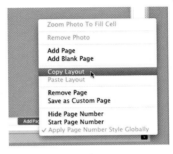

Figure 7-31

Guides

When you're setting up your books, you can use the guides and overlays to help position elements on the pages (see **Figure 7-33**). Use the check boxes to hide and show each type of guide, or turn on and off all the guides at once.

PAGE BLEED

The Page Bleed guides show the trim size of the book. Anything in the outer gray area of the preview will be trimmed when the finished book is cut to size (see Figure 7-33). Page bleed is not available when Book Settings specify PDF.

Figure 7-32

TEXT SAFE AREA

The Text Safe Area indicates the safe zone for placing text elements on the page. Book printing and bindery is not ultra-precise; you need to provide some margin for error. The thin gray line indicates the area that may be affected when the book is trimmed, so if you want to ensure something is not

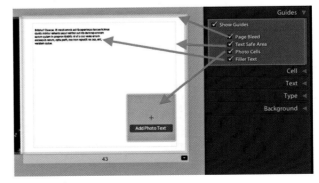

Figure 7-33

cut off, leave it within this line (see Figure 7-33). In Book Preferences (discussed earlier in this chapter) there's a setting to constrain text cells to within the Text Safe Area.

PHOTO CELLS

You can preview photo cells with a gray background, which doesn't print. This helps you see exactly where the outer edges of the cells are on the page, especially when you're using Zoom to Fit (see Figure 7-33).

FILLER TEXT

Before you insert text on a page, you can use the Filler Text guide to show the position of text cells and the type styling currently applied (see Figure 7-33). This type of guide is visible only prior to the moment you click a text cell, and it does not print. You can style a cell without selecting the text by clicking on its outer frame; as soon as you click in the text cell the Filler Text disappears and does not return.

Cell panel

The Cell panel contains the Padding controls (see **Figure 7-34**). You will use this panel frequently! Using padding, you can position elements on a page with great precision. A cell (photo or text) must be selected first. You can then drag the sliders or enter numeric values for Left, Right, Top, and Bottom. Use the small check boxes to Link padding sliders to the same values.

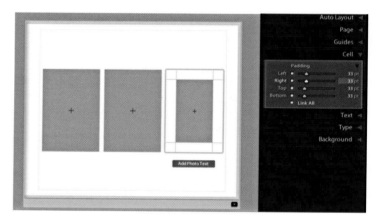

Figure 7-34

Check the Link All box at the bottom if you want to use the same padding for *all* sides of the cell. When Link All is enabled, the photo is automatically scaled as you change padding. When Link All is not checked *and* Zoom Photo to Fill Cell is not checked (on the photo cell's contextual pop-up menu), changing padding will not scale the photo—effectively applying a crop.

Once you've customized the cells on a page to have the desired padding you can save the layout as a custom page. Right-click or

Figure 7-35

Ctrl+click the page and choose Save as Custom Page (see **Figure 7-35**). Saved pages will appear under the Custom Pages section of the Page panel flyout menu (see Figure 7-28).

Drag to change padding
You can click and drag in the layout to change cell padding.

SELECTING AND DESELECTING CELLS AND PAGES

To select a cell, click within its boundary. To select a page, click one of its outer edges or anywhere in the area around the page number at the bottom of the page preview. Hold ⌘, Ctrl, or Shift and click to select multiple cells or pages at once (see Figure 7-34). A yellow border surrounds selected cells and pages.

EDIT→SELECT ALL TEXT CELLS AND SELECT ALL PHOTO CELLS

This command allows you to select all the cells of each type in the current layout (see **Figure 7-36**). This can be very helpful; for example, you can change padding on all photo cells at once, or change the padding and type styling on all text cells at once, etc.

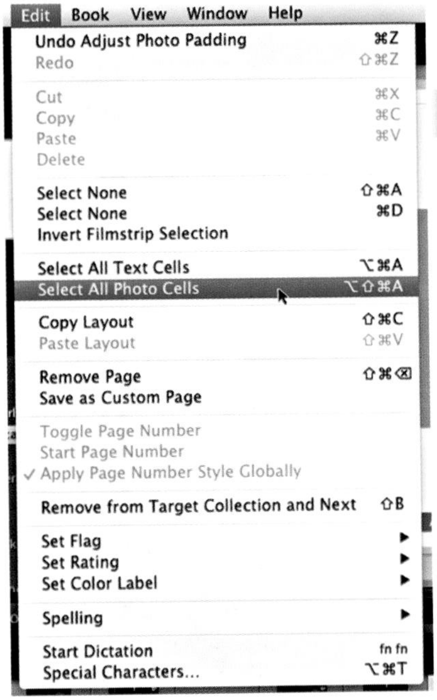

DESELECTING CELLS AND PAGES

To deselect a single item, hold Shift and click it. To deselect everything, click anywhere in the background of the main preview area.

Figure 7-36

MODIFYING PHOTOS IN CELLS

You can drag and drop photos from the Filmstrip to a cell and from one cell to another. Click to select a photo and a zoom control appears, allowing you to drag the slider to change the magnification of the photo within the cell (see **Figure 7-37**). (You can't enter numeric values.) Click and drag photos to reposition them within their cells.

REMOVING A PHOTO FROM A CELL

To remove a photo from a cell, select it and press Delete, or right-click or Ctrl+click on it and select the command from the pop-up menu.

Figure 7-37

PHOTO CONTEXTUAL MENU

Right-click or Ctrl+click on a photo for quick access to commonly used commands (see **Figure 7-38**).

RESOLUTION WARNINGS

Depending on the size of the cell, the resolution of the photo that's placed in it, and the specified zoom level for the photo, you may see a warning indicator at the top right corner of the page preview (see **Figure 7-39**). A warning indicator lets you know when a photo is enlarged beyond the recommended size for printing with good quality. You can choose to ignore the warning, but understand that your printed photos may appear pixelated; that is, you may be able to see the individual pixels in the image. Otherwise, your only options are to make the photo smaller or use a different one.

Figure 7-38

Text panel: Add text to photos and pages

The Text panel is where you add Photo Text and Page Text (see **Figure 7-40**). You must have a cell or page selected first; otherwise, the controls are dimmed and inaccessible.

Figure 7-39

PHOTO TEXT

Adding photo text inserts additional text cells positioned below, above, or over the photos. To apply photo text, select one or more photo cells in the layout and then check the box to enable Photo Text. **New in Lightroom 5:** There is now an Add Photo Text button that appears when a photo cell is selected that you can click and start entering your text right from the main preview area (see **Figure 7-41**).

CONFIGURE PHOTO TEXT

Using the menu at the right, choose what kind of text to use for the caption (see **Figure 7-42**). **New in Lightroom 5:** The photo text menu taps into your existing text templates that are available in all of the output modules. You can choose an existing text template or select Edit from the bottom of the menu and create a new custom template with the Text

Figure 7-40

Template editor. Creating custom text templates with the Text Template editor is discussed further in Chapter 9. (Once the dynamic text is rendered, you can manually edit it further.)

OFFSET

Drag the Offset slider or enter a numeric value. This controls the vertical position of the cell, with respect to its cell placement and the outer cell edge, or the photo's edge if Align with Photo is checked below. As you drag, you can see the results in the main preview. **New in Lightroom 5:** You can also interactively drag the text cell up and down on the page by placing your cursor over the edge of the cell and clicking and dragging up or down to set the offset.

Figure 7-41

ALIGN WITH PHOTO

Check the box for Align with Photo if you want to have the edges of the caption cell aligned with the edges of the photo, based on the padding values in effect in the Cell panel (see **Figure 7-43**). If Align with Photo is unchecked, the position of the caption cell will disregard the padding values and will be aligned with the outer edge of the photo cell instead (see **Figure 7-44**). If you're not using any padding, Align with Photo setting will have no apparent effect.

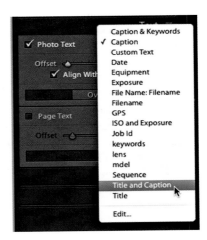

Figure 7-42

Figure 7-43

Figure 7-44

ABOVE, OVER, BELOW

To change the cell placement for the selected caption, use the buttons at the bottom of the panel section (see **Figure 7-45**).

TURN TEXT ON AND OFF

To turn off the text cells for selected photos uncheck the box; your text remains saved in case you want to turn it on again later.

PAGE TEXT

Page Text is a text cell that goes across the width of the page (see **Figure 7-46**). By default, their width is constrained by the Text Safe Area; this is a setting in Book Preferences. To apply a Page Caption, select one or more pages in the layout and then check the box for Page Caption. Drag the Offset slider to adjust the vertical position (or manually drag the cell up or down on the page). Type directly in the cell to enter your text. Each page can only have one page text cell applied.

Figure 7-45

 Copy and paste page captions

If you want the same page caption for multiple pages you need to use Copy/Paste to individually place the text into the cells on each page. There's no automated way to do this.

Figure 7-46

Type: Style your text

The Type panel gives you extensive control over the styling of text on your pages (see **Figure 7-47**). Use the Type panel to modify any text element in the document; the settings shown apply to the currently selected text cell. When you change these options on one cell, they remain the default for new cells as they are created. As you change these options you can see the effect on the selected text cell in the live preview. Click the black disclosure triangle button to the right to show additional options.

 Multiple styles within one cell

You can apply different Type styles to different text even when it's all within the same cell. Just select the specific type you want to modify and the Type controls will apply only to the selected text.

Figure 7-47

FONT AND STYLE

Choose a font in the top menu; the default is Myriad Pro. In the second menu underneath the font, choose the style and/or weight for the selected font. The choices shown here will depend on the font family selected above. (Font menu previews are not available.)

CHARACTER COLOR

To change the color of any selected text, click the swatch to the right to open the color picker. Using the color picker is discussed in detail in Chapter 4.

 Sample colors from your photos
You can choose a color from anywhere on the screen if you click inside the color picker, and then, while still holding down your mouse button, drag outside the color picker to sample colors. This is a great way to match the color of your text to a color in a photo.

SIZE

Drag the Size slider or enter a numeric value, specified in points (pt) to make the text larger or smaller.

OPACITY

Use the Opacity slider, or enter a numeric value, to set the opacity/transparency for the selected text. Semi-transparent type looks great when it's very large and overlaid on top of a photo.

 Make the panels wider
When you're adjusting the Type settings by dragging the sliders, it's easier if you make the panels much wider. Place your cursor over the inside edge of the right panels and drag inward toward the main preview area. Using wider panels provides greater sensitivity for the sliders.

TRACKING

The Tracking control sets the overall spacing for a selected line of text. All the characters are spaced the same using the specified amount, measured in em spaces.

BASELINE

The baseline is an invisible line on which the bottoms of all the characters sit. Applying a baseline shift allows you to adjust the selected text up or down in relation to the baseline. You can use this to create text as superscript (above) or subscript (below).

LEADING

Pronounced like "heading," the Leading setting sets the amount of vertical space between baselines of multiple lines of text. If you only have one line of text, the Leading setting won't do anything. Or, to use Auto Leading, click the button below.

KERNING

Kerning sets the horizontal spacing between two characters. Place your cursor between them and adjust the kerning to fine-tune their positions measured in em widths. Especially for large headlines and page titles, well-kerned text is a hallmark of good design and can make the difference between your book appearing amateurish or masterful. To use Auto Kerning, click the button below.

COLUMNS

Use this setting to format the selected text in multiple vertical columns, side by side. This is mainly used for large blocks of body copy.

GUTTER

The Gutter value sets the spacing between columns, measured in points. (In a page layout, the gutter can also refer to the space between pages in a spread, nearest the spine.)

ALIGNMENT AND JUSTIFICATION

The buttons at the bottom of the Type panel set the alignment and justification of the text (see Figure 7-47). Some templates allow vertical type.

TYPE TAT

The Targeted Adjustment Tool (TAT) in the Type panel allows you to adjust text settings without manipulating the sliders directly (see **Figure 7-48**). The TAT applies relative changes—if you're modifying text with different settings they are all changes relative to their original type values. Click the TAT to activate it, place your cursor over the text, and then click and drag to change the type settings as follows:

- Drag horizontally to change the Size of selected text.

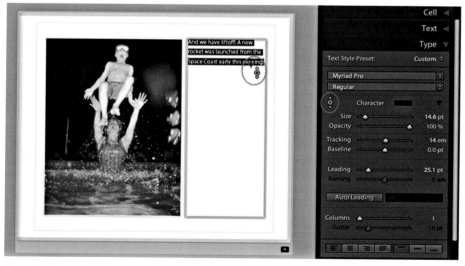

Figure 7-48

- Drag vertically to change Leading.

- Press and hold the ⌘ or Ctrl key while dragging horizontally to change Tracking.

- Press and hold the ⌘ or Ctrl key while dragging vertically to change Baseline Shift.

- With the text insertion cursor placed between two characters, drag horizontally to change Kerning.

- With a text cell selected, you can press Option or Alt to temporarily deactivate the TAT so you can select different type on the page.

Press Esc or click the tool icon to deactivate the TAT.

TEXT STYLE PRESETS

Figure 7-49

You can save your type settings as presets for quick retrieval later. With the settings applied that you want to save, at the top of the Type panel open the Text Style Preset menu and choose Save Current Settings as New Preset (see **Figure 7-49**).

 Include Text Style Presets in Auto Layout Presets
When you create a custom Auto Layout Preset (described earlier in this chapter) you can include a setting for the default Text Style Preset to use for Photo Captions. This can make building layouts *much* faster and easier!

Background panel

On the Background panel (see **Figure 7-50**) you can add background elements to your book pages. You can use a background graphic or photo and/or a solid color. Backgrounds can be applied to all the pages in the book or to individual pages.

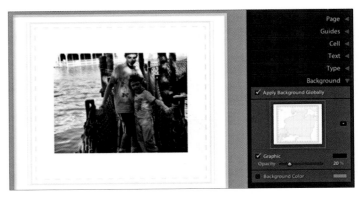

Figure 7-50

APPLY BACKGROUND GLOBALLY

With this box checked, when you apply a background it will go on all the pages in the current layout. If you leave this box unchecked, you can use a different background for individual pages.

07

BACKGROUNDS ON INDIVIDUAL PAGES

If you want a common background for most of the pages (but not all), check this box first, apply the background, and then *uncheck* it to change the backgrounds for individual pages. Any background previously placed on a page will remain until you remove it.

With such simple controls, the concept here can take some getting used to. Whether a background is applied to all the pages or to individual pages depends on the order in which you apply the settings. If you've applied a background to all pages and then override individual pages, those individual overrides will remain until you again apply a global change.

BACKGROUND PREVIEW

In the center of the Background panel a preview is shown of either the global background (if the above option is checked) or the background for the selected page.

Drag and drop a photo from the Filmstrip onto the Background panel preview to set it as the background.

REMOVING A BACKGROUND GRAPHIC

Right-click or Ctrl+click on the thumbnail preview in the panel and select the option to remove the background from the page (see **Figure 7-51**). If the Apply Background Globally box is checked, this removes the background from all the pages. With one or more individual pages selected and Apply Background Globally unchecked, removing the background does so only for those pages. If you've removed a background from one page and *then* check the Apply Background Globally box, the background will be removed from all the pages.

Figure 7-51

BACKGROUNDS MENU

Lightroom comes with many background graphics you can insert into your book layouts. Click the black triangle button to the right of the preview (or anywhere in the Background preview) and choose one from the menu (see **Figure 7-52**). Also, after you've applied your own photos as backgrounds they are retained in this list.

Figure 7-52

GRAPHIC SETTINGS

Below the background preview are settings that control the appearance of the placed graphic or photo. You can check or uncheck the box to hide and show the graphic either globally or on a page-by-page basis. To the right is a color swatch; you can apply a color to the graphic. At the bottom of the panel section is a slider that controls the Opacity of the background graphic. This is useful when you want to create a "ghosted" effect or when you want the background graphic to interact with the background color (discussed in the following section).

BACKGROUND COLOR

07

You can also apply a solid background color. Check the box to enable it, and then click the color swatch at the right to choose a color using the color picker. If you click and drag your mouse cursor with the color picker open, you can sample a color form anywhere on the screen. The color picker is explained in detail in Chapter 4.

About covers

There are separate templates for the front and back outside covers of your book. The outside covers (Front and Back) are shown at the beginning of the layout preview (see **Figure 7-53**). You can change the template and photos used for the front and back covers, just like

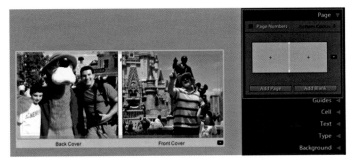

Figure 7-53

regular pages. You cannot place a photo on the inside front or inside back cover.

Note: When you're working with the Book Settings set to PDF, there are no inside covers shown in the preview.

BLURB LAST PAGE

When you're making a Blurb book, you can choose to allow them to put their logo on the last page of the book or use your own photo. (They offer a significant discount if you let them add their logo, but you'll lose one page of photos from your book; the last page becomes un-editable when the option is checked in the Book Settings panel.) When you choose Blurb in the Book menu, this option is enabled by default.

 Cover options

Depending on the size of the book you're making, Blurb has covers available in hardcover, hardcover with a dust jacket (a removable, folded paper cover over the top of a non-printed hard cover), and soft cover. If you're using another printer they may have other cover options available.

07

CHANGING THE COVER TEMPLATE

Like the inside pages, pre-built templates are provided for the covers. To choose a different cover design, use the Page panel (see **Figure 7-54**). There are 12 cover templates included; using cell padding and type styling you can really do a lot with these.

CHANGING COVER PHOTOS

When you use Auto Layout, by default, the cover will use the first and

Figure 7-54

last photos in the Filmstrip. To replace the photos just drag and drop the new ones into place from the Filmstrip. To add multiple instances of any photo in a layout you must drag from the Filmstrip. The counters in the Filmstrip will update to reflect the photo is used multiple times in the book. (If you drag and drop a photo from an inside page onto the cover, the two will be swapped, just like regular pages.)

Create Saved Book

At the top of the main preview area in the Book module is a horizontal bar that displays the saved state of the current

Figure 7-55

book (see **Figure 7-55**). If you haven't yet saved the book, it will say Unsaved Book; otherwise, it will display the name of the current saved Book. Since creating a book can be time-consuming, you should save the book early in your workflow. As you continue making modifications to the book settings, Lightroom automatically saves all your changes to the Saved Book.

Once you've saved the book, you can return to it at any time by clicking it in the Collections panel, and all your photos and the settings will be reloaded.

CLEAR BOOK

If the book has not been saved, you can click the button to Clear Book at the top right of the main preview. This removes all the photos and pages from the current working book. The button is not available when you're working within a saved book.

SAVING A BOOK

A saved Book contains the photos you've included along with their layout template and the sort order. A saved Book references the templates in use, but it does not contain the templates themselves. Remember that even if you update a saved book, you may still need to update templates (and presets) independently, and vice versa.

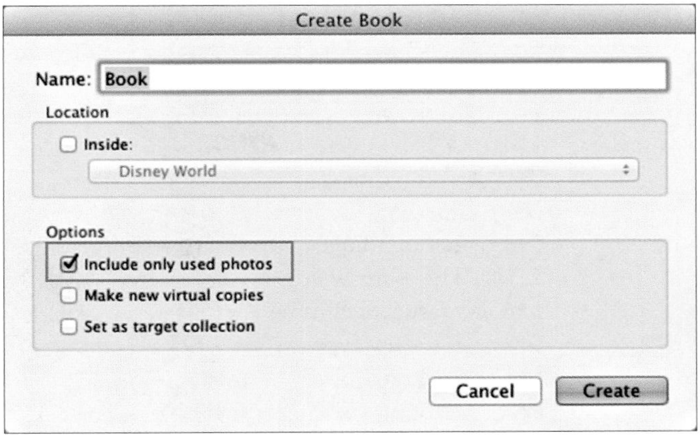

Figure 7-56

To save a Book, click the button at the right labeled Create Saved Book. This opens a dialog box containing options for saving the Book (see **Figure 7-56**). You can also save the Book by clicking the + button at the top of the Collections panel and choosing the Create Book menu option.

In the dialog box, you can specify the Placement options to choose where the new Book will be saved.

INCLUDE ONLY USED PHOTOS

The most important setting in the Create Book dialog is for "Include only used photos." If there are unused photos in the Filmstrip when you save the book, this box is checked by default. If you leave it this way, any photos not placed on pages at the time you save the Book will be removed when the Book is saved. (If all the photos in the Filmstrip are used in the Book, this option doesn't show.) I prefer to turn off this option unless I've already made my final selections. You can also choose to create new virtual copies for the photos in the Book (which I usually don't do, because I want the photos in the Book to remain linked to the photos and VCs I process in Develop or Quick Develop).

MODIFY A SAVED BOOK

There are many ways to change a previously saved book. Keep in mind that as you work on a saved book, any changes you make are automatically saved as you go. For example, you can modify any of the Book Settings and Lightroom will automatically rebuild the layout based on your changes. Depending on the number of photos in the book, this can be time-consuming. Also, you'll need to be prepared for the possibility that some of your carefully placed cells, such as captions, will be repositioned on the new pages and you'll probably need to go through them to refine their positioning. There's no way to directly synchronize settings between books; you need to use presets to apply those types of changes.

ADD MORE PHOTOS TO AN EXISTING BOOK

You can click and drag photos from any source in the catalog onto a saved Book to add them to that book, but they don't automatically get placed onto pages. It's usually easiest to do this from Library, but since the Collections panel is in Book as well, if the photos you want to add are already in one or more other collections, load those collections and then drag the thumbnails from the Filmstrip onto the saved book. You can also access other folders and collections from the Recent Sources list from the top of the Filmstrip as discussed in Chapter 3.

MAKE A NEW BOOK FROM A SAVED BOOK

Remember that a saved Book contains all the settings for the layout as well as references to all the photos. To make an all-new book from an existing one, you can use the Create Book option on the collections panel menu to duplicate the book. You can then modify it however you wish and the changes will be saved into the new book.

 Option or Alt drag

You can duplicate a Book (or any other collection) in the Collections panel by holding Option or Alt and dragging it to a new location. If you drag it to a different collection set, the original name will be retained. If you click and drag within the same location, Lightroom automatically appends the Book name to include "Copy".

EXPORT BOOK TO PDF

You can export books as PDF files. This is useful when you want to proof a book, use a printer other than Blurb, share a book by email or as a web download, show the book on your iPad, etc. When PDF is set in the Book menu on the Book Settings panel, you can configure the settings for the PDF output (see **Figure 7-57**). There is no page limit for PDF books saved from Lightroom.

Figure 7-57

Export PDF before sending to Blurb

Even if you've set Blurb as the destination in the Book menu in the Book Settings panel, you can Export as PDF by clicking the button at the bottom of the left panels. First switch to PDF in the Book menu and apply the settings you want to use, then switch back to Blurb in the Book panel. The exported PDF will use the most recent PDF settings in the panel.

PDF SETTINGS

If you've read the chapters on Export and Print and/or used those modules before, these settings will be familiar to you.

JPEG Quality: Use the slider or enter a numeric value to use for JPEG compression. Higher values produce larger files with better image quality. Quality 100 is equivalent to Photoshop's Quality 12 and can produce very large files. You should do some testing with your own photos to see where the optimal quality level is, but in general, if you're saving the PDF only to be viewed on-screen you can use settings in the 50-60 range. For printing, you can usually use settings of 80-100 with excellent quality on most photos. Using a JPEG Quality setting of 100 produces the best possible quality, but the files are *much* larger and the difference in printed quality is often negligible.

Color Profile: Choose the color space to use for the exported PDF here. If you are sending the PDF to a vendor for printing, try to get a custom profile from them and add it to the menu using the Other option (but only if they specify the profile is to be used for output). If you don't have a specific vendor profile, you can safely use sRGB for most printing conditions. If your print vendor supports it, Adobe RGB will most often provide the best color fidelity. (ProPhoto is recommended only for expert use.) Lightroom 5 can only output files using RGB color; you can't add CMYK profiles to the menu.

The contents of this menu appear similar to that of the menus in the Print to JPEG option (Print module) and the Color Space setting in the Export window; however, the contents of these menus are all separate. Adding a color profile to one menu does not populate that profile in the other modules' menus.

> **Use ColorMatch RGB for conversion to CMYK**
> If you're planning to have your PDF converted to CMYK prior to printing the book, use the ColorMatch profile. It's RGB, but contains colors much closer to the CMYK space than the other mainstream RGB spaces, so the colors will undergo much less of a visual shift when converted from RGB to CMYK . ColorMatch is a common default profile on Mac and can also be installed on Windows.

File Resolution: Drag the slider or type a numeric value. Resolution is discussed in detail in Chapters 5 and 9. Some very general guidelines: if you're going to have the book printed, using 300 ppi is fine; if you're saving the book PDF to be viewed, you can use lower resolutions.

Sharpening: Lightroom's output sharpening is also explained in Chapters 5 and 9. (I *always* apply print sharpening unless I'm going to process the files further in other software.) If you're using the PDF as a proof for a book you're later going to upload to Blurb, use Standard Glossy.

EXPORTING THE PDF
After you've applied your desired settings, click the Export as PDF button at the bottom of the right panels to save the files. Separate files are saved for cover and inside pages. You can open the PDFs in Adobe Reader or any other compatible software.

Send Book to Blurb

When you're ready, you can upload your book directly to Blurb for printing. The button for Send Book to Blurb… (see **Figure 7-58**) is available when Blurb is selected in the Book menu in the Book Settings panel. (If the menu is set to PDF that will show in the button instead.) Before you click the button, be sure you're happy with your book layout and that all your order settings are correct in the Book Settings panel. Also be sure you have an active Internet connection. (Note that Blurb has a 20-page minimum for a book to be uploaded.) Following are the steps required to perform the upload to Blurb:

Step 1. Click the Send Book to Blurb… button. This opens a dialog box where you sign in to your Blurb account, or create a new account. If you already have a Blurb account, enter your credentials and click the button to Sign In. If you don't already have a Blurb account, click the button that says Not a Member at the bottom left of the window and you can then create a new account in the same dialog box.

Figure 7-58

Step 2. In both cases, after you Sign In, the next screen asks you to enter a Title, Subtitle, and Author for the book. Book Title and Book Author are required.

Step 3. With the correct information entered, the Upload Book button becomes available at the bottom right of the dialog box. When you click this button, Lightroom renders all the pages for the book and uploads them to the Blurb servers. Your default web browser is then opened to a page on the Blurb Web site where you complete the order. (You can also change some printing options on the Blurb order page.)

You can upload a book to Blurb without paying; if you don't submit the order the files are removed from the Blurb servers after 15 days.

COLOR SPACE AND OUTPUT SHARPENING FOR BLURB UPLOADS

When you upload a book directly to Blurb, Lightroom converts the files to sRGB and applies Standard sharpening for Glossy paper. (If you make a PDF proof before uploading to Blurb, use these same settings.)

Next steps

When you get your printed book it's time to celebrate! A lot of work goes into producing any book (and sometimes a lot of money, too!) I recommend you take some time to enjoy the fruits of your labor. And don't forget to share! If you've made books for clients or as gifts, you might also want to keep a copy or two for yourself.

BLURB STORE

If you're interested in selling your book, when you print with Blurb you can also add them to their online store. Add links from your blog and website; announce it in your newsletter. Once a book is done, the work of promoting it has only just begun!

07

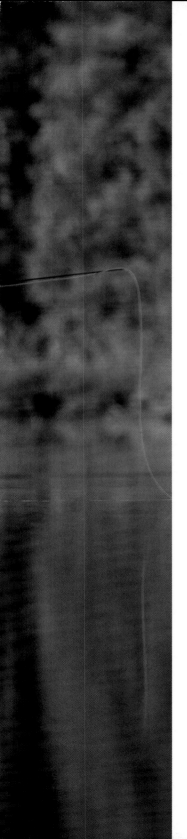

CHAPTER 08
Slideshow

08

SLIDESHOW: Present your photos and videos on screen

With Lightroom's Slideshow module you can create simple, attractive slideshows. In addition to photos, you can now include video clips in Lightroom 5. You can further enhance the look of your slideshow with text and other overlays, and configure a variety of background options. You can play your slideshow in Lightroom along with a synchronized audio soundtrack, and you can export Lightroom slideshows as video, PDF, or a series of JPEG files.

New in Lightroom 5: The ability to include video files in a slideshow is the next logical step in Lightroom's expanding support for video. Video files are treated exactly the same as photos in a slideshow, except that the video clip will play within the slideshow for the duration its slide is on screen (you may want to trim the length of the video to match the settings of your slideshow's slide duration). You could even create a slideshow entirely of video clips. We'll discuss how to handle audio included in a video clip later in the chapter.

After entering the Slideshow module, you'll probably want to start working with all the panels visible so you can see all the available options (see **Figure 8–1**). The left panel set contains Preview, Templates, and Collections. The right panels contain all the controls for customizing slideshows.

08

Figure 8-1

 Download all figures
All figures in this book are available for download at:
www.lightroomers.com/lightroom5book

Make a Slideshow

Working in Slideshow is similar to working in the other output modules: you pick a template to start, and then customize the layout to suit your needs. The general Slideshow workflow is:

Step 1. In Library, collect the photos and videos that will go into the slideshow. I like to create a regular collection of just the photos I want to use. It's easiest to organize and apply metadata to files in the Library module first; in particular, adding titles and captions.

Step 2. In the Slideshow Filmstrip (or Grid view of the Library module), you can click and drag photos to rearrange the playback sequence, or you can use a random order.

Step 3. From the Template Browser, choose a layout to begin designing the slides.

Step 4. Using the panels on the right side of the window, customize the slideshow design and add text or other optional overlay elements. Save custom layout as a template for reuse.

Step 5. (Optional) Add an audio soundtrack.

Step 6. Set the Slideshow playback options, such as timing and transitions.

Step 7. Preview your slideshow and make any desired adjustments to settings.

Step 8. Play the finished slideshow from within Lightroom and/or export it out to the hard disk.

What's New in Slideshow

- **Add video clips to a slideshow**
- **Easier manual slideshow control**
- **Improved soundtrack synchronization**

08

Preview

The Preview panel (see **Figure 8–2**) shows a small preview of the current layout, and also shows previews of Slideshow templates as you hover over them in the Template Browser. For the largest previews possible in the panel, click and drag the outer edge of the left panel set to make it wider.

ABOUT SLIDESHOW ASPECT RATIOS

The settings in Lightroom's Slideshow module are automatically derived from the current display settings on your computer, most importantly including

Figure 8-2

351

the aspect ratio of the screen. There are no controls for manually setting a fixed aspect ratio for slideshows, regardless of the template you use.

If you set up a slideshow on a computer with a widescreen format display, and then open it in another copy of Lightroom running on a display with a more traditional 4:3 aspect ratio (such as an LCD projector), the position of slideshow elements will change automatically. If you export a slideshow to files using one aspect ratio and then open the files on a computer with a different aspect ratio, the size of the slideshow may not fit ideally within the different display format.

For this reason, it's best to set up your slideshows on a computer with a display aspect ratio consistent with that of the system on which it will ultimately be shown. Obviously, if you're exporting and sharing slideshows with other people, you'll have limited control over this, and unfortunately this means that sometimes your slideshow won't look like you intended. Since the Slideshow module is dependent on your own monitor settings, if you want to ensure the slideshow will look the same on the intended display you'll need to find out those specifications and build the slideshow using settings with a matching aspect ratio.

Template Browser

The Template Browser panel (see **Figure 8–3**) lists the Slideshow templates installed with Lightroom along with templates you've created yourself. The Lightroom Templates folder contains a few basic, pre-built layouts; you can use them as they are, or you can simply use them as a starting point for customizing your own layout.

The default folder for your own custom slideshow layout is called User Templates. If you haven't yet saved any of your own Slideshow templates, this folder will be empty. Later, after you've saved your own templates, they can either be stored in User Templates or you can save them in folders with unique names.

The + symbol next to a template name indicates it's the one that will be used for Impromptu Slideshow, which is discussed toward the end of this chapter.

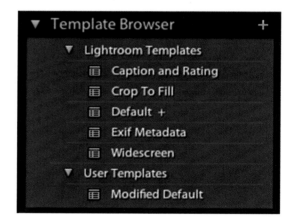

Figure 8-3

PREVIEWING TEMPLATES

In the Template Browser panel, move your mouse over the templates to see them in the Preview panel above, and then click to choose a template to use as the basis for the new slideshow. The template will load in the main preview area.

SAVING A NEW TEMPLATE

To save a new template, click the + button on the right side of the panel header. In the New Template window, type a name for the template, and choose a folder from the menu below. When you're done click Create.

THE ACTIVE TEMPLATE

When you click a template in the list, all its settings are loaded for the current set of photos. At this point, the slideshow is related to the template by common settings and the template becomes highlighted in the list. As soon as you change any settings, the current layout becomes disassociated from the template so the template name is no longer highlighted.

08

MANAGING SLIDESHOW TEMPLATES

There are several commands available for managing the templates in the panel (see **Figure 8–4**). This pop-up menu is accessed with a right-click or Ctrl+click on any template in the list. Note, the options in the contextual menu differ between the pre-built templates and the custom ones you create.

RENAMING A TEMPLATE

To rename a template, right-click or Ctrl+click its name in the list and choose Rename from the pop-up menu. Type in a new name and click OK, or press Return or Enter.

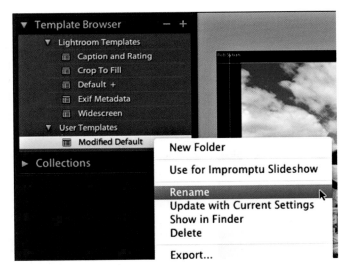

UPDATING A TEMPLATE

From the pop-up menu, you can also update a user template already in the list using all the current settings in the Slideshow module. Choose the option Update with Current Settings. Note that you can't choose

Figure 8-4

which settings to update—all the current settings are used. If you update a template with current settings, its name will become highlighted to indicate the current settings are identical to those stored within the template.

DELETING A TEMPLATE

To delete a template, right-click or Ctrl+click on the template name and choose Delete from the pop-up menu. Note that you won't get a confirmation dialog for this, but if you make a mistake or change your mind, you can use the Undo command under the Edit menu (or press ⌘+Z or Ctrl+Z) to undo the deletion.

MANAGING TEMPLATE FOLDERS

You can make a new folder for your templates by clicking the + sign in the Template Browser panel, choosing New Template Folder from the Slideshow menu, or right-clicking an existing template and choosing New Folder from the pop-up menu. (When you do this by clicking one of your own templates in the list, the selected template is automatically moved to the new folder.)

You can also drag and drop to move your own custom user templates between folders you create.

COPYING THE BUILT-IN LIGHTROOM TEMPLATES

You cannot update, delete, or rename the items in the Lightroom Templates folder. If you choose the New Folder command from the pop-up menu when clicking on a Lightroom Template, that template gets copied into the new folder. You can also drag and drop any Lightroom template onto a user folder to copy it into that folder. In both cases, you can then modify the template from there, including renaming, updating settings, etc.

Collections

The Collections panel in Slideshow displays the same list of collections available in all the other modules.

CREATING SLIDESHOW COLLECTIONS

If you create a new collection from within the Slideshow module, it gets added to the panel as a Saved Slideshow with a unique Slideshow collection icon (see **Figure 8–5**).

To save a new Slideshow collection, click the + button at the right of the Collections panel header and select Create Slideshow from the menu. (This does the same thing as clicking the Create Saved Slideshow button in the bar at the top of the main preview area, which is discussed later in this chapter.) In the resulting dialog box, give your new Slideshow a name and, optionally, change the settings—in most cases leaving the defaults is OK.

Figure 8-5

MODIFYING COLLECTIONS

To modify any of the collections in the panel, right-click or Ctrl+click on the collection or collection set name and choose a command from the pop-up menu. Collections and related menu commands are discussed in much more detail in Chapter 3.

Slideshow Toolbar

To show and hide the Toolbar, press T. The Slideshow Toolbar contains controls for navigating within the slideshow; choosing which photos to use; a play/pause button; rotate overlay buttons; and the add text button. See **Figure 8–6**.

Figure 8-6

SLIDE NAVIGATION CONTROLS

At the far left of the Toolbar, the square button serves as a shortcut to go to the first photo in the Filmstrip. To the right of that are two arrows you can use to go forward and back in the slideshow (the arrow keys on the keyboard can do this, too). These buttons simply change the active photo in the Filmstrip, which updates the slideshow preview to show that image with its associated slide contents.

USE: CONTENT SELECTION MENU

The Use: menu allows you to change the source of photos to be included in the slideshow via a pop-up menu (see **Figure 8–7**). You can choose from All Filmstrip Photos, Selected Photos, or Flagged Photos. With All Filmstrip Photos, everything visible in the Filmstrip will be included in the Slideshow. If you use Selected Photos, make sure you have some photos selected in the Filmstrip; otherwise the Slideshow will

be empty. Same goes for Flagged Photos: this option only includes photos from the Filmstrip with the flag status set to Pick (not the Reject flag); if photos are not flagged as Pick, they will be excluded from the slideshow.

Figure 8-7

Check filters

Any filters applied will also have an effect on the items visible in the Filmstrip. You can hide or show items with the filters on the top right of the Filmstrip in conjunction with the setting on the Use: menu. However, I almost always work from a unique collection made just for the current slideshow. This collection contains all of—and only—the photos I want in the slideshow, manually sorted in the order I want them displayed, so I use All Filmstrip Photos.

08

PLAY/PAUSE BUTTON

Press this button to preview the slideshow in the main preview area, starting from the currently selected photo. While the preview is playing, this button changes to Pause. Alternatively, press the Spacebar to Play/Pause the slideshow.

ROTATE BUTTONS

Click these buttons to rotate selected overlay item(s) counterclockwise or clockwise on the slide. If no overlays are selected, the buttons are dimmed. There's more about working with overlays later in this chapter.

ADD TEXT TO SLIDE

The button labeled ABC allows you to create a new text overlay. This overlay will be applied to all the slides in the current slideshow. Clicking the button displays additional options via a pop-up menu on the Toolbar (see **Figure 8–8**). From the pop-up menu, choose the type of text overlay you want to apply. For a custom text overlay that will display the same text on all slides, you'll then type or copy/paste the desired text into the field. Press Enter or Return when you're done entering text. Other types of text overlays that pull unique text from each file's metadata are discussed in more detail later in this chapter.

Figure 8-8

Options

Customize your slideshow design using the panels on the right side of the window. Changing options affects all the slides in the current slideshow—you can't selectively change settings for individual slides. It usually makes sense to work from top to bottom, but inevitably there will be some going back and forth. If you're not sure how a specific control works, try it! Changing an option in a panel will update the main preview. Keep tweaking the controls until you like the way the slideshow looks. Starting in the Options panel (see **Figure 8–9**), set how the photos are placed on the slides.

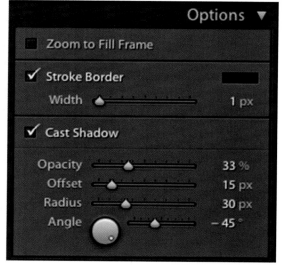

Figure 8-9

Solo mode
Remember that you can right-click or Ctrl+click on a panel header to enable Solo Mode; this is especially useful in Slideshow. As you work top to bottom on the right panels, it's easier to stay focused on the current task if the other panels are closed.

Fine slider control
You'll get a lot more control over the sliders in the right panel set if you widen the panels to their maximum width. Put your cursor over the edge of any panel; when the cursor changes to a double arrow, click and drag to the left to make the right panel set wider.

ZOOM TO FILL FRAME

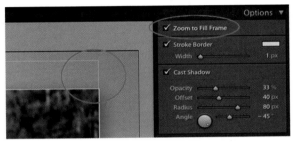

Zoom to Fill Frame will crop the files to fit within the visible area of the slide defined by the margins set in the Layout panel. Note that this doesn't change the actual crop of the photo or video, only what's visible on the slide. With Zoom to Fill enabled, you can click and drag to reposition each file

Figure 8-10

within the live area. A thin outline shows the edges of the full size file (see **Figure 8–10**).

STROKE BORDER

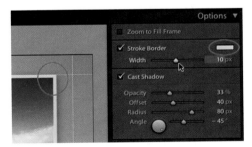

Check this box to add a solid outline around the photos. Set the width of the border (measured in pixels) by dragging the slider or by typing in a numeric value. To set the color of the border, click the rectangular swatch to the right of the panel (see **Figure 8–11**). This opens the color picker; click to choose a color. When you're done making changes in the color picker, click the X in the upper left corner or simply press

Figure 8-11

Return/Enter. If you want to cancel any changes you made in the color picker, press Esc. (The color picker is explained in detail in Chapter 4.)

CAST SHADOW

The bottom portion of the Options panel contains the settings for Cast Shadow. These shadows are displayed "behind" the photos, as if the photos were floating in front of the background with the shadow cast against it. (These won't be visible on very dark backgrounds.) Check the box to turn the cast shadow on, and then use the settings below to customize the appearance of the shadow for your desired effect.

OPACITY

Opacity sets the overall strength of the cast shadow. 100% opacity is solid black, and lower opacities make the shadow lighter and transparent over the background. You can't apply a color to the Cast Shadows; they're always neutral gray or black.

OFFSET

Offset determines how far away from the edge of the photo the shadow extends. Larger offsets give the appearance of more depth between the photo and the background.

RADIUS

Radius defines the softness of the edge of the shadow. A radius of zero provides a completely hard edge with 90-degree corners. Larger radius values apply more feathering of the shadow's edge.

ANGLE

Simulates a single light source positioned to illuminate the slide. The circle shows this as if the slide is lying flat and the light is above. You can click and drag inside the circle to position this virtual light source, or use the slider or enter a numeric value. Like Radius, the effect of the Angle will be more or less obvious depending on the Offset.

Layout

The Layout panel (see **Figure 8–12**) is where you set the slide margins, which determine the file's distance from the edges of the slide. The same margins are used for all slides.

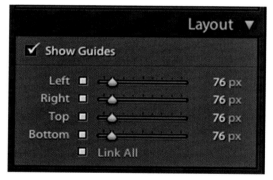

Figure 8-12

SHOW GUIDES

Tick the check box to Show Guides or uncheck the box to hide them. Whether the guides are visible or invisible, you can click and drag in the main preview to change the margins.

LAYOUT MARGINS

Slide margins are measured in pixels and the limits are dependent on your screen resolution and aspect ratio. You can individually set the widths for Left, Right, Top, and Bottom margins using the respective sliders or by entering numeric values. You can check the boxes next to the sliders to link the values of individual margins to another: top/bottom, left/right, etc.

LINK ALL

To quickly apply the same value for all margins, check the Link All box.

Overlays

In the Overlays panel (see **Figure 8–13**) you can apply text and graphical elements that appear on the slides along with the photos. Like the other panels, Overlays is split into distinct sections that control different options.

As mentioned before, overlays apply to all slides in the current slideshow; you can't apply different overlays to individual slides. However, some types of overlays, such as titles or captions, can display different content depending on the metadata associated with the photo on that slide.

 Use metadata to show different info on each slide
You can apply unique content to various metadata fields on each photo or video in the Metadata panel of Library.

IDENTITY PLATE

As also explained in other chapters, Lightroom's identity plates are graphical and text elements that you can create, customize, and apply in a variety of places throughout the program. Just like with the Book, Print, and Web modules, Slideshow allows you to place an optional identity plate on your slides, and you can access the common Identity Plate Editor from within this panel in the Slideshow module. So if you've made identity plates elsewhere, you can apply them in Slideshow, and if you make new ones here, they will be available from the other modules as well.

Figure 8-13

In Slideshow, identity plates are most often used to "brand" the presentation, but if you think creatively there are many other possible uses. A slideshow can only include one identity plate, so this is an example of a situation where you might save your own custom slideshow templates for quick access later.

Check the box to enable the identity plate in the slideshow. (When the box is unchecked, the identity plate is inactive and the controls are dimmed.)

The preview box in the panel will show the identity plate currently selected (see Figure 8–13). A checkerboard pattern in the background indicates areas of transparency, where slide layout elements behind the identity plate can show through. With a text identity plate, everything but the characters will be transparent; when you're using a graphical identity plate, areas of transparency will be determined based on the image you've loaded.

CHOOSE AN IDENTITY PLATE

Click anywhere in the preview box and choose from the pop-up menu. The default is your Main Identity Plate, if one has been previously configured using the main Identity Plate Editor.

CREATE A NEW TEXT IDENTITY PLATE

The following example explains how to place your name on the slides using a new text identity plate.

Step 1. Click anywhere in the identity plate preview and from the pop-up menu, choose Edit… (you can also use the same command to edit an existing identity plate). This opens the Identity Plate Editor, which works the same in all the modules.

Step 2. In the Identity Plate Editor window (see **Figure 8–14**), set the radio button to "Use a styled text identity plate". Type your name, studio name, or any other text you want in the text area. You can then customize the settings for Font, Style, Size, and Color. To change any of these settings for existing text it must first be selected. By selecting individual parts of the text, you can style the different parts with multiple fonts, sizes and colors.

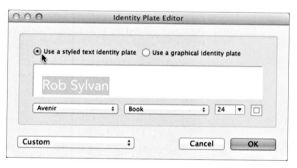

Figure 8-14

Step 3. When you're done, before closing the editor window, be sure to save a preset. Click on the menu at the bottom left of the window (if you've made changes, it will say "Custom") and then choose Save As…. Enter a name for your identity plate preset and click Save.

Step 4. Click OK to exit the editor window and apply the changes.

Back in the Overlays panel, the preview shows your selected identity plate.

Graphical identity plates

In addition to text, you can use graphic files as identity plates, which gives you the most control. Design them in Photoshop or another graphic program, save them as PNG files, and then bring them into the Lightroom's Identity Plate Editor. This technique is explained further in Chapter 9.

OVERRIDE COLOR

Below the preview box is an option for Override Color, which (as the name implies) will override all colors contained in the identity plate with a color you set here. To apply a color, first check the box, and then click the rectangular color swatch to the right. This opens the color picker where you can click to set the color. Click the X to close the color picker when you're done. (Using the color picker is explained in detail in Chapter 4.)

OPACITY AND SCALE

Sliders are provided to set the identity plate's Opacity and Scale. Opacity sets the level of transparency for the identity plate. At 100% it's totally opaque; nothing in the background will be visible through the identity plate. With lower opacity percentages you can see the other elements showing through. To scale the identity plate you can drag the slider or enter a numeric value. The scale value is a percentage of the total slide width.

MOVING, SCALING, AND ROTATING THE IDENTITY PLATE INTERACTIVELY

To reposition the identity plate in the slide layout, just click and drag it to the position you want. Also, when you've clicked to select the identity plate in the layout, control handles appear (see **Figure 8–15**). Click and drag any of the handles to scale the identity plate directly in the main preview. You can also rotate the selected identity plate by clicking the rotate buttons in the Toolbar.

Figure 8-15

Overlay anchor points

When an identity plate or text overlay is selected, you'll see a small square with a straight line connecting it to the overlay box (see **Figure 8–16**). This is an anchor point to aid positioning the overlay precisely on the slide. If you click the anchor point box and drag it around the slide, you will feel it "snap" to various key positions such as the corners and centers of the slide edges and photos. As you move it, also notice that it becomes attached to different corners of the text overlay. Clicking on the anchor point itself changes the box to orange with a black dot in the center. This means you have fixed the point in that spot. You can then move the text box around without the anchor point moving. This is helpful for long text boxes that you want to have the anchor in the center of the slide.

Figure 8-16

08

Once you've snapped the point to a location, you then snap the text overlay to the point, using the straight line as a visual reference. The benefit to this method is that the point always remains snapped to the center or edges of the photo or the slide, independent of the size or position of the text overlay itself. When you need to resize or move a text overlay to a precise position, you'll find that this straight-line, snapping behavior makes it very easy, without the need for rulers or math.

RENDER BEHIND IMAGE

At the bottom of the Identity Plate section is an option to "Render behind image". This layering control is useful when you want to use a large identity plate as part of the slide background design. When this option is enabled, the identity plate will be placed behind the photos and in front of the background.

WATERMARKING

You can apply a watermark to the photos in your slideshow. Check the box in the Watermarking section of the Overlays panel, and then choose a watermark from the pop-up menu. (You can also create a new watermark or modify an existing one using the Edit Watermarks… command in the pop-up menu.)

Unlike identity plates and other overlays, you can't position watermarks interactively—their positions are determined entirely by the settings saved in the watermark preset. Watermarks applied in the Slideshow module will only appear over the visible area of each file and will not extend onto any surrounding areas in the slide layout, regardless of the size you specify for the watermark. Also, the position of the watermark on a file is based on the outer edge of the margins set in the Layout panel, which can place the watermark outside the live area of the photo if Stroke Border is enabled and a large width is specified for the Stroke Border.

Using the Watermark Editor is covered in depth in Chapter 5.

RATING STARS

Enabling this option will display rating stars on the slides for photos that have them applied (see **Figure 8–17**). If a photo doesn't have stars applied, nothing will show in the overlay. You can change the color of the stars by clicking the color swatch to open the color picker. You can also change Opacity and Scale for the stars overlay. Rotating the stars is possible; with the Rating Stars overlay selected, use the rotate buttons on the Toolbar.

Figure 8-17

TEXT OVERLAYS

Check the box to display text overlays on the slides. The check box hides or shows *all* text overlays in the layout.

When an individual text overlay is selected in the layout preview, the controls in the Text Overlays section affect only the selected overlay. With no overlay selected, the controls in this panel section are dimmed.

When you insert a text overlay, it gets added to all the slides in the current slideshow. You can add as many text overlays as you want by repeatedly clicking the ABC button.

ADD TEXT TO SLIDE

To add a new text overlay, first make sure the Toolbar is showing (press the T key to hide/show the Toolbar). On the Toolbar, click the ABC button or use the command under the Slideshow menu in the main menu bar.

The default text type is Custom Text, which is shown in the pop-up menu in the Toolbar. With a Custom Text overlay selected, the text entry field to the right becomes active. Type your text into the box and press Return or Enter when you're done.

Or, choose another type of text template from the menu. To use photo metadata for the text overlay, click the pop-up menu (see **Figure 8–18**) and choose the type of metadata to display. The options shown use tokens, which are variable placeholders for specific types of metadata. There are tokens for Equipment, Date, Exposure, Caption, and many others, all of which use the specific metadata unique to each photo in the text overlay. This way, each photo in the slideshow can display different text, as opposed to a Custom Text overlay,

Figure 8-18

which remains the same on all slides. Creating custom text templates with the Text Template editor is discussed further in Chapter 9.

> **Titles and captions for photos**
> If you want to show individual Titles or Captions for the photos, they need to be entered in those corresponding metadata fields (in the Library module). You can't enter them in the Slideshow module.

> **Multi-line captions**
> In the Library Metadata panel, you can insert line breaks if you want to have multi-line captions. On Mac, use Shift+Return; on Windows use Ctrl+Enter.

POSITIONING AND STYLING YOUR TEXT OVERLAYS

New text overlays are inserted at the bottom left corner of the slide, using default font values for your operating system. Once you've inserted a text overlay, you can click and drag to move and/or resize it with the control handles. (Also see the information about using anchor points earlier in this chapter.) You can rotate text overlays, too; with the desired overlay selected, click one of the rotate buttons in the Toolbar.

When you've positioned your text overlay where you want it, you can use the Text Overlay controls on the panel to change Color, Opacity, Font, and Face (the font style) for the selected overlay.

 Arrow nudge
You can use the arrow keys on your keyboard to nudge overlays up, down, left, and right in small increments.

DELETING TEXT OVERLAYS
To delete an existing text overlay, select it with your mouse and press Delete on the keyboard. **When you delete it from one slide, it is deleted from all slides. If you delete the wrong overlay, just use Undo.**

SHADOW (MAC ONLY)
You can add shadows to text overlays on Mac OS X. These shadows are displayed "behind" the overlays, as if the object is floating in front of the background or photo, with the shadow cast against it (see **Figure 8–19**). Check the box to turn overlay shadows on or off. Then use the settings below to customize the appearance of the cast shadow for your desired effect. These settings are the same as for the Cast Shadow for photos, described earlier in this chapter.

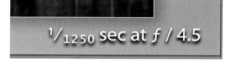

Figure 8-19

 Use consistent shadow settings
If you apply shadows behind photos and overlays, you should usually use the same settings in both panels—at the very least for the Angle setting. Otherwise, your shadows will appear as though they are coming from different light sources, which could be a distraction. (Or, could be a cool design effect!)

Backdrop
On the Backdrop panel you can customize the background for the slides. For a solid black background, simply uncheck all the options. Otherwise, use

Figure 8-20

the provided controls (see **Figure 8–20**) to apply styling for Color Wash, Background Image and Background Color. The three settings can be combined for all kinds of background effects.

COLOR WASH

This setting applies a gradient across the background, which smoothly transitions between the color you choose here and the main Background Color (see **Figure 8–21**). To apply a Color Wash, first check the box to enable it, and then click the swatch to open the color picker. Use the Opacity and Angle controls to fine-tune the strength and direction of the Color Wash.

Figure 8-21

BACKGROUND IMAGE

Here you can select a photo from within the current catalog to use as the slide background (see **Figure 8–22**). Click and drag a photo from the Filmstrip to place it into the background. You can modify the opacity of the background photo to blend it over the top of the Background Color and Color Wash. No controls are provided for the scaling or positioning of the background photo; if you need precise positioning you can use the Crop tool in Develop to crop a virtual copy exactly the way you want it.

Figure 8-22

Removing a background image

Once a background image is dragged onto the panel, it's difficult to remove. Of course, you can drag a different image to replace it, just turn off the option to hide it, or use a different template, but the image remains associated with the current panel settings. However, if you use a virtual copy (VC) as the background, deleting the VC from the catalog removes it from the Background Image panel. The background image is retained in Lightroom's memory; in some cases you may need to quit and restart Lightroom for it to be removed, and even this may work only if the slideshow has not been saved.

BACKGROUND COLOR

This value sets a solid color for the background. Click the swatch to open the color picker; click or enter a numeric value to set the Background Color.

 Keep backgrounds simple

Usually, the goal of the presentation is to prominently feature the photos! To that end, keep your backgrounds and other elements simple and clean, so they don't distract from the images.

Titles

The Titles panel (see **Figure 8–23**) provides options for adding intro and ending screens for your slideshow. A title screen can be just a simple, solid-color background or you can use identity plates to apply text or graphics. Using Photoshop or another graphics program, you can design elaborate intro and ending screens. Considering the ability to use straight text and/or graphics files, the options here are extensive.

However, one significant shortcoming of the Titles feature is that you can't independently control the duration of title screens—they will have the same timing as the rest of the slides. (However, if your slideshow isn't set to automatically repeat, the ending screen will show indefinitely.)

To enable one or both title screens, tick the appropriate check box next to it. When you enable one of the Titles elements, you see a quick preview in the main preview area. You can then apply settings for each screen independently. These settings are a limited subset of the same controls used for the Identity Plate panel discussed earlier in this chapter. You can change the background of the Title and Ending screens with the color swatches to the right (the default is black).

Figure 8-23

08

⇒ **Extend title preview time**
If you click and hold the knob on the Scale slider the preview will remain on screen until you release the mouse button.

⇒ **Creating text credits and other special title screens**
If you want to make titles or credit screens, you should consider setting up the text using a text editor program first, then copy and paste the text into the Identity Plate Editor for Titles. Text copied and pasted from a text editor into Lightroom will usually retain properties such as font style and alignment.

Better yet, use Photoshop to create graphics files, import them to the catalog, and make virtual copies. With multiple virtual copies placed one after another, you can give the appearance of prolonging the duration of special screens within your presentation.

Overall, you get a lot more flexibility and control if you use imported images for key elements in your slideshow, rather than relying only on the options in the Slideshow module.

Playback
This panel provides controls for slideshow playback from Lightroom (see **Figure 8–24**).

SOUNDTRACK
To add audio to the playback, check the box to enable the Soundtrack. You can assign only one audio file to each slideshow; if you need a soundtrack using multiple songs or audio clips you need to edit them into one file first, using other software. Lightroom can use MP3 or AAC format audio files, but can't work with audio files that are encrypted by digital rights management (DRM) encoding.

Figure 8-24

SELECT MUSIC
Click the button labeled Select Music. This opens a dialog box from which you can choose a single audio file from any connected hard drive.

⚠ **Linked music file**
The audio file is not stored in the catalog. If the drive containing the audio file is later offline, or the audio file has been renamed or deleted from disk, you'll have to reselect it or the audio won't play.

FIT TO MUSIC

To the right is a button labeled Fit to Music, which will adjust the Slides duration based on the current Fades setting to ensure all slides will display within the length of the selected audio track. This feature has been improved in Lightroom 5, but you may still need to tweak the settings after previewing the slideshow. Set your Fades setting before clicking Fit to Music.

 Re-fit the music if you change anything
If you later change soundtrack files or add/remove photos from the slideshow, click the Fit to Music button again to re-sync the slideshow duration with the audio track.

AUDIO BALANCE

The Audio Balance slider allows you to control how the audio contained in your video clips will interact with the soundtrack you add to your slideshow. If you move the slider all the way to the Video side, then the volume of the soundtrack is muted during a video slide so that the full audio in the video clip can be heard. Shifting the slider all the way to the Music side will mute any audio in the video clip and continue to play the soundtrack at full volume. Moving the slider anywhere in between allows you to combine the audio in the video with the soundtrack at a level you prefer.

SLIDE DURATION

To have the slides advance automatically, leave the Manual Slideshow box unchecked. To manually advance the slides during playback, check the Manual Slideshow box. No audio will play with Manual Slideshow checked and you can advance the slideshow as you wish with the arrow keys.

SLIDES

Using the Slides setting, you can manually set the amount of time each slide will be displayed, or click the Fit to Music button above and the timing will be calculated automatically.

FADES

The Fades slider determines the length of the transition between outgoing and incoming slides when automatic Slide Duration is enabled. Fades don't show when manually advancing the slideshow. If you are using Fit to Music, the Fades setting has a direct relationship to the Slide setting: lowering one value will increase the other, in order to force equal timing for all slides. If you change the Fades setting (or any of the slide timing settings) or the audio track, or add or remove photos, you will need to click Fit to Music again for Lightroom to recalculate the slide duration.

RANDOM ORDER

If you check the Random Order box, all the slides will display in a random order when the slideshow is played from Lightroom. This option has no effect on the sequence of exported files.

If you're presenting other people's photos submitted by a group of people, Random Order might be a good idea as it doesn't show any preference. If you have a specific sequence you want to use, leave Random Order turned off.

08

REPEAT

The Repeat check box sets the slideshow to automatically play again after reaching the last slide (or the ending screen, if applicable). You don't have the option to set a specific number of loops. When Repeat is enabled, you must stop the slideshow manually; see the next section on playing slideshows.

 Random and repeated photos

If you enable Random Order and Repeat, the random order will also apply during each loop of the total sequence, so it's possible that the same photo will be shown twice in a row. This might not be obvious; it may appear that one photo is being displayed for longer than the others.

PREPARE PREVIEWS IN ADVANCE

This option forces Lightroom to build new previews for all photos used in the slideshow, prior to beginning playback. Depending on the number of photos involved, this could take from a just few seconds to an extended period of time. A progress indicator appears when you click to play the slideshow and playback will not begin until all previews are rendered successfully.

The purpose of this option is to help avoid erratic delays during playback when a photo loads that has not had the necessary level of previews built. For example, if you have some photos for which slideshow previews already exist and some that don't, there will be a delay in playing those photos while the preview is rendered.

My preference is to play the slideshow once with this option enabled, and then disable it for subsequent presentations. Note that if you change photos or layout options you'll need to rebuild the previews.

 Save a new template

After you've designed a slideshow you like, be sure to save it as a template. When you save a slideshow template, all the current settings at the time the template is saved will be included in the template. Click the + button on the Template Browser panel header; be sure to give the template a meaningful name.

 ... or update an existing template

To save changes you've made to an existing template, right-click or Ctrl+click on the template, and from the pop-up menu choose Update with Current Settings.

Preview and Play Your Slideshow

You can see how the slideshow will look by previewing it in the main content area. This is essentially the same as playing the slideshow, but it doesn't blackout or fill the screen while playing. In most cases, while you're previewing the slideshow this way, you can also make adjustments to settings and the changes are applied—in real time—as the preview continues.

08

PREVIEW

To start previewing the slideshow, click the Preview button at the bottom of the right panel or the arrow button on the toolbar; both buttons do the same thing (see **Figure 8–25**). To exit the preview, press the Stop button in the Toolbar or just press Esc on the keyboard. (You'll need to click in the main preview area or press Esc to exit preview mode anyway, whether or not the preview is actually playing.)

Figure 8-25

PLAY

To play the slideshow full-screen and in high quality, click the play button at the bottom of the right panel (see Figure 8–25), or press the Return or Enter key. This blacks out the display, starts the slideshow immediately, and presents all the slides full-screen. You can pause the slideshow while it's playing by pressing the space bar; press it again to resume. To end the slideshow and return to the regular window mode, press Esc or click anywhere on the screen.

 Play the slideshow on a secondary display
If you have dual monitors connected to your computer, you can play the slideshow only on the second screen, instead of on your main display. In the Slideshow module, under the Window→Secondary Display menu, choose the option for Slideshow, or press ⌘+Option+Shift+Enter or Ctrl+Alt+Shift+Enter.

 You can apply attributes during playback
To apply attributes while a slideshow is playing, you can use the keyboard shortcuts for ratings (0-5), flags (P, X, U), and color labels (6-9). This is an effective way to quickly apply attributes based on real-time audience or client feedback.

 Playback problems
If the slideshow stops playing, shows blank slides, or jumps back to the first slide at the wrong time, it's likely because large previews haven't been rendered for those photos. To avoid this, you can enable the option for Prepare Previews in Advance by checking the box at the bottom of the Playback panel.

Impromptu Slideshow

Impromptu Slideshow is a command that you can run from anywhere in Lightroom to immediately begin playback of a slideshow using the current image source and Slideshow module settings. In the Slideshow module Template Browser, the template with the + next to it is the layout that will be used for the Impromptu Slideshow. To choose a template for the Impromptu Slideshow, right-click or Ctrl+click on it and select that option from the pop-up menu. Press ⌘ +Enter or Ctrl+Enter to run the Impromptu Slideshow (this keyboard shortcut will work from within any module except Book).

Create Saved Slideshow

At the top of the main preview area in the Slideshow module is a horizontal bar that displays the status of the current slideshow (see **Figure 8–26**). If you haven't yet saved the slideshow, it will say Unsaved Slideshow; otherwise, it will display the name of the saved Slideshow.

Figure 8-26

08

Saving a slideshow makes a special addition to the Collections panel. A saved Slideshow contains the photos you've included along with their saved sort order, and the Use: menu options that were active at the time it was saved. A saved Slideshow stores the state of the settings at the time it was saved, and remembers which template you used, but it does not contain the template itself. Remember that if you update a saved Slideshow, you may still need to update a template if you've made changes you want to quickly reload at a later time, especially if you want to apply it to another collection of photos.

To save a Slideshow, click the button at the right labeled Create Saved Slideshow. This opens a dialog box containing options for saving the slideshow (see **Figure 8–27**). You can also save the Slideshow by clicking the + button at the top of the Collections panel and choosing the Create Slideshow menu option. In the dialog box with options for saving the Slideshow, you can specify nesting the saved Slideshow under a collection or collection set using the Placement options.

Under the Slideshow Options, you can choose to include only the photos that were used in the current slideshow, based on the Use: menu setting. You can also choose to create new virtual copies for the photos in the slideshow (which I usually don't do, because I want the photos in the slideshow to remain linked to the originals I process in Develop).

Figure 8-27

Once you've saved the Slideshow, you can return to it at any time in the future and all your photos and the slideshow settings will remain intact.

Exporting Slideshows

Besides playing the slideshow from within Lightroom, you can also export new files using the slideshow layout. The exported files will use all the settings in place at the time of the export, and will generate new files on the selected hard drive. You have three options for exporting slideshows from Lightroom: PDF, JPEG, and video.

EXPORT PDF SLIDESHOW

Click the Export PDF button at the bottom of the left panel set. A dialog box appears, providing options for the exported file (see **Figure 8–28**). If you want Adobe Acrobat and Acrobat Reader to auto-play the slideshow, and show it full-screen, you must enable the option for "Automatically show full screen". (You can change these kinds of settings by editing the resulting PDF file with the full version of Acrobat.) The PDF file will not contain a Soundtrack.

EXPORT JPEG SLIDESHOW

Select the menu command Slideshow→Export JPEG Slideshow, or hold the Option or Alt key to change the Export PDF button to Export JPEG. Each slide will be saved as a single JPEG file. Title and ending screens are not created. Output sharpening is not an available option. The Save dialog box provides controls for the size and compression level of the files (see **Figure 8–29**).

EXPORT VIDEO SLIDESHOW

To export a slideshow as a video, click the Export Video button at the bottom of the left panel or select the menu command Slideshow→ Export Video Slideshow. When you export a slideshow as video, a single .mp4 movie file (H.264) is created containing the entire slideshow with all title screens, slides, and transitions. If a music file was selected, it will be included as well. (However, if the music track is longer than the slideshow, it will fade out automatically and the movie will end after the last slide.) The Save dialog box allows you to specify the location to save the new movie file

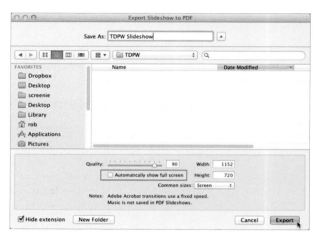

Figure 8-28

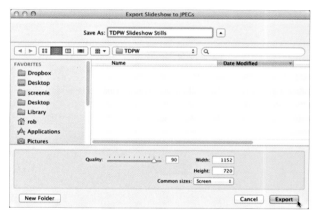

Figure 8-29

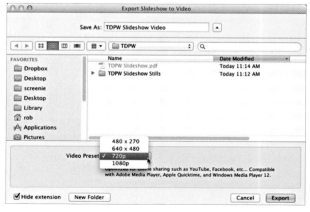

Figure 8-30

and provides a menu to select the size of the video (see **Figure 8–30**). These movies can be shared online or further optimized for mobile devices using video editing software and compression utilities.

Next steps

For quick slideshows that are easy to set up and look good for most kinds of presentations, the Slideshow module can often provide an ideal solution. However, Lightroom isn't really designed to compete with dedicated, comprehensive slideshow software. Lightroom's Slideshow functionality has not been significantly updated from version 3, so in some cases you may need to look elsewhere for more advanced slideshow capabilities. If you want to use other software to create slideshows, simply export your photos from Lightroom using the methods described in Chapter 5. The References section of the Appendix contains listings of some good options for standalone slideshow applications.

08

CHAPTER 09
Print

09

PRINT: Make professional prints yourself or at a lab

Prior to our digital age, the intrinsic nature of viewing a photograph has always meant viewing a print. Many still believe a photograph isn't truly finished until it's printed. The content of this chapter presumes you want to print your own photos or have them printed by someone else; we'll look at both scenarios.

If you're a wedding or portrait photographer, you're concerned with presenting proof images to clients prior to making the final prints. Lightroom excels at this. If you're a nature or landscape photographer, you're probably most interested in the perfect reproduction of fine detail and subtle tones within each individual photograph. Lightroom handles this with grace. Whether you need to print one photo or lots of them, you'll find Lightroom's capabilities are up to the task.

 Download all figures

All figures in this book are available for download at:
www.lightroomers.com/lightroom5book

Lightroom's Print module provides some of the most modern, sophisticated, and automated controls available for printing. In particular, the resizing, sharpening, and color management controls are made as simple as they can be. And, of course, you can save print layout templates for repeated use. In this chapter we'll go through all the features of the Print module and I'll do my best to explain all the controls in order to give you some ideas for how to apply them in your own printing scenarios.

Figure 9-1

Like everything else in Lightroom, printing can take some getting used to. Lightroom's printing procedures are very different—and notably better—than most other programs. But regardless of whether you're making your own prints or having prints made at a lab, setting up your print jobs in Lightroom is faster and easier, and offers more capabilities than ever before.

The Print module is set up like the other output modules: Preview, Templates, and Collections are on the left side, and all the controls for customizing the print job are on the right (see **Figure 9–1**). Like the Web module, the panels on the right side of Print change significantly depending on the layout style selected.

 Finish your master file first

At the risk of stating the obvious, be sure that you're happy with how your photos look before printing them. What's not so obvious is that in the digital photography workflow, your master file should never be modified with output-specific settings. When you're satisfied that each master photo looks the way you want it (using a calibrated monitor, of course) you can then make an unlimited number of derivative copies to adjust for each set of printing conditions. I'll say it again: **Never modify your master file for any specific type of output.** We'll discuss how to create virtual copies through the soft proofing process to make output specific adjustments later in the chapter.

09

Making a print

Lightroom's Print workflow has been thoughtfully engineered and often is the simplest, most straightforward way to make great digital prints using your own printer or to prepare files for printing at a lab. In both scenarios, the steps in the Print module are essentially the same, up to the last step where you either print the job or generate files for a lab to print.

Before setting up each print job, give some thought to the optimal process and the settings you will use. Are you printing just one photo, or multiple photos? What size and kind of paper will you use? Will all the photos be printed at the same size, or different sizes? Do you need to print textual information or graphics along with the images?

Following is an overview of the typical Print workflow (see Figure 9–1).

Step 1. In Library, organize the photos you want to print and put them into a collection.

Step 2. (Optional) In Develop, soft proof and adjust photos as desired.

Step 3. In the Print module, select a template or layout style.

Step 4. Use Page Setup to set the paper size and orientation for the print job.

Step 5. Modify the print layout, as necessary, to arrange the photos how you want them on the paper.

Step 6. (Optional) Add overlays for identity plates, text information, graphic elements, cut lines, etc.

Step 7. Set the output options in the Print Job panel.

Step 8. Print the job to your own printer, or use Print to JPEG to make files to send to an outside service provider.

These steps and their associated controls are explained in more detail throughout the remainder of this chapter.

Use Lightroom to create files for a lab

Many photographers, including seasoned pros who also make their own prints, often have good reasons to send their photos to a lab or other vendor for printing. Lightroom can assist with this by giving you complete control for setting up the final files that you will provide to the lab. One of the essential features of Lightroom's Print module is the ability to lay out all kinds of different print jobs. You can use Lightroom to set up contact sheets and proofs, picture packages containing prints at various sizes, and fine art enlargements, and then generate the final files for the vendor to print.

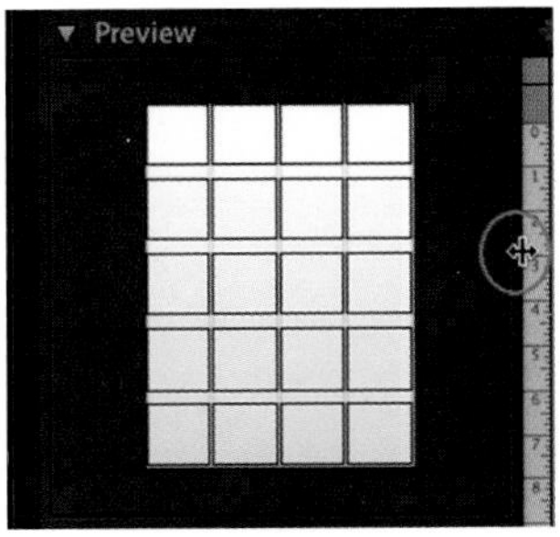

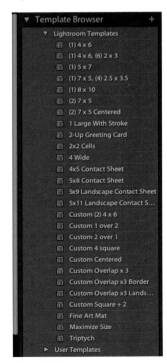

Figure 9-2

Preview

The Preview panel (see **Figure 9–2**) shows a small preview of the current print layout, and also shows previews of Print templates as you move your cursor over them in the Template Browser. For larger previews in the panel, you can click and drag the inner edge of the left panel set to make it wider.

Template Browser

As with the other output modules, your work in Print will usually start by selecting one of the available templates, which store saved layout settings. Print templates are listed in the Template Browser panel (see **Figure 9–3**). Lightroom comes with multiple print layout templates, some of which are more useful than others depending on the printing needs you have. The default templates are made using Lightroom's three built-in layout styles. User Templates is the default folder for your own custom Print layouts. If you haven't yet saved any of your own Print templates, this folder will be empty. After you've saved your own templates, they can be stored in User Templates or other folders with unique names.

Print templates are dependent on layout styles. The placement of photos on the pages depends entirely on the layout style used by the template; we'll look more at them later. After choosing a

Figure 9-3

template (or layout style) as a starting point, you'll customize your print layout using the panels on the right side of the window.

Templates include the paper size and orientation specified in Page Setup. When you're starting from built-in templates, this is one of the settings you will frequently need to change.

PREVIEWING TEMPLATES
As you hover your cursor over the list of installed templates, you can see them in the Preview panel. Choose the template that is closest to your intended layout.

LOADING A TEMPLATE
Click the name of a template to load it. When you click a template, Lightroom also loads the layout style associated with that template. (Conversely, if you click a layout style, Lightroom loads the default template for that style, or the most recent custom settings used.)

THE ACTIVE TEMPLATE
When you click a template in the list, all its settings are loaded for the current set of photos. At this point, the print layout is related to the template by common settings and the template becomes highlighted in the list. As soon as you change any settings, the current layout becomes disassociated from the template and the template name is no longer highlighted.

SAVING A NEW TEMPLATE
To save a new template, click the + button on the right side of the panel header. In the New Template window, type a name for the template, and choose a folder from the menu below. When you're done click Create.

MANAGING PRINT TEMPLATES
There are several commands available for managing the templates in the panel (see **Figure 9–4**). Right-click or Ctrl+click on any template in the list to open a pop-up menu containing the available options. There are more options available for custom user templates.

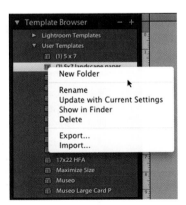

Figure 9-4

RENAMING A TEMPLATE
To rename a user template, right-click or Ctrl+click its name in the list and choose Rename from the pop-up menu. Type in a new name and click OK, or press Return or Enter.

UPDATING A TEMPLATE
From the pop-up menu, you can also update a user template already in the list with all the current settings in the Print module. Choose the option for Update with Current Settings. You can't choose which settings to update—all the current settings are used. If

you update a template, its name will become highlighted to indicate the current settings are identical to those stored within the template.

DELETING A TEMPLATE

To delete a user template, right-click or Ctrl+click on the template name and choose Delete from the pop-up menu. Note that you won't get a confirmation dialog for this, but if you make a mistake or change your mind, you can use the Undo command under the Edit menu (or press ⌘+Z or Ctrl+Z) to undo the deletion.

MANAGING TEMPLATE FOLDERS

You can make a new folder for your user templates with the New Folder command on the + button or the pop-up menu. (When you do this by clicking one of your own templates in the list, the selected template is automatically moved to the new folder.) You can also drag and drop to move user templates between folders.

COPYING THE BUILT-IN LIGHTROOM TEMPLATES

You cannot update, delete, or rename the items in the Lightroom Templates folder. If you choose the New Folder command from the pop-up menu when clicking on a Lightroom Template, that template gets copied into the new folder. You can also drag and drop any Lightroom template onto a user folder to copy it into that folder. In both cases, you can then modify the template from there, including renaming, updating settings, etc.

EXPORT TEMPLATE

You can export templates from the output modules using the command on the pop-up menu. This saves new files on your hard drive (using the .lrtemplate extension), making it easier to transfer templates between machines.

Collections

The Collections panel in the Print module shows the same list of collections available in all the other modules (see **Figure 9–5**).

Figure 9-5

SAVING A PRINT

When you create a new collection from within the Print module, it gets added to the panel as a Saved Print with a unique Print collection icon (see Figure 9–5). To save a new Print, click the + button at the right of the Collections panel header. This does the same thing as clicking the Create Saved Print button in the bar at the top of the main preview area, discussed later in this chapter. The Saved Print references the current template and the Use: menu setting in the Toolbar.

MODIFYING COLLECTIONS

To modify any of the collections in the panel, right-click or Ctrl+click on the collection or collection set name and choose a command from the pop-up menu. Collections and related menu commands are discussed in much more detail in Chapter 3.

Use virtual copies for printing

There are many situations where using virtual copies (VCs) can streamline your print workflow. When you need to adjust one or more photos to meet the criteria of a particular print job, using a VC is a good idea. In general, once you have finished a master photo and applied all the adjustments to make it look the way you want, any further modifications for specific purposes (including printing) should always be done using VCs. From your finished master files, make virtual copies for different print jobs— you can use VCs for alternate crops, making triptychs and other multi-image layouts and apply adjustments specific to the current printing conditions, all without affecting your original master photos. (Soft Proofing in Develop helps you create and adjust VCs for printing; there's a lot more about VCs and Soft Proofing in Chapter 4.) Using VCs, your work can be economically retained for future use, or you can delete them when you're done. Through it all, your master file is never altered and you can return to it to make new derivative VCs later as needed.

 Use Quick Develop for Print adjustments to multiple files

To adjust settings for multiple VCs at once, use Quick Develop in the Library module. Quick Develop adjustments are *relative*, meaning they are applied on top of the values of any existing adjustments. So even if the selected master photos were all using different adjustments, you can apply the same relative change to all of them for printing. See Chapter 3 for more about working in Quick Develop.

Page Setup

The most important control for specifying the size of the printed pages, and thus the size of the photos that can fit on them, is Page Setup. You need to apply a Page Setup as one of the first steps in the printing workflow; all the other measurements will be determined based on the Page Setup. Click the Page Setup... button at the bottom of the left panel group (see **Figure 9–6**).

Figure 9-6

In the Page Setup dialog box, choose the correct paper size and orientation for the current print job. After selecting your printer, you can then choose from preset paper sizes provided by the printer driver software, or set up a custom page size. You also need to specify the paper source and orientation (see **Figure 9–7**). Depending on your operating system and printer, the controls for this may vary, but the common goal is to precisely specify the size of the paper and the direction the images will be placed on the page. The settings you choose here dictate the parameters that Lightroom will use for layout purposes.

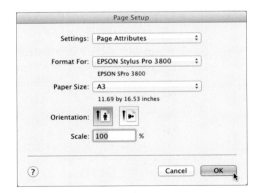

Figure 9-7

Borderless printing

If you want to print borderless, you need to choose a borderless option in Page Setup first (which is the printer driver). The settings you choose in the printer driver (via Page Setup) determine the minimum margins Lightroom can use, and when borderless is chosen it allows Lightroom's margins to go to zero. If you're framing the print, don't print borderless; be sure to leave an inch or so of blank paper around all the outside margins to make mounting easier.

Main preview area

In the center of the window, the main preview area shows the Print layout with all current settings applied. In most cases, this preview is identical to what you'll see on the printed page; however, sometimes there may be slight differences in the output due to the way different printers handle margins. If the Info Overlay is enabled (as shown on **Figure 9–8**) it will also display page information. When you're changing settings, be sure to check the preview frequently and, for multi-page print jobs, check all the pages.

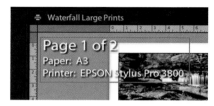

Figure 9-8

Print Toolbar

Depending on the number of photos and the layout options used, you may often end up with a print job comprised of multiple pages. All layout styles provide support for multi-page jobs. The Toolbar shows how many pages are in the current job (see **Figure 9–9**) and indicates which page you're previewing. There are arrow buttons for moving forward and back in multi-page print jobs. Click the square button to go to the first page.

Figure 9-9

The Use: menu on the Toolbar helps you choose which photos to use in the current print job (see **Figure 9–10**). If you're working from a collection and want to print everything, you can leave this set to All Filmstrip Photos. Or, using the Filmstrip you can select or deselect photos and then choose Selected Photos in the Use menu. You can also print only photos with a Pick flag.

Figure 9-10

Layout Style

Occasionally, before you choose a template, you will select an option from the Layout Style panel at the top right of the Print module (see **Figure 9–11**). The selection of a layout style determines the options available for the print job. Lightroom offers the following built-in layout styles, each providing different controls for a particular purpose.

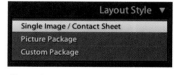

Figure 9-11

SINGLE IMAGE / CONTACT SHEET

Use the Single Image / Contact Sheet layout when you want to print a single photo or multiple photos all at the same size. This layout style places photos in cells of the same size using a fixed-grid layout.

PICTURE PACKAGE

Use the Picture Package layout to print one photo per page in multiple sizes. With Picture Package you have more control over the size and positioning of the printed photos on the paper than with Single Image/Contact Sheet, but with only one photo per layout (just like ordering school pictures).

CUSTOM PACKAGE

Custom Package allows you to totally customize the size and placement of photos on each page of the print job. This is by far the most flexible style; with a Custom Package you can print different photos at different sizes on any number of pages.

The right panels change depending on the selection in the Layout Style panel.

 Enable Solo Mode
Right-click or Ctrl+click on any panel header and click the pop-up menu option to enable Solo Mode.

Single Image / Contact Sheet

In the Single Image / Contact Sheet layout style, photos are arranged in layout cells all of the same size, arranged in a grid (see **Figure 9–12**). The Layout panel settings determine the maximum size possible for the longest side of each photo. You can rotate photos and/or scale them to fit into the grid cells differently, but all the grid cells remain the same size. This style is ideal for printing one single image, such as when making fine art prints.

SORT ORDER

The order of the photos placed in the rows and columns of the grid is based on the current sort order, which can be controlled by changing the sort order in the Library module for that grouping of photos, or manually by dragging photos to rearrange them in the Filmstrip (assuming you are working from within a regular collection or a single folder). I find it easiest to press the G key to jump to Grid view, change the sort order, and then return to the Print module.

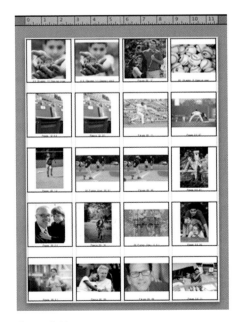
Figure 9-12

Following are descriptions of the panel controls available when working with a Single Image / Contact Sheet layout style.

Image Settings

The settings on this panel configure how the photos are placed within the grid cells (see **Figure 9–13**).

Figure 9-13

ZOOM TO FILL

This setting enlarges each photo to fill the entire grid cell. Depending on the aspect ratio of the cell, this can result in cropping the photo within the cell (see **Figure 9–14**). You can click and drag to reposition the photo within the cell (the photo is not actually cropped; it just appears that way in the layout).

ROTATE TO FIT

The Rotate to Fit option rotates photos as necessary to use the most available space in the cell. Individual photos are rotated so their longest edge corresponds with the longest side of the cell (see **Figure 9–15**).

REPEAT ONE PHOTO PER PAGE

With multiple images selected, enabling this option forces Lightroom to place only one photo on each page of the print job. If you have more than one photo selected, enabling this option produces a multi-page job. Depending on the number of rows and columns you specify, this could result in just one photo on the page, or multiple copies of the same photo repeated at the same size in all the cells (see **Figure 9–16**).

STROKE BORDER

Enable this option to add a solid, outline border to the printed photos (see **Figure 9–17**). Use the slider or type in a numeric value to set the width of the border. Click the rectangular color swatch to open the color picker and set a color. (The color picker is explained in detail in the section about Local Adjustments in Chapter 4.)

Figure 9-14

Figure 9-15

Layout

The Layout panel contains settings for adjusting the grid layout (see **Figure 9–18**). These measurement settings all work in conjunction—changing one setting will usually also change the others, and sometimes it's impossible to get everything you want if the numbers don't add up. This is one area in Lightroom that often requires doing some

09

math and you'll likely need to work the settings back and forth until you get the exact settings you're looking for.

RULER UNITS

Use the pop-up menu to specify inches, centimeters, millimeters, points, or picas.

MARGINS

The Margins values establish the outer page margins in the specified units. The minimum allowable margins are determined by the settings you choose in the printer driver via the Page Setup button. Note, minimum margins will vary by printer and paper size, and the minimum size may not be uniform around all sides of the print.

Figure 9-16

PAGE GRID

When you're using the Single Image / Contact Sheet layout style, this setting specifies the number of rows and columns used to place the photos on the page. Along with the other measurements, the number of rows and columns in the grid determines the allowable size of the cells.

CELL SPACING

If there is more than one cell on the page, this sets the amount of vertical and horizontal space between the cells. If the Page Grid is set to one row and one column, these settings are unavailable.

Figure 9-17

CELL SIZE

The Cell Size value sets the size of the cells in which the photos are placed. The cell sizes possible are determined by the other measurements. If you have a specific size you want the cell(s) to be, type to enter a numeric value. Cell spacing will be adjusted accordingly. If you enter a number and Lightroom refuses to accept it, you must adjust one or more of the other measurements.

KEEP SQUARE

Check this option to force all the cells to be square. Changing any of the margin and cell size values will also change the size of the other dimension so they are always the same.

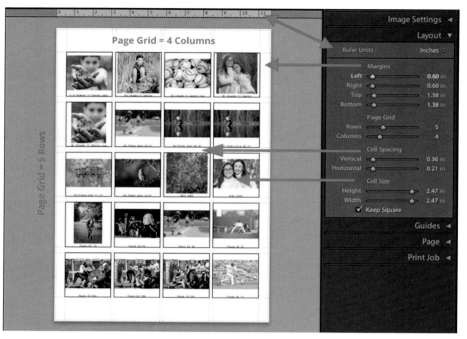

Figure 9-18

Guides

Check or uncheck the boxes on this panel to show or hide the available guides and measurement indicators (see **Figure 9–19**). None of the elements in the Guides panel will appear on a print. You can also click and drag the guide lines to modify the layout.

RULERS

This guide turns rulers on and off in the top and left sides of the main preview.

PAGE BLEED

In traditional lithographic printing, bleed refers to the amount that an image(s) extends beyond the edges of the page. Bleeds are used

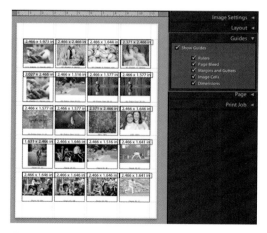

Figure 9-19

to provide wiggle room for misalignment when printing full-page images, so that the image is ensured to go all the way to the edge when the page is trimmed. In Lightroom, this Page Bleed is really a "page margin"; however, with the other use of the term "margin" in the Print module this could become confusing.

If this box is checked, the page bleed is shown as a gray margin on the page, which actually is showing the margins of the maximum printable area based on the Page Setup. It's not possible to place a photo to extend beyond this area.

MARGINS AND GUTTERS

These guides show the effect of the settings in the Layout panel. Margins are the spaces around the outer edges of the paper; gutters are the spaces between cells on the page. With this box checked, lines are displayed in the preview to show the edges of margins and gutters.

IMAGE CELLS

Show and hide the cell borders in the preview, which appear as solid black outlines but do not print. Toggle the check box on and off to see how cells are shown.

DIMENSIONS

Enable this option to display the sizes of the photos as they are placed within the cells. If Print Resolution is unchecked in the Print Job panel (discussed later in this chapter), this will also display the print resolution of each photo at its current size.

Page

With the settings on the Page panel you can add other elements to the printed page along with the photos (see **Figure 9–20**).

Figure 9-20

PAGE BACKGROUND COLOR

You can specify a solid color to print on the page background around the photos. Tick the box to enable the feature, and then click the color swatch to set the color using the color picker (see **Figure 9–21**).

Figure 9-21

IDENTITY PLATE

As in all the output modules, you can add a graphical or textual overlay, such as a logo, your studio name, etc. to your prints. First, check the box to enable the Identity Plate, and then click the preview to choose one from the drop-down list, or to make a new one. The Identity Plate in the Print module works exactly the same as in the Slideshow and Web modules.

ANGLE

The default is 0 degrees; click the number for a pop-up menu with preset rotation values (see **Figure 9–22**).

Figure 9-22

OVERRIDE COLOR

Enabling this option will fill a text identity plate with the specified color, regardless of the colors originally used.

OPACITY

Opacity sets the level of transparency for the identity plate. This is useful when you're using the identity plate as a watermark.

SCALE

Enter a value to enlarge or reduce the identity plate. You can also click and drag in the main preview to reposition and/or resize your identity plate. Note that you can't do this if you have multiples of the same image on the page and have Render on Every Image selected; see below.

RENDER BEHIND IMAGE

When checked, the identity plate will be placed behind the photo(s). This can be useful for adding custom borders or background designs.

RENDER ON EVERY IMAGE

Applies the selected identity plate to every photo in the layout. Enable this if you're applying logos/watermarks, borders or other graphics on the photos.

 Printing custom borders or graphics on your photos
In addition to the main identity plate, in the Print module (and other output modules) you can make unlimited, additional identity plates. You can use identity plates to overlay customized borders or other graphical elements on your photos (see **Figure 9–23**). Design your border or other artwork in Photoshop, making sure to leave areas transparent so the photo can show through. Save the file from Photoshop as a PNG (I find that the PNG-24 option under Save for Web works well)and bring it into Lightroom as an identity plate. On the Page panel, you can then

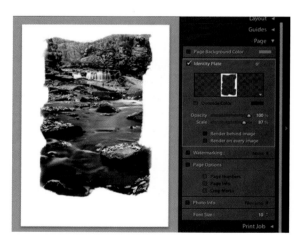

Figure 9-23

specify your graphic as the current identity plate. Now that we can import PNG files into Lightroom it makes it much easier to track and manage these types of files.

WATERMARKING

Check the box to apply a watermark and then select one from the list. The selected watermark is applied to each photo in the print job. Creating watermarks is discussed in detail in Chapter 5.

PAGE OPTIONS

Use the Page Options to add the following elements to the prints. Note that when you use Page Numbers and Page Info, the cell sizes are automatically adjusted to make room for them.

PAGE NUMBERS

With this option enabled, the Print module will add a number to the bottom right corner of each page in a multi-page job.

PAGE INFO

Shows print job information such as sharpening, color management settings, and printer.

CROP MARKS

Places crop marks outside the corners of the cell(s).

PHOTO INFO

This is text displayed below each photo in the layout. The text is placed within each cell, so adding Photo Info slightly reduces the size of the photo. If you need an exact photo size and are also using Photo Info, you'll need to compensate accordingly. To apply Photo Info, check the box, and then choose the kind of information to show using the pop-up menu (see **Figure 9–24**).

To make your own style of Photo Info, choose Edit... from the pop-up menu. This opens the Text Template Editor (see **Figure 9–25**). Here you can configure a wide range of information to show with each photo. When you're done setting up your text template, be sure to save it by clicking the Preset menu at the top of the window and choose "Save Current Settings As New Preset."

Figure 9-24

FONT SIZE

This sets the size of the type in points for the Page Options and Photo Info text elements. All type options use the same size, and you can't choose the font.

Picture Package

Use a Picture Package when you want to print multiple copies of a single photo at different sizes (see **Figure 9–26**), just like when ordering a package of school photos (such as one 8x10, two 4x6, and a bunch of wallet size of the same pose). With Picture Package, each individual photo in the print job goes in its own layout of photo cells. If you have, for example, six pictures to print, Picture Package starts by making six pages of identical layouts, each layout for one photo.

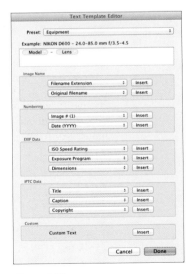

Figure 9-25

The number of pages in the job is shown on the Toolbar. A Picture Package can consist of multiple pages, and each page in the package can contain a different layout of photo cells. Note, to put multiple different photos at different sizes all on one page you should use Custom Package, which is covered later in this chapter.

Picture Package is a good solution for wedding, portrait, and event photographers who need to print client photos in a variety of sizes.

Figure 9-26

The panels and settings for Picture Package are similar to those of Single Image / Contact Sheet, with a couple of important differences.

MANUAL LAYOUT IN PICTURE PACKAGE

In Picture Package, you can click and drag the photo cells to rearrange or scale the cells on the page. Click within the cell and drag it around to reposition it; you will feel it "snap" to positions within the page grid. Click and drag one of the control handles to change the print size of the cells, which also scales the photo within the cell accordingly (see **Figure 9–27**). Hold Shift to constrain the photo to its original aspect ratio. This is the easiest way to put together your rough layout, but for more precision you'll probably need to go to the right-side panels to fine-tune the numeric settings.

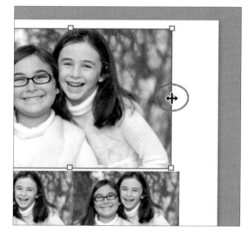

Figure 9-27

Also, in a Picture Package, if any cells are overlapping, a warning icon is shown at the top right of the page preview (see **Figure 9–28**). However, Picture Package allows you to print with photos overlapping. (Think about the creative possibilities here.)

To duplicate a cell within a Picture Package layout, hold Option or Alt and click and drag the cell. A copy will be placed in the position where you release the mouse. You can then change the settings for that cell if needed.

Figure 9-28

You can drag and drop a photo from the filmstrip to add to the layout, which will change all the cells on the page to that photo.

Image Settings

Use these settings to configure how each photo is placed within the cells (see **Figure 9–29**).

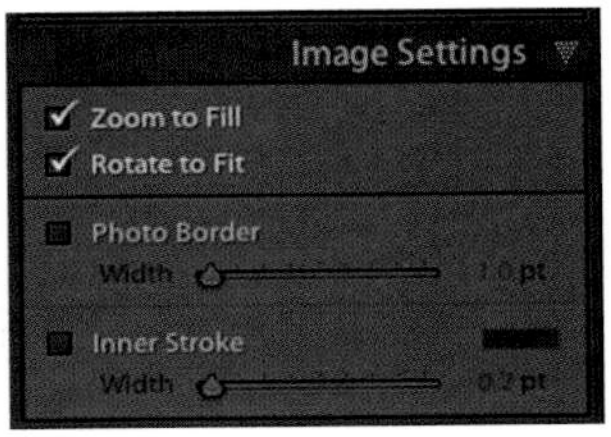

NOTE: All the photos in the Picture Package will use the same settings.

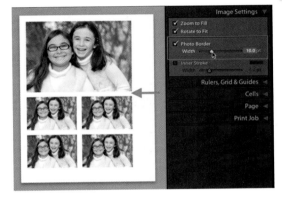

ZOOM TO FILL AND ROTATE TO FIT

Zoom to Fill and Rotate to Fit function the same as in Single Image / Contact Sheet, discussed earlier in this chapter.

Figure 9-29

PHOTO BORDER

You can set the width of an outer border (really a margin) around each photo, specified in points. You can't apply a color—this "border" will reveal the Page Background between photos. If you haven't set a background color it will show white (see **Figure 9–30**). Uncheck the box if you don't want the border between photos.

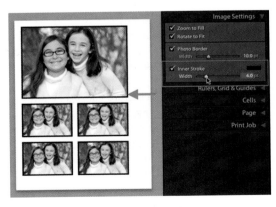

INNER STROKE

This is an additional border that's placed along the edge of the photo, inside the Photo Border described above (see **Figure 9–31**). Tick the box to enable it, then drag the slider or enter a numeric value to set the width. To choose a color for the Inner Stroke, click the swatch to open the color picker.

Figure 9-30

Rulers, Grid & Guides

These settings provide visual aids to help you position the photos on the page (see **Figure 9–32**).

RULER UNITS

You can use this menu to change the ruler units to Inches, Centimeters, Millimeters, Points and Picas. You can also right-click or Ctrl+click on a ruler to access this menu.

Figure 9-31

GRID SNAP

When repositioning cells you can have them set to snap to the layout grid or to other cells, making positioning much easier. Use the menu to turn Grid Snap Off or snap to other Cells or to the Grid (see **Figure 9–33**).

SHOW GUIDES

Tick the check box for Show Guides to enable them.

Figure 9-32

RULERS

Tick the box to show the rulers, or use the shortcut ⌘+R or Ctrl+R. Use the pop-up menu above to select the ruler units.

PAGE BLEED

This turns on and off the visual preview for the working area of the printed page. If your Page Setup contains a bleed, you'll see it shown in the preview as a gray area around the margins of the page.

Figure 9-33

PAGE GRID

This check box hides and shows the Grid, which is displayed in light blue lines behind the photos.

IMAGE CELLS

When this is enabled, outlines show around the cells on each page. (These will not print.)

DIMENSIONS

When enabled, this displays the size (and resolution, if applicable) for each photo on the page, in ppi. If Print Resolution is enabled on the Print Job panel (covered later in this chapter) the resolution ppi is not displayed.

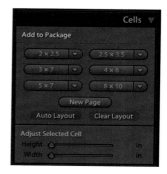

Figure 9-34

Cells

This panel provides controls for adding and removing cells and pages to and from the Picture Package, and for adjusting the size of selected cells (see **Figure 9–34**).

ADDING CELLS

The top section of the panel is labeled "Add to Package." There are six buttons showing size dimensions. Click a button to place a new cell, using the size shown, on the current page. To the right of each button is a pop-up menu (see **Figure 9–35**) where you can choose a different size to assign to that button. From the pop-up menu, click Edit... to make a new size of your own.

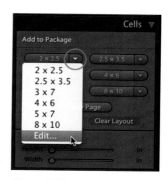

Figure 9-35

You can click a button multiple times to add more cells of that size to the page. If the new cell you're adding won't fit on the current page, a new page is automatically added.

ADDING PAGES

To create a new, blank page in the current package click the New Page button (see **Figure 9–36**). When you do this, each new page is associated with a single photo. The main preview shows the pages for only one photo at a time. The maximum number of pages you can use for each photo is six; this applies whether you use New Page or by auto-adding cells. To navigate between pages (by changing the selected photo in the Filmstrip), use the forward and back buttons on the Toolbar, the left and right arrow keys on your keyboard, or hover your cursor over the page numbers on the Toolbar and drag the scrubby slider left or right.

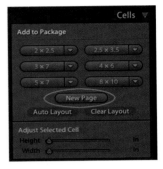

Figure 9-36

To delete a page from the layout, place your cursor over it, then click the X at the top left of the page (see **Figure 9–37**).

AUTO LAYOUT

Clicking the Auto Layout button to the left and below New Page tells Lightroom to arrange the existing photos/cells in the most economical manner possible. This affects all cells and all pages; if you do this and then change your

Figure 9-37

mind, you can Undo using the command under the Edit menu or the shortcut.

CLEAR LAYOUT

Clear Layout, below and to the right of New Page, removes all the cells from all pages. This also deletes all but the first page in the current layout.

ADJUST SELECTED CELL

The Adjust Selected Cell sliders in the bottom section of the panel allow you to resize the currently selected cell. It's often difficult, if not impossible, to set the sliders to an exact number by dragging them. Click on the value and then you can type in a number. Remember to press Return or Enter when you're done typing.

Page

This panel offers most of the same controls as Single Image / Contact Sheet covered earlier in this chapter: Page Background Color, Identity Plate, and Watermarking; see the previous descriptions of those controls. In addition, when using a Picture Package you can also check the box to apply Cut Guides (see **Figure 9–38**). When Cut Guides are enabled, you can use the adjacent pop-up menu to choose either solid lines or corner crop marks. Page Options and Photo Info are not available in Picture Package.

Figure 9-38

Custom Package

For total control over the photos and their position on each page, use a Custom Package (see **Figure 9–39**). Custom Package works similarly to the Picture Package style, with the main difference being that you can use multiple different photos in a single layout. The controls in Picture Package that are not available in Custom Package are Zoom to Fit and Auto Layout; these functions are irrelevant in the Custom Package. There are also two controls in the Custom Package Cells panel that are not in Picture Package: Rotate Cell and Lock to Photo Aspect Ratio. The Rotate Cell button simply rotates the cell between horizontal and vertical orientations. When Lock to Photo Aspect Ratio is checked the cell's dimensions are constrained to the same aspect ratio as the photo within the cell.

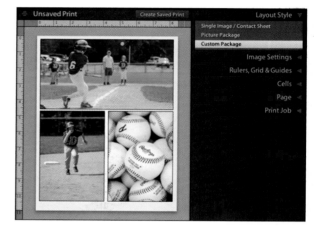

Figure 9-39

CREATE A CUSTOM PACKAGE

The easiest way to start laying out a Custom Package is to simply drag and drop photos on the page, then resize and position where you want them. You can also place cells first (using the controls on the Cells panel as described in Picture Package), then drag and drop your photos into them.

OVERLAPPING PHOTOS

Like Picture Package, in Custom package it's possible to have photos overlapping. However, in Custom Package you can right-click or Ctrl+click

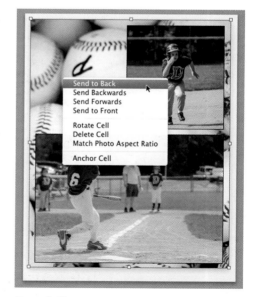

Figure 9-40

for a contextual pop-up menu with many additional options. From this menu, for example, you can change the stacking order of the pictures by sending them forward or back, rotate or delete the cell, automatically match the cell to the photo aspect ratio, or anchor the cell (see **Figure 9–40**).

 Import graphics files to make layered packages
Custom Package allows you to put together all kinds of creative print layouts. Instead of simply having photos in your catalog, you can create and import a set of graphics files, created in Photoshop, etc., that you use to combine with your photos to make beautiful, interesting print layouts all within Lightroom.

ANCHORING CELLS
Anchoring a cell places it and the photo it contains in the same position on all pages. With this feature, along with the fact that you can overlap images, you can create all kinds of elaborate layouts, including customized background, logo or branding elements, etc. that extend far beyond what you can do with identity plates or watermarks.

 Save or update your template
All the settings described above can be stored within a Lightroom Print template. After you've configured everything the way you want (and presumably, tested the results) you should, in most cases, save a template for later, or update a template you've previously saved. It's good practice to name your print templates based on the layout style and print options they were created with.

Figure 9-41

Print Job
After laying out your page(s), configure the options on the Print Job panel (see **Figure 9–41**). The choices you make here will determine the destination and quality of the printed output.

PRINT TO
This pop-up menu determines whether Lightroom will output the print job to your printer or generate a JPEG file (see **Figure 9–42**). Changing the Print to: setting determines the options available below.

Figure 9-42

DRAFT MODE PRINTING
When Draft Mode Printing is enabled, the Lightroom previews are used for the prints, not the full-resolution files on disk. This can be handy sometimes, such as when you just need a quick contact sheet or layout proofs. Draft Mode Printing can dramatically speed print time but, of course, produces lower quality output. With Draft Mode enabled, the rest of the Print Job options become disabled. Use Draft Mode Printing if you only need a very rough print of the photos. Otherwise, for the best quality prints leave Draft Mode Printing unchecked.

PRINT RESOLUTION

Check the option for Print Resolution to specify an output resolution in pixels per inch (ppi). When this is enabled, all the photos in the print job will be resampled to the specified resolution as they are output, regardless of their native resolutions. The maximum Print Resolution you can set in Lightroom 5 is 1440 ppi; the minimum is 72 ppi. As also described elsewhere in this book, the importance of higher resolution determines the ability to resolve more detail and thus make larger prints with good quality. Resolution is also discussed in Chapter 5.

About resampling and interpolation

Depending on the native resolutions of the photos you're printing, changing their output resolution will almost always result in either downsampling or upsampling. In downsampling for reductions, pixel data is discarded. Printing photos at a reduced size is rarely problematic—the main concern is when making enlargements. During upsampling for enlargements, Lightroom interpolates the original image data to make new pixels for the output. The maximum enlargement potential depends on the original resolution of the file.

09

If a photo falls between 180 ppi and 480 ppi at final print size, it's often best to print the file at its native resolution. If the native resolution is higher than this range, with most printers and drivers, there's no benefit to downsampling to lower resolutions. Resampling up or down can cause a very slight softening of a photo, but in moderate amounts this is nothing to be too concerned about, and sometimes resampling is necessary to produce the best possible print. When upsampling is applied, Lightroom does a fantastic job.

RESOLUTION FOR DIFFERENT TYPES OF PRINTING

The resolution requirements for high-quality reproduction depend on the type of printing and the intended viewing distance. For example, to reproduce high-quality photographs in a book like this one, the image files should be somewhere around 300 ppi at final print size. A high quality inkjet print most often requires resolution between 180 and 360 ppi at final print size. Typical lab prints (RA4) are often printed at 300 ppi; 200 ppi is also common. Very large prints, from which a viewer needs to stand several feet to view, can often be printed at 180 ppi or less with good results. Huge, building-size billboards can be printed using resolutions of 100 ppi and even lower.

So ideally, you should always use a resolution specific to the type of printing you're using. If you're working with a lab or other vendor, ask them what resolution to use. If you're making your own inkjet prints, using a resolution between 180 and 360 is appropriate for most photos. If you have your own printer you should do some tests using your own images to gain a thorough understanding of the effect of resolution and resampling on the appearance of a print.

LEAVING PRINT RESOLUTION UNCHECKED

It's usually OK to print multiple photos that have different native resolutions all at once, provided they are all within the specified tolerances described above. When you don't resample, the image resolution will simply be scaled to produce the specified output size. For example, a 10 x 10 inch file at 100 ppi is the same as a 1 x 1 inch file at 1000 ppi. A photo with a resolution of 1000 x 3000 pixels is 10 x 30 inches at 100 ppi, 5 x 15 inches at 200 ppi, and 2 x 6 inches at 500 ppi.

 **Guide dimensions**
To see the native resolution each photo will print at, check the Dimensions option in the Guides panel. (When Print Resolution is checked, the resolution does not show.)

 **Continuity in ganged prints**
If you're printing a group of photos with varying native resolutions, you may want to resample all of them to the same resolution so that the printed results appear similar.

PRINT SHARPENING

Tick the check box to have Lightroom apply output sharpening during the print job. Choose an amount (Low, Standard, or High) and a media type (Matte or Glossy paper; Matte applies stronger sharpening). **If you're printing to glossy or semi-gloss paper (this includes luster), use Glossy.** For art papers and canvas, use Matte. Using these simple menu selections, Lightroom is often capable of applying the ideal sharpening for print. Make a few test prints using different settings to determine what works best for certain photos.

 **Don't over-sharpen**
If you've already used Photoshop or a third-party plugin to resize and sharpen your files for printing and you're not enlarging or reducing them on the Lightroom print job leave Lightroom's Print Sharpening off.

16-BIT OUTPUT (MAC OS X ONLY)

Some recent-model printer drivers can process 16-bit files, which can produce the best possible output quality on certain printers. 16-bit output is especially beneficial for eliminating banding in photos with smooth, gradual transitions. Check your printer documentation to see it supports 16-bit print files and, if so, check this box to use it. Note that your printing times will increase, and depending on the photo you may or may not see a visible improvement in quality.

COLOR MANAGEMENT

You have two options for Color Management when printing from Lightroom: 1) let Lightroom handle the color output using an ICC profile, or 2) let the printer driver do all the color management. For the most accurate color, in nearly all cases I recommend using ICC profiles and having Lightroom perform the color management. Use the controls in the Color Management section to choose the Profile and Rendering Intent. You can click the black triangle button at the top right of the panel to show additional information about the Color Management settings (see **Figure 9–43**).

MANAGED BY PRINTER

If you can't, or don't want to, have Lightroom handle color management, set the pop-up menu to Managed by Printer. Lightroom's color management controls become disabled.

Figure 9-43

You then make all your color management settings in the printer driver screens. In this instance it is imperative that you enable color adjustment in the printer driver.

 When to use printer color management
I use Epson's Advanced Black and White driver options for making black and white prints and have been very pleased with the results. In this case, I turn off Lightroom's color management altogether and use only the driver settings to handle the output. You should also set the menu to Managed by Printer if you're sending the files to a raster image processor (or "RIP", such as ImagePrint, Qimage, ColorBurst, etc.) and want color management handled there.

USING A PRINTER PROFILE

A printer profile is a small computer file residing on your hard drive that describes the color characteristics of a printer and paper combination. To have Lightroom handle the color management during output, select a profile from the pop-up menu (see **Figure 9–44**). If none are listed in the menu, select Other... A dialog box appears that allows you to add profiles into Lightroom. In the Choose Profiles window, all the available profiles on your computer are shown (see **Figure 9–45**). Check the boxes for the printer/paper profile(s) you want to add to Lightroom and click OK. When added, they will remain in the Profile pop-up for future use. (The profiles in the menu are shared with the Soft Proofing panel.)

If you use Lightroom's color management with an ICC profile, it's critical that you disable all color management in the printer driver; see the next section on Print.

Figure 9-44

 Obtaining printer profiles
If the correct printer profiles are not installed on your computer, you can usually download them from your printer and/or paper manufacturer's website. For example, if you're using an Epson printer and Epson paper, you can get the profile from the Epson website. If you're using an Epson printer and Ilford paper, you will need to look on the Ilford site for the correct profile. Make sure to use the profile made specifically for your model of printer. Unfortunately, in rare cases, none will be available, and you'll need to use the closest alternative, make a custom profile, or use Managed by Printer.

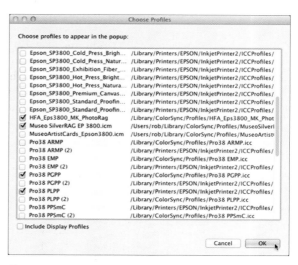

Figure 9-45

Soft Proofing

For the most predictable results when printing, use the Soft Proofing feature in the Develop module. Soft proofing provides a reasonable simulation of the printed output on-screen, and with practice, you can train your eye to accurately predict how your prints will look. When you use Soft Proofing, be sure the selected profile matches the one used for the proof; if you're printing a Proof Copy this is determined automatically.

RENDERING INTENT

Next, choose the Rendering Intent. This setting determines how the colors in the photo are translated to the printer's color space. The two available rendering intents in Lightroom are Perceptual and Relative. Perceptual rendering compresses the range of all colors in the photo to preserve their visual appearance on the print. Relative leaves the colors that the printer can reproduce as-is, and only clips the out-of-gamut colors to their nearest equivalent. Generally speaking, to preserve color relationships use Perceptual and to preserve tonal relationships use Relative. (If the colors of your photos are all within the gamut of the printer, use Relative.) There's more about color management and rendering intents in Chapters 1, 4, and 5.

09

 Printing Develop Soft Proofs

If you're printing a photo or virtual copy you've soft proofed in Develop, the rendering intents you specified for each photo will override the setting used here. Because of this, you can now print photos using both rendering intents together on a single sheet.

PRINT ADJUSTMENT

At the bottom of the Print Job panel are the Print Adjustment controls (see **Figure 9–46**). These adjustments are specifically designed for printing and are intended to address the very common problem of prints coming out too dark due to incorrect display settings and/or the characteristics of the chosen printer.

To apply a Print Adjustment, check the box and click the black triangle button at the right to expand the controls. Use the sliders to increase the Brightness and Contrast. The results of these adjustments are not shown in Lightroom; they are applied as Lightroom outputs the file and can be seen only in the resulting print. If you suffer from dark prints and can not otherwise resolve the issue, a Brightness increase of +15 and a Contrast increase of +10 might be reasonable values to start with; you'll have to experiment by doing a few test prints to determine the optimal settings for each printer and paper combination. The ideal adjustments are not specific to an individual photo; they are specific to a printer/paper combination so the effect of the Print Adjustments will be affected by your choice of profile and rendering intent.

Figure 9-46

These adjustments are not meant to take the place of proper color management practices: if you're using a correctly calibrated display and you've used Soft Proofing to make adjustments in the Develop module, you most often won't need to use these controls.

Print Adjustment settings are stored in templates and Saved Prints.

Print and Printer...

When you've applied and double-checked all the settings for your print job, click the Print or the Printer... button at the bottom of the right panel (see **Figure 9–47**). (If you're printing to JPEG files, see the next section.) Clicking the Printer... button opens the print dialog box for your operating system and allows you to see and/or change printer driver settings.

Figure 9-47

09

Note, if you used an earlier version of Lightroom these buttons were formerly named Print One and Print... respectively. The names have changed in Lightroom 5, but the functionality is exactly the same as before.

 Print to PDF

There is no button or native functionality in the Print module to print directly to PDF, but it can be done . On a Mac, simply use the PDF button on the main print Print dialog box. On Windows, you need a dedicated PDF printer driver; these can be freely obtained on the web or you could use the full version of Adobe Acrobat. You can print any layout to a PDF using these methods, which allows you to send the file(s) to vendors or other outside parties for printing or review.

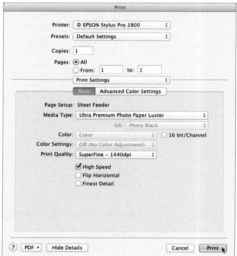

Figure 9-48

PRINT TO PRINTER

With the Print to: menu set to Printer, when you click the Printer... button at the bottom of the right panel group the printer driver dialog box appears. Because printer driver dialog boxes vary in the extreme, I can't go into further detail on this here, but general settings to check include paper size, media type and color management settings. I've included screenshots for Epson 3800 on Mac and on Windows (see **Figures 9–48** and **9–49**); consult your printer documentation for more about its specific settings.

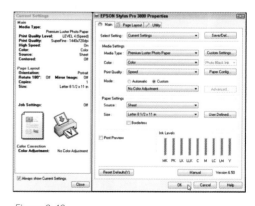

Figure 9-49

In the driver, apply the appropriate settings for the print job. **If you're using Lightroom's color management, you need to take special precautions to make sure that color management is completely turned off in the printer driver.** The vast majority of color problems on prints are due to "double color management". Depending on your printer and driver software, this will be found in different places. While working in the dialog boxes, most printer drivers allow you to save your custom settings for the driver. Along with saving a Lightroom template, saving your printer driver settings will make the process faster on future jobs.

Lastly, you'll need to click Print (OK on Windows) in the printer driver one more time to spool the job to the printer.

 Update your template
All the printer driver settings also get stored with the print template when it's saved, so be sure to save/update your template when you're done.

09

PRINT

When you click Print, Lightroom bypasses the print dialog and immediately outputs the job using the most recent settings. This can be a real time-saver; just be sure you have the correct settings in place before clicking.

PRINT SETTINGS (BUTTON ON MAC OS X ONLY)

This button at the bottom of the left panel (next to Page Setup) opens the printer driver dialog directly. When you're using Print, you can access the Print Settings to change them without using the main Printer… button. These settings are retained until you change them.

Print to JPEG File

Printing JPEG files from Lightroom is very useful when preparing files to be printed by a lab or service bureau. You can save out JPEG files using all the current print layout and settings, and instead of outputting the job to your own printer, save one or more files to your hard drive. This offers the benefits of allowing you to "gang up" multiple photos on single sheets (saving money) and specifying precise color management options (for better color reproduction). Perform your print layout steps as described earlier in this chapter, up to the point where you are setting the options in the Print Job panel, and then choose JPEG File in the Print to: menu. With Print to JPEG file selected, the Print Job panel options allow you to specify the following options (see **Figure 9–50**). (If you're going to send these files to a lab, you should ask for a list of specifications to guide you.)

Figure 9-50

DRAFT MODE PRINTING

Selecting this option causes Lightroom to use its previews for the output instead of the image data from the files on disk. The results are of much lower quality, but the output is much faster. This option is most useful for printing contact sheets, where you have a large number of thumbnails on a single page and output quality isn't as critical.

FILE RESOLUTION

This sets the resolution in ppi for the output file. Use the specs provided by your lab for this.

PRINT SHARPENING

Check the box to enable output sharpening, and use the pop-up menu to select the amount of sharpening to apply. I usually use Standard.

MEDIA TYPE

Choose the kind of paper to be used: Glossy or Matte. (If you're printing on semi-gloss, satin, or "luster" paper, choose Glossy.)

JPEG QUALITY

Unless your vendor has specified otherwise, I recommend you use Quality set at 80 if upload speed and storage is an issue, or up to 100 if only concerned about quality for making JPEG print files. 80 is equivalent to Photoshop's level 10 setting, and 100 is equivalent to level 12 for JPEG quality.

CUSTOM FILE DIMENSIONS

This lets you specify an output size for the JPEG file. When unchecked, Lightroom relies on the settings entered into the printer driver to determine the layout and margins. When saving out as a JPEG the printer driver settings (and limitations) are not really relevant. If you want to create a JPEG layout at a non-standard size or at a size that your own printer does not support, then you'll want to check the box and enter the desired size. Margins will be set to zero when checked.

COLOR MANAGEMENT

Try to get a printer profile from your lab. Install it on your computer using the instructions they provide, and then select Other... from the menu to add it to the profile list (as per the instructions earlier in this chapter). Keep in mind that many lab profiles are intended only for soft proofing purposes, and you should verify with the vendor the profile needed for output.

If you can't get a custom profile, you'll at least need to know what kind of printer the lab is using to make your prints. If you are having RA4 prints made (Lambda, LightJet, Frontier, Chromira, etc.) you can safely use sRGB and Relative Intent. If you are having inkjet prints made (Epson, Canon, HP, etc.), it's usually OK to use Adobe RGB and Relative Intent.

PRINT ADJUSTMENT

The Print Adjustment controls work exactly the same when printing to JPEG as to your printer. I would urge you to work with your print provider to solve any dark print issues before using this option.

PRINT TO FILE

When all the correct settings have been entered, click the Print to File button (see Figure 9–50). Lightroom will prompt you to choose a location to save the files. When you're ready, click Save. Lightroom will output JPEG file(s) for each page of your print job. After you get the prints back from the lab, you can decide for yourself whether it's worth saving these JPEG files for future use. (I usually don't, because it's so easy to make print files from Lightroom whenever it's necessary.)

Create Saved Print

At the top of the main preview area in the Print module is a horizontal bar that displays the saved state of the current print job. If you haven't yet saved the print, it will say Unsaved Print; otherwise it will display the name of the saved print.

Saving a print makes a special addition to the Collections panel. A saved print contains the photos you've included along with their saved sort order, and the Use: menu options that were active at the time it was saved. A saved print references the template in use, but it does not contain the template itself. Remember that even if you update a saved print, you may still need to update a template independently, and vice versa.

To save a print, click the button at the right labeled Create Saved Print. This opens a dialog box containing options for saving the print. You can also save the print by clicking the + button at the top of the Collections panel and choosing the Create Print menu option.

In the dialog box, you can specify the Location options to choose where the new Print will be saved. In the Options section, you can choose to include only the photos that were used in the current Use: menu setting. You can also choose to have this saved print designated as the target collection, which makes it easy to add new photos to this collection if desired.

Once you've saved the print, you can return to it at any time by clicking it in the Collections panel, and all your photos and the print settings will be reloaded.

Print troubleshooting

Whether you make your own prints or have them done at a lab there are a number of things that can go wrong, resulting in prints with less than optimal quality. Problems with printed output are most often due to incorrect settings in Lightroom, the printer driver, or both. In most cases, you can and should expect excellent quality if you've taken the right steps. Prints that don't look good could always have been done better, whether in your initial capture, Develop work, or preparing the print job. That said, all printers are not created equal, and some labs are definitely better than others. Following are suggestions for handling some of the most common problems you might experience with your prints.

09

09

PRINTS TOO DARK

Prints that come out too dark are almost always a result of the monitor being set too bright. If what you see on-screen is not an accurate representation of the actual tones in the file, when you get the print everything will be darker than you expect. The best solution is to use a hardware monitor calibration system and set your monitor luminance to between 90 and 110 cd/m2. Although at first this may seem very dim, you will get used to the lower brightness and you'll find that your prints look much closer to what you'd expect.

COLOR LOOKS WRONG

The most common cause of incorrect color output is "double color management." When you use Lightroom and a printer profile to handle color management (as I recommend) you need to be sure to disable all color management functions in the printer driver. Depending on your printer model and driver version, there will be different methods for doing this, but in general, you want to look for settings that say "No Color Management" or "Color Matching: OFF", etc.

IMAGE LOOKS PIXELATED

If you can see the pixels in the printed photo it's because the output resolution was too low. Every digital image has a finite size at which it can be printed without showing its pixels. Sometimes you can upsample the image (increase Resolution in the Print Job panel) but there are limitations. In some cases, unfortunately, you won't be able to print to the enlargement you want using the selected file.

IMAGE LOOKS SOFT OR BLURRY

It's possible that the image was not sharp to begin with. Other times, if the image has been heavily upsampled, softening will result. Try printing at a smaller size, if possible. If you print to JPEG and find the results appear too soft try increasing the Resolution value to 720 ppi and Quality at 100, and then import the resulting JPEG and export again at final resolution and quality.

VISIBLE HALOES AROUND THE EDGES OF SHAPES

Haloes are most often caused by overly aggressive sharpening. Try backing off the amount of sharpening being applied in Develop and/or the Print module.

PRINT ANOMALIES

Some users have reported seeing differences in prints made from Lightroom versus those from Photoshop or other software. Problems have been reported on a few printers from Epson, HP, and Canon. There are several possible reasons for this. First, some older printer drivers may have trouble with Lightroom's output. In cases where the problem lies with Lightroom's printing pipeline, Adobe has worked diligently to iron out the bugs. Unfortunately, this hasn't always been the case with problems in printer drivers. Printer manufacturers notoriously blame the operating system (and vice versa), so these kinds of problems are resolved slowly, if ever. Search the name of your printer model along with "Lightroom printing," etc., to see if people are discussing problems with your particular printer.

Next steps

After you've made prints you may want to mount them for hanging or put them in a portfolio. Many times, the print is the final culmination of the photographic process. But it doesn't need to be! With Lightroom, you have many other ways to present and share your work with others. See the chapters on Book, Slideshow, and Web to learn more about your other options for presenting your photography.

09

CHAPTER 10
Web

WEB: Create browser-based photo galleries

You can use Lightroom's Web module to create photo galleries for your own website and disc-based presentations.

Before you start making a Web gallery, it's a good idea to do some organizing in Library first. Decide which photos to use and get them sorted into collections in the order you want them to appear in the Web gallery. (It's usually easier to organize photos in Library before going to the Web module.) With the photos all chosen and sorted, you can then use the controls in the Web module to create the gallery.

You don't need to know anything about coding to build galleries with the Web module. When you're done customizing a gallery in the Web module, Lightroom will generate all the required HTML, CSS, Flash, and images. You can use Lightroom's built-in FTP service to transfer all the gallery files to your website's hosting server (you will need the FTP account information to do this) or you can export the finished gallery files to your hard drive, where you can view the pages locally using a standard web browser (and you can upload to a server later if you wish). These and many other options are discussed in detail in this chapter.

Like the other output modules, the Web module workspace contains template and collection organization on the left, and customization controls on the right (see **Figure 10–1**). Whenever you switch to the Web module, the most recent settings are reloaded for you.

Figure 10-1

⚠ **Video export and playback not supported in Web**
You currently can't use the built-in features of the Web module to play or embed video clips using the provided Web galleries. If you include a video clip in the selected files for a Web gallery, a still frame will be used. (This frame can be selected using the Set Poster Frame command described in Chapter 3.)

 ## Build a Lightroom Web Gallery

Following is an overview of the typical workflow you'll use to create a Web gallery. The Web module steps are detailed throughout the remainder of the chapter.

Step 1. In Library, organize the photos that will go into the gallery.

Step 2. Go into the Web module and make sure all the panels are visible.

Step 3. Check that the correct photos are showing in the Filmstrip in the order you want them and reorganize as necessary.

Step 4. Choose a template and/or layout style to start the design process.

Step 5. Use the panels on the right side of the window to design the look and feel of the gallery by setting layout options, sizes, and colors; adding type; and setting font styles, etc.

Step 6. Preview your gallery pages and make changes if necessary.

Step 7. Upload the gallery to your web server or export the files to a hard drive.

Preview panel

The Preview panel (see **Figure 10–2**) shows a preview of the current layout, and also shows previews of other Web templates as you mouse over them in the *Template Browser* (see below). For the largest previews possible in the panel, click and drag the outer edge of the left panel set to make it wider.

Template Browser

As with the other output modules, your work in Web usually starts by selecting one of the available templates, which store saved layout settings. Web templates are listed in the Template Browser panel (see **Figure 10–3**). The default templates use Lightroom's built-in HTML and Flash layout styles. User Templates is the default folder for your own custom Web galleries. (If you haven't yet saved any of your own Web templates, this folder will be empty. After you've saved your own templates they can be stored in User Templates or other folders with unique names.)

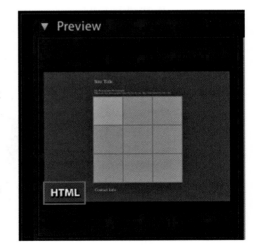

Figure 10-2

Web templates are dependent on layout styles. The functionality and design of your Web gallery depends entirely on the layout style used by the template; we'll look more at them later. After choosing a template (or Layout Style) as a starting point, you'll customize your gallery design using the panels on the right side of the window.

Figure 10-3

PREVIEWING TEMPLATES

As you move your mouse over the list of installed templates, you can see them in the Preview panel. The bottom left of the preview displays either "HTML" or an "*f*" for Flash (see Figure 10–2). HTML and Flash templates are discussed later in this chapter.

LOADING A TEMPLATE

Click the name of a template to load it. When you click a template, Lightroom also loads the layout style associated with that template. (Conversely, if you click a Layout Style, Lightroom will load the default template for that style.)

THE ACTIVE TEMPLATE

When you click a template in the list, all its settings are loaded for the current set of photos. At this point, the gallery is related to the template by common settings and the template becomes highlighted in the list. As soon as you change any settings, the current layout becomes disassociated from the template and the template name is no longer highlighted.

SAVING A NEW TEMPLATE

To save a new template, click the + button on the right side of the panel header. In the New Template window, type a name for the template, and choose a folder from the menu below. When you're done click Create.

MANAGING WEB TEMPLATES

There are several commands available for managing the templates in the panel (see Figure 10–3). Right-click or Ctrl+click on any template in the list to open a pop-up menu containing the available options. There are more options available for user templates than for the preinstalled templates.

RENAMING A TEMPLATE

To rename a user template, right-click or Ctrl+click its name in the list and choose Rename from the pop-up menu. Type in a new name and click OK, or press Return or Enter.

UPDATING A TEMPLATE

From the pop-up menu, you can also update a user template already in the list with all the current settings in the Web module. Choose the option for Update with Current

Settings. You can't choose which settings to update—all the current settings are used. If you update a template, its name will become highlighted to indicate the current settings are identical to those stored within the template.

DELETING A TEMPLATE

To delete a user template, right-click or Ctrl+click on the template name and choose Delete from the pop-up menu. Note that you won't get a confirmation dialog for this, but if you make a mistake or change your mind, you can use the Undo command under the Edit menu (or press ⌘+Z or Ctrl+Z) to undo the deletion.

MANAGING TEMPLATE FOLDERS

You can make a new folder for your templates with the New Folder command on the + button or the pop-up menu. (When you do this by clicking one of your own templates in the list, the selected template is automatically moved to the new folder.)

You can also drag and drop to move user templates between folders.

COPYING THE BUILT-IN LIGHTROOM TEMPLATES

You cannot update, delete, or rename the items in the Lightroom Templates folder. If you choose the New Folder command from the pop-up menu when clicking on a Lightroom Template, that template gets copied into the new folder. You can also drag and drop any Lightroom template onto a user folder to copy it into that folder. In both cases, you can then modify the template from there, including renaming, updating settings, etc.

EXPORT TEMPLATE

You can export templates from the output modules using the command on the pop-up menu. This saves new files on your hard drive (using the .lrtemplate extension), making it easier to transfer templates between machines.

Figure 10-4

Collections

The Collections panel in the Web module shows the same list of collections available in all the other modules (see **Figure 10–4**).

Using collections for Web galleries has some distinct advantages over folder sources. If you use a folder, chances are it will contain photos you don't want in the Web gallery; you'd need to hide those using filters. With a collection, you can include just the photos you want in the Web gallery and easily sort them into your preferred order.

Using metadata for smart Web collections

I recommend using a smart collection based on workflow keywords (as explained in Chapter 3). Web galleries are often updated frequently, so they make good candidates for the use of smart collections. Simply apply a unique keyword with the name of the Web gallery to which you want the photo to belong. (Of course, you can use regular collections instead, and just drag and drop to add photos for your Web gallery.) Smart collections need to be created in the Library module first; you can't make them from within the Web module. (However, you can modify the settings for existing smart collections from within the Web module's Collections panel, but keep in mind this will also affect those smart collections elsewhere.)

It isn't possible to apply keywords to photos from within the Web module, so if you're using workflow keywords to manage your smart collections for Web galleries, you need to apply those keywords to photos in Library first. You can, however, apply and/or change attributes—ratings, flags, and labels—from within the Web module, using the keyboard shortcuts described in Chapter 3, so consider including these in the smart collection criteria.

Alternatively, you can create a regular collection before entering the Web module, and many people find this to be an easy way to manually gather specific photos together in the Library module before heading to Web. I do this quite often. However, there is also special type of regular collection, called a Web Gallery, which you can create in the Web module from the photos in the Filmstrip.

CREATING SAVED WEB GALLERY COLLECTIONS

When you create a new collection from within the Web module, it gets added to the panel as a Saved Web Gallery with a unique Web collection icon (see **Figure 10–5**). To do this, click the + button at the right of the Collections panel header. This does the same thing as clicking the Create Saved Web Gallery button in the bar at the top of the main preview area, discussed later in this chapter.

The Saved Web Gallery references the current template and the Use: menu setting in the Toolbar. A Web Gallery behaves the same as a regular collection, but has the added benefit of remembering all your Web module settings. You can also double-click the special Web Gallery icon to jump to the Web module from anywhere else in Lightroom.

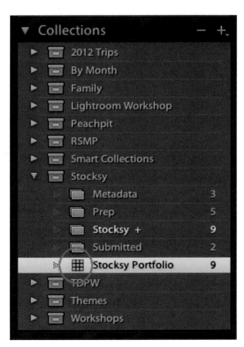

Figure 10-5

MODIFYING COLLECTIONS

To modify any of the collections in the panel, right-click or Ctrl+click on the collection or collection set name and choose a command from the pop-up menu. Collections and related menu commands are discussed in much more detail in Chapter 3.

Main preview area

In the center of the window, the main preview area shows the Web gallery with all current settings applied. In most cases, this preview is identical to what you'll see in a web browser; however, sometimes there may be slight differences due to the way different browsers render HTML. The previews are fully interactive: you can click any of the links in the preview to navigate between all the pages of the Web gallery. When you're building your gallery and changing settings, be sure to click in the preview area to see all the pages.

Web Toolbar

Press T to show and hide the Toolbar. The Web Toolbar (see **Figure 10–6**) provides controls to jump to the first page of the gallery, navigate between next and previous photos, and choose the content to include. At the far right of the Web Toolbar the name of the current layout style is shown.

Figure 10-6

GALLERY NAVIGATION CONTROLS

At the far left of the Toolbar, the square button functions as a shortcut to go to the first page in the gallery. To the right of that are two arrows you can use to go to previous and next photos. These buttons simply change the active photo in the filmstrip. If you have photos selected in the Filmstrip, these arrows will cycle through the current selection only. Depending on the gallery template you're working with, these may or may not update the gallery preview to display that image with its associated web page content. With many templates, you must click the links in the main preview area to navigate through the pages.

USE: MENU

The Use: menu allows you to change the content to be included in the Web gallery (see **Figure 10–7**). You can choose from All Filmstrip Photos, Selected Photos, or Flagged Photos. With All Filmstrip Photos, everything visible in the Filmstrip will be included in the gallery. If you use Selected Photos, make sure you have some photos selected in the Filmstrip; otherwise the gallery will be empty. Same goes for Flagged Photos: this option includes only photos with the flag status set to Pick (not the Reject flag).

Figure 10-7

Use a small group of photos for setup

If you're building a Web gallery with lots of photos, changing templates and settings can result in slow performance. For the fastest response from the Web module, consider using a small, temporary set of photos to create your layouts. You can easily do this with Use: Selected Photos and just select a few of your photos from the full collection using the Filmstrip. Then, when you've finished your setup, save or update your template and change Use: back to All Filmstrip Photos.

Layout Style

The first panel in the top position in the right panel group is Layout Style (see **Figure 10–8**). This panel lists the available layout styles (those installed on your computer and compatible with the current version of Lightroom).

A Web layout style determines the program code and screen layout used for the gallery; every Web template is based on a specific Layout Style. Different layout styles provide widely varying options.

Figure 10-8

There are two basic categories of Lightroom Web Galleries: those that use Flash and those that use only HTML, which (as their names imply) use different code to compile and display the gallery. Adobe Flash is a proprietary scripting language that provides capability for sophisticated Web graphics, elaborate animation, and interactivity; it requires the Flash browser plug-in to operate. Standard HTML is much more widely supported by common browsers and doesn't need any special software to display. Lightroom comes with several preinstalled Flash and HTML layouts.

FLASH GALLERIES

Flash templates can offer strong visual appeal and customization of design elements and transitions between photos. The biggest disadvantage of Flash galleries is they're not widely supported by mobile devices such as the iPad and iPhone. If you want your galleries to be viewed by people using these devices, you can rule out using Flash. Also, Flash galleries are not well-suited for search engine indexing due to the programming code embedded within the Flash file used to display photos—in a Flash gallery, your photo metadata, including keywords and captions, is not visible to search engines. Secondarily, some people still resist using Flash, or have browser problems with Flash versions.

In the best cases, Flash galleries will take longer to load than HTML galleries. Besides these performance issues, I also think many Flash designs become too elaborate for effective photo presentation; the interface can easily distract from the photos themselves. Finally, Adobe has announced that they will no longer be actively developing the technology for the Flash platform—its days as a programming language are numbered. I strongly encourage you to avoid using Flash galleries.

Note: The Airtight galleries that come with Lightroom are built using Flash.

HTML GALLERIES

HTML galleries are very search engine friendly—a search engine crawling the Web can find your HTML pages and read through their content, allowing the search engine to index the pages *and the photos themselves*. The potential drawback to pure HTML photo galleries is that you might not always like the way they look, and you can't easily include fancy transitions and animated effects. However, I think this is far outweighed by the speed and compatibility that straight HTML offers. If you want to have your photos found by people searching the web and have the most possible viewers be able to see them—and you want a simple, clean layout—stick with HTML.

Note: It is possible to build fantastic websites using a combination of Flash and HTML; in many cases this is a great solution. However, you can't do this with Lightroom alone and will need to use other software and/or web services.

Find More Galleries Online

You can add more Web galleries to Lightroom; your options for creating attractive, functional Web galleries are greatly expanded when you use one of the growing number of third-party Web galleries available online.

These third-party galleries proves a wide range of options ranging from more advanced control over gallery styling to e-commerce capabilities and even full-blown website construction. Some add-on galleries are free; the best ones are available for relatively minimal costs. Many add-on galleries are modular and designed to work together by assembling different components to customize the solution to your needs. At the time of this writing, the most comprehensive third-party Lightroom Web gallery add-ons currently available are from The Turning Gate (TTG); new gallery packages are being released from this and other developers with increasing frequency.

There is a button for **Find More Galleries Online...** (see **Figure 10–9**). Clicking this button launches your default web browser and opens the page on the Adobe Exchange website with listings of add-on Lightroom Web Galleries. From this page you can download more galleries, which, when correctly installed, will be shown in the Layout Style panel.

There are more Lightroom Web Galleries available than are listed on the Adobe Exchange site; you can do a web search for "Lightroom Web Galleries" and see the Appendix for a list of resources for additional options.

Figure 10-9

When you install additional Web galleries, they are displayed in the Layout Styles panel. You can save templates from them just like with the built-in galleries.

Add-on Web galleries provide their own documentation and help for their controls and operation.

 Different layout styles provide different options
The controls provided on the right-side panels will change—sometimes drastically— depending on the layout style in use. If you're looking for an option that's not there, it's probably because it doesn't exist in the current Layout Style. Learning how to use a new Web gallery style, especially those downloaded from a third party, is mostly about understanding the different options available and memorizing where they're located.

Customize your Web gallery

Use the panels on the right side of the Web module to customize your gallery. The following panel and settings descriptions are based on the default Lightroom HTML Gallery layout style.

Site Info

The Site Info panel (see **Figure 10–10**) provides controls for setting type on the page (see **Figure 10–11**). Next to the name of each text element, there's a small triangle button, from which you can access a list of text values recently used for that element.

In most of the default templates, each line of text is styled differently, and in many layout styles there are no controls provided for modifying the style of these text elements. (However, if you know CSS you can change the styles after you render the gallery files.)

To remove any type element from the layout, simply leave the text field blank; if there's text in the field, select and delete it, and the element will be deleted from the page.

Note: You can't use HTML or any other code in these fields.

 Type directly on the page
In addition to entering text in the panel, you can select the text in the main preview and edit it directly on the page.

Figure 10-10

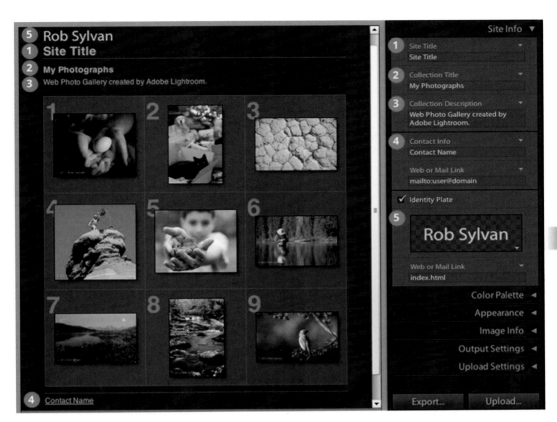

Figure 10-11

SITE TITLE

This text appears at the top of the page and is the largest text element. (See label 1 in Figure 10-11.) If you're not using an identity plate (explained later in this chapter) you can use this area to place your name or your client's name. The limit for this field is 500 characters.

COLLECTION TITLE

This reference to "Collection Title" in the Web module has no direct relationship to the items in the Collections panel. (See label 2 in Figure 10-11.) You can use whatever text you want here, regardless of how the photo collection itself may be named. There's no automated method for populating this field with the name of a collection listed in the Collections panel. The limit for this field is 500 characters, including spaces.

COLLECTION DESCRIPTION

You can enter more details about the photo gallery here. (See label 3 in Figure 10-11.) The limit for this field is 19,920 characters.

CONTACT INFO

This is the text used for the link at the bottom left of the page. (See label 4 in Figure 10-11.) You could enter text like "Email Me" and insert an email link below, or use "Home Page" and provide a link to your website's main page. Of course, you can use whatever text you want here; it doesn't have to be contact information and it doesn't need to contain a link. The limit for this field is 19,920 characters.

WEB OR MAIL LINK

This is the invisible hyperlink attached to the Contact Info text above. (See label 4 in Figure 10-11.) In order for the link to work correctly, the value of this field must be a correctly formatted URL. If you're using an email link, use the format *mailto:myemailaddress@mydomain.com*. If you're using a link to a web page, use the full address, such as *http://www.mywebsiteaddress.com*. The limit for this field is 19,920 characters.

IDENTITY PLATE

The bottom section of the Site Info panel allows you to apply and customize an identity plate (see **Figure 10–12** and label 5 in Figure 10-11). This applies to the default HTML template; in other layout styles, the Identity Plate section may be absent or in a different location.

Figure 10-12

Step 1. Check the box to enable Identity Plate. You can click on the small preview to see a list of saved identity plates. To make a new one, click Edit… in the menu.

Step 2. In the Identity Plate Editor (see **Figure 10–13**), choose whether to use a text or graphical identity plate. If you select the text option for your identity plate, type the text you want to use, then use the controls provided to style the text. The text must be selected to apply the styling.

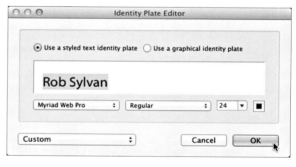

Figure 10-13

To use a graphic, you must first create an image file in other software such as Photoshop. Lightroom supports identity plate graphics using JPEG, PNG, GIF, BMP, and TIF. Click the Locate… button to find a file on your hard drive, or drag and drop a file from your desktop into the window.

Step 3. When you're done setting up your new identity plate, click the button at the bottom left that says Custom (see **Figure 10–14**), then choose Save As… Give your new identity plate a meaningful name, like "My Web Gallery ID plate", click Save, and then click OK to apply the new identity plate to your Web gallery.

Your new identity plate will become available in all areas in Lightroom where you can specify an identity plate for a layout, including Book, Slideshow, and Print. (Identity plates are covered in those chapters as well.)

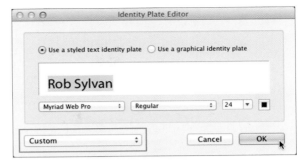

Figure 10-14

WEB OR MAIL LINK

After applying the identity plate, you can enter a link to a web page or email address that will be loaded when it's clicked; format the link using the instructions in the previous section. If you don't want to include a link on your identity plate, leave this field blank.

 Provide a link to your Home Page

In the Site Info panel, the default HTML Lightroom Web templates provide the two places just described to create links to other web pages or email. If you are adding Web galleries to an existing site, I recommend you be sure to use either the identity plate or the Web or Mail Link to include a link to the home page of the site. Otherwise, the Web gallery will be isolated from the rest of your website, offering users no way to get anywhere outside that specific Web gallery. This condition varies in other layout styles; some provide other ways to add outbound links from your gallery.

Color Palette

This panel allows you to specify colors for various elements within your layout (see **Figure 10–15**). The main elements to which you can apply color are listed down the left side of the panel. You can specify colors for the following items:

Figure 10-15

Text: entered in the Site Info panel

Detail Text: links and text on the large image pages

Background: the main page background

Detail Matte: the area surrounding the large image

Cells: thumbnail backgrounds

Rollover: the color used for highlighting thumbnail cells as the user moves her cursor over each cell

Grid Lines: lines separating thumbnail grid cells

Numbers: numbers in the background of grid cells

QUICK GUIDE TO USING THE COLOR PICKER

Next to each element is a rectangular color swatch. (If you're using the HTML default template these will all be varying shades of gray and are easy to overlook.) To change the color of an element, click its swatch. A color picker box appears with the name of the selected element along the top (see **Figure 10–16**). Choose the color from the picker; when you're done, click the X in the upper left corner of the color picker or press Return or Enter. If you want to cancel changes you made in the color picker, press Esc. The color picker is covered in detail in Chapter 4.

10

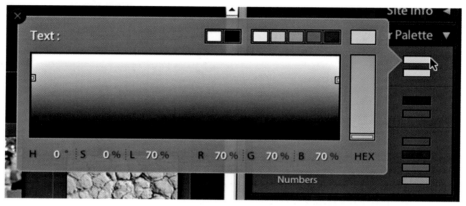

Figure 10-16

 **Changing from grayscale to color**
If the color currently selected is a shade of gray, white, or black, and you want to apply a color, you first need to click somewhere in the saturation elevator (the vertical slider) at the right side of the color picker. Then you'll see a full-color spectrum. Click inside the spectrum to choose the hue range you want, and then use the elevator to increase or decrease saturation.

Hiding page elements
You can't actually "turn off" or remove any of these page elements using the Color Palette panel. However, you can effectively *hide* elements by making them the same color as their backgrounds. For a precise match, manually enter numeric values for the colors. Note that these elements will still be included in the HTML code, even though they are not visible on the page.

Appearance

The Appearance panel is split into three sections (see **Figure 10–17**): Common Settings, Grid Pages, and Image Pages.

I usually start customizing the gallery design by styling the thumbnail pages. Most HTML templates use "index" pages for thumbnails, which link to individual pages that show each full-size photo. (Flash templates often have the thumbnails on the same page as the full-size photo.) In both types of layout styles, with Lightroom's built-in templates you can't change the size of the thumbnails, but you usually can change how many thumbnails will show on a single page. (Some third-party layout styles allow you to adjust the size and presentation of thumbnails.)

 Use Advanced Settings

There are advanced CSS controls not visible in the default view. Use the shortcut ⌘+Option+Shift+/ or Ctrl+Alt+Shift+/ to show Advanced Settings on the Appearance panel. If you're an experienced coder integrating your Lightroom Web Gallery with other existing web pages, these controls are invaluable.

Figure 10-17

COMMON SETTINGS

Common Settings are applied to all photos within the current gallery.

DROP SHADOW

Use the checkbox to show or hide a drop shadow behind each photo. (This single setting applies to both thumbnails and large image pages). In the default HTML gallery you don't have any options for styling the drop shadow.

SECTION BORDERS

Section Borders are placed between the different areas of the page, depending on the Layout Style, and can be turned on and off. To change the colors of the Section Borders, click the swatch to open the color picker.

GRID PAGES

The middle section of the Appearance panel contains the options for Grid Pages within the gallery (see Figure 10–17). The grid you see in the panel represents rows and columns on your thumbnail pages. Click in the grid to change the number of rows and columns. (Don't click and drag in the box—just click!) If you're viewing a grid page as you do this, the main preview will be updated automatically.

PANEL ALERTS

If you see a warning exclamation point to the right of the Grid Pages text, it's because you're looking at a large Image Page and not a Grid Page. If you see the warning to the right of the Image Pages text (see Figure 10–17) it's because you're viewing the Grid Page and not the large Image Page. The warning is to let you know that if you change those settings, you won't see the changes reflected in the preview until you switch back to a page with the corresponding view.

GALLERIES WITH MULTIPLE PAGES

If you have more images than can fit on one page of thumbnails, Lightroom will automatically add more pages—and any necessary links to those pages—at the bottom right corner of the page footer (see **Figure 10–18**). To see the page numbers and Previous and Next links, be sure the bottom of the page is visible in the main preview area; you may need to scroll down.

Figure 10-18

How many columns?

One challenge in setting up the Grid Page is deciding the ideal number of rows and columns to use, based on the number of photos you're including and the anticipated resolution and aspect ratio of your target audience display. Though you have the option to use eight columns, I recommend that you generally refrain from doing this, because it's likely that many people will need to scroll sideways to see all the photos. Most people aren't used to scrolling sideways on web pages, so they might never realize there are more photos hiding there. When possible, it's usually best to arrange your Grid Pages in three or four columns unless you know the target screen is wide enough to accommodate more.

SHOW CELL NUMBERS

Below the grid is a checkbox that turns Cell Numbers on and off. You can't change the type style for these numbers.

PHOTO BORDERS

Photo Borders can be applied to the thumbnails; click the swatch to change the color. You can't change the width of the Grid Page Photo Borders in the default HTML layout style.

IMAGE PAGES

The bottom area of the Appearance panel has controls for customizing Image Pages (see Figure 10–17). These settings affect the styles for the pages that contain a single, large photo. Again, if you see a warning triangle, it's because you're not looking at a large image page: click one of the thumbnails in the main preview and when the large image page loads, the warning will go away.

SIZE

The Size of the large image is set by dragging the slider or by clicking in the text field to manually enter a value. The slider sets the length of the *longest side* of each photo in the gallery. The length of the short side is scaled proportionally.

Choosing the ideal size
Having just one Size slider has several implications. First, if you have both horizontal and vertical photos in the gallery, you can't set their sizes to different values. And if you're inclined to make the images really big so they fill the screen, this may work great for the horizontal photos, but not so well for verticals. Viewers might not be able to see the whole photo at once, and having to scroll over a large photo can significantly degrade the viewer experience. The difficulties of choosing the optimal size are compounded if you have very wide panoramic images, square images, etc. You'll need to decide carefully whether or not to present images of different aspect ratios within a single gallery.

PHOTO BORDERS
Especially on the large image pages, adding Photo Borders can improve the overall presentation. The controls here work the same as Photo Borders for Grid Pages. I often use very wide, white borders to set off the photos from the darker backgrounds (see **Figure 10–19**).

10

Figure 10-19

Image Info
This panel provides options for two labels with textual information to be included on the large image pages (see **Figure 10–20**).

LABELS
Check the boxes to enable or disable Title and Caption text labels. Keep in mind that these Web gallery "titles and captions" are not necessarily referring to the metadata fields

Figure 10-20

by the same names, (though by default, that's what they display). In Figure 10-20 I changed the Title area to display the photo's file name (labeled number 1), and changed the Caption area to show exposure information (labeled number 2).

TITLE
On the large image pages, the Title is displayed above the photo. Use the drop-down menus to choose what information will be shown.

CAPTION
On the large image pages, the Caption is shown below the photo. Use the drop-down menus to choose what information will be shown.

Clicking the Edit… menu item opens the **Text Template Editor** (see **Figure 10–21**), where you can configure your own titling presets using a wide range of metadata and custom text entries. Text Templates are used for placing dynamic text on Web gallery pages. The Text Template Editor is very similar to the Filenaming Template Editor, which is explained in detail in Chapter 3.

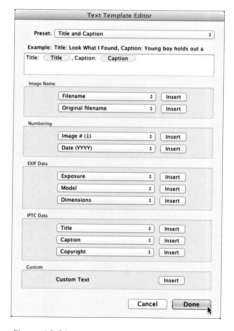

Figure 10-21

Combining elements
Using custom text templates, you can create any combination of text elements, such as putting Title and Caption metadata fields in one element, leaving the other element free for something else.

Output Settings

This panel provides controls that affect how Lightroom processes the photos when exporting the gallery (see **Figure 10–22**).

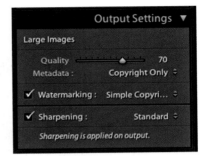

Figure 10-22

LARGE IMAGES

A "large image" is the single, large photo that shows on its own page when a thumbnail is clicked. On this panel section you can apply settings specific to the large images.

QUALITY

The Quality setting determines the level of JPEG compression for the large images. There is a direct correlation between the Quality setting and the resulting file size. Higher quality equals larger files; lower quality equals smaller files. JPEG compression works best with large areas of solid color. Photos with very fine detail always produce larger file sizes than those with less detail, even at the same Quality setting. For most photos, you can usually get very good quality at settings between 50 and 80, though some images start to show ugly compression artifacts in this range. Between 80 and 100, each incremental increase to the Quality level starts to significantly increase file size with limited improvement in the appearance of the image. For most photos, a JPEG quality level of 80 is a practical upper limit for web images.

METADATA

The Metadata pop-up menu (see **Figure 10–23**) gives you a simple selection of what metadata will be embedded within the newly exported JPEG files for the gallery. Note that this metadata is totally independent from any other metadata you may also be displaying on the pages—this setting specifically controls which metadata is included *in the image files themselves*. "All" will include all metadata you've assigned to the file, including keywords, captions, titles, ratings, etc. "Copyright Only" is just that—everything else will be omitted from the exported image files.

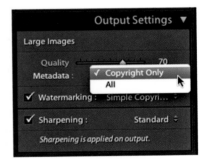

Figure 10-23

Reduce file size by omitting metadata
Depending on the amount of metadata you've applied to a photo, using Copyright Only can reduce the size of the exported files by a significant percentage. This is especially useful when fast loading is more important than having lots of metadata and when

you're working under strict file size limitations. (Lightroom doesn't provide a preview of what the difference in file size will be with and without all the metadata; if file size is a concern, you'll need to compare the sizes of the exported files to see where they end up.)

WATERMARKING

To apply a watermark to the photos in your Web gallery, check the box to enable the option and then choose a watermark from the pop-up menu, or make a new one. Watermarks are covered in detail in Chapter 5.

SHARPENING

To apply output sharpening to the files, check the Sharpening box and choose the desired amount from the menu. You only have three choices: Low, Standard, or High. With these simple controls Lightroom is very good at applying the optimal amount of sharpening for the size of the images being output for the gallery. This is especially true if you've done a good job sharpening the images at earlier stages of the workflow. Lightroom applies sharpening as the last step, after rendering the thumbnails and large images at the sizes specified by the Layout Style. I usually use a sharpening setting of High for Web galleries.

Upload Settings

When you've got your gallery set up the way you want, you can use Lightroom to upload the entire gallery to your web server. Lightroom will render all the files for the gallery and then put them on the server using the account settings and directory locations you specify.

To do this, you need to have a web hosting account set up, and have FTP access to the web server. You also need to know a few things about the way the files and folders are structured on the server. If you're going to be publishing Web galleries to your own hosting account, I strongly recommend that you first understand the basics of web hosting, hyperlinks, and FTP file transfers.

With innumerable variables related to the setup and configuration of web hosting servers, I can't possibly cover every scenario here. However, there are some settings and procedures that apply in most all cases. You will need to choose the server and enter optional Subfolder information using the Upload Settings panel (see **Figure 10–24**).

Figure 10-24

FTP SERVER

The first and most important configuration settings to make are those for the FTP server. Click the pop-up menu and choose a server if one has been previously saved, or select Edit… to open the Configure FTP File Transfer window.

CONFIGURE FTP FILE TRANSFER

In this dialog box (see **Figure 10–25**), enter the server name or IP address, the username, and the password for the FTP account. If you plan to save a preset for this server, I recommend that you only enable the option to store the password in the preset if you are absolutely confident in the security of

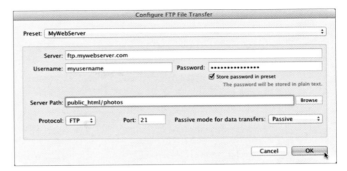

Figure 10-25

your computer (and where that data is backed up). This information in the wrong hands could do more damage to your website than just messing with your web galleries.

The Server Path is very important. If you don't know what to enter here, leave it blank for now, and check with your hosting provider. Otherwise, if you know you need to put the files in a folder other than the site root, enter that directory path in the Server Path field. Most often this will be something like /www/ or /public_html/. The presence or absence of leading and training slashes can be of vital importance; check your hosting account documentation as necessary.

SELECT A SERVER PATH MANUALLY

To select a Server Path folder directly from your web server, click the Browse button. Lightroom will connect to your server, if possible. A new window opens with a connection progress bar at the bottom left. (If Lightroom can't connect, an error message will eventually be displayed; you'll need to check your Internet connection and account settings in the main FTP configuration window.) When Lightroom is finished interacting with the server, a list of directories will be shown, from which you can locate the folder to be used as the Server Path. Highlight the desired directory in the list and click the Select button.

Back in the main window, in most cases you can leave the fields for Protocol, Port, and Passive Mode for Data Transfers at their default values. If Lightroom has trouble connecting to your server, these settings may need to be changed.

 Save a preset

Before leaving the Configure FTP File Transfer screen, be sure to save the FTP server settings as a new preset. At the top of the window, click the Preset: menu, and select Save Current Settings as New Preset. Be sure to give your preset a meaningful name.

Click OK to apply the FTP settings (or Cancel to leave the dialog box without saving changes).

If you're not sure what to use for any of the settings, refer to your web hosting help files or ask your server administrator.

PUT IN SUBFOLDER:

In the Upload Settings panel (see Figure 10–24), you can choose to put the uploaded files into a subfolder (the default is a folder named "photos"). If you previously entered a value in the Server Path field in the main FTP setup window, the new subfolder(s) will be created under that folder. If you don't want to put the gallery in a subfolder, leave this box unchecked.

 Always use web-friendly names for folders

When you're creating any folders (and files) for web use, don't use spaces, punctuation (other than hyphens and underscores), or any special characters. Otherwise, web browsers might not be able to access your pages.

Creating multiple subfolders

You can create a series of nested folders all at once by entering their names into the text field, separated by slashes, for example: photos/trips/moab/

FULL PATH

At the bottom of the Upload Settings panel, the Full Path: text shows the server directory path where the Web gallery will be uploaded (see Figure 10–24).

 Update your template

All the panel settings—including Upload Settings—will be stored in a saved Web template. In future sessions, you will only need to tweak a couple of settings to publish brand new galleries!

Create Saved Web Gallery

At the top of the main preview area in the Web module is a horizontal bar that displays the saved state of the current gallery (see **Figure 10–26**). If you haven't yet saved the gallery, it will say Unsaved Web Gallery; otherwise it will display the name of the saved gallery.

Figure 10-26

Saving a gallery makes a special addition to the Collections panel. A saved gallery contains the photos you've included along with their saved sort order, and the Use: menu options that were active at the time it was saved. A saved gallery references a template, but does not contain the template itself. Remember that even if you update a saved gallery, you may still need to update a template independently.

To save a gallery, click the button at the right labeled Create Saved Web Gallery. This opens a dialog box containing options for saving the gallery (see **Figure 10–27**). You can also save the gallery by clicking the + button at the top of the Collections panel and choosing the Create Web Gallery menu option.

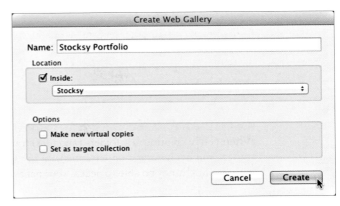

Figure 10-27

10

In the Create Web Gallery dialog box, you can specify the Placement options to choose where the new gallery will be saved. In the Web Gallery Options section, you can choose to create new virtual copies for the photos in the gallery, (which I usually don't do, because I want the photos in the gallery to remain linked to the originals I process in Develop).

Once you've saved the Web Gallery, you can return to it at any time by clicking it in the Collections panel, and all your photos and the gallery settings will be reloaded.

Preview in Browser

There may be times when you want to preview the gallery in a real web browser outside of Lightroom. In addition to previewing the Web gallery within Lightroom's image display area, you can also test it in the default web browser on your computer. (This is set in your operating system's preferences.) On the bottom of the left panel track is a button labeled "Preview in Browser…". Clicking this will render your gallery and load it into the default browser on your computer.

Previewing in a browser requires Lightroom to render temporary files for all the photos and can be quite slow. I recommend that you instead use the Web module's built-in preview whenever possible, or use a limited number of photos for your test previews.

 Testing in multiple browsers
If you want to test the gallery in multiple browsers, you can export the gallery to disk and open the files in any browser(s) of your choosing.

Export…

You can export Web galleries from Lightroom even if you don't have a web hosting account set up. In a Web export the files are saved to your hard drive but not to a web server. Click the Export… button at the bottom right of the window to export the current Web gallery to disk (see **Figure 10–28**).

Figure 10-28

A dialog box appears, asking you to choose the location and name for the new folder that will contain all the gallery files. Enter a name and click Save. Lightroom will generate all the necessary files for the Web gallery you've created, including all the files and subfolders required.

The exported gallery is self-contained—Lightroom packages all the files within a single, top-level directory, and all the links are relative to one another within that folder, so you can do all kinds of useful things with exported Web galleries. You can export a Web gallery now, and upload it to a server later. (If you have a dedicated FTP program and are comfortable with its operation, this might be the fastest/easiest way to upload Lightroom galleries to your server.)

ABOUT RELATIVE HYPERLINKS

The links that Lightroom generates within Web galleries are always *relative* to each file. In other words, all the pages in the Web gallery are linked by directory path locations relative to one another. This allows viewing the gallery without an Internet connection, and the presentation looks and works just the same as if it was being accessed from a web server. This also means that if you change the folders or files after the gallery has been generated, the links will be broken. Making changes to Web gallery links requires you to either generate a new gallery, or use dedicated web development software (such as Adobe Dreamweaver) to modify the files.

 Offline galleries

Lightroom Web galleries also make great offline presentations, even without an Internet connection. You can export Web galleries and copy them to a USB flash drive or burn them to disc for presentation to clients, galleries, and prospective vendors. From the disc or other removable media, people can open your gallery index page in a browser on their own computer and navigate throughout the gallery just as if it was delivered from a web server.

Upload

When you're done setting up your Web gallery and with the FTP settings properly configured, click the Upload... button (see **Figure 10–29**) to upload the gallery to the server selected in the Upload Settings panel. Lightroom will generate all the files required for the gallery, including JPEG images and HTML pages (and Flash files, if necessary) and will upload them to your web server in the location specified.

Figure 10-29

Uploading does not save a local copy to your hard drive. When you use the Web module to upload gallery files directly to your server, no files are stored on your hard drive. If this matters to you, you have two options: 1) use Export instead, and manually upload the files using an FTP program, or 2) after using Lightroom to upload, use an FTP program to download copies to your local disk.

UPDATING EXISTING WEB GALLERIES

When you make changes to a Lightroom Web gallery and want to update it on the server (or export it) every file must be rewritten. You don't have the option to add just a single photo, or change one line of text, without regenerating the entire gallery. Usually, this is not a problem—as long as you're not in a hurry. Keep in mind that if you make changes to a Web gallery and need to reupload to your server, the entire gallery will be rewritten. If you've made changes to those files outside Lightroom, such as changing CSS, hyperlinks, etc. you need to be very careful with this.

 Do a few test runs before sharing the link
It's likely that even with lots of experience under your belt you will occasionally do web uploads or exports that for one reason or another don't turn out how you wanted. This is normal and should not be feared! If you're under the gun—like when presenting to a client—it's a good idea to do a few trial runs with any new templates and settings you haven't used before uploading the final gallery files and sharing the link. Just like in all website development, thorough testing is necessary to be sure everything's right before announcing your gallery to the world!

Next steps

With a little practice, you can use Lightroom's Web module to create great-looking Web galleries easily. However, Lightroom's built-in Web galleries have some significant limitations, some of which might be deal breakers depending on your needs.

Most importantly, each gallery you create with Lightroom's built-in templates generates an independent, stand-alone collection of files with no direct links to any other separate galleries. This means if you create a collection of photos and generate a Web gallery with those, and then do the same with another collection of photos, the two collections will have no way of linking directly to one another. When you upload the galleries to your web server, you need to create some kind of separate master index page to provide links to all the individual galleries. Of course, there are add-on, third-party Web galleries and plug-ins that can do this, or if you're able to work with HTML yourself this may not be a problem, but understand that the default functionality that comes with Lightroom's Web module does not provide the capability to generate index pages that link together separate galleries.

Also, the HTML and Flash code generated by the Web module is anything but what would be called "clean." Around the Internet, all web pages are not created equal, and compared to best practices in writing web code, Lightroom's HTML is typically messy, convoluted, and hard to customize, even for experienced coders.

For these reasons, after you've made a few Web galleries using Lightroom's built-in functionality, you may well start looking at additional resources for more advanced capabilities. Check the Appendix for a list of links to get you started.

CHAPTER 11
Catalogs

11

WORKING WITH LIGHTROOM CATALOGS: Advanced photo management techniques

Although we've discussed catalog-related issues at various points throughout this book, the topic of working with Lightroom catalogs deserves its own chapter. For some photographers, there comes a point when working with just one catalog is not ideal for their workflow. Unfortunately, for other folks, even correctly managing a single catalog becomes confusing and difficult. In my teaching and consulting work I've repeatedly seen how many people struggle with catalog management at one point or another. It doesn't need to be so difficult!

Since Lightroom relies on the catalog to function, ignoring this aspect of Lightroom can be a recipe for disaster. The good folks at Adobe have gone to great efforts to make using Lightroom (and catalogs) as easy as possible (and it usually is), but when something goes wrong, many photographers find themselves in uncharted territory. Most people simply have no prior experience dealing with image databases. In this chapter, you'll learn lots more about Lightroom catalogs and how to use them to manage your photo library.

REVIEW OF LIGHTROOM DATA ARCHITECTURE

Always bear in mind that a Lightroom catalog is a database file on your hard drive. When Lightroom is launched for the first time, an empty catalog is created in the Pictures folder under your user account. When you launch Lightroom, it looks for a catalog to load. Whenever you're working in Lightroom, you're working in a catalog; you'll be working from the default catalog until you change this. You can use as many Lightroom catalogs as you desire and they can be stored on any hard drive attached to your computer. You cannot open a catalog over a network.

A Lightroom catalog contains records of the photos and videos you've imported, but it does not contain the actual photo and video files (these are always stored on some drive of your choosing). All the work you do in the catalog is done by reference: Lightroom continually reads from each image file and/or video clip on the hard drive while you work. The original image data in these files are never modified. As you work, Lightroom continually renders previews, which are also saved on the hard drive in a special cache file next to the catalog file. The previews you see in Lightroom are generated using the current adjustments you've made. All this information is stored in the catalog, along with your history, collections, virtual copies, etc. You can also save each photo's adjustment information out to the photo's own metadata on the hard disk, but Lightroom always treats the catalog file as the primary source of information about your photos. (If necessary, review Chapters 1 and 2 for more on this.)

ESSENTIAL FILE MAINTENANCE

If your catalog is lost, deleted, or corrupted, the work you've done in the catalog will be lost. This is why it's imperative to a) make regular backups of your catalog and image files, b) keep your catalog clean and optimized, and c) consider saving metadata to your photos on disk as you work. (These subjects are covered in detail in various places earlier in this book.)

ABOUT CATALOG LOCATIONS AND NAMING

Lightroom can open and work with a catalog in any location on a local hard drive. Also, you can use any name for a Lightroom catalog. (Obviously, you don't want to have multiple catalogs with the same name.) You don't have to use any specific names, though… if you use just one catalog, sticking with the default name is fine!

 Use care when renaming existing catalogs

The catalog and the preview package have a symbiotic relationship: the names and locations of the preview files are stored in the catalog. If you rename the catalog in the Mac Finder or Windows Explorer, Lightroom won't be able to match the catalog to the existing preview cache with the old name, and will need to rebuild the previews for all the photos in the catalog. You can avoid this by renaming the preview cache to match the new name of the catalog. For example, if your catalog file is named *Lightroom 5 Catalog.lrcat* then the preview cache will be named *Lightroom 5 Catalog Previews. lrdata*. If you rename the catalog to My *Lightroom Catalog.lrcat* then you just need to rename the preview cache to My *Lightroom Catalog Previews.lrdata*. You'd obviously only do this with Lightroom closed.

If you rename a catalog and preview cache I suggest double-clicking the catalog file to open it into Lightroom. This allows you to double-check that everything works as it should right away. With the catalog open in Lightroom, you might also want to update Lightroom's Default Catalog preferences to use this newly named catalog (we'll cover the Default Catalog a little later in this chapter).

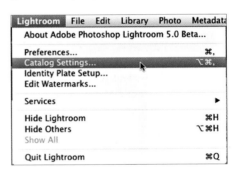

Figure 11-1

Catalog Settings

Each Lightroom catalog has its own settings. With Lightroom running, you can find Catalog Settings under the Lightroom menu for Mac (see **Figure 11–1**) and the Edit menu on Windows (see **Figure 11–2**). As you're working in Lightroom, you should expect to work in this dialog box from time to time; more often when you're using multiple catalogs and different computers. The Catalog Settings dialog box provides controls grouped into General, File Handling, and Metadata categories. Keep in mind that Catalog Settings apply *only to the catalog currently open* (unlike the Lightroom Preferences, which apply to all catalogs).

Figure 11-2

GENERAL

The first section in the Catalog Settings panel provides information about the catalog and the settings for Lightroom's automatic catalog backups (see **Figure 11–3**).

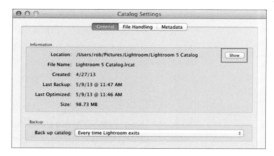

INFORMATION

This section is one of the most important parts of the Catalog Settings. It tells you the name and

Figure 11-3

location of the current catalog. As you're working with Lightroom, especially when using multiple catalogs, you can look here to confirm you're using the correct catalog. Even if you only use one catalog, there are situations in which looking at this information is vitally relevant—for example, if you open Lightroom and things don't look like you remembered them from your last work session. If you ever suspect the wrong catalog is loaded, or just want to confirm the location on disk for the current catalog, look here. (Opening different catalogs and setting the default catalog is covered later in this chapter.)

To the right of the Location information is a button labeled Show. Click this button to open the folder containing the catalog in the Mac Finder or Windows Explorer.

BACKUP

A menu is provided with options for choosing the frequency of backup reminders for this catalog. Choose an option from this menu to set how often Lightroom reminds you to perform a catalog backup. We'll look at catalog backups in detail in a moment.

FILE HANDLING

The File Handling section provides options for previews and import numbering defaults (see **Figure 11–4**).

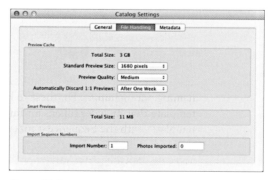

PREVIEW CACHE

Lightroom previews are essentially JPEG files saved on your hard drive and read from the cache as you work. Use the drop-down menus to choose the settings for Lightroom's previews. The Standard preview is the one used for Loupe

Figure 11-4

previews in every module except Develop. (For a review of Lightroom's preview sizes and how they're used in different modules, see Chapters 1, 2, 3, and 4.) The default standard preview size is 1440 pixels on the long edge. Depending on the screen resolution of your monitor you can set this larger or smaller.

For example, on my laptop, which has a monitor resolution of 1680 x 1050, I set the Standard Preview size to 1680, but on my higher resolution desktop monitor I use 2048. Preview Quality sets the JPEG quality used to render previews. The default is Medium, and this is strongly recommended because it is the best compromise between the visual quality of the preview and the amount of disk space each preview requires. If you need a smaller cache size to preserve your disk space and want the slight benefit that comes from the faster read time of smaller files, you could try the Low setting and see if you can live with the lower quality of the previews.

Lightroom's 1:1 previews are used when you zoom in to 1:1 and greater in the Library module. These previews are pixel-for-pixel from the original image data and are the largest that Lightroom renders. They can take up a significant amount of disk space, so it's practical to discard 1:1 previews you haven't used in a while. Use the menu to select how often to purge the 1:1 previews from your hard disk. (I keep this set to After One Week.) When 1:1 previews have been discarded, they will need to be rebuilt when you later zoom in to 1:1 or greater, and Lightroom does this automatically when needed, or you can manually create them anytime via the Build 1:1 Previews option under the Library→Previews menu.

11

SMART PREVIEWS

New in Lightroom 5: Smart previews offer a new way to create workflows involving offline files. We were introduced to smart previews in Chapter 1 when learning Lightroom fundamentals, in Chapter 2 on importing (as that is the first opportunity you have to create them), and again in Chapter 3 when discussing how to manage your photos. In Chapter 4 we learned that we could use smart previews to work in Develop with photos that were currently offline (such as those stored on a disconnected drive).

Recall that smart previews are stored in their own special cache file alongside the catalog and the regular preview cache. The middle section of the File Handling tab displays a running tally of the file size of the smart preview cache. You can delete smart previews at any time by selecting the photos that have a smart preview in Grid view of the Library module and going to Library→Previews→Discard smart previews.

IMPORT SEQUENCE NUMBERS

These fields set the values for optional sequence numbers you can use for automatic file naming during import. For these to have any effect, you must be using a file naming template that includes tokens for Import # and/or Image #. (If you use file naming templates with the Sequence # token you don't need to change these values.)

You can manually enter values for these fields, but they're really designed to be used automatically, in conjunction with the associated filename tokens. The values are automatically incremented as you perform multiple imports, provided the tokens were used in the file naming. (Otherwise these will not change from their default values of 1.)

Import Number keeps track of the number of imports completed and sets a number to be inserted into the filenames for each import. Photos Imported tracks the number of photos imported and thus sets the starting image number to be used for the next import. This feature is particularly useful when you're importing photos from a single shoot captured across multiple cards.

METADATA

This panel of Catalog Settings provides controls for how Lightroom handles various metadata (see **Figure 11–5**).

EDITING

Offer suggestions from recently entered values: check or uncheck this box to enable/disable Lightroom's auto-suggestion feature. By default, as you type, Lightroom will try to insert and/or automatically complete words and phrases

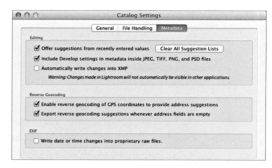

Figure 11-5

based on text you've previously entered. All these text values are tracked in lists within the catalog; if you find the values being retrieved are not relevant to your current project and are hindering your workflow you can click the button to Clear All Suggestion Lists.

Include Develop settings in metadata inside JPEG, TIFF, and PSD files: When you Save Metadata to Files, Lightroom can insert its adjustment instructions directly into the metadata of these file types. However, these adjustments will only be read and respected by other software that supports XMP standards, such as Bridge and Adobe Camera Raw. When you view or open these types of files using those programs, if you've saved Lightroom metadata into them, the previews will reflect those changes. However, if you save Lightroom metadata into one of these file types and then open them directly into Photoshop, your changes will not be visible, since Photoshop ignores this particular metadata. Even so, I always leave this option enabled, as there's no harm in writing Lightroom's Develop metadata into the files along with Library metadata, and if you're going to import them into another catalog or view them with other Adobe software you'll likely want to retain the Lightroom adjustments.

Automatically write changes to XMP: When this option is enabled, Lightroom automatically saves your metadata to the files as you work. On the surface this seems like a brilliant idea and you may wonder why it is not checked by default. The main reason it is no longer checked by default is that when checked it has the potential to affect performance because it means Lightroom is writing to the catalog file and writing to each file's own XMP metadata at the same time in the background.

As computer power increases this becomes less noticeable and less of an issue. I personally leave this unchecked because I have confidence in my catalog backup system and I don't want Lightroom to write to each one of my photos. That said, I have seen this option really save the day for some people who (for whatever reason) lost their Lightroom catalog and had to start over completely from scratch. Because all of the changes were written to each photo's XMP metadata, all of that information was imported into the new catalog when they started over again. Needless to say that was a huge time-saver for them. It is worth noting that there are some things that cannot be written into a file's XMP metadata, such as flag status, regular collection membership, virtual copies, and all of the individual history states from the beginning of time. So, it is still really important to have a solid catalog (and photo) backup plan, but if you feel safer wearing a belt with your suspenders then this is a good option for you.

REVERSE GEOCODING

Lightroom's Map module and associated metadata features provide the ability to perform Reverse Geocoding, which enters suggested IPTC location data when GPS coordinates are added to a photo (Internet connection required). If you prefer not to have location data automatically entered for photos with GPS coordinates, this can be disabled here.

Enabling the option to "Export reverse geocoding suggestions whenever address fields are empty" will automatically insert the location data suggested by reverse geocoding into exported photos unless you have changed those fields. Set this option in conjunction with your choice of Metadata options in the Export window, discussed in Chapter 5.

EXIF

This option enables/disables Lightroom's ability to directly change capture time data within original raw files from your camera. When this is enabled, and you change the capture time in the Library module, the data in the raw files is directly altered. (This is the only type of change Lightroom can make to native raw files.) Some people aren't comfortable with this option; disabling it will change the capture times only in catalog and XMP metadata.

Catalog backups

It's essential that you practice good backup habits when working with your photo libraries. You need to regularly back up your Lightroom catalog(s) and the original source files (photos and videos). You may also want to maintain backups of your presets and other Lightroom configuration files.

LIGHTROOM BACKUPS

Lightroom provides its own functionality to make backups of the catalog. The only time these Lightroom catalog backups can occur is when the program quits. Depending on the options set in your Catalog Settings (see previous section) you will receive occasional reminders about backups (see **Figure 11–6**). When you're shutting down Lightroom and you see this dialog box, you can choose to perform a backup, or skip it (see **Figure 11–7**). When you allow Lightroom to do a catalog backup, you can also have the catalog tested and optimized, both of which are essential maintenance functions. (I always leave these options enabled.)

Understand that it's only the current catalog file that gets backed up; Lightroom can't make backups of your image and video files. Also, Lightroom does not provide the capability to back up previews or settings files; if you want to back those up you'll need to use a different method, which we'll look at in a bit.

When you allow Lightroom to make a backup, the catalog file is copied either to a subfolder in the same folder as

Figure 11-6

the original catalog (by default) or to a location of your choice. To change the backup location, click the Choose button in the backup dialog box. Each copied catalog file is put in a subfolder named for the date and time it was created (see **Figure 11–8**).

Figure 11-7

Back up frequently

I recommend you back up your catalog after every work session where you make any significant changes. I have my Catalog Settings set to "Every time Lightroom exits"—I just skip a backup if it's not needed or I am in a hurry to shut down. This may seem like overkill, but it is easy, free, and it just may save your bacon someday.

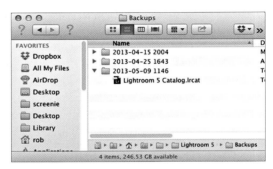

Figure 11-8

Back up before and after major changes

Any time you're planning to do major work to a catalog, such as upgrading to a new version, adding or deleting lots of collections, making major changes to keywords, etc., it's a good idea to do a catalog backup immediately before *and* after making the changes. This gives you the flexibility of "rolling back" the changes and reverting to the previous version if something goes wrong.

Make backups onto another disk

If your catalog backups are on the same hard drive as the master catalog and the drive fails, you'll lose everything, unless you have also frequently replicated all those files to another drive. I can't emphasize strongly enough how important it is to always be sure to save backups onto additional media. It is not a matter of *if* your drive fails, but *when*.

GENERAL BACKUP STRATEGIES

The way we maintain our backups is one of the more personalized aspects of the digital photography workflow. (There are some excellent books dealing with the subject in great detail; see the Appendix for links.) Saving and backing up your work is covered in detail in many places throughout this book. Here are a few reminders:

- Always have at least two current, valid copies of each file, on different media. (Three is better.) This applies to Lightroom catalogs as well as image and video files.

- If possible, keep one set of backups off-site, or separate from your master working files in another physical location.

- Keep the most recent versions of each file. Too many old backups take up unnecessary space and can create confusion.

- In general, don't use simple drag and drop to copy files for backups. Use dedicated backup software to synchronize data between hard drives. This is much faster and more reliable than drag and drop. Recommendations are provided in the Appendix.

- Verify and optimize the data in your catalogs and on your hard drives on a regular basis.

 Delete old backups

You really only need to keep the few most recent Lightroom catalog backups. Lightroom doesn't provide an automated way to limit the number of catalog backups saved. If you're allowing Lightroom to make catalog backups, make sure they're always going into the same folder(s), verify them periodically by opening them into Lightroom, and then delete older backups (set your default catalog preferences to something other than Load Most Recent to ensure the correct catalog opens when you launch Lightroom).

RESTORING A LIGHTROOM CATALOG FROM BACKUP

If you have a problem with your master catalog that can't be corrected and you want to restore a backup, use these steps as a guide:

Step 1. Quarantine the bad catalog. Find the folder on the hard drive containing the catalog you no longer want to use and either move it or rename the folder it's contained in. You don't want to get it confused with your backup. Collect the previews and any other temporary Lightroom files from this folder as well, but don't delete any of these files until you've successfully restored the backup.

Step 2. Locate the backup to be restored. Go to your main backup folder containing either your Lightroom catalog backups, or another hard drive where you've used one of the above methods for backup.

Step 3. Copy (don't move) the backup to the location where the previous master was stored. You should be moving just the single catalog file only. Don't worry about the preview package; Lightroom will make a new one.

Step 4. With the backup in the correct location, double-click to open it in Lightroom.

Step 5. With the catalog opened, confirm all is OK with this restored backup. If not, quit Lightroom and repeat the steps beginning at Step 2 using a different backup copy.

Step 6. (Optional) When you've confirmed the restored backup is OK, go into the Lightroom Preferences and verify that the setting for the Default Catalog opening at launch is set to the current catalog.

Step 7. Delete the old (bad) files.

 Don't delete journal or temp files right away

When Lightroom crashes or is forced to quit, journal files often remain in the Lightroom catalog folder. Lightroom uses these the next time the catalog is opened. In cases where the catalog needs to be repaired, these files are essential. If you ever see these kinds of files in the catalog folder, don't delete them until you successfully run Lightroom again and quit the program normally. After starting and quitting Lightroom you can delete any journal or temp files that may remain left over from a previous session.

 Take your time

I've stated this many times throughout this book, but it bears repeating again: really think things through before you act. When you're working with backup files that have the same name as the original master, it's easy to get confused as to which is which. Take each step slowly and carefully. Whenever possible, it's best to not try to resolve backup issues when you're in a hurry or under pressure—most times, things just get worse.

BACKING UP YOUR PRESETS, CONFIGURATION FILES, AND PROFILES

Lightroom does not provide any way to make backups of the configuration files, presets, and template files you have created. Your best option is to create aliases (shortcuts) to the folders containing these files, and back them up manually. Of course, if you're making regular backups of your system disk where the application is installed, you shouldn't be at great risk of losing them. However, synchronizing your configuration files between multiple computers is another challenge unto itself, which you can learn about later in this chapter.

There is a third-party plug-in worth checking out called TPG-LR-Backup available from the Photographer's Toolbox (link mentioned in the Appendix) that automates the process of backing up these configuration and preset files for you (as well as deleting old backup copies too).

Maintaining catalog integrity

Like all databases, a Lightroom catalog should undergo occasional maintenance. As you work within a catalog, many changes occur to the data—new data is created, old data is discarded or marked for deletion, and existing data is modified. There's a huge amount of underlying processing happening when you make even the simplest change in a Lightroom catalog. For these reasons, you should take steps to keep your catalog healthy.

KEEP YOUR CATALOG CLEAN

If you have missing folders or missing photos, you should figure out what happened and fix the references to those missing files or remove them. Same goes for unused collections, virtual copies, etc., which you should periodically purge from the catalog. Try not to leave junk hanging around in the catalog. It is easy to say, "I'll clean that up tomorrow," but before you know it you've got a huge mess on your hands and you may not remember clearly how things got that way.

TESTING INTEGRITY

Performing the data validation tests and correcting database errors is the most important reason to allow Lightroom to perform its own backups. Even if you back up your catalog(s) using dedicated hard drive backup software, you should also allow Lightroom to do its own backups from time to time. This allows Lightroom's integrity test to run, and it ensures the Lightroom catalog was closed at the time it was backed up. It is fine to let your backup software back up the copies Lightroom makes too.

11

You can also test the integrity of a catalog as it's being opened. In the Select Catalog dialog (as specified in Preferences or by holding Option or Alt when starting Lightroom), enable the option to test integrity (see Figure 11-11).

OPTIMIZE CATALOG

You can optimize your catalog as part of the backup process, but even if you don't do a backup, the Optimize Catalog command can be run from under the File menu.

The Optimize Catalog command runs the SQL Vacuum procedure, which cleans, compacts, and repairs the catalog. Regardless of your backup frequency, I recommend you optimize your catalog every now and then to keep things running smoothly.

If your catalog is running slowly or you're experiencing frequent crashes or Lightroom freezes, optimizing the catalog can often help. Sometimes it won't help, though, and you need to take additional steps to determine the cause of the problem.

CATALOG TROUBLESHOOTING

If you don't have a lot of experience using databases—especially for image editing and asset management—it may come as a shock if a problem with the Lightroom catalog makes your photos inaccessible. It is entirely possible that a Lightroom catalog could become corrupted and not be able to be opened or worked with in any way. But in the vast majority of cases, a problem with the Lightroom catalog does not indicate a problem with the image files. (Of course, in some cases an image file could itself be corrupt, but that is a separate issue.)

If you launch Lightroom or open a catalog and receive an error message, STOP! Before you click anything, you need to slow down and consider what's happened. Most of the time when Lightroom finds a problem with a catalog it can be fixed; sometimes it can't. This is why maintaining your backups is so critical.

When catalogs become corrupted, it's most often a result of one of the following situations occurring:

1. Lightroom crashed or was forced to quit with a catalog open;

2. A hard drive was disconnected or otherwise taken offline with the catalog open; or

3. Other problems on the hard drive, such as a failing drive, have affected the files.

It's imperative that you determine the cause of the corruption before continuing. Otherwise, the same thing could happen all over again. If your catalog was corrupted because of a Lightroom crash, you can probably repair it or safely restore your most recent backup. Otherwise, take the time to resolve any other computer problems before continuing with Lightroom.

REBUILDING PREVIEWS

It's possible that the Lightroom previews package will become corrupted. When this happens, Lightroom will perform erratically and may even crash. There might be nothing wrong with the catalog itself.

11

In most cases where I'm diagnosing a Lightroom catalog problem, the first step is to delete the preview package from the Lightroom catalog folder. Allowing Lightroom to rebuild the previews file often solves many problems that initially appear to be catalog-related.

READ-ONLY FILES

Sometimes, operating system software can mark files as read-only without your intervention. The reasons this happens are far outside the scope of this book. However, I can tell you that I've seen several instances where Lightroom catalogs became set to read-only for no clear reason. When this happens, you may or may not get clear error messages stating what's wrong.

Make sure the disk is not write-protected. Then make sure all the directories and all your image files are also not set to read-only. The methods for doing this will depend on your operating system; most of the time you can use Get Info (Mac Finder) or Properties (Windows Explorer) to change the read/write options for folders and files. If not, you'll have to search online for more information.

 Lightroom catalogs are not supposed to become corrupt
I hate to say it, but most of the problems people encounter are of their own making. I've been using Lightroom from the beginning, using many, many catalogs with many tens of thousands of images, and I have never seen one of my catalogs become corrupted. I have seen it happen to other people, though, and in those cases it was usually due to the catalog being stored on an external drive that accidentally became disconnected while the catalog was open.

If you're regularly having problems with catalog corruption, there's something else going on. You'd do well to look for more help in one of the many excellent online resources. See the Appendix for links.

 Creating a new catalog from a corrupt one
Even from an un-repairable catalog, sometimes you may be able to generate a brand new catalog using all the data from the current one. If you keep getting catalog corruption or error messages, try using the Export as Catalog command discussed later in this chapter. Many times, creating a good, new catalog from an old, bad one is the most straightforward fix. Keep in mind that Publish Services are not included in catalog export, so any publish service connections would have to be rebuilt from scratch.

Upgrading catalogs

Every time you upgrade Lightroom to a major release (2.0, 3.0, 4.0, 5.0, etc.) you must also upgrade the catalog. You can upgrade a copy of a Lightroom catalog from any older version to any newer version at any time (you can't go from new version to old version though).

When you upgrade a catalog, a copy is first made of the original file. No changes are ever made to the original catalog. During the upgrade process, Lightroom copies all your data from the old catalog and puts it into the new catalog. The new catalog also contains all the updated program code for the newer version of Lightroom. You then move forward with the new upgraded copy.

In an effort to be more efficient, the new version of Lightroom takes control of the existing preview cache and associates it with the newly upgraded copy of the catalog (so the new version has one less thing to do). If you should open the old catalog again with the old version of Lightroom it will have to regenerate all of the previews. Most people move forward without looking back, but you should make a copy of the preview cache to a different folder before upgrading if you have a need to hold on to the old version for awhile.

To upgrade a catalog, simply open it with a newer version of Lightroom. (If you've just upgraded the application, Lightroom should automatically find your catalog from the previous version.) You can do this with the Open command under the File menu or by double-clicking a catalog in the Mac Finder or Windows Explorer. You'll be presented with a dialog box with notification that a catalog upgrade is required to use that catalog with the version of Lightroom you're running (see **Figure 11–9**).

If you're using the default catalog name, Lightroom will automatically change the name of the upgraded catalog file to reflect the current version. For example, *Lightroom 4 Catalog* would become *Lightroom 5 Catalog*.

Figure 11-9

If you're using a custom name, Lightroom will append a hyphen and sequence number at the end of the new catalog name. For example, Master Lightroom Catalog would become Master Lightroom Catalog-2.

By default, Lightroom will create the new catalog in the same folder as the original. If desired, you can choose a different location and/or filename for the new catalog by clicking the Change button. When you're ready, click the Upgrade button.

After upgrading a catalog and confirming everything is OK, you should delete the old catalog(s) from your system. Archive it first if this makes you nervous. You can also uninstall the old version of the software.

USING MULTIPLE CATALOGS

For most photographers, working with one main, master Lightroom catalog is best, but there are many possible exceptions. For example, some photographers might use different catalogs for work and personal photos, or a unique catalog for each client. A wedding or sports photographer might use a catalog for each event. Some photographers use separate catalogs for each calendar year of photos.

I strongly prefer to have my entire photo library indexed within one master catalog—when I open Lightroom, I want access to everything in one place—but I use working catalogs very frequently. There's no inherent risk in keeping everything in one master catalog; I have nearly 90,000 photos in my master catalog, and personally know photographers with several hundred thousand photos in theirs. There's no known upper limit to the number of photos your catalog can contain, but obviously there are some very real performance implications (computer hardware is the biggest variable affecting performance).

Even if you use only one master catalog for your entire photo collection, there will be times when using temporary working catalogs will come in very handy. One example is when traveling, using Lightroom on a laptop, and then returning home to your main computer. Travel photographers often use a new project catalog for each trip.

You can use one or many catalogs to manage your photo library; you could split or re-combine your catalogs however you like, an unlimited number of times. This is something you need to decide carefully. (The best way to combine data from multiple catalogs is Export from Catalog and Import from Catalog, which you'll learn about in a moment.)

 Not for beginners
You should only consider using multiple catalogs when you've really got a handle on the database concepts of Lightroom.

ONE PHOTO IN MULTIPLE CATALOGS
Although a single photo can potentially be imported into any number of different catalogs, I don't recommend it. For your own sanity and efficiency you really only want to have any given photo managed by a single catalog.

 Find catalogs and eliminate unused ones
To find all the Lightroom catalogs on your computer, search in Mac Finder or Windows Explorer for folders and files containing the file extension .lrcat. If you haven't been deleting old catalog backups there will likely be many, many catalogs on your hard drive. Searching for .lrcat files is a good way to locate them. Just be careful when you're deleting them—since your backups will have exactly the same filenames as the original catalogs from which they were made, it's easy to accidentally delete the wrong one!

OPEN A DIFFERENT CATALOG
Lightroom can have only one catalog open at a time. To open another catalog, use the Open Catalog command under the File menu. Or, in the Mac Finder or Windows Explorer, double-click on a catalog file. When opening a different catalog, Lightroom must quit and restart. If you've specified backup options, you will see the Backup dialog when Lightroom is quitting out of the first catalog.

 Always know the name and location of the catalog you're using
Many photographers have had big problems unknowingly using more than one catalog! As you can imagine, this can result in significant confusion and frustration, but if you're paying attention it's easy enough to avoid. The best way to ensure you're using the right catalog is to verify the name and location in the Catalog Settings dialog box. If your catalogs have unique names, you can also check the name shown in the window title bar in Lightroom's standard window mode.

CHOOSING A DIFFERENT CATALOG AT STARTUP

When Lightroom launches, it must load a catalog. In the Lightroom Preferences, you can set the default catalog. You can choose Load most recent catalog (the default), select a specific recent catalog from the list, or have Lightroom open the prompt dialog when the program starts (see **Figure 11–10**). I strongly urge you to have Lightroom choose a specific catalog. Using Load most recent catalog means that Lightroom automatically chooses the last catalog you opened, but you may not realize this until it is too late. You need to be in the driver's seat on this decision, so make it now and save yourself some trouble.

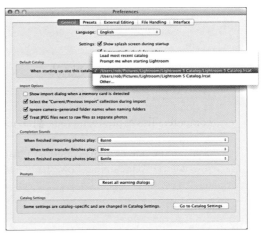

Figure 11-10

You can also press Option (Mac)/ Ctrl (Win) when launching Lightroom to load the Select Catalog… dialog box, from which you can select a specific catalog or make a new one (see **Figure 11–11**). If you wish, you can make the catalog you select the new default catalog by checking the Always load this catalog on startup box.

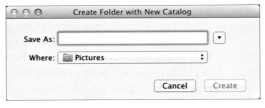

Figure 11-11

CREATE A NEW CATALOG

You can create a new, empty Lightroom catalog at any time. Use the New Catalog command under the File menu. You'll be prompted to enter a name for the new catalog and a folder location on disk (see **Figure 11–12**). When Lightroom creates the catalog, it will first create a new folder using the name you provided, and then place the new catalog file inside that folder, also using the same name.

Figure 11-12

 Use meaningful names for catalogs
If you use multiple catalogs, name each one for its specific purpose and keep the names simple and functional. For example, if you're shooting a wedding, name the catalog for the client; if you're traveling, name it for the trip, etc.

Export as Catalog

From within the Library module, you can export
one or more photos, folders, and collections as
new catalogs. When you use the Export as Catalog
command, all the catalog data for the selected files
is copied to the new catalog, including collections
and smart collections, virtual copies, stacks, and
keywords. Optionally, you can also copy the
original image files.

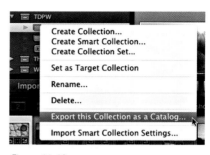

Figure 11-13

Step 1. Choose the item(s) to be exported to the
new catalog. To export individual images into a
new catalog, they must be selected; you can then
choose the Export as Catalog… option under the
File menu. Or, right-click or Ctrl+click on a folder
or collection name (see **Figure 11–13**). Also, if

Figure 11-14

you press Option or Alt, you'll see the standard Import and Export buttons (bottom left,
Library) change to Import Catalog and Export Catalog (see **Figure 11–14**).

Step 2. In the resulting dialog box, you
must type a name and location on disk
for the new catalog to be saved (see
Figure 11–15). A folder will be created
using that name. Inside the folder
will be the new catalog and preview
package, using the same base name you
entered here. You also can choose from
the following options:

Figure 11-15

Export selected photos only: When
this is checked, only selected photos
will be exported to the new catalog. Otherwise, *all photos from the currently selected source*
will go into the new catalog. A text display above the check boxes indicates the results
of your choice here. This option is not visible if no photos are selected when you run the
Export as Catalog command.

Export negative files: In this instance, "negative files" simply means the source files
on disk. When this is checked, Lightroom will make copies of the files and the new
catalog will link to those files, not the originals. If this is left unchecked, the new catalog
references will remain linked to the original files on disk. This option is useful when you
want to take copies of the photos with you.

Build / Include Smart Previews: Check this option when you want to include any
available smart previews or have Lightroom create new smart previews as part of this
catalog export. This new option also gives you the freedom to skip including negative
files and only include smart previews for a compact travel package that still allows you to
continue working on your photos.

11

Include available previews: When this option is checked, Lightroom will also copy the regular previews from the old preview package into the new one. I don't usually do this; I'm OK with having new previews rendered when the new catalog is opened.

Export catalogs to share them
Using this method, you can easily create self-contained, portable sets of files. Exporting catalogs is a great way to share work between different people, multiple computers, etc.

Publish services and settings are not exported
Lightroom does not provide a way to transfer Publish Services and/or related settings between catalogs.

Import from Catalog

Using the Import from Catalog command is an essential technique for transferring Lightroom data between catalogs. (There's currently no way to synchronize two Lightroom catalogs.) When you do an Import from Catalog, any folders, collections, virtual copies,

Figure 11-16

and filter settings from the catalog being imported are transferred to the current catalog. This means that you can use working catalogs for any purpose, using all of Lightroom's functions, and can later merge all that data into another catalog. You can import from catalogs made with earlier versions into Lightroom 5, though depending on the version you'll be prompted to upgrade those catalogs first (see **Figure 11–16**).

Merging multiple catalogs into one
If you've been working with multiple catalogs and want to combine them, you can use Import from Catalog to merge them all into one. You can then delete (or archive) the individual old catalogs.

Following are the basic steps to import data from one catalog to another:

Figure 11-17

Step 1. Choose the Import from Another Catalog command from under the File menu, or press the Option or Alt key and the regular Import button (bottom left, Library) changes to say Import Catalog (see **Figure 11–17**).

Step 2. A dialog box opens prompting you to select the catalog to import from. Find the catalog on your hard drive and click the Choose button (Mac) or the Open button (Windows); see **Figure 11–18**.

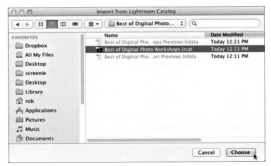

Figure 11-18

Step 3. The window that opens next is the Import from Catalog dialog box (see **Figure 11–19**). You can resize/maximize this window to show more of its contents. You have options for which files will be imported, how the files will be handled, and what to do about any existing files in the current catalog. (For a review of import options, see Chapter 2.)

Figure 11-19

Step 4. Choose what to import. If necessary, choose from the folder list at the top left to check or uncheck entire folders for the import. With image thumbnails showing (click Show Preview at bottom left) you can also check or uncheck individual photos (see **Figure 11–20**).

11

Step 5. Below, under File Handling, choose whether to have Lightroom Copy the files to a new location, or Add new photos to catalog without moving (see Figure 11–20). If you're importing from a catalog on one hard drive to a catalog on another drive, you'll likely also want to have Lightroom perform the file copies for you.

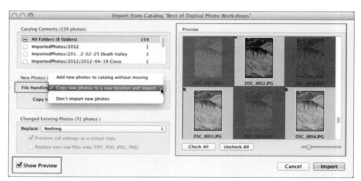

Figure 11-20

Step 6. In the last section, Changed Existing Photos, Lightroom will indicate photos that exist in both catalogs but have different settings applied (see **Figure 11–21**). If none are found, this option is disabled. If Lightroom detects duplicate photos in both catalogs that have

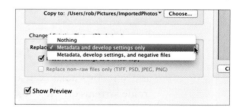

Figure 11-21

different settings applied, you have the choice of keeping the version in your open catalog or using the one that's coming in from the imported catalog. In the latter case, there's a check box to Preserve Old Settings as a Virtual Copy, which is a good idea if you're not certain which the correct version is. Using the drop-down menu you can choose which types of settings to override using the new metadata coming in.

Step 7. When you're ready, click the Import button at the bottom right of the window and the import process begins. Just like with a regular import, the import window immediately closes and you'll be taken back to the Library module where you can see the new photos and any other catalog data as they are being added.

Duplicate collection names

One thing to watch out for when you're importing photos from one catalog into another: if collections with the same name exist in both catalogs, the photos being imported will be merged into the collection with the same name in your main catalog. Depending on how you've set up collection and sets, this could produce an unintended outcome. If you have collections with the same name in both catalogs, and you don't want the photos to be merged in that collection, you'll need to change the name of the collection in one or the other catalog before doing the import. See Chapter 3 for more about collections.

Working with Lightroom on multiple computers

Many photographers work on multiple computers. The most common scenario is that you have a main editing workstation at your home or studio, where you keep your master catalog(s) and all your image and video files, and a laptop or other portable device that you work on when you're out and about.

A single Lightroom license allows you to install and use Lightroom on up to two computers. Even if you have one Mac and one Windows machine, you can easily use Lightroom on multiple computers.

Using Lightroom on multiple computers requires an understanding of using multiple catalogs, creating new catalogs, using Import from Catalog and Export as Catalog, etc. If you skipped here from elsewhere in the book and haven't read those previous sections of this chapter, I suggest you do so before continuing this section.

USING ONE MASTER PHOTO LIBRARY ON DIFFERENT COMPUTERS

If you store all your photos and catalogs on external hard drives, it's easy to connect the drives to different computers as the need arises. If you're using all Mac or all Windows machines, all you need to do is connect the drive to another computer and double-click the catalog to open it in the local copy of Lightroom. With this method you can easily work on your main photo library on any number of computers.

However, if you're planning to connect your photo library hard drives to both Mac and Windows machines you'll need to use special procedures because of differences in file systems on the two operating systems. To support both operating systems, it's best to format your hard drives as ExFAT. This allows you to work seamlessly with both platforms. If your drives are already formatted using another method and are unreadable by the other system as a result, you might be able to use special utility software to accomplish this. However, this is a kludgey workaround and you might have problems with Lightroom as a result. You'd be better off updating your backups and then reformatting each drive and re-copying the files to get everything onto ExFAT.

USING PROJECT CATALOGS FOR WORKING ON THE ROAD

When traveling, I use a temporary, working catalog on my laptop specific to each trip. Each day, at the end of shooting I download the photos and import them into the trip catalog, apply my standard Develop presets, add my metadata preset, and do some basic keywording. All the files (including the catalog) are then backed up immediately to an external hard drive or USB flash drive.

11

Back at home, depending on the number of files involved, I either connect my laptop to my studio computer over the network, or, more often, connect my external backup drive directly to my main machine. In my master Lightroom catalog I use "Import from Catalog" to copy the files to my main working drives and import them into the master catalog.

When this is done, I sync my master hard drive to a duplicate drive, and then I delete everything from my laptop and traveling backup drive so they're ready for the next trip.

 ## Road Trip Workflow

Following is the set of procedures I use when out shooting on location and downloading to my laptop computer. You can use this same set of steps for any situation where you're using temporary working or project catalogs. Depending on your own computer hardware and software setup, you can follow this workflow verbatim, or use it as a basis for developing your own methods.

MAKE A NEW TRIP CATALOG/PROJECT CATALOG

The steps for making a project catalog are the same as those described earlier in this chapter in the section on creating new catalogs; for reference, see the figures there.

Step 1. On the laptop, launch Lightroom and select File→New Catalog.

Step 2. A dialog box appears, asking you to provide a name and location for the new catalog. This will also be the name given to the folder containing the catalog and preview files. Using your standard naming convention, give the catalog a name, as you would a folder. For example, Death Valley_0213. **Do not specify a file extension.**

Save the new catalog in a place you can easily find. If you always use the same location, such as your Desktop or Pictures folder, your catalog will be easy to find. You may also use an external portable drive to manage project catalogs, but I prefer to use the internal drive of my laptop for these, and use the external drive for backups. Whichever storage location you prefer on the road, when you get home it's always easiest to use an external drive to get the photos into your master archives.

Step 3. Click Save. Lightroom creates the new catalog with the same base filename as the folder.

IMPORT TO THE TEMPORARY PROJECT CATALOG

Step 1. Always verify you're working in the correct catalog.

Step 2. Import new photos into the project catalog using the methods and settings described in Chapter 2. As desired, you can create subfolders for individual days or locations. Just be sure that all the image files/folders are put in the main project folder and are all organized the same way.

Step 3. After every import, carefully verify that all the desired files have been successfully copied, renamed, converted, etc. Immediately back up your catalog and image files to a second hard drive as soon as each import is completed.

Step 4. While traveling, you can work on your photos as you see fit, including working in the Develop and output modules. For redundancy, you can Save Metadata to Disk as you work (review Chapters 3 and 4 for more about this).

Step 5. While on the road, make regular backups of your trip folder onto a portable hard drive or flash drive. You can do this with drag and drop, but dedicated sync software is preferred. Just be sure your backups all remain current throughout the trip.

Reformat your card in the camera
After backing up your image files and confirming their integrity, remember to reformat your card in the *camera* before each new shooting session.

IMPORT PROJECT FILES TO YOUR MASTER CATALOG

The steps for importing from another catalog are the same as those described earlier in this chapter; for reference, see the figures there.

Step 1. When you return to your main workstation, make sure that the trip/project catalog on the laptop is fully up-to-date. Then do a complete backup or sync onto the portable hard drive. Make sure all the files on the external drive are the most recent versions.

Step 2. Connect the external portable hard drive to your main computer with your master catalog.

Step 3. Open your Master catalog. Select File→Import from Catalog. Locate the trip/project catalog on the external drive and click Choose (or double-click the file) to select it as the import source.

Step 4. In the Import from Catalog dialog box, you can optionally Show Previews to see the image thumbnails. In the File Handling section, select "Copy new photos to new location and import" You're going to have Lightroom make the file copies for you. In Copy to:, select Choose; navigate to your main photo drive and select the parent folder that the trip folders will be placed into.

Step 5. Click Import. Lightroom copies your photos and videos from the external portable drive into the selected folder on the hard drive and merges the data from your project catalog into your master catalog.

Step 6. After the import has completed, check all the photos and folders. If you had collections in the project catalog, those will be imported as well. Confirm that the folders and the number of photos in each are consistent with the files in the working project catalog on the laptop or external drive. If anything is out of place, you can rename folders and/or drag and drop to rearrange them if necessary (see Chapter 3 for a review) or do additional imports.

Step 7. Remember to synchronize the backups for your main photo library hard drives.

Step 8. On the laptop, you can now delete all the temporary project catalogs, files, and folders for the trip or event.

Once you've done this process a few times, it becomes much easier, and you can tweak the steps to suit your personal preferences.

 Taking your master photo library on the road
If your master Lightroom catalog is on an external drive—and backed up properly—you can easily take your main working photo library on the road with you. You can also use the Export as Catalog command if you prefer to take smaller subsets of photos to work on while traveling; when you return home, just use the Import from Catalog to sync the changes you made while on the road.

MOVING PRESETS AND PROFILES BETWEEN MACHINES

Transferring a Lightroom catalog from one computer to another is relatively easy; it's just one file. Keeping your Lightroom presets and other configuration files synced between machines is a bit more complex and time-consuming.

When you're going to use Lightroom catalogs on different machines, first make sure all installations of Lightroom are running the same version. You can check this with the About Lightroom option under the Lightroom menu on Mac and the Help menu on Windows (see **Figure 11–22**).

You'll probably also want to keep your presets and profiles (especially camera and lens correction profiles) the same on all computers. The challenge is keeping them in sync, since you may frequently create new presets and templates. There is currently no automated method for syncing presets between machines.

 Go to the Presets panel of the Lightroom Preferences and click the Show Lightroom Presets Folder button to locate the folder. You can then copy the presets (or entire folders) to the same place on the other computer.

Figure 11-22

The default locations of the Lightroom presets, plug-ins, and other configuration files are:

- **Mac OS X:** Macintosh HD/Users/YourUserName/Library/Application Support/ Adobe/Lightroom

- **Windows: C:** \Users\YourUserName\App Data\Roaming\Adobe\Lightroom

The default locations of camera and lens profiles are:

- **Mac OS X:** Macintosh HD/Library/Application Support/Adobe/CameraRaw/ CameraProfiles

- **Windows: C:** \ProgramData\Adobe\CameraRaw\CameraProfiles

Note: Custom (user added) camera profiles under Windows are stored in C:\Users\YourUserName\AppData\Roaming\Adobe\CameraRaw\CameraProfiles. Custom lens profiles are in the same parent folder, under LensProfiles.

You can copy the contents of your Lightroom presets and profiles folder from one machine to another using a USB flash drive or other removable media. Also, you can set up this folder for cloud sharing using a service such as Dropbox. These are easy ways to keep your presets in sync on multiple computers.

Storing presets in the catalog

In Lightroom Preferences there's an option to store presets within the catalog. To some degree, this does make your presets a bit more portable; however, it also *makes those presets specific to a single catalog.* For most Lightroom users I recommend leaving that option unchecked so that all presets and templates are stored in the default central location to all catalogs.

Next steps

If you've read all the way through this book, congratulations! You're well on your way to mastering Lightroom.

As you've no doubt seen already, Lightroom is a highly modular and extensible application. What you may not know is that from the beginning it has been programmed to be modified by outside developers. There are many ways to add and change Lightroom's functionality. As discussed in earlier chapters, using plug-ins is one major way to add features to Lightroom, but there are also many ways to hack Lightroom configuration files to customize even further. Unfortunately, due to time and space restrictions, these are topics that must be covered elsewhere. If you're the technical type who really wants to get under the hood, I encourage you to stay up-to-date using the myriad online Lightroom resources and communities. I've included links to the best of them in the Appendix.

I hope you enjoy working with Lightroom 5 and I wish you all the best in your photographic endeavors!

Favorite Shortcuts

From anywhere in Lightroom:

G Library Grid

E Library Loupe

D Develop Loupe

R Develop Crop

Tab Hide/show side panels

Shift+Tab Hide/show all panels

Right-click Open contextual menu or Ctrl+click

T Hide/show Toolbar

L Cycle Lights Out

F toggle Fullscreen

Shift+F Fullscreen

Shift+Command F Fullscreen and hide panels

Numbers 0-5 Apply star rating

P, U, X Apply Pick/Unflagged/Reject flag

B Add to/remove from Target Collection

⌘+B or Ctrl+B Go to Target Collection

Delete Remove photo or virtual copy

Return or Enter Finish typing into a text field

Esc Close a text field, import screen color picker, Targeted Adjustment Tool, etc. without saving

⌘+Z or Ctrl+Z Undo

⌘+Option+Left Arrow Go back or Ctrl+Alt+Left Arrow

⌘+Option+Right Arrow Go forward or Ctrl+Alt+Right Arrow

⌘+' or Ctrl+' Create virtual copy

⌘+= or Ctrl+= Zoom in

⌘+- or Ctrl+- Zoom out

⌘+E or Ctrl+E Edit selected photo in Photoshop (or other primary external editor)

⌘+R Show selected file(s) in Finder or Ctrl+R or Explorer

⌘+Shift+S Synchronize selected photos or Ctrl+Shift+S

⌘+, or Ctrl+, Open Lightroom Preferences

In Library:

Arrows Move between photos

Shift+Arrows Select contiguous photos

⌘+A or Ctrl+A Select All

⌘+D or Ctrl+D Select None

Shift+Command+D or Shift+Control+D Select only active photo

⌘+G or Ctrl+G Stack selected photos

⌘+Shift+G Unstack selected photos or Ctrl+Shift+G

C Compare two images

N Survey multiple images

J Cycle grid cell styles

I Cycle info overlay in Loupe and Compare views

\ Hide/show Filter Bar

⌘+L or Ctrl+L Enable/disable filters

⌘+N or Ctrl+N New collection

Shift+I Set video in point

Shift+O Set video out point

Space Play/pause video

V Apply Black & White color treatment (works in Develop too)

Z Zoom in/out (works in Develop too)

In Develop:

W White balance selector

A Constrain aspect ratio

Q Spot Removal

M Graduated filter

K Local adjustment brush

[Smaller brush

] Larger brush

Option or Alt Erase from brush mask

H Hide/show tool overlay and edit pins

O Cycle crop guide overlay

Shift+O Cycle crop guide overlay orientation

O Hide/show adjustment brush mask overlay

Shift+O Cycle mask overlay colors

Y Show Before/After

\ Toggle Before/After in main preview

Lightroom Preferences

The Lightroom Preferences control the behavior of the program; they are not specific to any single catalog. The more you use Lightroom, the more likely it is you'll want to tweak things a bit to suit your taste and your computer setup. Throughout the chapters of this book I've referenced specific Preferences in the context of the controls and functions they affect. Following are additional sample figures provided for reference, as well as showing the Preferences I normally use and brief descriptions of the available options.

WHAT'S NEW IN PREFERENCES

In Lightroom 5 there have been a couple additions to the Preferences. Here's a quick overview:

- Select the "Current/Previous Import" collection during import

- When tether transfer finishes play

GENERAL

The General tab (see **Figure A-1**) contains a couple of the most important controls for how Lightroom functions. The Default Catalog is set using the menu near the top. The default setting is Load Most Recent Catalog.

Figure A-1

 Choose a specific catalog as your default
I can't urge you strongly enough to change this to your specific catalog file. If you use more than one catalog then I recommend using the Prompt me when starting Lightroom option. Whatever you do, don't use Load most recent catalog.

The Load most recent setting can backfire on you if you are not aware of what catalog file you are opening when you launch Lightroom. See Chapter 11 for more about Catalogs.

Another key function provided here is whether or not to **Show import dialog when a memory card is detected**. When this is checked, Lightroom will open the Import window when removable media is found—not just cameras or memory cards. This can also apply to USB flash drives, smartphone, and DVDs. I normally leave this off because I like to manually open the Import dialog when I want it open.

Select the "Current/Previous Import" collection during import: When this is checked, Lightroom will switch your view to the Current/Previous Import collection in the Catalog panel after you click the Import button. This is the same way previous versions of Lightroom behaved after import. However, if you uncheck that option you will remain in whatever folder or collection you were working in before you started the import. It is nice to have the choice.

Treat JPEG files next to raw files as separate photos: If you shoot raw+JPEG, turn this on. If unchecked, Lightroom will copy the JPEG from the memory card to your computer, but you will only see the raw version in the catalog.

Completion Sounds: Choose a sound from the menus to have Lightroom play a sound when it's done importing, exporting, or when finished transferring photos from a tethered shoot. Since I don't normally sit and watch imports and exports as they proceed, I find this very handy.

Reset all warning dialogs: If you've ever checked one of those boxes in the warning dialogs that say Don't Show Again, this is the way to get them to start showing again.

Go to Catalog Settings: This button will open the Catalog Settings dialog box, which is covered in great detail in Chapter 11.

PRESETS

This panel section (see **Figure A-2**) controls how Lightroom handles presets and default settings. In the top section of the panel, if you check the box to Apply auto tone adjustments, Lightroom will always do this by default for photos without settings applied by a preset or another default. If you want to develop a fully automated workflow, and like the way Lightroom's auto tone works with your photos, this might be a good feature to enable. (I always leave it off.)

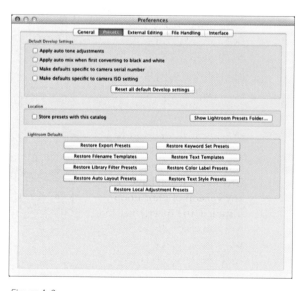

Figure A-2

When checked, the Apply auto mix when first converting to black and white tells Lightroom to take a stab at adjusting the sliders in the B&W panel of the Develop module to create a new starting point based on what Lightroom thinks will look good for a B&W photo. When unchecked, Lightroom simply converts the photo to B&W and leaves the sliders zeroed out. I prefer to leave this unchecked and make my own decision from the zeroed out setting. You can always manually click the Auto button in the B&W panel to see what Lightroom does.

The check boxes for Make defaults specific… pertain to how Lightroom applies Develop defaults. Lightroom reads the EXIF metadata for each photo so it can easily recall different stored settings based on the camera and ISO used for the shot. With these features enabled you have a huge range of customization available when creating your own custom defaults. See Chapter 4 for lots more about Default settings.

I recommend leaving Store presets with catalog unchecked so that all presets (and templates) are stored in a central location that is accessed by all catalogs. You can click the Show Lightroom Presets Folder… button to open the folder containing all your presets, which is a great way to make a backup copy of your presets or if you need to transfer them to a new computer. At the bottom of the Presets panel are buttons to restore the original default presets installed with Lightroom. If you should ever find your default presets are missing you can click the respective button on this panel to have them restored. This most commonly happens if you check the Store presets with this catalog button, which creates a subset of preinstalled presets in a folder next to your catalog file, but leaves all your custom presets behind (if you had any at the time),

EXTERNAL EDITING

If you find yourself frequently sending files out of Lightroom and into other software you'll need to configure this panel to suit your needs (see **Figure A-3**). The defaults here are intended to maintain the maximum amount of data in the copies sent to Photoshop (or other editors). As explained in Chapter 5, if you have any version of Photoshop installed, the newest version will automatically become the primary external editor. In the section below for Additional External Editor, you can specify as many other

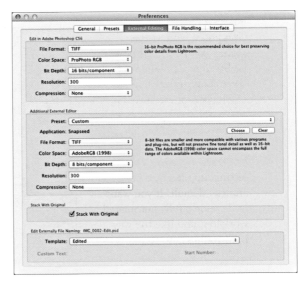

Figure A-3

editors as you want. For each program, just save a new preset using the menu. The option for Stack With Original makes finding externally edited photos easier. At the bottom of the window is a menu for customizing the automatic filenames used when you edit in an external program.

FILE HANDLING

At the top of the window (see **Figure A-4**) are the default settings Lightroom uses when you convert files to DNG. The option for Embed Fast Load Data is important if you use DNG in your workflow; it can significantly speed up the response time when you're working in Develop, so I always leave this on. Otherwise, I've always left the DNG settings at their defaults and never been disappointed. See the section later in this Appendix for more about DNG.

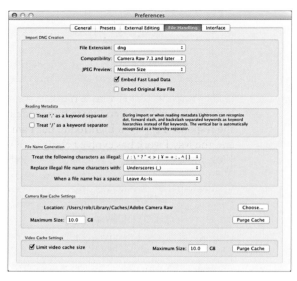

Figure A-4

Starting in Lightroom 4 the Camera Raw Cache uses much smaller files than previous versions. Instead of fewer, larger files measured in MB, the cache files are now many small files measured in the hundreds of kb. This change has improved performance, and the default setting here will be fine for most people. The large cache files used by previous versions of Lightroom will continue to be supported and read from when necessary, but they will no longer be created. Also, Camera Raw Cache files are now JPEG compressed (they used to be uncompressed). There is also a Preference control for Video Cache Size limit. If you're interested in achieving top performance from Lightroom, you should learn more about managing the caches on the Adobe website (helpx.adobe.com/lightroom/kb/optimize-performance-lightroom.html) and forums.

INTERFACE

Chapter 1 describes some of the features these settings control. In general, these settings turn on and off different elements of the interface, and control the color and shading of features like Lights Out. You'll need to experiment with these a bit to arrive at the settings you're most happy with; my settings are shown in **Figure A-5**.

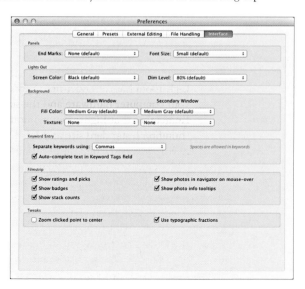

Figure A-5

Of special note is the check box at the bottom left for Zoom clicked point to center. As the name implies, when this is checked and you click to zoom into a preview, wherever you clicked is shifted so it's in the center of the preview area.

Optimizing Lightroom performance

Lightroom 5's processing has been re-engineered to provide faster response and better quality than earlier versions. That said, with each new release Lightroom's powerhouse features demand more and more from computers. I've always been pretty satisfied with the response I get from Lightroom, but I am also meticulous about my computer setup and the way I work has evolved along with my expectations—I'm careful about what I click and when. If you're experiencing anything less than satisfactory performance from Lightroom, there's probably something you can do about it. The steps to improving Lightroom's responsiveness generally fall into three categories: optimize your computer setup, apply the correct settings in Lightroom to get the best performance, and regularly maintain your Lightroom catalogs and operating system. Here are a few ways you can ensure Lightroom is running the best it can:

1. Keep ample free space on your system hard drive (where the Lightroom application is installed) and the drive that holds the Lightroom database and preview files. This is true for all photo-editing and imaging applications. Also, the read/write speed of your drive makes a difference; 7200 rpm is the practical minimum for fast performance with Lightroom.

2. Load your machine with as much RAM as it will hold (or that you can afford). Lightroom likes to have lots of memory available.

3. If you have 4 GB of RAM or more, and your operating system supports 64-bit processing, make sure you're running Lightroom in 64-bit mode. If you're not sure what this means, you can find more information about it in the Adobe documentation. Lightroom 5 is 64-bit by default.

4. Take control of your previews. Each time you make an adjustment to a photo, Lightroom has to render new previews. The speed it can do this depends on your computer hardware and the size of the original files you're working with. Remember that Lightroom maintains three separate previews for each image: thumbnail, standard size and 1:1. Lightroom will generate any previews it needs on the fly, sometimes this means you'll see a delay as Lightroom builds a preview. If Lightroom already has all the necessary previews rendered, moving between images should be quick. Using the commands on the Library →Previews menu or the contextual menu (discussed in Chapter 3), you can instruct Lightroom to discard and re-render the previews whenever you choose.

5. In Catalog Settings→File Handling (see Chapter 11), you can set the size of your standard preview, based on your screen size and how fast you want the preview redrawing to be. No need to use larger standard previews than what your display system is capable of handling. But you should use only the size and

quality of previews you need. Changing from the default Catalog Settings to make your previews very large and very high quality can really slow Lightroom down if your computer can't handle it. If you're using a very large monitor, you'll need a fast computer to keep up with the previews Lightroom is trying to generate as you work.

6. Increase the setting for your Camera Raw cache, in Preferences→File Handling (see previous section). I usually work with this set to between 10 GB and 30 GB; people have reported big improvements with cache sizes even larger than this.

7. Optimize your catalog periodically—maybe every eight to ten days of work— using the command on File menu, as described in Chapter 11. In addition to optimizing your catalogs, performing regular maintenance on your hard drives is always a good idea.

8. When working in Lightroom, try not to select folders/subfolders with large numbers of images when you don't need to, because Lightroom will reread all the files in the chosen source, attempting to get information about all previews and metadata. For example, if you click the All Photographs source from the Catalog panel, and you have many thousands of photos in the catalog, reading all those files can take a while. Click on a folder that contains only the images you want to work with. (Using Collections is a more efficient way to organize your photos and videos; see Chapter 3.)

9. Keep your catalog on an internal drive. I often recommend keeping your catalog on an external drive along with all your photos; this is a matter of convenience, not performance. Once you're comfortable managing your catalogs, keeping them on an internal drive is almost always faster than external. (But, like with the cache settings, if you do choose to work with your catalog on an external drive, using a fast interface such as FireWire 800 or USB 3.0 is best. If you use older versions of USB or FireWire, you'll see a noticeable decrease in speed.)

10. Close user interface elements you don't need. For example, if you don't look at the Histogram in the Library module, keep it closed. That way Lightroom won't have to redraw it each time to select a new photo. The same applies to the Filmstrip, the Navigator window, the Detail preview in the Develop module, and the Metadata panel in the Library module.

The Adobe website has lots more detailed specifications about the optimal hardware and software setups for Lightroom.

Adobe DNG

DNG stands for Digital Negative, an open source file format developed and standardized by Adobe. Adobe has consistently demonstrated a commitment to improving and advancing the format.

The latest DNG spec (1.4 at the time of this writing) provides functionality for much faster processing, smaller files, and enormous flexibility. Especially if you capture raw, you should seriously consider integrating DNG in your workflow. Some people use DNG just for archival copies; I believe this is missing the real benefit. I use DNG for my master working files. DNG also offers the additional benefit of being able to directly save XMP metadata into the DNG file, eliminating the need for sidecar files that would be required to save edits for raw files. Most common raw formats converted to DNG preserve all the original image data.

I always capture in raw, then convert the raw files to DNG as one of the first steps in my workflow. I'm a big believer in DNG, and it's great for my workflow, but you should investigate and learn more about it yourself.

With the new DNG spec you can also resize DNGs as they are created and apply optional lossy compression.

CONVERTING RAW FILES TO DNG IN LIBRARY

You can convert camera raw files to DNG during import, or from within the Library module, without needing to do an export. (Actually, you can convert to DNG at any point in your workflow.)

Library menu→Convert Photo(s) to DNG
Select the photos to be converted and, after choosing the menu command, in the dialog box apply the settings for the conversion. (I prefer and usually recommend using the default settings.) Always keep Embed Fast Load Data checked.

 Use DNG as your raw format and TIF as your layered work format
From these two master file formats you can produce derivatives of any kind, for any purpose.

Glossary

Absorption - When light waves penetrate the surface of an object and do not reflect.

Aerial perspective - The appearance of distance due to atmospheric haze.

Analogous - Colors that are close to one another in hue.

Aperture - The opening in a camera lens that lets light through.

Aperture Priority - Exposure mode where the photographer sets the aperture value and the camera determines the shutter speed for the exposure.

APS - Advanced Photo System; a class of digital camera sensor sizes smaller than full frame.

Asset management - The hardware, software, and organizational systems used to store digital files.

Backlight - When the main source of light is behind the subject.

Background - The part of the picture farthest from the camera.

Ball head - A type of tripod head that connects the camera to the tripod with a large rotating ball secured by clamps.

Body of work - A collection of imagery representing the artist's unique vision.

Bokeh - The way a particular lens blurs objects when they are completely out of focus.

Bracketing - Making a series of images with slight changes in settings.

Build quality - The standards of materials and construction used to manufacture camera equipment.

Camera body - The main part of a camera system that houses the recording media and exposure controls.

Camera shake - Blur in a photograph caused by movement of the camera during exposure.

Center of interest - The part of the photograph that provokes the greatest intellectual stimulation.

Chiaroscuro - The appearance of depth and dimension caused by variation in light and shadow.

Chromatic aberration - Color fringes along object edges in a photograph caused by light waves striking the image sensor at differing angles.

Clipping - Lack of detail in the brightest or darkest parts of the photograph. Highlight clipping is pure white; shadow clipping is pure black.

Colorcast - An undesirable tint affecting the overall color of a photo, most often caused by incorrect white balance settings.

Color management - Systems of computer hardware and software designed to translate color values between electronic devices. The CMS is the built-in color management system on your computer.

Color profile - A small piece of computer code that describes to the CMS the colors of an image file or an imaging device.

Color space - The numeric model of color used for an image file or device.

Color wheel - A visual representation of the relationships of color.

Compact flash (CF) card - A memory card on which most dSLR cameras can store captured images. See also Secure Digital (SD) card.

Complementary - Colors opposite each other on the color wheel.

Composite - An image made by combining multiple original images. Panoramic and HDR photos are composites.

Continuous mode - A camera drive mode where multiple captures are made when the photographer holds down the shutter button.

Contrast - Difference and variation in the visual qualities of a photograph. Contrast is most often used to describe variation in tone.

Cool light - Light with a blue tint; high color values on the Kelvin scale.

Cross-processing - A style of developing photos that warms and cools the shadows and highlights separately.

Deep focus - A long distance of sharpness in a photo.

Depth of field - The area of sharp focus within a scene.

Depth of Field Preview - A button on the camera body that stops down the lens to the selected aperture showing how much of the picture will be in sharp focus.

Diaphragm - In a camera lens, overlapping leaves made of metal or plastic that open and close to create the aperture.

Diffraction - When light waves bend and scatter as they pass through an object.

Diffused light - Light that appears soft because the waves are coming from many directions. The opposite of direct light.

Diffuser - A light modifier photographers use to soften direct light.

Direct light - Light that strongly appears to come from one direction, often creating strong shadows.

Hue - The named color of an object; red, orange, and purple are hues.

Dominance - When an element takes the leading role in a photographic composition, based mainly on size within the frame.

Dust spots - Undesirable artifacts that appear in a photograph caused by dust on the image sensor.

Dynamic range - The range of light values in a scene, or the range of light that a camera can capture.

Equivalent exposures/equivalence - Photos showing the same balance of tone and color but made using different camera settings.

Establishing shot - A wide-angle photo showing the larger environment or scene in which subsequent closer images are made.

Exposure - A combination of camera settings and lighting that produces the captured image. Exposure is affected by many variables including ISO, aperture, and shutter speed.

Exposure compensation - In Auto-exposure shooting modes, manually overriding the camera's metered exposure to either increase or decrease the exposure value. In Aperture Priority mode, applying exposure compensation affects the shutter speed. In Shutter Priority, exposure compensation affects the aperture setting.

Exposure mode - Sets how the camera will determine the correct exposure values based on available light and other factors.

Figure/ground reversal - Eye motion within a composition caused by the proximity of foreground and background objects and their competing dominance.

Fill light - Adding a small amount of light to reveal more detail in shaded areas.

Filling the frame - Allowing the main subject matter to extend beyond the edges of the frame.

Filter factor - The amount of exposure lost as light passes through a lens filter.

Focal length - The distance between the main focusing element and the image sensor.

Focal point - The part of the picture where the eye is first attracted.

Foreground - The part of the picture closest to the camera.

Frame - The box created by the edges of a picture.

Frame in a frame - When an object creates an additional frame around another part of the picture.

Front light - Light striking the front of the object as seen from the camera position.

F-stop - The size of the aperture.

Full frame - A digital camera sensor size approximately the same size as a 35mm film frame.

Gamut - The range of available colors.

Global adjustments - Changes applied to all parts of a picture during post-processing.

Golden hour - The time of warm light after sunrise and before sunset. See also magic hour.

Harmony - Visually pleasing color relationships.

HDR (High Dynamic Range) - Scenes that contain a wider range of light values than the camera can capture in a single exposure.

High key - A photo that is primarily light in tonal values.

Histogram - A bar graph showing the range of brightness values in a photo.

HSL - Hue, saturation, luminance. A common model for describing and manipulating digital color values.

Image stabilization - Camera and lens technology that allows longer shutter speeds without blur by stabilizing the image as the exposure is made. See also vibration reduction.

Intersection - Where lines in a composition converge.

JPEG - A common image file format for the display and transfer of photos on the Internet and for printing.

Kelvin scale - A scale by which the color of light is measured.

Lens - One or more glass or plastic discs that gather and focus light onto a specific point inside the camera.

Live View - A real-time preview of the framed shot displayed on the camera's rear LCD panel.

Local adjustments - Changes made only to localized areas in a photo during post-processing.

Low key - A photo that is primarily dark in tone.

Macro photography/macro - Traditionally, photos made at 1:1 or greater magnification. Currently used to describe extreme close-up photography at any magnification ratio.

Magic hour - See golden hour.

Magnification factor - The amount of apparent enlargement caused by using a 35mm focal-length measurement on an APS-sized camera. Also referred to as crop factor.

Manual mode - An exposure mode that requires the photographer to manually enter both aperture and shutter speed values.

Medium format - A class of cameras larger than 35mm but smaller than large format. Medium format cameras come in several physical frame sizes.

Merger - In a composition, when elements appear to blend into one another due to sharing the same tone or color.

Metadata - Textual information embedded in a digital image file that describes the contents of the file.

Mirror lockup - A camera setting that reduces blur caused by mirror slap.

Mirror slap - Blur in a photo caused by the action of the mirror moving up as the shutter button is pressed.

Neutral density (ND) filter - A lens filter that reduces the amount of light coming into the lens without changing the color.

Nodal point - For panoramic photography, the point around which the lens can pivot to make photos without significant distortion.

Noise - Undesirable colored blobs or grainy speckles in a digital image. Most often caused by high ISO, low light, or underexposure.

Normal focal length - A lens that renders approximately the same appearance of perspective as the human eye.

Overexposed - A photo that appears brighter than the actual scene.

Pan/tilt head - A type of tripod head with separate controls for up/down, side-to-side, and rotation movements.

Panning - Moving the camera in a linear direction during the exposure.

Panoramic - A photograph showing a very wide angle of view, often created by combining multiple captures into a single image.

Patterns - Repeating, geometric graphics in a photo.

Photo editing - Selecting and separating the best photos from a shoot.

Photography - From Greek words meaning "writing with light."

Plane of critical focus - The distance at which the lens is precisely focused and the most sharp.

Polarizing filter - A lens filter that realigns the light waves coming into the camera so that they are parallel, reducing haze and glare.

Post-processing - Manipulating photographs after they are captured by the camera.

Previsualization - Imagining what a photograph will look like before making it.

Prime lens - A lens that only offers one focal length. Also called a "fixed" lens or fixed focal length lens.

Proportion - The size relationships of objects in a composition.

Quality of light - A combination of direction, intensity, diffusion, and color.

Raw - A capture format that preserves all the original data from the camera sensor.

Resolution - The amount of detail in a digital image.

Saturation - The purity of color, as opposed to neutral gray.

Scale - The size of objects within a composition.

Secure Digital (SD) card - A memory card on which many dSLR cameras can store captured images. See also compact flash (CF) card.

Selective focus - Using a wide aperture and a specific focusing distance to make parts of the photo sharp and others blurry.

Sharpening - Increasing the contrast along edges of objects in the photograph.

Shoot to the right - A technique used to capture the most possible image data by slightly overexposing the digital capture. Refers to the appearance of tonal data concentrated to the right of the histogram.

Shooting mode - The main setting that determines how the camera will calculate exposure settings (or not). Common shooting modes are Aperture Priority (Av or A, for "aperture value" or "aperture"), Shutter Priority (Tv or S, for "time value" or "shutter"), Manual, and Program. Shutter curtain Panels of fabric or plastic that move across the recording surface to expose a picture when the shutter is released.

Shutter Priority - A shooting mode where the photographer sets the shutter speed and the camera determines the aperture setting for the exposure.

Shutter speed - How long the camera's shutter is open and exposing the recording surface to light.

Sidelight - Light coming from the side of an object.

Silhouette - A featureless, dark shape created by backlighting.

Specular light - Direct light that is not significantly affected by anything in its path. The midday sun on a clear day is a specular light source.

Split neutral density filter - A lens filter with only part of the surface tinted, used to darken just a portion of the framed composition in order to provide a balanced exposure.

Stitching - Combining multiple photos to form a panoramic image.

Stops - Changes in exposure measured by doubling or halving the previous value.

Subject - The theme or message of a photo.

Subject matter - The objects in a photograph.

Targeted Adjustment Tool (TAT) - A tool in Lightroom that allows you click and drag in an image to adjust its appearance interactively.

Telephoto - Lenses whose physical focal length is shorter than the apparent focal length suggested by the magnification.

Tempo - The pace at which the eye travels between objects in a composition.

Texture - Random, organic surfaces that elicit a tactile sensation when viewed.

Tones - The range of brightness in a photo, from darkest to lightest, without regard to color.

Transmit - Allowing light to pass through an object.

Underexposed - A photograph that appears darker than the actual scene.

UV filter - A lens filter that limits the amount of ultraviolet light rays entering the lens. Used to reduce haze and protect the front lens element.

Vibration reduction - See image stabilization.

Warm light - Light with a yellow, orange, or golden color; low values on the Kelvin scale.

White balance - The method by which cameras and software compensate for the color of light in a scene with the intention of producing a balanced, "neutral" color rendition.

Workflow - A sequence of steps taken to produce a specific outcome.

Zoom lens - A lens that offers varying focal length and magnification.

Zooming - Enlarging or reducing the scene as it appears in the camera

Resources

ADOBE

Lightroom Journal blog
http://blogs.adobe.com/lightroomjournal

Adobe Lightroom Exchange
www.exchange.lightroomers.com (this redirects to the Adobe site)

Lens profiles, DNG Editor, and more at Adobe Labs
http://labs.adobe.com

Adobe raw file format support
http://www.adobe.com/products/photoshop/cameraraw.html

Adobe customer support
http://helpx.adobe.com/lightroom.html
www.adobe.com/go/intlsupport
http://forums.adobe.com/community/lightroom
http://feedback.photoshop.com/photoshop_family

Adobe channel on YouTube
www.youtube.com/user/AdobeLightroom

LIGHTROOM HELP, TUTORIALS, AND DISCUSSION

www.lightroomers.com
www.lightroomqueen.com
www.lightroomkillertips.com
www.photoshopuser.com
www.lightroom-blog.com
www.lightroomsecrets.com
www.thelightroomlab.com
www.laurashoe.com
www.luminous-landscape.com/forum
www.lightroomforums.net

LIGHTROOM PRESETS

www.presetsheaven.com
www.lightroompresets.com

LIGHTROOM PLUG-INS

www.photographers-toolbox.com
www.lightroomsolutions.com
www.regex.info/blog/lightroom-goodies
www.lrbplugins.com
www.mosaicarchive.com

LIGHTROOM WEB GALLERIES

www.slideshowpro.net/products/slideshowpro
www.photographers-toolbox.com
www.theturninggate.net

DIGITAL PHOTOGRAPHY WORKFLOW

www.dpBestFlow.com

COLOR MANAGEMENT

www.xrite.com
www.rawworkflow.com
www.color.org
www.chromix.com

BACKUP AND DISK UTILITY SOFTWARE

Carbon Copy Cloner for Mac www.bombich.com
Chronosync for Mac www.econtechnologies.com
ViceVersa Pro for Windows www.tgrmn.com
SyncBack www.2brightsparks.com/syncback
Find duplicate files www.easyduplicatefinder.com and www.hardcoded.net/dupeguru

KEYWORD LISTS

Controlled Vocabulary www.controlledvocabulary.com
Nick Potter www.nickpotter.net/lightroom-keywords

GPS AND LOCATION DATA RESOURCES

www.gpsbabel.org
www.gpsvisualizer.com

MISCELLANEOUS

Metadata resources www.iptc.org
Check machine requirements at Apple http://support.apple.com/kb/ht3696
ProShow slideshow software www.photodex.com

A

B

G

S

Vertical correction, 196–198
vibration reduction, 470
Video Cache settings, 153
Video panel, Export window, 265
videos
  Capture Frame command, 154
  deleting, Library module, 109–110
  editing, 151–155
  exporting, 155, 265
  file formats, 17, 151
  metadata for, 140
  moving between folders, Library module, 108
  Poster Frame, setting, 153–154
  Quick Develop panel settings for, 154
  on secondary displays, 153
  slideshows, exporting as, 372
  trimming, 153–154
view modes, 57, 86
view options, Loupe view, 96
vignetting, post-crop, 203–204
virtual copies (VCs), 115, 238–239, 381
Volume Browser display options, 102
volumes, in Folders panel, 102–103

W

warm light, 470
Warning icon, 5
Watermark Editor window, 275–278
watermarking
  applying to exported files, 275
  applying to photos in print job, 388
  effects, 277–278
  image options, 276
  slideshow overlays, 362
  styles, 276
  text options, 276–277
  for Web galleries, 426
Web gallery resources, 472
Web module
  Appearance panel, 420–423
  Collections panel, 411–413
  Color Palette panel, 419–420
  customizing galleries, 416
  exporting files to hard drive, 429–430
  Image Info panel, 423–425
  Layout Style panel, 414–415
  main preview area, 413

Output Settings panel, 425–426
  overview, 26, 407–409
  Preview panel, 409
  previewing in browsers, 429
  saving Web galleries, 428–429
  Site Info panel, 416–419
  third-party galleries, adding, 415–416
  Toolbar, 413–414
  Upload Settings panel, 426–428
  uploading galleries, 430
  workflow, 409
white balance, 159–160, 171–173, 470
White Balance Tool, 173–174
workflows, defined, 470
workspace. *See also* panels
  Develop module, 164–165
  Filmstrip, 32
  main application window, 24
  main preview area, 27
  Map module, 299
  menus, commands, and shortcuts, 35–36
  modules, 26–27
  Navigator panel, 31–32
  overview, 23
  Secondary Display feature, 24
  toolbars, 36–37
  viewing additional functions, 37

X

XMP metadata, 18, 120, 148–149, 438

Z

zoom lenses, 470
zoom level, 307, 320
zoom ratios, 31, 85–86, 230
zooming, defined, 470
zooming in/out, Loupe view, 94–95